BRUNEI

T0291316

SOCIAL SECURITY AND LABOR PROTECTION SYSTEM, POLICIES, LAWS AND REGULATIONS HANDBOOK

STRATEGIC INFORMATION AND REGULATIONS

International Business Publications, USA
Washington DC, USA - Bandar Seri Begawan

BRUNEI

SOCIAL SECURITY AND LABOR PROTECTION SYSTEM, POLICIES, LAWS AND REGULATIONS HANDBOOK

STRATEGIC INFORMATION AND REGULATIONS

UPDATED ANNUALLY

We express our sincere appreciation to all government agencies and international organizations which provided information and other materials for this handbook

Cover Design: International Business Publications, USA

2017 Updated Reprint International Business Publications, USA
ISBN 978-1-5145-3053-5

For additional analytical, business and investment opportunities information,
please contact Global Investment & Business Center, USA
at (703) 370-8082. Fax: (703) 370-8083. E-mail: ibpusa3@gmail.com
Global Business and Investment Info Databank - www.ibpus.com

For additional analytical, business and investment opportunities information,
please contact Global Investment & Business Center, USA
at (703) 370-8082. Fax: (703) 370-8083. E-mail: ibpusa3@gmail.com
Global Business and Investment Info Databank - www.ibpus.com

Printed in the USA

For additional analytical, business and investment opportunities information,
please contact Global Investment & Business Center, USA
at (703) 370-8082. Fax: (703) 370-8083. E-mail: ibpusa3@gmail.com
Global Business and Investment Info Databank - www.ibpus.com

BRUNEI

SOCIAL SECURITY AND LABOR PROTECTION SYSTEM, POLICIES, LAWS AND REGULATIONS HANDBOOK

STRATEGIC INFORMATION AND REGULATIONS

TABLE OF CONTENTS

For additional analytical, business and investment opportunities information,
please contact Global Investment & Business Center, USA
at (703) 370-8082. Fax: (703) 370-8083. E-mail: ibpusa3@gmail.com
Global Business and Investment Info Databank - www.ibpus.com

For additional analytical, business and investment opportunities information,
please contact Global Investment & Business Center, USA
at (703) 370-8082. Fax: (703) 370-8083. E-mail: ibpusa3@gmail.com
Global Business and Investment Info Databank - www.ibpus.com

For additional analytical, business and investment opportunities information,
please contact Global Investment & Business Center, USA
at (703) 370-8082. Fax: (703) 370-8083. E-mail: ibpusa3@gmail.com
Global Business and Investment Info Databank - www.ibpus.com

For additional analytical, business and investment opportunities information,
please contact Global Investment & Business Center, USA
at (703) 370-8082. Fax: (703) 370-8083. E-mail: ibpusa3@gmail.com
Global Business and Investment Info Databank - www.ibpus.com

STRATEGIC AND BUSINESS PROFILE

BRUNEI DARUSSALAM

Capital and largest city	Bandar Seri Begawan 4°53.417′N 114°56.533′E4.890283°N 114.942217°E
Official languages	Malay
Recognised	English
Other languages	• Brunei Malay • Tutong • Kedayan • Belait • Murut • Dusun • Bisaya • Melanau • Iban • Penan
Ethnic groups (2004)	• 66.3% Malays • 11.2% Chinese • 3.4% Indigenous • 19.1% other
Demonym	Bruneian
Government	Unitary Islamic absolute monarchy
- Sultan	Hassanal Bolkiah
- Crown Prince	Al-Muhtadee Billah
Legislature	Legislative Council
Formation	
- Sultanate	14th century
- British protectorate	1888
- Independence from the United Kingdom	1 January 1984
Area	
- Total	5,765 km^2 (172nd) 2,226 sq mi
- Water (%)	8.6
Population	
- Jul 2013 estimate	415,717 (175th)
- Density	67.3/km^2 (134th) 174.4/sq mi
GDP (PPP)	2012 estimate
- Total	$21.907 billion
- Per capita	$50,440
GDP (nominal)	2012 estimate
- Total	$17.092 billion
- Per capita	$39,355
HDI (2013)	▲0.855 very high · 30th
Currency	Brunei dollar (BND)
Time zone	BDT (UTC+8)

For additional analytical, business and investment opportunities information, please contact Global Investment & Business Center, USA at (703) 370-8082. Fax: (703) 370-8083. E-mail: ibpusa3@gmail.com Global Business and Investment Info Databank - www.ibpus.com

Drives on the	left
Calling code	+673
ISO 3166 code	BN
Internet TLD	.bn

Brunei officially the **Nation of Brunei, the Abode of Peace** is a sovereign state located on the north coast of the island of Borneo in Southeast Asia. Apart from its coastline with the South China Sea, it is completely surrounded by the state of Sarawak, Malaysia; and it is separated into two parts by the Sarawak district of Limbang. It is the only sovereign state completely on the island of Borneo; the remainder of the island's territory is divided between the nations of Malaysia and Indonesia. Brunei's population was 408,786 in July 2012.

At the peak of Bruneian Empire, Sultan Bolkiah (reigned 1485–1528) is alleged to have had control over the northern regions of Borneo, including modern-day Sarawak and Sabah, as well as the Sulu archipelago off the northeast tip of Borneo, Seludong (modern-day Manila), and the islands off the northwest tip of Borneo. The maritime state was visited by Spain's Magellan Expedition in 1521 and fought against Spain in 1578's Castille War.

During the 19th century the Bruneian Empire began to decline. The Sultanate ceded Sarawak to James Brooke as a reward for his aid in putting down a rebellion and named him as rajah, and it ceded Sabah to the British North Borneo Chartered Company. In 1888 Brunei became a British protectorate and was assigned a British Resident as colonial manager in 1906. After the Japanese occupation during World War II, in 1959 a new constitution was written. In 1962 a small armed rebellion against the monarchy was ended with the help of the British.

Brunei regained its independence from the United Kingdom on 1 January 1984. Economic growth during the 1990s and 2000s, averaging 56% from 1999 to 2008, has transformed Brunei into a newly industrialised country. It has developed wealth from extensive petroleum and natural gas fields. Brunei has the second-highest Human Development Index among the South East Asia nations after Singapore, and is classified as a developed country. According to the International Monetary Fund (IMF), Brunei is ranked fifth in the world by gross domestic product per capita at purchasing power parity. The IMF estimated in 2011 that Brunei was one of two countries (the other being Libya) with a public debt at 0% of the national GDP. *Forbes* also ranks Brunei as the fifth-richest nation out of 182, based on its petroleum and natural gas fields

Brunei can trace its beginnings to the 7th century, when it was a subject state of the Srivijayan empire under the name Po-ni. It later became a vassal state of Majapahit before embracing Islam in the 15th century. At the peak of its empire, the sultanate had control that extended over the coastal regions of modern-day Sarawak and Sabah, the Sulu archipelago, and the islands off the northwest tip of Borneo. The thalassocracy was visited by Ferdinand Magellan in 1521 and fought the Castille War in 1578 against Spain. Its empire began to decline with the forced ceding of Sarawak to James Brooke and the ceding of Sabah to the British North Borneo Chartered Company. After the loss of Limbang, Brunei finally became a British protectorate in 1888, receiving a resident in 1906. In the post-occupation years, it formalised a constitution and fought an armed rebellion. Brunei regained its independence from the United Kingdom on 1 January 1984. Economic growth during the 1970s and 1990s, averaging 56% from 1999 to 2008, has transformed Brunei Darussalam into a newly industrialised country.

Brunei has the second highest Human Development Index among the South East Asia nations, after Singapore and is classified as a Developed Country. According to the International Monetary Fund (IMF), Brunei is ranked 4th in the world by gross domestic product per capita at purchasing power parity.

According to legend, Brunei was founded by Awang Alak Betatar. His move from Garang [location required] to the Brunei river estuary led to the discovery of Brunei. His first exclamation upon landing on the shore, as the legend goes, was "Baru nah!" (Which in English loosely-translates as "that's it!" or "there") and thus, the name "Brunei" was derived from his words.

It was renamed "Barunai" in the 14th Century, possibly influenced by the Sanskrit word varunai (वरुण), meaning "seafarers", later to become "Brunei". The word "Borneo" is of the same origin. In the country's full name "Negara Brunei Darussalam" "Darussalam" means "Abode of Peace" in Arabic, while "Negara" means "Country" in Malay. "Negara" derives from the Sanskrit Nagara , meaning "city".

Brunei Darussalam, the host of the 1995 BIMP-EAGA EXPO is a stable and prosperous country which offers not only a well-developed infrastructure but also a strategic location within the Asean region. The country is chugging full steam ahead to diversify its economy away from an over-dependence on oil and gas, and has put in place flexible and realistic policies to facilitate foreign and local investment. The cost of utilities are the lowest in the region, while political stability, extensive economic and natural resources and a business environment attuned to the requirements of foreign investors go towards making Brunei an excellent investment choice

At present the country's economy is dominated by the oil and liquefied natural gas industries and government expenditure patterns. Brunei exports crude oil, petroleum products and LNG mainly to Japan, the United States and the Asean countries. The second most important industry is construction, a direct result of the government's investment in development and infrastructure projects. Gearing up towards putting on the mantle of a developed country in January 1996, Brunei allocated in its 1991-95 Five Year Plan a hefty B$5 billion for national development, over a billion dollars more than in the previous budget. About B$510 million was allotted for 619 projects while B$550 million or 10 percent of the development budget went to industry and commerce. Some B$100 million alone was reserved for industrial promotion and development.

STABLE, CONDUCIVE ENVIRONMENT

The oil-rich country, lying on the north-western edge of the Borneo island, has never experienced typhoons, earthquakes or severe floods. Profitable investment can be had as the country levies no personal income tax, no sales tax, payroll, manufacturing or export tax.

Competitive investment incentives are available for investors throughout the business cycle marked by the start up, growth, maturity and expansion stages. The tax advantages at start up and the on-going incentives during growth and expansion are among the most competitive around. There is no difficulty in securing approval for foreign workers, from labourers to managers. With a small labour pool of 284,500 Brunei people and Bruneians showing a marked preference for the public sector as employer, the country has had to rely on foreign workers. These make up a third of its work force.

In line with moves to promote the private sector, it is encouraging to note the contribution from the non-oil and gas sector of the economy has risen, contributing about 25 percent to GDP compared to the oil and gas sector's 46 percent. In terms of infrastructure, Brunei is ready for vigorous economy activity. At its two main ports at Muara and Kuala Belait, goods can be shipped direct to Hong Kong, Singapore and other Asian destinations. Muara, a deep-water port 29 km away from the capital of Bandar Seri Begawan, has seen continual increase in container traffic over the past two decades.

For additional analytical, business and investment opportunities information, please contact Global Investment & Business Center, USA at (703) 370-8082. Fax: (703) 370-8083. E-mail: ibpusa3@gmail.com Global Business and Investment Info Databank - www.ibpus.com

The Brunei International Airport at Bandar offers expanded passenger and cargo facilities. Its new terminal can accommodate 1.5 million passengers and 50,000 tonnes of cargo a year, which is expected to suffice till the end of the decade. A 2,000-km road network serving the whole country undergoes continual expansion. A main highway runs the entire length of its coastline, linking Muara, the port entry point at one end, and Belait, the oil-production centre, at another end.

Telecommunications-wise, Brunei has one of the best systems in the region with plans for major upgrading. Telephone availability is about one to every three people.

Two earth satellite stations provide direct telephone, telex and facsimile links to most parts of the world. Operating systems include an analogue telephone exchange, fibreoptic cable links with Singapore and Manila, a packet switching exchange for access to high-speed computer bases overseas, cellular mobile telephone and paging systems. Direct phone links are also available in the more remote parts of the country via microwave and solar-powered telephones.

PIONEER INDUSTRY INCENTIVES

Companies granted pioneer status enjoy tax holidays of up to eight years. Brunei's regulations governing foreign participation in equity are the most flexible in the region, with 100 percent foreign ownership permitted. A pioneer company is also exempt from customs duty on items to be installed in the pioneer factory and from paying import duties on raw materials not available locally or produced in Brunei for the manufacture of pioneer products.

GEOGRAPHY

Location: Southeastern Asia, bordering the South China Sea and Malaysia
Geographic coordinates: 4 30 N, 114 40 E
Map references: Southeast Asia

Area:
total: 5,770 sq km
land: 5,270 sq km
water: 500 sq km

Area—comparative: slightly smaller than Delaware

Land boundaries:
total: 381 km
border countries: Malaysia 381 km

Coastline: 161 km
Land use:
arable land: 1%
other: 12%

permanent crops: 1%
permanent pastures: 1%
forests and woodland: 85%

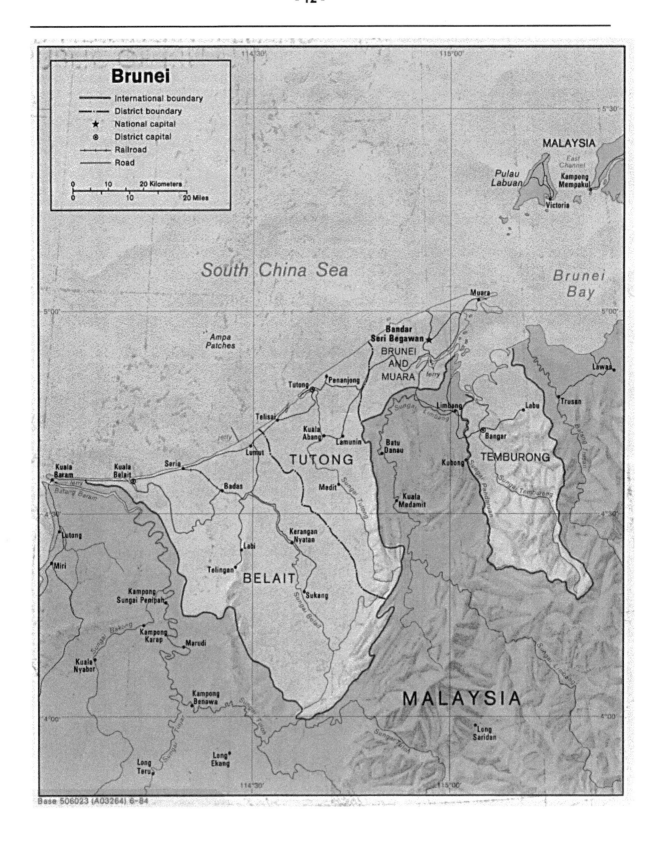

For additional analytical, business and investment opportunities information,
please contact Global Investment & Business Center, USA
at (703) 370-8082. Fax: (703) 370-8083. E-mail: ibpusa3@gmail.com
Global Business and Investment Info Databank - www.ibpus.com

Irrigated land: 10 sq km
Natural hazards: typhoons, earthquakes, and severe flooding are very rare
Environment—current issues: seasonal smoke/haze resulting from forest fires in Indonesia

Environment—international agreements:
party to: Endangered Species, Law of the Sea, Ozone Layer Protection, Ship Pollution
signed, but not ratified: none of the selected agreements

Geography—note: close to vital sea lanes through South China Sea linking Indian and Pacific Oceans; two parts physically separated by Malaysia; almost an enclave of Malaysia

PEOPLE

Population: 322,982

Age structure:
0-14 years: 33% (male 54,154; female 51,766)
15-64 years: 63% (male 106,492; female 95,921)
65 years and over: 4% (male 7,945; female 6,704)

Population growth rate: 2.38%
Birth rate: 24.69 births/1,000 population
Death rate: 5.21 deaths/1,000 population
Net migration rate: 4.35 migrant(s)/1,000 population

Sex ratio:
at birth: 1.06 male(s)/female
under 15 years: 1.05 male(s)/female
15-64 years: 1.11 male(s)/female
65 years and over: 1.19 male(s)/female
total population: 1.09 male(s)/female

Infant mortality rate: 22.83 deaths/1,000 live births

Life expectancy at birth:
total population: 71.84 years
male: 70.35 years
female: 73.42 years

Total fertility rate: 3.33 children born/woman

Nationality:
noun: Bruneian(s)
adjective: Bruneian

Ethnic groups: Malay 64%, Chinese 20%, other 16%
Religions: Muslim (official) 63%, Buddhism 14%, Christian 8%, indigenous beliefs and other 15% (1981)
Languages: Malay (official), English, Chinese

Literacy:
definition: age 15 and over can read and write
total population: 88.2%
male: 92.6% *female:* 83.4%

GOVERNMENT

Country name:
conventional long form: Negara Brunei Darussalam
conventional short form: Brunei

Data code: BX
Government type: constitutional sultanate
Capital: Bandar Seri Begawan

Administrative divisions: 4 districts (daerah-daerah, singular—daerah); Belait, Brunei and Muara, Temburong, Tutong

Independence: 1 January 1984 (from UK)
National holiday: National Day, 23 February (1984)

Constitution: 29 September 1959 (some provisions suspended under a State of Emergency since December 1962, others since independence on 1 January 1984)

Legal system: based on English common law; for Muslims, Islamic Shari'a law supersedes civil law in a number of areas

Suffrage: none

Executive branch:
Brunei

Sultan	HASSANAL Bolkiah, Sir
Prime Minister	HASSANAL Bolkiah, Sir
Min. of Communications	Awang ABU BAKAR bin Apong
Min. of Culture, Youth, & Sports	MOHAMMAD bin Daud, Gen. (Ret.)
Min. of Defense	HASSANAL Bolkiah, Sir
Min. of Development	ABDULLAH bin Begawan
Min. of Education	Abdul RAHMAN bin Mohamed Taib
Min. of Energy	YAHYA bin Begawan
Min. of Finance	HASSANAL Bolkiah, Sir
Min. of Finance II	ABDUL RAHMAN bin Ibrahim
Min. of Foreign Affairs	MOHAMED Bolkiah, Prince
Min. of Foreign Affairs II	LIM Jock Seng
Min. of Health	SUYOI bin Osman
Min. of Home Affairs	ADANAN bin Begawan
Min. of Industry & Primary Resources	AHMAD bin Jumat, Dr.
Min. of Religious Affairs	MOHD ZAIN bin Serudin, Dr.
Senior Min. in the Prime Minister's Office	Al Muhtadee BILLAH, Crown Prince

| Ambassador to the US | PUTEH ibni Mohammad Alam |
| Permanent Representative to the UN, New York | SHOFRY bin Abdul Ghafor |

Legislative branch: unicameral Legislative Council or Majlis Masyuarat Megeri (a privy council that serves only in a consultative capacity; NA seats; members appointed by the monarch)
elections: last held in March 1962
note: in 1970 the Council was changed to an appointive body by decree of the monarch; an elected Legislative Council is being considered as part of constitutional reform, but elections are unlikely for several years

Judicial branch: Supreme Court, chief justice and judges are sworn in by the monarch for three-year terms

Political parties and leaders: Brunei Solidarity National Party or PPKB in Malay [Haji Mohd HATTA bin Haji Zainal Abidin, president]; the PPKB is the only legal political party in Brunei; it was registered in 1985, but became largely inactive after 1988; it has less than 200 registered party members; other parties include Brunei People's Party or PRB (banned in 1962) and Brunei National Democratic Party (registered in May 1985, deregistered by the Brunei Government in 1988)

International organization participation: APEC, ASEAN, C, CCC, ESCAP, G-77, IBRD, ICAO, ICRM, IDB, IFRCS, IMF, IMO, Inmarsat, Intelsat, Interpol, IOC, ISO (correspondent), ITU, NAM, OIC, OPCW, UN, UNCTAD, UPU, WHO, WIPO, WMO, WTrO

Diplomatic representation in the US:
chief of mission: Ambassador Pengiran Anak Dato Haji PUTEH Ibni Mohammad Alam
chancery: Watergate, Suite 300, 3rd floor, 2600 Virginia Avenue NW, Washington, DC 20037
telephone: (202) 342-0159
FAX: (202) 342-0158

Diplomatic representation from the US:
chief of mission: Ambassador Glen Robert RASE
embassy: Third Floor, Teck Guan Plaza, Jalan Sultan, Bandar Seri Begawan
mailing address: PSC 470 (BSB), FPO AP 96534-0001
telephone: [673] (2) 229670 *FAX:* [673] (2) 225293

Flag description: yellow with two diagonal bands of white (top, almost double width) and black starting from the upper hoist side; the national emblem in red is superimposed at the center; the emblem includes a swallow-tailed flag on top of a winged column within an upturned crescent above a scroll and flanked by two upraised hands

ECONOMY

Brunei has a small well-to-do economy that depends on revenue from natural resource extraction but encompasses a mixture of foreign and domestic entrepreneurship, government regulation, welfare measures, and village tradition. Crude oil and natural gas production account for 60% of GDP and more than 90% of exports. Per capita GDP is among the highest in Asia, and substantial income from overseas investment supplements income from domestic production. For Bruneian citizens the government provides for all medical services and free education through the university level. The government of Brunei has been emphasizing through policy and resource investments it strong desire to diversity its economy both within the oil and gas sector and to new sectors.

GDP (purchasing power parity):
$22.25 billion (2013 est.)
country comparison to the world: 128
$21.93 billion (2012 est.)
$21.73 billion (2011 est.)
note: data are in 2013 US dollars

GDP (official exchange rate):
$16.56 billion (2013 est.)

GDP - real growth rate:
1.4% (2013 est.)
country comparison to the world: 164
0.9% (2012 est.)
3.4% (2011 est.)

GDP - per capita (PPP):
$54,800 (2013 est.)
country comparison to the world: 12
$54,900 (2012 est.)
$55,200 (2011 est.)
note: data are in 2013 US dollars

GDP - composition, by end use:
household consumption: 22.1%
government consumption: 18.2%
investment in fixed capital: 14.6%
investment in inventories: 0%
exports of goods and services: 78.4%
imports of goods and services: -33.3%
(2013 est.)

GDP - composition, by sector of origin:
agriculture: 0.7%
industry: 70.9%
services: 28.4% (2013 est.)

Agriculture - products:
rice, vegetables, fruits; chickens, water buffalo, cattle, goats, eggs

Industries:
petroleum, petroleum refining, liquefied natural gas, construction, agriculture, transportation

Industrial production growth rate:
1.5% (2013 est.)
country comparison to the world: 135

For additional analytical, business and investment opportunities information, please contact Global Investment & Business Center, USA at (703) 370-8082. Fax: (703) 370-8083. E-mail: ibpusa3@gmail.com Global Business and Investment Info Databank - www.ibpus.com

Labor force:
205,800 (est.)
country comparison to the world: 169

Labor force - by occupation:
agriculture: 4.2%
industry: 62.8%
services: 33%

Unemployment rate:
2.6%
country comparison to the world: 21
2.7%

Budget:
revenues: $6.992 billion
expenditures: $5.366 billion (2013 est.)

Taxes and other revenues:
42.2% of GDP (2013 est.)
country comparison to the world: 29

Budget surplus (+) or deficit (-):
9.8% of GDP (2013 est.)
country comparison to the world: 5

Fiscal year:
1 April - 31 March

Inflation rate (consumer prices):
1% (2013 est.)
country comparison to the world: 24
0.5% (2012 est.)

Commercial bank prime lending rate:
5.5% (31 December 2013 est.)
country comparison to the world: 142
5.5% (31 December 2012 est.)

Stock of narrow money:
$3.472 billion (31 December 2013 est.)
country comparison to the world: 113
$3.509 billion (31 December 2012 est.)

Stock of broad money:
$11.92 billion (31 December 2013 est.)
country comparison to the world: 99
$11.41 billion (31 December 2012 est.)

For additional analytical, business and investment opportunities information,
please contact Global Investment & Business Center, USA
at (703) 370-8082. Fax: (703) 370-8083. E-mail: ibpusa3@gmail.com
Global Business and Investment Info Databank - www.ibpus.com

Stock of domestic credit:
$2.846 billion (31 December 2013 est.)
country comparison to the world: 127
$2.351 billion (31 December 2012 est.)

Current account balance:
$3.977 billion
country comparison to the world: 31

Exports:
$12.75 billion
country comparison to the world: 86
$9.88 billion

Exports - commodities:
crude oil, natural gas, garments

Exports - partners:
Japan 45.7%, South Korea 15.1%, Australia 9.1%, NZ 6.6%, India 5.8%, Vietnam 4.7% (2012)

Imports:
$3.02 billion (est.)
country comparison to the world: 147

Imports - commodities:
iron and steel, motor vehicles, machinery and transport equipment, manufactured goods, food, chemicals

Imports - partners:
Singapore 26.3%, China 21.3%, UK 21.3%, Malaysia 11.8%

Debt - external:
$0 (2005)
country comparison to the world: 202

Exchange rates:
Bruneian dollars (BND) per US dollar -
1.23 (2013 est.)
1.2496 (2012 est.)
1.3635 (2010 est.)
1.45 (2009)

ENERGY

Electricity - production:
3.723 billion kWh (est.)
country comparison to the world: 126

Electricity - consumption:

For additional analytical, business and investment opportunities information,
please contact Global Investment & Business Center, USA
at (703) 370-8082. Fax: (703) 370-8083. E-mail: ibpusa3@gmail.com
Global Business and Investment Info Databank - www.ibpus.com

3.391 billion kWh (est.)
country comparison to the world: 127

Electricity - exports:
0 kWh (est.)
country comparison to the world: 111

Electricity - imports:
0 kWh (est.)
country comparison to the world: 123

Electricity - installed generating capacity:
759,000 kW (est.)
country comparison to the world: 129

Electricity - from fossil fuels:
100% of total installed capacity (est.)
country comparison to the world: 9

Electricity - from nuclear fuels:
0% of total installed capacity (est.)
country comparison to the world: 57

Electricity - from hydroelectric plants:
0% of total installed capacity (2010 est.)
country comparison to the world: 161

Electricity - from other renewable sources:
0% of total installed capacity (est.)
country comparison to the world: 162

Crude oil - production:
141,000 bbl/day (est.)
country comparison to the world: 45

Crude oil - exports:
147,900 bbl/day (est.)
country comparison to the world: 35

Crude oil - imports:
0 bbl/day (est.)
country comparison to the world: 166

Crude oil - proved reserves:
1.1 billion bbl (1 January 2013 est.)
country comparison to the world: 41

Refined petroleum products - production:
13,500 bbl/day (est.)

For additional analytical, business and investment opportunities information,
please contact Global Investment & Business Center, USA
at (703) 370-8082. Fax: (703) 370-8083. E-mail: ibpusa3@gmail.com
Global Business and Investment Info Databank - www.ibpus.com

country comparison to the world: 101

Refined petroleum products - consumption:
14,640 bbl/day (est.)
country comparison to the world: 144

Refined petroleum products - exports:
0 bbl/day (est.)
country comparison to the world: 159

Refined petroleum products - imports:
3,198 bbl/day (est.)
country comparison to the world: 169

Natural gas - production:
12.44 billion cu m (est.)
country comparison to the world: 38

Natural gas - consumption:
2.97 billion cu m (est.)
country comparison to the world: 73

Natural gas - exports:
9.42 billion cu m (est.)
country comparison to the world: 25

Natural gas - imports:
0 cu m (est.)
country comparison to the world: 167

Natural gas - proved reserves:
390.8 billion cu m (1 January 2013 est.)
country comparison to the world: 35

Carbon dioxide emissions from consumption of energy:
8.656 million Mt (2011 est.)

COMMUNICATION

Telephones - main lines in use:
70,933
country comparison to the world: 154

Telephones - mobile cellular:
469,700
country comparison to the world: 170

Telephone system:
general assessment: service throughout the country is good; international service is good

For additional analytical, business and investment opportunities information,
please contact Global Investment & Business Center, USA
at (703) 370-8082. Fax: (703) 370-8083. E-mail: ibpusa3@gmail.com
Global Business and Investment Info Databank - www.ibpus.com

to Southeast Asia, Middle East, Western Europe, and the US
domestic: every service available
international: country code - 673; landing point for the SEA-ME-WE-3 optical telecommunications submarine cable that provides links to Asia, the Middle East, and Europe; the Asia-America Gateway submarine cable network provides new links to Asia and the US; satellite earth stations - 2 Intelsat (1 Indian Ocean and 1 Pacific Ocean)

Broadcast media:
state-controlled Radio Television Brunei (RTB) operates 5 channels; 3 Malaysian TV stations are available; foreign TV broadcasts are available via satellite and cable systems; RTB operates 5 radio networks and broadcasts on multiple frequencies; British Forces Broadcast Service (BFBS) provides radio broadcasts on 2 FM stations; some radio broadcast stations from Malaysia are available via repeaters (2009)

Internet country code:
.bn

Internet hosts:
49,457
country comparison to the world: 96

Internet users:
314,900
country comparison to the world: 128

TRANSPORTATION

Railways:
total: 13 km (private line)
narrow gauge: 13 km 0.610-m gauge

Highways:
total: 1,150 km *paved:* 399 km *unpaved:* 751 km

Waterways: 209 km; navigable by craft drawing less than 1.2 m
Pipelines: crude oil 135 km; petroleum products 418 km; natural gas 920 km
Ports and harbors: Bandar Seri Begawan, Kuala Belait, Muara, Seria, Tutong
Merchant marine:
total: 7 liquefied gas tankers (1,000 GRT or over) totaling 348,476 GRT/340,635 DWT

Airports: 2

Airports—with paved runways:
total: 1
over 3,047 m: 1
Airports—with unpaved runways:
total: 1 *914 to 1,523 m:* 1 **Heliports:** 3

MILITARY

Military branches: Land Forces, Navy, Air Force, Royal Brunei Police

Military manpower—military age: 18 years of age
Military manpower—availability:
males age 15-49: 88,628
Military manpower—fit for military service:
males age 15-49: 51,270
Military manpower—reaching military age annually:
males: 3,078
Military expenditures—dollar figure: $343 million
Military expenditures—percent of GDP: 6%

TRANSNATIONAL ISSUES

Disputes—international: possibly involved in a complex dispute over the Spratly Islands with China, Malaysia, Philippines, Taiwan, and Vietnam; in 1984, Brunei established an exclusive fishing zone that encompasses Louisa Reef in the southern Spratly Islands, but has not publicly claimed the island.

IMPORTANT INFORMATION FOR UNDERSTANDING BRUNEI

PROFILE
OFFICIAL NAME: Negara Brunei Darussalam

Geography
Area: 5,765 sq. km. (2,226 sq. mi.), slightly larger than Delaware.
Cities: *Capital*--Bandar Seri Begawan.
Terrain: East--flat coastal plain rises to mountains; west--hilly lowland with a few mountain ridges.
Climate: Equatorial; high temperatures, humidity, and rainfall.

People
Nationality: *Noun and adjective*--Bruneian(s).
Population : 383,000.
Annual growth rate: 3.5%.
Ethnic groups: Malay, Chinese, other indigenous groups.
Religion: Islam.
Languages: Malay, English, Chinese; Iban and other indigenous dialects.
Education: *Years compulsory*--9. *Literacy* (2006)--94.7%.
Health: *Life expectancy (years)*--74.4 (men), 77.4 (women) yrs. *Infant mortality rate* --12.25/1,000.

Government
Type: Malay Islamic Monarchy.
Independence: January 1, 1984.
Constitution: 1959.
Branches: *Executive*--Sultan is both head of state and Prime Minister, presiding over a fourteen-member cabinet. *Legislative*--a Legislative Council has been reactivated after a 20-year suspension to play an advisory role for the Sultan. *Judicial* (based on Indian penal code and English common law)--magistrate's courts, High Court, Court of Appeals, Judicial Committee of the Privy Council (sits in London).
Subdivisions: *Four districts*--Brunei-Muara, Belait, Tutong, and Temburong.

Economy
Natural resources: Oil and natural gas.
Trade: *Exports*--oil, liquefied natural gas, petroleum products, garments. Major markets--Japan, Korea, ASEAN, U.S. *Imports*--machinery and transport equipment, manufactured goods. *Major suppliers*--ASEAN, Japan, U.S., EU.

PEOPLE

Many cultural and linguistic differences make Brunei Malays distinct from the larger Malay populations in nearby Malaysia and Indonesia, even though they are ethnically related and share the Muslim religion.
Brunei has hereditary nobility, carrying the title Pengiran. The Sultan can award to commoners the title Pehin, the equivalent of a life peerage awarded in the United Kingdom. The Sultan also can award his subjects the Dato, the equivalent of a knighthood in the United Kingdom, and Datin, the equivalent of damehood.

Bruneians adhere to the practice of using complete full names with all titles, including the title Haji (for men) or Hajah (for women) for those who have made the Haj pilgrimage to Mecca. Many Brunei Malay women wear the tudong, a traditional head covering. Men wear the songkok, a traditional Malay cap. Men who have completed the Haj can wear a white songkok.
The requirements to attain Brunei citizenship include passing tests in Malay culture, customs, and language. Stateless permanent residents of Brunei are given International Certificates of Identity, which allow them to travel overseas. The majority of Brunei's Chinese are permanent residents, and many are stateless. An amendment to the National Registration and Immigration Act of 2002 allowed female Bruneian citizens for the first time to transfer their nationality to their children.

Oil wealth allows the Brunei Government to provide the population with one of Asia's finest health care systems. Malaria has been eradicated, and cholera is virtually nonexistent. There are five general hospitals--in Bandar Seri Begawan, Tutong, Kuala Belait, Bangar, and Seria--and there are numerous health clinics throughout the country.

Education starts with preschool, followed by 6 years of primary education and up to 7 years of secondary education. Nine years of education are mandatory. Most of Brunei's college students attend universities and other institutions abroad, but approximately 3,674 (2005) study at the University of Brunei Darussalam. Opened in 1985, the university has a faculty of more than 300 instructors and is located on a sprawling campus overlooking the South China Sea.
The official language is Malay, but English is widely understood and used in business. Other languages spoken are several Chinese dialects, Iban, and a number of native dialects. Islam is the official religion, but religious freedom is guaranteed under the constitution.

HISTORY

Historians believe there was a forerunner to the present Brunei Sultanate, which the Chinese called Po-ni. Chinese and Arabic records indicate that this ancient trading kingdom existed at the mouth of the Brunei River as early as the seventh or eighth century A.D. This early kingdom was apparently conquered by the Sumatran Hindu Empire of Srivijaya in the early ninth century, which later controlled northern Borneo and the Philippines. It was subjugated briefly by the Java-based Majapahit Empire but soon regained its independence and once again rose to prominence.

The Brunei Empire had its golden age from the 15th to the 17th centuries, when its control extended over the entire island of Borneo and north into the Philippines. Brunei was particularly powerful under the fifth sultan, Bolkiah (1473-1521), who was famed for his sea exploits and even briefly captured Manila; and under the ninth sultan, Hassan (1605-19), who fully developed an elaborate Royal Court structure, elements of which remain today.

After Sultan Hassan, Brunei entered a period of decline due to internal battles over royal succession as well as the rising influences of European colonial powers in the region that, among other things, disrupted traditional trading patterns, destroying the economic base of Brunei and many other Southeast Asian sultanates. In 1839, the English adventurer James Brooke arrived in Borneo and helped the Sultan put down a rebellion. As a reward, he became governor and later "Rajah" of Sarawak in northwest Borneo and gradually expanded the territory under his control.

Meanwhile, the British North Borneo Company was expanding its control over territory in northeast Borneo. In 1888, Brunei became a protectorate of the British Government, retaining internal independence but with British control over external affairs. In 1906, Brunei accepted a further measure of British control when executive power was transferred to a British resident, who advised the ruler on all matters except those concerning local custom and religion.

In 1959, a new constitution was written declaring Brunei a self-governing state, while its foreign affairs, security, and defense remained the responsibility of the United Kingdom. An attempt in 1962 to introduce a partially elected legislative body with limited powers was abandoned after the opposition political party, Parti Rakyat Brunei, launched an armed uprising, which the government put down with the help of British forces. In the late 1950s and early 1960s, the government also resisted pressures to join neighboring Sabah and Sarawak in the newly formed Malaysia. The Sultan eventually decided that Brunei would remain an independent state.

In 1967, Sultan Omar abdicated in favor of his eldest son, Hassanal Bolkiah, who became the 29th ruler. The former Sultan remained as Defense Minister and assumed the royal title Seri Begawan. In 1970, the national capital, Brunei Town, was renamed Bandar Seri Begawan in his honor. The Seri Begawan died in 1986.

On January 4, 1979, Brunei and the United Kingdom signed a new treaty of friendship and cooperation. On January 1, 1984, Brunei Darussalam became a fully independent state.

GOVERNMENT AND POLITICAL CONDITIONS

Under Brunei's 1959 constitution, the Sultan is the head of state with full executive authority, including emergency powers since 1962. The Sultan is assisted and advised by five councils, which he appoints. A Council of Ministers, or cabinet, which currently consists of 14 members (including the Sultan himself), assists in the administration of the government. The Sultan presides over the cabinet as Prime Minister and also holds the positions of Minister of Defense and Minister of Finance. His son, the Crown Prince, serves as Senior Minister. One of the Sultan's brothers, Prince Mohamed, serves as Minister of Foreign Affairs.

Brunei's legal system is based on English common law, with an independent judiciary, a body of written common law judgments and statutes, and legislation enacted by the sultan. The local magistrates' courts try most cases. More serious cases go before the High Court, which sits for about 2 weeks every few months. Brunei has an arrangement with the United Kingdom whereby United Kingdom judges are appointed as the judges for Brunei's High Court and Court of Appeal. Final appeal can be made to the Judicial Committee of the Privy Council in London in civil but not criminal cases. Brunei also has a separate system of Islamic courts that apply Sharia law in family and other matters involving Muslims.

The Government of Brunei assures continuing public support for the current form of government by providing economic benefits such as subsidized food, fuel, and housing; free education and medical care; and low-interest loans for government employees.

The Sultan said in a 1989 interview that he intended to proceed, with prudence, to establish more liberal institutions in the country and that he would reintroduce elections and a legislature when he "[could] see evidence of a genuine interest in politics on the part of a responsible majority of Bruneians." In 1994, a constitutional review committee submitted its findings to the Sultan, but these have not been made public. In 2004 the Sultan re-introduced an appointed Legislative Council with minimal powers. Five of the 31 seats on the Council are indirectly elected by village leaders.

Brunei's economy is almost totally supported by exports of crude oil and natural gas. The government uses its earnings in part to build up its foreign reserves, which at one time reportedly reached more than $30 billion. The country's wealth, coupled with its membership in the United Nations, Association of Southeast Asian Nations (ASEAN), the Asia Pacific Economic Cooperation (APEC) forum, and the Organization of the Islamic Conference give it an influence in the world disproportionate to its size.

Principal Government Officials
Sultan and Yang di-Pertuan, Prime Minister, Minister of Defense, and Minister of Finance--His Majesty Sultan Hassanal Bolkiah
Senior Minister--His Royal Highness Crown Prince Billah
Minister of Foreign Affairs--His Royal Highness Prince Mohamed Bolkiah
Ambassador to the United States--Pengiran Anak Dato Haji Puteh
Ambassador to the United Nations--Dr. Haji Emran bin Bahar
Brunei Darussalam maintains an embassy in the United States at 3520 International Court, NW, Washington, DC 20008; tel. 202-237-1838.

ECONOMY

Currency	Brunei dollar BND
Fixed exchange rates	1 Brunei dollar = 1 Singapore dollar
Fiscal year	1 April – 31 March (from April 2009)
Trade organisations	APEC, ASEAN, WTO. BIMP-EAGA
	Statistics
GDP	$20.38 billion PPP Rank: 123rd
GDP growth	2.8% Q1
GDP per capita	$51,600
GDP by sector	agriculture (0.7%), industry (73.3%), services (26%)
Inflation (CPI)	1.2%
Population below poverty line	1000 person
Labour force	188,800
Labour force by occupation	agriculture 4.5%, industry 63.1%, services 32.4%
Unemployment	3.7%
Main industries	petroleum, petroleum refining, liquefied natural gas, construction
Ease-of-doing-business rank	83rd
	External
Exports	$10.67 billion
Main export partners	Japan 46.5% South Korea 15.5% Australia 9.3% India 7.0% New Zealand 6.7% (est.)

Imports	$12.055 billion c.i.f.
Main import partners	Singapore 26.3% China 21.3% United Kingdom 21.3% Malaysia 11.8%
	Public finances
Public debt	$0
Revenues	$10.49 billion
Expenses	$5.427 billion
Credit rating	Not rated

Main data source: CIA World Fact Book *All values, unless otherwise stated, are in US dollars.*

Brunei is a country with a small, wealthy economy that is a mixture of foreign and domestic entrepreneurship, government regulation and welfare measures, and village tradition. It is almost totally supported by exports of crude oil and natural gas, with revenues from the petroleum sector accounting for over half of GDP. Per capita GDP is high, and substantial income from overseas investment supplements income from domestic production. The government provides for all medical services and subsidizes food and housing. The government has shown progress in its basic policy of diversifying the economy away from oil and gas. Brunei's leaders are concerned that steadily increased integration in the world economy will undermine internal social cohesion although it has taken steps to become a more prominent player by serving as chairman for the 2000 APEC (Asian Pacific Economic Cooperation) forum. Growth in 1999 was estimated at 2.5% due to higher oil prices in the second half.

Brunei is the third-largest oil producer in Southeast Asia, averaging about 180,000 barrels per day (29,000 m³/d). It also is the fourth-largest producer of liquefied natural gas in the world.

Brunei is the fourth-largest oil producer in Southeast Asia, averaging about 219,000 barrels a day in 2006. It also is the ninth-largest exporter of liquefied natural gas in the world. Like many oil producing countries, Brunei's economy has followed the swings of the world oil market. Economic growth has averaged around 2.8% in the 2000s, heavily dependent on oil and gas production. Oil production has averaged around 200,000 barrels a day during the 2000s, while liquefied natural gas output has been slightly under or over 1,000 trillion btu/day over the same period. Brunei is estimated to have oil reserves expected to last 25 years, and enough natural gas reserves to last 40 years.

Brunei Shell Petroleum (BSP), a joint venture owned in equal shares by the Brunei Government and the Royal Dutch/Shell group of companies, is the chief oil and gas production company in Brunei. It also operates the country's only refinery. BSP and four sister companies--including the liquefied natural gas producing firm BLNG--constitute the largest employer in Brunei after the government. BSP's small refinery has a distillation capacity of 10,000 barrels per day. This satisfies domestic demand for most petroleum products.

The French oil company Total (then known as ELF Aquitaine) became active in petroleum exploration in Brunei in the 1980s. The joint venture Total E&P Borneo BV currently produces approximately 35,000 barrels per day and 13% of Brunei's natural gas.

In 2003, Malaysia disputed Brunei-awarded oil exploration concessions for offshore blocks J and K (Total and Shell respectively), which led to the Brunei licensees ceasing exploration activities. Negotiations between the two countries are continuing in order to resolve the conflict. In 2006, Brunei awarded two on-shore blocks--one to a Canadian-led and the other to a Chinese-led

consortium. Australia, Indonesia, and Korea were the largest customers for Brunei's oil exports, taking over 67% of Brunei's total crude exports. Traditional customers Japan, the U.S., and China each took around 5% of total crude exports.
Almost all of Brunei's natural gas is liquefied at Brunei Shell's Liquefied Natural Gas (LNG) plant, which opened in 1972 and is one of the largest LNG plants in the world. Some 90% of Brunei's LNG produced is sold to Japan under a long-term agreement renewed in 1993.

The agreement calls for Brunei to provide over 5 million tons of LNG per year to three Japanese utilities, namely to TEPCo, Tokyo Electric Power Co. (J.TER or 5001), Tokyo Gas Co. (J.TYG or 9531) and Osaka Gas Co. (J.OSG or 9532). The Japanese company, Mitsubishi, is a joint venture partner with Shell and the Brunei Government in Brunei LNG, Brunei Coldgas, and Brunei Shell Tankers, which together produce the LNG and supply it to Japan. Since 1995, Brunei has supplied more than 700,000 tons of LNG to the Korea Gas Corporation (KOGAS) as well. In 1999, Brunei's natural gas production reached 90 cargoes per day. A small amount of natural gas is used for domestic power generation. Since 2001, Japan remains the dominant export market for natural gas. Brunei is the fourth-largest exporter of LNG in the Asia-Pacific region behind Indonesia, Malaysia, and Australia.

The government sought in the past decade to diversify the economy with limited success. Oil and gas and government spending still account for most of Brunei's economic activity. Brunei's non-petroleum industries include agriculture, forestry, fishing, aquaculture, and banking. The garment-for-export industry has been shrinking since the U.S. eliminated its garment quota system at the end of 2004. The Brunei Economic Development Board announced plans in 2003 to use proven gas reserves to establish downstream industrial projects. The government plans to build a power plant in the Sungai Liang region to power a proposed aluminum smelting plant that will depend on foreign investors. A second major project depending on foreign investment is in the planning stage: a giant container hub at the Muara Port facilities.

The government regulates the immigration of foreign labor out of concern it might disrupt Brunei's society. Work permits for foreigners are issued only for short periods and must be continually renewed. Despite these restrictions, the estimated 100,000 foreign temporary residents of Brunei make up a significant portion of the work force. The government reported a total work force of 180,400 in 2006, with a derived unemployment rate of 4.0%.

Oil and natural gas account for almost all exports. Since only a few products other than petroleum are produced locally, a wide variety of items must be imported. Nonetheless, Brunei has had a significant trade surplus in the 2000s. Official statistics show Singapore, Malaysia, Japan, the U.S., and the U.K. as the leading importers in 2005. The United States was the third-largest supplier of imports to Brunei in 2005.

Brunei's substantial foreign reserves are managed by the Brunei Investment Agency (BIA), an arm of the Ministry of Finance. BIA's guiding principle is to increase the real value of Brunei's foreign reserves while pursuing a diverse investment strategy, with holdings in the United States, Japan, Western Europe, and the Association of Southeast Asian Nations (ASEAN) countries.

The Brunei Government encourages more foreign investment. New enterprises that meet certain criteria can receive pioneer status, exempting profits from income tax for up to 5 years, depending on the amount of capital invested. The normal corporate income tax rate is 30%. There is no personal income tax or capital gains tax.

One of the government's priorities is to encourage the development of Brunei Malays as leaders of industry and commerce. There are no specific restrictions of foreign equity ownership, but local participation, both shared capital and management, is encouraged. Such participation helps when tendering for contracts with the government or Brunei Shell Petroleum.

Companies in Brunei must either be incorporated locally or registered as a branch of a foreign company and must be registered with the Registrar of Companies. Public companies must have a minimum of seven shareholders. Private companies must have a minimum of two but not more than 50 shareholders. At least half of the directors in a company must be residents of Brunei.

The government owns a cattle farm in Australia through which the country's beef supplies are processed. At 2,262 square miles, this ranch is larger than Brunei itself. Eggs and chickens are largely produced locally, but most of Brunei's other food needs must be imported. Agriculture, aquaculture, and fisheries are among the industrial sectors that the government has selected for highest priority in its efforts to diversify the economy.

Recently the government has announced plans for Brunei to become an international offshore financial center as well as a center for Islamic banking. Brunei is keen on the development of small and medium enterprises and also is investigating the possibility of establishing a "cyber park" to develop an information technology industry. Brunei has also promoted ecotourism to take advantage of the over 70% of Brunei's territory that remains primal tropical rainforest.

DEFENSE

The Sultan is both Minister of Defense and Supreme Commander of the Armed Forces (RBAF). All infantry, navy, and air combat units are made up of volunteers. There are two infantry battalions equipped with armored reconnaissance vehicles and armored personnel carriers and supported by Rapier air defense missiles and a flotilla of coastal patrol vessels armed with surface-to-surface missiles. Brunei has ordered, but not yet taken possession of, three offshore patrol vessels from the U.K.

Brunei has a defense agreement with the United Kingdom, under which a British Armed Forces Ghurka battalion (1,500 men) is permanently stationed in Seria, near the center of Brunei's oil industry. The RBAF has joint exercises, training programs, and other military cooperation with the United Kingdom and many other countries, including the United States. The U.S. and Brunei signed a memorandum of understanding (MOU) on defense cooperation in November 1994. The two countries conduct an annual military exercise called CARAT.

FOREIGN RELATIONS

Brunei joined ASEAN on January 7, 1984--one week after resuming full independence--and gives its ASEAN membership the highest priority in its foreign relations. Brunei joined the UN in September 1984. It also is a member of the Organization of the Islamic Conference (OIC) and of the Asia-Pacific Economic Cooperation (APEC) forum. Brunei hosted the APEC Economic Leaders' Meeting in November 2000 and the ASEAN Regional Forum (ARF) in July 2002.

U.S.-BRUNEI RELATIONS

Relations between the United States and Brunei date from the 1800s. On April 6, 1845, the U.S.S. Constitution visited Brunei. The two countries concluded a Treaty of Peace, Friendship, Commerce and Navigation in 1850, which remains in force today. The United States maintained a consulate in Brunei from 1865 to 1867.

The U.S. welcomed Brunei Darussalam's full independence from the United Kingdom on January 1, 1984, and opened an Embassy in Bandar Seri Begawan on that date. Brunei opened its embassy in Washington in March 1984. Brunei's armed forces engage in joint exercises, training programs, and other military cooperation with the U.S. A memorandum of understanding on defense cooperation was signed on November 29, 1994. The Sultan visited Washington in December 2002.

Principal U.S. Embassy Officials
Ambassador--Daniel L. Shields
Deputy Chief of Mission--John McIntyre
Management Officer--Michael Lampel

The U.S. Embassy in Bandar Seri Begawan is located on the third & fifth floors of the Teck Guan Plaza, at the corner of Jalan Sultan and Jalan MacArthur; tel: 673-2229670; fax: 673-2225293; e-mail: usembassy_bsb@state.gov

TRAVEL AND BUSINESS INFORMATION

The U.S. Department of State's Consular Information Program advises Americans traveling and residing abroad through Consular Information Sheets, Public Announcements, and Travel Warnings. **Consular Information Sheets** exist for all countries and include information on entry and exit requirements, currency regulations, health conditions, safety and security, crime, political disturbances, and the addresses of the U.S. embassies and consulates abroad. **Public Announcements** are issued to disseminate information quickly about terrorist threats and other relatively short-term conditions overseas that pose significant risks to the security of American travelers. **Travel Warnings** are issued when the State Department recommends that Americans avoid travel to a certain country because the situation is dangerous or unstable.

For the latest security information, Americans living and traveling abroad should regularly monitor the Department's Bureau of Consular Affairs Internet web site at http://www.travel.state.gov, where the current Worldwide Caution, Public Announcements, and Travel Warnings can be found. Consular Affairs Publications, which contain information on obtaining passports and planning a safe trip abroad, are also available at http://www.travel.state.gov. For additional information on international travel, see http://www.usa.gov/Citizen/Topics/Travel/International.shtml.

The Department of State encourages all U.S citizens traveling or residing abroad to register via the State Department's travel registration website or at the nearest U.S. embassy or consulate abroad. Registration will make your presence and whereabouts known in case it is necessary to contact you in an emergency and will enable you to receive up-to-date information on security conditions.

Emergency information concerning Americans traveling abroad may be obtained by calling 1-888-407-4747 toll free in the U.S. and Canada or the regular toll line 1-202-501-4444 for callers outside the U.S. and Canada.

The National Passport Information Center (NPIC) is the U.S. Department of State's single, centralized public contact center for U.S. passport information. Telephone: 1-877-4USA-PPT (1-877-487-2778). Customer service representatives and operators for TDD/TTY are available Monday-Friday, 7:00 a.m. to 12:00 midnight, Eastern Time, excluding federal holidays.

Travelers can check the latest health information with the U.S. Centers for Disease Control and Prevention in Atlanta, Georgia. A hotline at 877-FYI-TRIP (877-394-8747) and a web site at http://www.cdc.gov/travel/index.htm give the most recent health advisories, immunization recommendations or requirements, and advice on food and drinking water safety for regions and countries. A booklet entitled "Health Information for International Travel" (HHS publication number CDC-95-8280) is available from the U.S. Government Printing Office, Washington, DC 20402, tel. (202) 512-1800.

EU-BRUNEI RELATIONS

Official Name	Negara Brunei Darussalam
Population	0.38 million
Area	6000 km²
Gross Domestic Product	5 bn euros
GDP Per Capita	14.173 €
Real GDP (% growth)	3.0 %
Exports GDP %	0.85
Imports GDP %	0.27
Exports to Brunei from EU (mn €, 2001)	108 EU imports from Brunei (mn €)
Imports to EU from Brunei (mn €, 2001)	72
Human Development Index (rank of 175°)	33
Head of State	HM Paduka Seri Baginda Sultan Haji Hassanal Bolkiah Mu'izzadddin Waddaulah (Sultan, prime minister, minister of finance and defence)

FRAMEWORK

The framework for co-operation dialogue with Brunei is the EC-ASEAN Agreement of 1980. There is no bilateral cooperation agreement.

POLITICAL CONTEXT

Brunei Darussalam became independent from the United Kingdom on 1 January 1984, and a week later joined the Association of South-East Asian Nations (ASEAN). Brunei is a constitutional monarchy with the Sultan Yang Di-Pertuan – Hassanal Bolkiah as the Head of State, Prime Minister, Defence Minister, as well as Minister for Finance. The Sultan presides over a 10-member cabinet which he appoints himself. Five councils advise the Sultan on policy matters: the Religious Council, the Privy Council, the Council of Succession, the Legislative Council and the Council of Ministers (the cabinet). Since 1962 the Sultan has ruled by decree. Thus, the system of government revolves around the Sultan as the source of executive power.

On 25 September 2004, the Legislative Council met for the first time in 20 years, with 21 members appointed by the Sultan. It passed constitutional amendments, calling for a 45-seat council with 15 elected members. In a move towards political reform an appointed parliament was revived in 2004. The constitution provides for an expanded house with up to 15 elected MPs. However, no date has been set for elections.

Brunei is a Muslim country, with a Ministry of Religious Affairs established to foster and promote Islam. Brunei continues to play a peacekeeping role in the Philippines, and is taking part in efforts to monitor peace in the Indonesian region of Aceh.

EUROPEAN COMMUNITY ASSISTANCE

By virtue of its advanced level of economic development Brunei does not benefit from bilateral development or economic projects.

EC co-operation with Brunei has for the greater part been limited to joint EC- ASEAN projects.

The EC has given financial support to the ASEAN-EC Management Centre (AEMC), located in Brunei, the contract for which has come to an end.

TRADE AND ECONOMIC

Since 1929, when oil was discovered in Brunei, the country has flourished. During 1998 and as a consequence of the Asia crisis, however, both exports and imports decreased in comparison with previous years.

    □ **Key role of oil and gas**: Brunei suffered little directly from the Asian financial crisis of 1997. But, in 1998, the Sultanate was hit by the sharp fall in oil sales and the bankruptcy of a locally-owned oil and gas company, resulting in a contraction in GDP of 4%. Subsequently, economic activity recovered in step with the resumption of oil and gas extraction and, in recent years, the sharp rise in the oil price. The latest available data for GDP shows real annual growth around 3%. Oil reserves are officially estimated at 25 years, but, great hopes are placed in two new drilling concessions.

Economic structure: Almost everything the country needs is imported. Even the industrial labour force comes from abroad, mainly from India, the Philippines, Indonesia and Bangladesh as most of Brunei's citizens are employed as civil servants (60% of the population) and prefer the status related to that occupation. This also explains the apparent contradiction between the necessity to employ foreign manpower and the rising unemployment rate (officially at 4.7% but estimated at 9%).

    □ At the beginning of 2000, the government of the Sultanate announced an ambitious programme of **economic reforms** in order to reduce the dependence on oil and gas. Two initiatives have been taken up till know– to develop tourism and to support the creation of an off-shore financial centre in developing Islamic banking business.

    □ The tourism industry is, however, handicapped by the shortage of quality infrastructure, and the geographical insulation of the Sultanate.

Brunei's trade surplus fell by an estimated 74% in US dollar terms in 1999 as the price of oil and gas collapsed. A strengthening oil price and long-term contracts for natural gas, paid in US dollars, should, however, ensure that Brunei's trade position remains healthy.

At present Brunei produces oil and gas almost to the exclusion of other products. The government is trying hard, however, to develop manufactured exports, in particular cement and roofing (tiles) which are both protected sectors. The garment industry is struggling after the abolition of global quotas on the textile trade. The Sultan has announced financial reforms.

Brunei has signed a free-trade pact with New Zealand, Singapore and Chile. A Brunei Tourism Board has been set up

The domestic economy: Brunei's economic growth remains fairly sluggish, at 2.6% year on year but a recovery is likely to have taken place in the second quarter of 2005. The non-oil and gas sector is expanding more rapidly than the energy sector. High global oil prices have lifted transport prices, but overall inflation remains low.

Foreign trade and payments: High oil prices lay behind an increase in the merchandises-trade surplus in the first quarter of 2005.The oil and gas sector continues to account for the bulk of exports; garments exports were much lower than in the year-earlier period.

The investment policy in Brunei is largely open to foreign investors, as indicated by a favourable legal environment and a policy allowing full foreign ownership in a majority of economic sectors. Foreign investments have been more particularly in the last years as they are considered by the government as a key element to contribute to the targeted diversification of the country's economy.

As part of this strategy to attract foreign investments, an Economic Development Board (EDB) was created in 2001. The main sectors and projects promoted by the EDB and susceptible to attract foreign investments include port infrastructure, industry, communication (aviation hub), eco-tourism, and financial services. In parallel with the creation of the EDB, major policy changes have been made in the last years to promote foreign investments. August 2000 saw the introduction of an offshore legislation in Brunei. New laws were drafted covering international banking, insurance, offshore companies, trusts, limited partnerships and registered agents.

Changes in the legislation are too recent analyze its effects. The volume of FDI has doubled between 2001 and 2002, while the figures available until mid 2003 include that the trend is positive and that investments do not only target natural resources but also services.

BRUNEI LEGAL SYSTEM BASICS

The British Residential system was introduced in Brunei Darussalam by virtue of the Courts Enactment of 1906. Another enactment was later introduced, known as the 1908 Enactment and had repealed the 1906 Enactment. The purpose of this second Enactment was to amend the law relating to the constitution and powers of the Civil and Criminal Courts and the law and procedures to be administered in Brunei Darussalam (hereafter called the "State").

By virtue of section 3 of the 1908 Enactment, five courts were constituted in the State for the administration of Civil and Criminal justice. There were:

(1) The Court of the Resident

(2) Courts of Magistrate of the First Class

(3) Courts of Magistrate of the Second Class

(4) Courts of Native Magistrates

(5) Courts of Kathis.

The first court would be the Court of the Resident, which had and exercised original and appellate jurisdiction in civil and criminal matters. The Officer, which presided the Court of the Resident, should either be the Resident; or the District Judge of the District Court of Labuan or any District Judge of the Colony of the Straits Settlements[1].

The Court of the Resident had jurisdiction in all suits, matters and questions of a civil nature except the power to authorize any Court in the State to dissolve or annul a marriage lawfully solemnised in the United Kingdom of Great Britain and Ireland or in any British Colony, Protectorate or Possession[2].

Its appellate jurisdiction in both civil and criminal matters would be to hear and determine all appeals from the decisions of the lower Courts; and in doing so might exercise full powers or supervision and revision in respect of all proceedings in such Courts[3].

Section 8A of the 1908 Enactment stated that the Courts of Magistrates was of two kinds

i.e. Courts Magistrates of the First Class, and Courts Magistrates of the Second Class.

For the Court of Magistrate of the First Class, its criminal jurisdiction would be to try all offences for which the maximum term of imprisonment provided by law did not exceed a term of 7 years imprisonment of either description or which were punishable with fine only and for any other offence in respect of which jurisdiction was given by law; whereas

[1] Section 4 of the 1908 Enactment. [2] Section 5(i) of the 1908 Enactment. [3] Section 7 of the 1908 Enactment.

for civil jurisdiction it would hear and determine all suits when the amount in dispute or the value of the subject matter did not exceed $1,000 [4].

For additional analytical, business and investment opportunities information, please contact Global Investment & Business Center, USA at (703) 370-8082. Fax: (703) 370-8083. E-mail: ibpusa3@gmail.com Global Business and Investment Info Databank - www.ibpus.com

In addition to that, such Court had power to grant, alter, revoke and annul probates of wills and letters of administration in the estate of all persons leaving movable or immovable property in the State or the time of death having a fixed place of abode within the State where such estate does not exceed in value $2,500[5]. Such Court also had power to appoint and control guardians of infants and lunatics[6].

For its appellate jurisdiction, the Court of Magistrate of the First Class had power to hear and determine all appeals from the decisions of inferior Courts both in civil and criminal matters, and had power for revision and supervision in respect of all proceedings in such Courts[7].

For the Court of Magistrate of the Second Class, its criminal jurisdiction would be to try all offences for which the maximum term of imprisonment provided by law does not exceed 3 years imprisonment of either description or which were punishable with fine only of a sum not exceeding $100 and any offence in respect of which jurisdiction is given to the Court of a Magistrate of the Second Class.[8]

In its civil jurisdiction, the Court of Magistrate of the Second Class would hear and determine all suits when the amount in dispute or the value of the subject matter does not exceed $ 100.[9]

Unlike the Court of Magistrate of the First Class, the Court of Magistrate of the Second Class had no power to grant probate of wills or letters of administration, to appoint and control guardians of infants and lunatics, or even to hear appeals in civil or criminal matters[10].

As for the Court of a Native Magistrate, it could hear and determine all suits brought by or against Malays or other Asiatics in which the amount in dispute or the subject matter does not exceed $25 while its criminal jurisdiction would be to try and determine cases in which the maximum amount of imprisonment prescribed by law did not exceed three months[11].

And lastly, the Court of a Kathi that had such powers in all matters concerning Islamic religion, marriage and divorce as may be defined in his "Kuasa."[12].

[4] Section 8B (i) of the 1908 Enactment. [5] Section 8B (ii)(a) of the 1908 Enactment. [6] Section 8B (ii)(b) of the 1908 Enactment. [7] Section 8B (iii) of the 1908 Enactment. [8] Section 8C (i) of the 1908 Enactment. [9] Section 8C (i) of the 1908 Enactment. [10] Section 8C (ii) of the 1908 Enactment. [11] Section 9 of the 1908 Enactment. [12] Section 9 of the 1908 Enactment.

Sentences that might be imposed by the various Courts:

(1) Court of the Resident – any sentence authorized by law.

(2) Courts of Magistrate of the First Class – Imprisonment for a term not exceeding two years. Fine not exceeding $1,000. Whipping not exceeding 12 strokes.

(3) Courts of Magistrate of the Second Class – Imprisonment for a term not exceeding fourteen days. Fine not exceeding $50.

(4) Courts of Native Magistrates and Kathis – Fine not exceeding $10.[13]

Apart from the five courts mentioned earlier, there was the Supreme Court. The is court or any Judge thereof would have the original jurisdiction in the case of any offence charged to had been committed within the State for which the punishment of death is authorised by law[14].

The Supreme Court had civil appellate jurisdiction for an appeal from the final decision of the Court of the Resident in any civil action or proceeding where the amount in dispute or the subject matter exceeded$1,000 except in any of the following cases where no such appeal might be made:

(1) where the judgment or order was made by the consent of parties;

(2) where the judgment or order relates to costs only;

(3) where by any Enactment for the time being in force the judgment or order of the Court of the Resident was expressly declared to be final[15].

The criminal appellate jurisdiction of the Supreme Court would be to hear appeal from any decision of the Court of the Resident in the exercise of its original jurisdiction whereby any person had been convicted and sentenced to not less than two years imprisonment or to a fine of not less than $ 500[16].To make an appeal, the appellant would lodge a petition of appeal at the Court of the Resident addressed to the Supreme Court within seven days from the date when the judgment or order was pronounced or within such further time as may be allowed by the Court of the Resident[17]. Any judgment of order of the Court of Appeal or of the Supreme Court made under this Enactment should be executed, enforced and be given effect by the Court of the Resident[18].

However, under this Enactment there was still scope for an appeal against any judgment or order of the Court of Appeal in any civil matter. This appeal might be made to His Britannic Majesty in Council (i.e. Privy Council) subject to such rules and regulations as may be prescribed by order of His Majesty in Council[19].

[13] Section 13 of the 1908 Enactment. [14] Section 14 (i) of the 1908 Enactment. [15] Section 15 (i) of the 1908 Enactment. [16] Section 16 (1) of the 1908 Enactment. [17] Section 16(2) of the 1908 Enactment. [18] Section 17 of the 1908 Enactment. [19] Section 18 of the 1908 Enactment.

THE COMING OF ISLAM TO BRUNEI DARUSSALAM

Being a state where majority of the populations are Muslims, Islam has been made the official religion of Brunei Darussalam. To say that Islam has only been practiced in this country in recent years are quite incorrect as there are sources, which date the establishment of a Muslim sultanate rule. In fact, Islamic laws have always been the governing laws in Brunei Darussalam even before the coming of the British.

There are evidences which show that Islam had come to Brunei since the 10th century. However, its reception was slow probably because most of the populations during that time were still holding on to their beliefs in Hinduism. Muslims were comprised of just a small section of the population including those traders who came to Brunei[20]. And it was believed that the acceptance of the Sultans and nobles had started the spread of Islam among the community. Awang Alak Betatar, the first ruler of Brunei, embraced Islam when he married the princess of Johore [21]. He changed his name to Sultan Mohammad Shah and since then Islam slowly spread within Brunei.

Islam was quickly spread among most of the people in Brunei when Sultan Sharif Ali, the third Sultan of Brunei, ascended to the throne. Believed to be a descendant of the Prophet Muhammad (Peace Be Upon Him)[22], he was a pious person and was the one who had started to build mosque and had been the one who determined the direction of the Qiblat[23]. From then on Islam has become an important aspect in the life of people in Brunei where eventually it has become the official religion of Brunei Darussalam.

Other evidence that shows Brunei was indeed been governed by Islamic law can be seen in written and codified form. There exist two manuscripts, the first manuscript was called the "Hukum Kanun Brunei" which, contained 96 pages and is kept at the Language and Literature Bureau, whilst copy for reference can be found at the Brunei Museum reference no. A/BM/98/90[24]. While the second manuscript was known as "Undang-Undang dan Adat Brunei Lama" (Old Brunei Law and Custom). It consists of 68 pages and is now reserved in the Sarawak Museum[25].

The content of the first manuscript covered a wide range of laws including the Islamic laws of hudud and qisas. The overall content of the manuscript is in harmony with the Islamic law. For example: Clause One of the manuscript talks about relationship between people and its ruler, conditions of becoming a ruler, responsibilities of the people towards

[20] Prof. Dato Dr. Haji Mahmud Saedon A. Othman, *Ke Arah Pelaksanaan Undang-Undang Di Negara Brunei Darussalam*, Jurnal Undang-Undang Syariah Brunei Darussalam, Januari-Jun 2002 Jilid 2 Bil. 2 p.

[21] Pehin Jawatan Dalam Seri Maharaja Dato Seri Utama Dr. Haji Awang Mohd. Jamil Al-Sufri, *Tarsilah Brunei: Sejarah Awal dan Perkembangan Islam*, Jilid 1, Pusat Sejarah Brunei 2001, p. 33. [22] Ibid p. 80. [23] Ibid p. 90. [24] Prof. Dato' Dr. Hj Mahmud Saedon bin Awang Othman, *Undang-Undang Islam Dalam Kesultanan Melayu Brunei hingga Tahun 1959,* International Seminar on Brunei Malay Sultanate in Nusantara 1999, p.

its rulers; Clause Four talks about various kind of offences such as murder, stabbing, slaying, hitting, robbery, stealing and many other though no punishment for those offences were stated in this Clause; Clause Five talks about the punishment of qisas for murder and also for the murderer to be killed in return for his crime; Clause Seven talks about offence of stealing, the punishment of which would be to cut off certain part of his hand; Clause Twenty-Five talks about marriage, requirements of marriage and the words to be uttered during the marriage contract; Clause twenty-Six talks about number of witnesses in a marriage contract; Clause Thirty-One talks about the rule and conditions in sale and purchase contract; and other clauses which talks about wide ranges of laws that is in accordance with Islamic laws. [26]

The *Hukum Kanun Brunei* was written during the reign of Sultan Hassan though it was believed that it had been started even earlier than that. It was completed and enforced during the reign of Sultan Jalilul Akbar and then continued during the reign of his son, Sultan Jalilul Jabbar. With the enforcement of this law, Islamic law has been enforced and that it had became the basic law and policy of Brunei Darussalam at that time[27].

THE CONSTITUTION

The governing structure of Brunei Darussalam rests on the country's written Constitution along with the three pillars of its national philosophy, namely Malay, Islam and Monarchy.

Brunei Darussalam's written Constitution sets out its governing authorities along with their respective functions and responsibilities. Specifically, the Constitution sets out the executive authority over the affairs of Brunei Darussalam and further creates the Council of Ministers, the Religious Council, the Privy Council, the Legislative Council, the *Adat Istiadat* (Customs and

Traditions) Council and the Council of Succession. The basic order, structure, functions, responsibilities and underlying principles of the governing authorities are premised on what is prescribed in the Constitution. In relation to the law making process, it sets out the procedure within Brunei Darussalam with the recent rejuvenation of the Legislative Council, which will be discussed in detail later.

The Constitution of Brunei Darussalam was originally enacted in September 1959 much to the efforts of our then Sultan, Al-Marhum Sultan Haji Omar Ali Saifuddien Sa'adul Khairi Waddien, who is also the present Sultan's late father. The enactment of the 1959 Constitution represented the country's primary stepping stone in its move towards full independence, which eventually came in 1984.

Since 1959, the Constitution has been subject to a number of important amendments, in particular in 1971, 1984 and most recently in 2004. In fact, a newly revised Constitution was published in 2004 incorporating all the amendments that have been made since its birth year of 1959.

STATUTES/LEGISLATIVE ENACTMENTS

Brunei Darussalam has in place a set of acts compiled in volumes called "Laws of Brunei." At present, there are 193 Acts in place which are in loose leaf form kept in ring binder volumes that consist of legislations that were passed prior to Independence Day and those that were enacted after it. Some of the legislations are also Acts that were extended from the United Kingdom, some dating back as early as 1958. However, some have been notably repealed, either in whole or in part to reflect updates in the development of the law. There are however some old enactments that have been merely omitted from the Laws of Brunei as authorized by His Majesty for the Attorney General to omit. Nevertheless, its omission does not mean that they do not have the force of law and hence would still be considered valid unless it is otherwise provided.[1]

There are also a number of *Government Gazettes* which consists of: i) new laws that has not been revised to become an Act;

Since Brunei Darussalam at present pass their laws in accordance with article 83(3) of the Constitution, any new laws that has been approved by His Majesty will be published in *Government Gazette* form and will come into force on the date His Majesty approves of. Hence that new law will for the time being be referred to as an Order and not an Act.

The Law Revision Act is in place to govern the revision of such *Gazettes* to turn into Acts. After the 1st of January of every year, the Attorney General revises the law and publishes a revised edition of the new law to be included in the Laws of Brunei volumes. He also does this with existing law that has been amended so he will publish a new revised edition of that law incorporating all the recent amendments. [2]

The following constitutional and legislative documents are also considered part of the Laws of Brunei.[3] They are:

i) Treaty of Friendship and Co-operation between Brunei Darussalam and the

United Kingdom dated 7th January 1979;

ii) The Continental Shelf Proclamation 1954

iii) The North Borneo (Definition of Boundaries) Order in Council 1958; and

iv) The Sarawak (Definition of Boundaries) Order in Council 1958.

ISLAMIC LAWS

In Islam, the main source of law is the Holy Qur'an then followed by the tradition of the Prophets or Hadith as the second source of the Islamic Laws[4]. Other sources of law in Islam includes *Ijma'* or consensus of opinion[5], *Qiyas* (Analogical Deduction)[6], *Istihsan* or Equity in Islamic Law[7], *Maslahah Mursalah* (Consideration of Public Interest)[8], *'Urf* (Custom)[9], *Istishab* (presumption of Continuity)[10], *Saad al-Dhara'i* (Blocking the Means)[11].

Similarly, Islamic laws in Brunei Darussalam are guided mainly by the principles in the Holy Qur'an and the Prophet's tradition or Hadith as well as other sources mentioned earlier. Islam as the official religion in Brunei Darussalam is clearly stated in the Constitution of Brunei Darussalam:

[2] Section 7 of the Law Revision Act [3] Schedule to the Law Revision Act [4] Mohammad Hashim Kamali, *Principles of Islamic Jurisprudence*, Second Revised Edition, Ilmiah Publishers Sdn. Bhd., Kuala Lumpur 1998, p. 58. [5] ibid p.168. [6] ibid p.197. [7] ibid p.245. [8] ibid p.267. [9] ibid p.283. [10] ibid p.297. [11] ibid p.310.

"The official religion of Brunei Darussalam shall be the Islamic Religion: Provided that all other religions may be practiced in peace and harmony by the persons professing them.[12]"

Islamic law in Brunei is still governed under the Religious Council and Kadis Courts Act (Chapter 77), an Act which consolidates the law relating to the Religious Council and the Kadis Courts, the constitution and organization of religious authorities and the regulation of religious affairs.

Apart from this Act, there are also other legislations enforced in Brunei Darussalam to govern the conduct of Muslims in this country, these legislations are for example:

i) the Syariah Courts Act (Chapter 184), an Act which make specific provisions in respect of the establishment of Syariah Courts, appointments, powers of Syar'ie Judge and jurisdiction of Syariah Courts and other matters connected with the proceedings of Syariah Courts, and for the determination and confirmation of the new moon;

ii) the Syariah Courts Evidence Order, 2001, an Order relating to the law of evidence for the Syariah Courts;

iii) the Emergency (Islamic Family Law) Order, 1999, an Order that make certain provisions relating to Islamic family law in respect of marriage, divorce, maintenance, guardianship and other matters connected with family life;

iv) the Islamic Adoption of Children Order, 2001, an Order to make certain provisions on the law of adoption of children according to Islam; and

v) the Halal Meat Act (Chapter 183) an Act which regulate the supply and importation of halal meat and related matters.

SUBSIDIARY LEGISLATION

We also have in place as part of the Laws of Brunei, a number of subsidiary legislations which include rules, regulations, orders, proclamations or other documents that has the force of law and annexed to their relevant parent Acts. Other government departments whose work is relevant to that particular legislation would usually prepare the drafts for subsidiary legislations.

The power to make subsidiary legislation is conferred under section 13 of the Interpretation and General Clauses Act (CAP. 4). Section 16 further states that the subsidiary legislation should be published in the *Government Gazette.*

CASE LAW/JUDICIAL PRECEDENT

The Supreme Court of Brunei Darussalam is largely guided by the written Constitution and the Laws of Brunei in executing their responsibility of upholding the law in Brunei Darussalam. However where there are no written laws on a particular matter, the courts would then turn to principles of law that are found in case law or judicial precedent.

[12] Article 3(1) of the Constitution of Brunei Darussalam.

Cases heard in Brunei Darussalam are compiled in annual volumes of what are called "Judgments of Brunei Darussalam." Similar to other members in the family practicing the English Legal System, Brunei Darussalam also practice the doctrine of *stare decisis,* where decisions of a higher court are binding on the lower courts. The advantages of following binding precedent include certainty, flexibility, comprehensiveness and practicality in its practice. However, it is recognized that sometimes it can be difficult for lower courts that are bound by the decision and therefore cannot alter it. For that reason also, it may create more appeals.

The courts of Brunei Darussalam would also occasionally refer to cases from Malaysia, Singapore, India and the United Kingdom, all practicing the English legal system though the decisions in those cases would not be binding but instead would only be regarded as "persuasive authority" in the courts of Brunei Darussalam.

COMMON LAW OF ENGLAND

Under the Application of Laws Act, the Common Law of England and the doctrine of equity, together with the statutes of general application that are administered or in force in England, also have the force of law in Brunei Darussalam. This provision is however on the condition that the said common law, doctrine of equity and statutes of general application does not contradict the circumstances of Brunei Darussalam, its inhabitants and subject to such qualifications or local circumstances and custom may render necessary.

GOVERNMENT AND THE STATE

THE EXECUTIVE

As stated under section 4 of the Constitution, the supreme executive authority of Brunei Darussalam is vested in and shall be exercised by His Majesty the Sultan and Yang Di-Pertuan of Brunei Darussalam who is also the Prime Minister of Brunei Darussalam. Nevertheless, His Majesty the Sultan may still appoint Ministers or Deputy Ministers to exercise that executive authority whilst solely being responsible to him in the course of their duties. These appointed ministers shall also assist and advise His Majesty the Sultan in the event His Majesty discharges his executive authority.

THE LEGISLATIVE COUNCIL

Under the Constitution, any member of the Legislative Council may introduce any bill and a bill will only become law when His Majesty the Sultan has assented, signed and sealed the bill with the Seal of the State.

The Legislative Council was temporarily suspended in 1983 but was recently reestablished at its first official meeting in September 2004. During the period where the Council was inactive, laws were passed in the form of emergency orders by His Majesty in accordance with article 83(3) of the Constitution. The normal procedure of the law making process during this period would be initiated by a particular Ministry or Government Department who would either propose or prepare the draft legislation and would then pass it to the Attorney General's Chambers to give legal advice on. Where a Ministry or Governmental Department merely propose the drafting of such legislation, the Attorney General's Chambers will then prepare the draft based on substantive points the former provides. Once the draft is ready to be adopted, it will be presented to His Majesty for his approval. The draft legislation that His Majesty approves of will be passed in an **Emergency Order** form and will be published in the *Government Gazette*.

Every order made under article 83(3) however are deemed to have been validly made, to be fully effectual and to have had full force from the date on which such Proclamation or Order was declared or made and they are deemed to have been passed by the Legislative Council.[1]

The law making process by the Legislative Council is prescribed under Part VII of the Constitution. Basically, any member of the Legislative Council may

(i) introduce a new bill;
(ii) propose a motion for the Council to debate on; or

(iii) present any petition to the Council. The bill, motion or petition will then be debated on and disposed of in accordance with the Standing Orders of the Legislative Council.

[1] Article 83A

Every bill that is going to be introduced needs to be published in the gazette and within 7 days of the publication of the bill in a gazette, the bill shall then be laid before the Legislative Council.[2]

There are certain matters however that are generally excluded from being discussed by the Legislative Council, unless His Majesty the Sultan approves otherwise, and these include matters relating to the issue of bank notes, the establishment of any bank association, amendment of the constitution in relation to both those matters. Matters that would also be disqualified are where the issues are inconsistent with any obligations imposed upon His Majesty under any international treaty or agreement with another power of state. Other disqualified matters include those having the effect of lowering or adversely affecting the rights, positions, discretions, powers, privileges, sovereignty or prerogatives of His Majesty, the standing or prominence of Brunei Darussalam's national philosophy that is Malay Islamic Monarchy and the finances or currency of Brunei Darussalam.[3]

All questions proposed to the Legislative Council to decide upon shall be concluded by way of majority vote taken from the members that are present and voting. Once a bill has been debated on, the Legislative Council will then make a decision whether or not to pass it. If the Council rejects it, which is called a "negative resolution", the Speaker of the Council will then have to submit a report to His Majesty the Sultan incorporating a summary of the debate and the reasons why the Council reached such a resolution. Nevertheless, His Majesty may still declare the Bill to have effect, notwithstanding the negative resolution and he may order it to have effect either as an Act in the form in which it was introduced or to include any amendments that he may think fit to include.[4]

When the Legislative Council decides to pass the Bill, such Bill will only become law if His Majesty the Sultan assents to it, signs it and thereafter seals the Bill with the official State Seal. Again, the bill might take effect as an Act either in its original form as to how it was introduced or His Majesty the Sultan may still make amendments to it as he thinks fit. Such law once assented, signed and sealed by His Majesty shall come into operation on the date on which such assent shall be given.[5]

All the laws made through the Legislative Council shall be styled as "Acts" which will always have the enacting words as follows: "Be it enacted by His Majesty the Sultan and Yang DI-Pertuan with the advice and consent of the Legislative Council as follows."[6]

His Majesty the Sultan also has reserved powers over any bills that was not or has not yet been passed by the Legislative Council if in his opinion, the passing or expedited passing of the Bill is in the interests of public order, good faith and good government. In such

[2] Article 41, the Constitution [3] Article 42 [4] Article 43 [5] Article 45 [6] Article 46

cases, he can declare that bill/motion/petition /business to have effect as if it had been passed or carried by that Council even though it has not been done so.[7]

THE JUDICIARY

THE SUPREME COURT

The Supreme Court of Brunei Darussalam is the body wholly responsible for the administration of justice in civil law (as opposed to "syariah law") and strictly speaking has within its hierarchical structure, the Court of Appeal and the High Court. Within the same building of the Supreme Court, we can also find the Intermediate Courts and the Courts of Magistrates (also known as the Subordinates Courts).

The head of administration for the Judiciary Department is the Chief Registrar whereas the entire judicial system is presided over and supervised by the Chief Justice.

Introduction

The Supreme Court is governed by the Supreme Court Act[8] along with its Rules annexed to the Act. The Rules of the Supreme Court regulates the practice and procedure of the High Court and the Court of Appeal. The Supreme Court consists of the President of the Court of Appeal, the Chief Justice, the Judges and the Judicial Commissioners of the Supreme Court. The jurisdiction of the Supreme Court is over any original and appellate criminal and civil cases by the High Court and also appellate criminal and civil jurisdiction by the Court of Appeal.[9]

The judges of the High Court at present consist of the Chief Justice along with two judges who are often referred to as Justices. The Court of Appeal judges are the President and two other appellate judges.

Jurisdiction

The civil jurisdiction of the High Court consists of the original jurisdiction and authority similar to that held and exercised by the Chancery, Family and Queen's Bench Divisions of the High Court of England and shall also include any other jurisdiction, original or appellate as may be conferred upon it by any other written law.[10]

The criminal jurisdiction of the High Court consists of such jurisdiction, original or appellate, as may be conferred upon it by any written law, which includes the Penal Code, the Criminal Procedure Code or the Criminal Conduct (Recovery of Proceeds) Order. In the Criminal Procedure Code specifically,[11] the High Court will have jurisdiction over any offence that was committed wholly or partly within Brunei Darussalam, or committed on board any ship or aircraft registered in Brunei Darussalam,

[7] Article 47, The Constitution [8] CAP 5 of the Laws of Brunei [9] Section 6, Supreme Court Act [10] Section 16, Supreme Court Act [11] Section 7 of the Criminal Procedure Code

or committed on the high seas if the offence is one of piracy by the law of nations. The Court will also have jurisdiction over an offence whether or not it was committed in Brunei Darussalam if it was committed by a subject of His Majesty the Sultan or by a person who abets, or enters a conspiracy to commit, an offence of Brunei Darussalam whether or not any overt act in furtherance of such conspiracy takes place within Brunei Darussalam. The High Court may also pass any sentence authorized by law. [12]

Any civil or criminal appeals from the High Court can be brought to the Court of Appeal.

The civil jurisdiction of the Court of Appeal consists of appeals from a judgment or order of the High Court in a civil cause or matter and again, such other jurisdiction conferred upon it by any other written law. The criminal jurisdiction of the Court of Appeal consists of appeals from the High Court.[13]

Appeals

Any civil appeals made from the Court of Appeal can only be referred by His Majesty the Sultan to the Judicial Committee of Her Britannic Majesty's Privy Council. For criminal cases however, no such appeals from the Court can be further made. There can be no civil appeals made if the appeal is[14]:

(i) against an order made allowing for an extension of time for appealing against a judgment or order;
(ii) a judgment that has been expressed to be final by any law;

(iii) any order made with the consent of all parties to the case;

(iv) any order relating only to costs;
(v) made without leave of the High Court of the Court of Appeal where the amount or value of the subject matter does not exceed $10,000 or where it is from any interlocutory order of judgment.

Extended jurisdiction of the High Court

Along with the exercise of its own jurisdiction as mentioned above, the High Court also has a general supervisory and revisionary jurisdiction over the Intermediate Courts and the Magistrates' Courts. Any time during a proceeding in an Intermediate Court or a Magistrates' Court, a High Court judge can always call for and check the record of proceedings and thereafter can either transfer the matter or proceedings to the High Court of he could also give directions as to the further conduct of the proceeding by the Intermediate or Magistrates' Court. Upon the High Court calling for any record in this instance, all such proceedings in the Intermediate or Subordinate Courts shall be stayed pending further what the High Court will order later on. The High Court may also feel the need to call on any decision recorded or passed by the Intermediate or Magistrates' Courts to assess the correctness, legality or propriety of the decision recorded. If they are not satisfied with their findings, they can direct for a new trial or whatever action that is necessary to secure that substantial justice is done.[15]

[12] Section 10 of the Criminal Procedure Code [13] Section 18, 19, Supreme Court Act [14] Section 20, Supreme Court Act [15] Section 20A to 20E, Supreme Court Act

INTERMEDIATE COURTS

Introduction

The Intermediate Court is governed by the Intermediate Courts Act.[16] It is an open court to which the public generally has access to.[17] However, the same provisions with regards to power to hear proceedings in camera that was are mentioned below for Magistrates Court likewise applies to the Intermediate Courts. The Intermediate Court is presided over by a Judge who sits alone.[18] There are also registrars and deputy registrar who shall also be ex-officio commissioners for oaths and notaries public.[19]

Jurisdiction

The Intermediate Court's criminal jurisdiction[20] runs concurrently with the High Court. Hence, it has all the jurisdiction, powers, duties and authority as are vested, conferred and imposed on the High Court in the exercise of its **original** criminal jurisdiction.

The Court however does not have jurisdiction in respect of any offence that is punishable with death or with imprisonment for life. Nor does it have jurisdiction in respect of any offence that imposes a period of imprisonment that is longer than 20 years. If it so happens that after the trial ends and a conviction is secured, and it appears to the Court that the imprisonment imposed should be longer than 20 years or should carry a more serious penalty, then the Intermediate Court may commit the case to the High Court for sentencing.

Where the High Court and the Intermediate Court has concurrent jurisdiction in respect of any prosecution or proceeding, the Public Prosecutor or any person expressly authorized by him in writing, can direct in which those courts the proceeding should be instituted in.

The Intermediate Court exercises its original civil jurisdiction[21] in every action where the amount claimed or the value of the subject matter in dispute exceeds $15, 000 but does not exceed $100,000 or any higher sum that the Chief Justice may further prescribe. Similarly to the provisions for the Magistrate Court, to obtain this jurisdiction, one has to further prove that the cause of action arose in Brunei Darussalam or the defendant at the time the proceedings were instituted has some form of connection with Brunei Darussalam, be it being a resident or carrying on a business etc, or the facts of the case the proceedings are based on must be alleged to have occurred in Brunei Darussalam.

[16] CAP 162 of the Laws of Brunei [17] Section 7, Intermediate Courts Act [18] Section 10, Intermediate Courts Act [19] Section 11, Intermediate Courts Act [20] See Part IV of the Intermediate Courts Act [21] See Part V of the Intermediate Courts Act

The Court does not have civil jurisdiction over the recovery of immovable property or where there is a dispute as to a title registered under the Land Code, over the interpretation of a trust instrument, the grant or revocation of probate, over the interpretation of a will, over a declaratory decree, over the legitimacy of any person, over the guardianship or custody of a minor and over the validity or dissolution of any marriage.

In an action concerning immovable property that commenced in the Intermediate Court, a defendant may within one month apply to the High Court for the action to be transferred to the High Court if he feels that there is a dispute as to a title registered under the Land code. If a High Court judge is satisfied, he may order the action to be transferred to the High Court.

Also, not taking into account that the amount claimed should not be more than $100,000, an Intermediate Court has jurisdiction over any action for the recovery of immovable property with or without a claim for rent or profits if there is no dispute as to title registered under the Land Code.

Any judgement of an Intermediate Court should be regarded by the Parties as final and conclusive between themselves.

The Intermediate Court also has jurisdiction to grant probate and letters of administration in respect of the estate within Brunei Darussalam of a deceased person and the estate in respect of which the grant is applied for but it must be exclusive of what the deceased possessed of and over what the applicant is entitled to as a trustee and not a beneficiary, and without deducting anything on the account of debts due or owing, the amount claimed must not exceeds $250,000.

When a plaintiff has a cause of action for more than $100,000, which the Intermediate Court does not have jurisdiction over, it is possible for him to abandon the excess amount in order to bring it within the jurisdiction of the Intermediate Court. However he will not be able to recover any of the excess amounts that he abandoned. Nevertheless, if the amount is more than $100,000, the Intermediate Court can still have jurisdiction when and if the parties concerned agree by a signed memorandum filed in the Intermediate Court that it shall have jurisdiction, even though the amount claimed exceeds $100,000.

In an Intermediate Court proceeding, if the counterclaim or defence of any defendant involves a matter beyond the Intermediate Court's jurisdiction, any party may apply to the High Court within one month of being served the counterclaim, for an order that the whole proceedings, or just proceedings on the counterclaim defence to be transferred to the High Court.

Appeals

Civil appeals goes straight to the Court of Appeal as if it was an appeal from the High Court. However there will be no right of appeal entertained if the parties to the action have agreed in writing that the judgment of the court shall be final and conclusive between them.[22]

Criminal appeals also go to the Court of Appeal. The Court of Appeal can also review any sentencing that has been passed by the Intermediate Court on any person or provide an opinion on a point of law that has been referred to it.[23] The practice and procedure as contained in the

Supreme Court Rules for the High Court and the Court of Appeal shall also apply to the Intermediate Court.

MAGISTRATES' COURT

Introduction

The Magistrate Courts are governed by the Subordinate Courts Act[24], in terms of its civil jurisdiction and by the Criminal Procedure Code[25] in the exercise of its criminal jurisdiction. There is also in place a set of Subordinate Courts Rules regulating and prescribing the procedure (including methods for pleading) and the practice in the Magistrate Courts in the exercise of its civil jurisdiction. These Rules of Court extends to all matters of procedures, practice relating to or concerning the effect or operation in law of any procedure or practice, enforcement of judgments or orders, in any case within the cognizance of the Magistrate Court.

All magistrate courts are deemed to be open and allow public access, however there are some instances when a Court may still direct to have the whole proceedings or only in part to be in camera sitting only[26]. In particular, where references are made, whether orally or in writing, directly to any act, decision, grant, revocation, suspension, refusal, omission, authority or discretion by His Majesty the Sultan or if there are cases that intends to refer to any issue that may directly or indirectly concerns the inviolability, sanctity or interests of the position, dignity, standing, honour, eminence or sovereignty of His Majesty the Sultan, then the Magistrate Court shall hold such proceedings in camera, so long as His Majesty the Sultan has not himself issued a direction that such proceedings need not be heard in camera.

Jurisdiction

The Magistrate Court exercises its civil jurisdiction[27] over every civil proceeding where the amount claimed or the value of the subject matter in dispute does not exceed B$30,000. However, if the matter is heard before the Chief Magistrate, Chief Registrar, Deputy Chief Registrar, Senior Magistrate or the Senior Registrar this prescribed limit would be B$50,000.

[22] Section 26, Intermediate Courts Act [23] Section 27, Intermediate Courts Act [24] CAP 6 of the Laws of Brunei [25] CAP 7 of the Laws of Brunei [26] Section 7, Subordinate Courts Act [27] See Section 17 of the Subordinate Courts Act

For the court to have jurisdiction of the case, the cause of action need to have arose in Brunei Darussalam, the defendant at the time the proceedings were instituted has some form of connection with Brunei Darussalam, be it being a resident or carrying on a business etc, and the facts of the case the proceedings are based on must be alleged to have occurred in Brunei Darussalam.

Furthermore, a Magistrate Court also has jurisdiction in any proceedings for the recovery of immovable property where the rent payable in respect of such property does not exceed $500 per month. This excludes cases where there is a genuine dispute as to title registered under the Land Code.

A Magistrate Court does not have any civil jurisdiction over acts done by the order of His Majesty the Sultan, over the recovery of immovable property where there is a genuine dispute as to the title registered under the Land Code, over cases involving specific performance and rescission of contracts, over the cancellation or rectification of instruments, over the interpretation of trust instruments and the enforcement of administration of trusts, the grant of probate or letters of administration in respect of a deceased person, over the interpretation of wills, administration of estate of any deceased person and lastly it does not have civil jurisdiction over declaratory decrees.

The Magistrate's court criminal jurisdiction[28] is similar to the High Court's criminal jurisdiction as mentioned above. Namely, the court will have jurisdiction over any offence that was committed wholly or partly within Brunei Darussalam, or committed on board any ship or aircraft registered in Brunei Darussalam, or committed on the high seas if the offence is one of piracy by the law of nations. The Court will also have jurisdiction over an offence whether or not it was committed in Brunei Darussalam if it was committed by a subject of His Majesty the Sultan or by a person who abets, or enters a conspiracy to commit, an offence of Brunei Darussalam whether or not any overt act in furtherance of such conspiracy takes place within Brunei Darussalam. Furthermore, the types of offences the magistrate court may try are any offence that is shown in the eighth column of the First Schedule of the Criminal Procedure Code to be so triable. However, if the offence it is given the power to try carries a maximum punishment the court has no power to award, it shall then commit the defendant for trial by the High Court if it holds the opinion that the punishment it has power to award is inadequate.

The criminal jurisdiction of magistrates conferred by the Criminal Procedure Code include hearing, trying, determining and disposing of summarily prosecutions for offences cognized by such magistrate and inquiring into offences committed with a view to committal for trial by the High Court. Magistrates also have the power and authority to inquire into complaints of offences, summon and examine relevant witnesses, summon and issue warrants for the apprehension of criminals and offenders, and deal with them according to law, issue search warrants, hold inquests and do all other matters and things which a magistrate is empowered to do by this Code or any other Act.

[28] See section 7 of the Criminal Procedure Code

Appeals

Any appeal in a civil matter in the Magistrate Court goes to the High Court.[29] Such appeals that has right to do so are cases where a Magistrate Court has given a final judgment in any proceedings for the recovery of immovable property or in any proceedings where the amount in dispute exceeds $500. Leave for appeal is needed from a judge with respect of an interlocutory order, from a final judgment of a Magistrate Court where the amount claimed or the value of the subject matter in dispute does not exceed $500. Leave from the judge is also required from an order relating to costs and also for any orders that were made by consent of the parties.

It is important for the appellant to keep in mind that he must also fulfill all other conditions of appeal imposed in accordance with the Rules of Court of the Supreme Court Act.

In a criminal matter, if a defendant, the complainant or the Public Prosecutor is not satisfied with any judgment, sentence or order given by the magistrate, he may appeal to the High Court against such judgment, sentence or order for any error in law or in fact, or on the ground that the sentence is either to extensive or too inadequate.

A Magistrate Court can also, at any time before or during any civil proceeding, request a legal opinion from the High Court if it desires to do so. Either the Magistrate initiates the request or it can also be made on the application of any of the parties. They shall forward a statement of the facts of the case and specify the exact points on which legal opinion is being sought. The High Court will then make a declaration or order in response to the query as it thinks fit.[30]

APPOINTMENT OF JUDGES, REGISTRARS AND OTHER RELEVANT PERSONS WITHIN THE SUPREME COURTS, INTERMEDIATE COURTS AND SUBORDINATE COURTS

The High Court and Court of Appeal judges are appointed by His Majesty the Sultan by instrument under his sign manual and the State Seal.[31] To become a judge of the Supreme Court, one has to be or has been a judge of a Court having unlimited jurisdiction over civil and criminal matters in some part of the Commonwealth or a Court having jurisdiction in appeals from any such Court. He must also have been entitled to practice as an advocate in such a court for a period of not less than 7 years. The judges of the Supreme Court hold their positions until the age of 65 or at a later time where His Majesty may approve of.

His Majesty may also from time to time appoint someone who satisfies the same conditions as mentioned above for the Supreme Court judges to be a Judicial Commissioner of the Supreme Court.[32] The Judicial Commissioner has the power to act as a Judge of the Supreme Court and all things done by him in accordance with the terms

[29] Section 17, Subordinate Courts Act [30] Section 22, Subordinate Courts Act [31] Section 7, Supreme Court Act [32] Section 11, Supreme Court Act

of this appointment will be deemed to have the same validity and effect as if it has been done by a judge.

An Intermediate Court judge is also appointed by His Majesty. To qualify for appointment, he must have been entitled to practice in a court having unlimited jurisdiction in civil and criminal matters in Brunei Darussalam or some part of the Commonwealth for not less then 5 years.[33]

Finally, magistrates are also appointed by His Majesty, in particular a Chief Magistrate who shall have seniority over all other Magistrates and Coroners. His Majesty can also appoint any fit and proper person to be a Coroner who shall have the same power to act as a Magistrate for the purpose of discharging the functions of a Magistrate. Hence, their actions shall have the same validity and effect as if they had been done by a Magistrate.[34]

SYARIAH COURT

The Syariah Courts in Brunei Darussalam consist of the Syariah Subordinate Courts, the Syariah High Court and the Syariah Appeal Court. These courts will have such jurisdiction, powers, duties and authority as are conferred and imposed by the Syariah Courts Act (Chapter 184) as well as by any other written law.[35]

For appointment of Judges in the Syariah Courts, Part II of this Act, among others, talks about the appointment of Chief Syar'ie Judge, the Syariah Appeal Court Judges, Syariah High court Judges and Syariah Subordinate Courts Judges.

Section 8(1) of this Act, stated that His Majesty the Sultan and Yang Di-Pertuan may, on the advice of the President of the Majlis Ugama Islam and after consultation with the Majlis, appoint a Chief Syar'ie Judge.[36] To be qualified as a Chief Syar'ie Judge, a person must be a citizen of Brunei Darussalam; and he has served as either a Judge of a Syariah Court, or Kadi, or in both capacities, for a cumulative period of not less than 7 years prior to his appointment or that he is a person learned in *Hukum Syara*[37].

For Syariah Appeal Court Judges, section 9(1) of this Act, stated that His Majesty the Sultan and Yang Di-Pertuan may, on the advice of the President of the Majlis and after consultation with the Majlis, appoint and re-appoint not more than 5 Muslims to form a standing panel of Judges, for a period of not exceeding 3 years. For each proceeding in the Syariah Appeal Court, the Chief Syar'ie Judge shall elect 2 of them to constitute a quorum of Judges. Again, a person qualified to be appointed as one of the Judges in the Syariah Appeal Court must be a citizen of Brunei Darussalam and he has served as either a Judge of a Syariah Court, or Kadi, or in both capacities, for a cumulative period of not

[33] Section 10, Intermediate Courts Act [34] Section 9-11, Subordinate Courts Act [35] Section 6(1) of the Syariah Courts Act (Chapter 184). [36] Section 8(1) of the Syariah Courts Act (Chapter 184). [37] Section 8(2) of the Syariah Courts Act (Chapter 184).

less than 7 years prior to his appointment, or that he is a person learned in *Hukum Syara*[38].

Section 10(1) of this Act provides for appointment of Syariah High court Judges whereby His Majesty the Sultan and Yang Di-Pertuan may, on the advice of the President of the Majlis and after consultation with the Majlis, appoint Judges of the Syariah High Court. To be qualified as one, a person must be a citizen of Brunei Darussalam; and has, for a cumulative of not less than 7 years prior to his appointment, served as either a Judge of a Syariah Subordinate Court, or Kadi, or registrar, or Syar'ie Prosecutor, or in more than one of such capacities; or that he is a person learned in Hukum Syara[39].

And for appointment of Syariah Subordinate Courts Judges, section 11 of this Act provides that His Majesty the Sultan and Yang Di-Pertuan may, on the advice of the President of the Majlis and after consultation with the Majlis, appoint Judges of the Syariah Subordinate Courts.

Under this Act, the Chief Syar'ie Judge and Syariah High Court Judges shall hold office until the age of 65 years or until such later time as may be approved by His Majesty the Sultan and Yang Di-Pertuan[40]. However, any Syar'ie Judges including the Chief Syar'ie Judge, may at any time resign from his office by sending to His Majesty the Sultan and Yang Di-Pertuan a letter of resignation under his hand, through the Majlis or the Chief Syar'ie Judge, but he may not be removed from his office or his service terminated except in accordance with the provisions of subsections (3), (4) and (5) of section 12(1) of this Act.

As mentioned earlier, Syariah Courts in Brunei Darussalam consists of Syariah Subordinate Courts, the Syariah High Court and the Syariah Appeal Court each with its own jurisdictions.

The Syariah High Court has both criminal and civil jurisdiction. In its criminal jurisdiction it shall try any offence punishable under any written law which provides for syariah criminal offences, under any written law relating to Islamic family law or under any other written law which confers on it jurisdiction to try any offence, and may impose any punishment provided therein[41].

In its civil jurisdiction, the Syariah High Court shall hear and determine all actions and proceedings relating to –

(i) betrothal, marriage (including *ta'at balik*), divorce, *khulu'*, *fasakh*, *cerai ta'liq*, determination of turns, *li'an*, *illa* or any matrimonial matter;

(ii) any disposition of or claim to any property arising out of any matter set out in the above paragraph.

[38] Section 9(2) of the Syariah Courts Act (Chapter 184). [39] Section 10(2) of the Syariah Courts Act (Chapter 184). [40] Section 12(1) of the Syariah Courts Act (Chapter 184). [41] Section 15*(a)* of the Syariah Courts Act (Chapter 184).

(iii) maintenance of dependants, legitimacy (*ithbatun nasab*) or guardianship or custody (*hadanah*) of infants;

(iv) division of or claims to *harta sepencarian*;
(v) wills or gifts during *maradal-maut* of a deceased Muslim;
(vi) gift *inter vivos* (*hibah*), or settlement (*sulh*) made without adequate monetary consideration or value by Muslim;

(vii) *waqaf* or *nazar*;

(viii) division of and inheritance of property, testate or intestate;

(ix) determination or persons entitled to part of the estate of a deceased Muslim or part of the property which such persons are respectively entitled to; or
(x) other matters in respect of which jurisdiction is conferred by any written law.[42]

For Syariah Subordinate Courts, their criminal jurisdiction are to try offence punishable under any written law which provides for syariah criminal offences, prescribing offences where the maximum punishment provided for does not exceed $10,000 or imprisonment for a period not exceeding 7 years or both and may impose any punishment provided therefor[43].

In their civil jurisdiction, the Syariah Subordinate Courts shall hear and determine all actions and proceedings which the Syariah High Court is empowered to hear and determine, where the amount or value of the subject-matter in dispute does not exceed $500,000 or is not capable of estimation in terms of money[44]. This jurisdiction may, form time to time, be increased by His Majesty the Sultan and Yang Di-Pertuan on the recommendation of the Chief Syar'ie Judge, by notifying it in the *Gazette*[45].

Jurisdiction of the Syariah Appeal Court shall be to hear and determine any appeal against any decision made by the Syariah High Court in the exercise of its original jurisdiction[46]. Whenever an appeal against a decision of the Syariah Subordinate Court has been determined by the Syariah High Court, the Syariah Appeal Court may, on application by any party, grant leave for any question of law in the public interest which has arisen in the course of the appeal, and where the decision of the Syariah High Court has affected the determination of the appeal, to be referred to the Syariah Appeal Court for its decision. Whenever leave is granted by the Syariah Appeal Court, it shall hear and determine the questions allowed to be referred for its decision and make any order which the Syariah High Court might have made, and as it thinks just for the disposal of the appeal.

[42] Section 15*(b)* –do-. [43] Section 16(1)*(a)* of the Syariah Courts Act (Chapter 184). [44] Section 16(1)*(b)* Ibid. [45] Section 16(2) Ibid. [46] Section 20(1) Ibid.

For additional analytical, business and investment opportunities information,
please contact Global Investment & Business Center, USA
at (703) 370-8082. Fax: (703) 370-8083. E-mail: ibpusa3@gmail.com
Global Business and Investment Info Databank - www.ibpus.com

Apart from having its original jurisdiction, the Syariah High Court shall have supervisory and revisionary jurisdiction over all Syariah Subordinate Courts[47]. Similarly, the Syariah Appeal Court shall have that same power over the Syariah High Court[48].

OTHER RELEVANT LEGAL DEPARTMENTS

The Attorney General's Chambers

The Attorney General is the principal legal adviser to the Government of His Majesty the Sultan and shall advise on all legal matters connected with the affairs of Brunei Darussalam or by the Government of Brunei Darussalam.[49] He is assisted by the Solicitor General and counsels, in advising the Government and representing the Government in civil and criminal cases. The Attorney General is also responsible for the drafting of legislation. In carrying out the task of legislative drafting, the Attorney General's Chambers work closely with other Government Ministries and Departments.

The Attorney General is vested with the power under the Constitution to institute, proceed and discontinue once instituted, any criminal proceedings. All criminal prosecutions are instituted in the name of the Public Prosecutor. In carrying out this duty, the Attorney General is not subject to the direction or control of any other person or authority. He is assisted by Deputy Public Prosecutors in the conduct of criminal trials held in the Supreme Court and the Subordinate Courts.

The Attorney General basically has the exercisable power to institute, conduct or discontinue, at his discretion, any proceedings of an offence other than proceedings before a Syariah Court or a Court Martial, subject to the provisions of any other written law.

In addition, the Public Prosecutor and his Deputies also advise, and direct prosecution undertaken by the police and other law enforcement departments including rendering advice in their investigations.

Apart from carrying out the above duties, the Attorney General's Chambers also provides services to the public by maintaining the following registries; Companies, Business names, Trade Marks, Industrial designs, Inventions, Power of Attorney, Marriages, Bills of Sales.

There are five legal divisions in the Attorney-General's Chambers: Civil Division, Criminal Justice Division, International Law Division, Legislative Drafting Division and the Registry Division.

Syariah department

In 1980, a Committee of Harmonizing Laws In Accordance With Islam[50], was formed. To increase this effort, a Legal Unit[51] chaired by the Chief Kadi was established in 1988 by the Ministry of Religious Affairs its task mainly to replace the earlier committee. In 1993, a Committee for the establishment of Syariah Supreme Court known as the Action Committee Towards the Establishment of Syariah Supreme Court[52] was formed. Another committee known as the Islamic Family Law Legislative Committee[53] was later established in 1995, its tasks are to study, legislate and prepare Islamic family laws as well as other laws governed by the Kadis Court. This Legal Unit, in 1997, was eventually alleviated to its present position as a separate department in the Ministry of Religious Affairs now known as the Islamic Legal Unit.[54]

Among the duties of this Unit are to study, examine and do research on provisions in the Laws of Brunei now enforced to see whether or not there is any conflict with *Hukum Syara'*; prepare proposed draft amendment for any legal provision that conflict with *Hukum Syara'* and prepare draft legislation in accordance with *Hukum Syara'* if there is no such legislation available yet. This Unit is also appointed secretariat for several committees that had been mentioned above. Apart from that, this Unit also gives advice concerning Islamic laws to the Syariah Courts, the Faith Control Unit (Unit Kawalan Akidah), the Prosecution Section, the Investigation Section, the Family Counseling Section, the Attorney General's Chambers as well as other government departments and private firms.[55]

LEGAL PROCEDURE

CRIMINAL PROSECUTION

As stated in the Criminal Procedure Code, the general direction and control over criminal prosecutions and proceedings in Brunei Darussalam is under the responsibility of the Attorney General who is also the Public Prosecutor. His Majesty may also from time to time appoint Deputy Public Prosecutors who will be under the general control and direction of the Public Prosecutor. Deputy Public Prosecutors are conferred the powers under the Criminal Procedure Code as are delegated to them by the Public Prosecutor.

The Public Prosecutor may also by notification in the *Government Gazette* delegate all or any of his powers vested to him under the Criminal Procedure Code to any Deputy Public Prosecutor. Thus the exercise of these powers by the Deputy Public Prosecutor would be treated as if they had been exercised by the Public Prosecutor so long as Public Prosecutor does not revoke the delegation.

The Criminal Procedure Code also specifically states that every criminal prosecution and every inquiry can also be conducted by some other person expressly authorized in writing by the Public Prosecutor or His Majesty the Sultan. In those cases, a police officer or an officer of a Government Department in relation to minor cases and cases that is relevant to that particular Government Department, such as the Customs Department, the Immigration Department, the Narcotics Control Bureau and the Anti-Corruptions Bureau who do have their own prosecuting officers also conduct criminal prosecution for their relevant cases.

CRIMINAL PROCEDURE

INVESTIGATIONS

The Police are given powers to search a property and in doing so they are required to prepare a list of the things that have been seized and this document is to be signed by the officer in charge of the search and seizure. The owner of the property being searched must be present at the time the search is conducted. [1]

The police officer during the investigation stage can also take a written statement from a witness or a suspect and the person being interviewed is required to answer all questions posed to him in relation to the case being investigated on. The police officer is required to repeat the statement back to the person being questioned and he must thereafter sign the statement. [2] All statements made can be used as evidence if the person questioned becomes a witness during proceedings thereafter.[3]

[1] Section 69 of the Criminal Procedure Code [2] Section 116 of the Criminal Procedure Code [3] Section 117 of the Criminal Procedure Code

When interviewing a potential defendant, the police officer is always required to read out the defendant's rights to him after the charge is explained to him. The Courts only accept voluntarily made statements whether or not the contents of the statement are true. There is no right of silence in Brunei Darussalam as the Courts may as a consequence treat silence as a detrimental factor for the defendant.

Once a suspect is arrested, he shall be placed in remand or released on bail. If the remand is ordered by the Magistrate, the defendant cannot be remanded for more than 15 days. On the other hand, if it was ordered by the High Court, there is no time limit.[4]

PRE-TRIAL PROCEDURE

With the exception of some offences that would need the prior sanction of the Public Prosecutor or the official complaint of a concerned public servant, a Judge or magistrate may take cognizance of an offence upon receiving a complaint launched by a complainant[5], upon his own knowledge or suspicion that an such offence has been committed or when any person who is in custody without process, has been brought before him for committing an offence that the Judge or magistrate has jurisdiction to inquire into or try.[6]

Once the Judge or magistrate takes cognizance of the offence and is satisfied that there is sufficient ground for proceeding, he will either issue a summons for the accused to attend court or if it is in relation to an offence that requires a warrant to be issued first, he would then issue the warrant in the first instance and also issue a summons that specifies the accused to appear at a certain time before him or some other Judge or magistrate having jurisdiction over the case. [7]

Preliminary Inquiries

Preliminary inquiries are always held for offences against the State, murder or any offence which carries a death penalty. [8]

Preliminary Inquiries are generally held for a magistrate to determine whether there is sufficient evidence to commit the case for trial in the High Court (filteration). Other cases like trafficking of drugs and rape cases go straight to the High Court without any preliminary inquiries. All other cases are generally tried summarily in the Magistrate Court.

At a preliminary inquiry, the Prosecutor will present its case and set out all the evidence, including examining witnesses, in support of its case to the Magistrate. The defendant is allowed to cross examine the witnesses who can then also be re-examined by the Prosecutor. If the magistrate, after hearing all the evidence, feels that there are insufficient grounds for committing the accused, he could either discharge him or he can

[4] Section 223 of the Criminal Procedure Code [5] Section 133 of the Criminal Procedure Code [6] Section 131 of the Criminal Procedure Code [7] Section 136 of the Criminal Procedure Code [8] Section 138 of the Criminal Procedure Code

still order that the defendant be tried before himself or before some other magistrate. In the latter case, he will consequently frame a charge and call upon the defendant to plead to those charges.

[9] However if the magistrate finds that there are sufficient grounds for committing him for trial, he shall then commit the accused for trial before the High Court.[10]

If the accused is committed to trial to High Court, the magistrate will give the accused the opportunity to give a list of witnesses he wishes to be summoned to give evidence for his trial. The final list of witnesses shall be included in the record of the magistrate.[11]

Once the accused has been committed for trial, the committing magistrate shall then send the original record and all the relevant documents, weapons (if any) or any other thing which is to be produced in evidence to the Court the accused is committed to. A list of all the exhibits is also forwarded with the record. The record will specifically contain the following information[12]:

i) the serial number of the case;

ii) the date of the commission of the offence;

iii) the date of the complaint, if any;

iv) the name, age, sex, residence, if known, and nationality (or race) of the accused;

v) the offence complained of and the offence proved, and the value of the

property, if any, in respect of which the offence has been committed;

vi) the date of the summons or warrant and of the return day of the summons, if any, or on which the accused was first arrested;

vii) the date on which the accused first appeared or was brought before a magistrate;

viii) the name and title of the officer or other person conducting the prosecution;

ix) the date of making each adjournment or postponement, if any, and the date to

which such adjournment or postponement was made and the grounds for making the same;

x) the date on which the proceedings terminated;

xi) the order made;

xii) the depositions;

xiii) the statement, if any, of the accused;

xiv) the charge; and

xv) the list of witnesses as provided by the accused.

The law also allows for committal without the consideration of evidence. This method is referred to as paper committal and is done through the submission of written statements only. [13] Hence a written statement can be substituted for oral evidence and it would have

[9] Section 141 of the Criminal Procedure Code [10] Section 144 of the Criminal Procedure Code [11] Section 145 of the Criminal Procedure Code [12] Section 147 of the Criminal Procedure Code [13] Section 151A and 151B of the Criminal Procedure Code

a similar effect to be admissible under the Evidence Act. It must however satisfy the following conditions:

a) the statement must be signed by the person who made it;

b) the statement must contain a declaration by that person that the information he has written is true to the best of this knowledge and belief;

c) a copy of the statement must be given to each of the other parties to the proceedings not less then 7 days before the statement is tendered in evidence;

d) none of the other parties objects to the statement being tendered in evidence.

Bail applications[14]

The defendant or his counsel may also apply for bail (whilst investigations are still being carried out) before a magistrate, High Court Judge or Intermediate Court Judge, depending on the seriousness of the case. In deciding to grant that application, the magistrate will consider two opposing factors. [15] On one hand, the Court must remember that the accused is innocent only until proved otherwise. However, the Court shall also take into consideration that the interests of justice will be perverted if the accused absconds or tampers with the witnesses.

At present, all magistrates have the power to grant bail for all type of cases by virtue of their appointments as Registrars of the Supreme Court. However, in practice, bail applications in serious cases that are triable in the High Court or Intermediate Court will be remitted to either court for such applications to be heard. These particular points will be taken into account on deciding whether or not the defendant should be released on bail:

i) Is the offence bailable or non bailable under Schedule 1 of the Criminal

Procedure Code? However, the Court still has discretion to grant bail for non-bailable offences;

ii) The nature and gravity of the offence;

iii) The number of charges;

iv) The likelihood of the accused absconding;

v) The previous record of the accused;

vi) Strength of evidence; and

vii) Other relevant factors like the age and health of the accused.

The usual conditions attached to bail are cash bail, the duty to report to the nearest police station at a prescribed number of times a week, the assurance that the accused will not tamper with witnesses and to not approach certain places, to surrender his passport and other travel documents and to remain indoors between certain hours.

Pre-Trial Review

Sometimes, a pre-trial review is also held by the High Court Judge prior to the trial. There is no legislative requirement for this and hence is not mandatory but in practice is usually held for High Court and Intermediate Court cases where the Judge will go

[14] Sections 346-353 of the Criminal Procedure Code [15] Public Prosecutor V Haji Sadikin (2000) JCBD Vol. 1 349

through the relevant documents such as the list of witnesses, list of exhibits and agreed facts (if any) with both the prosecution and the defence.

Withdrawal of Charges

At any time before a judgment is entered, charges against the defendant and all evidence against him may be discharged. If the discharge is one not amounting to an acquittal, this would mean that prosecution can be made at another time based on the same factors. [16] The power to withdraw a charge only lies with the prosecution. The person who reported the offence and initiated the prosecution cannot withdraw his claim once a police report or a statement has been prepared.

TRIAL PROCEDURE

Chapter XIX of the Criminal Procedure Code governs the procedure for trials in Brunei Darussalam.

When the defendant first appears before the Court, the charge containing the particulars to the offence or offences he is accused of shall be read out and explained to him and he shall then be asked to enter his plea, guilty or not guilty. If the accused pleads guilty, the plea will be recorded and he may be convicted thereon. However, the Judge would first need to hear the complainant and other evidence first as it considers necessary and he would also make sure the defendant truly understands the nature and consequences of his plea and intends to admit, without qualification, the offence or offences alleged against him.

Where the defendant pleads not guilty, a trial will be held ad witnesses would be called to give evidence. At the start of the trial, the prosecution will first open the case by stating briefly the nature of the offence charged and disclosing the evidence, including the appearance of witnesses, by which he proposed to prove guilt of the defendant. The burden of proof lies with the prosecution beyond reasonable doubt. If the defendant is not represented by counsel, (there is no legal aid in Brunei Darussalam with the exception of cases carrying a death penalty where the defendant will be provided a defence counsel) the Court will assist the defendant in the cross examination of witnesses.

At the close of the prosecution's case, the Court will lay down the choices for the defendant, either to given his own evidence or maintain his silence. Usually, if they choose to keep silent, and where the evidence against him is strong, a conviction will be given. However, if he decides to give his own evidence, he will then in turn open his case by stating the facts or law on which he intends to rely and make whatever comments in response to the evidence put forward by the prosecution. Before summing up his case, he would then be called upon to enter his defence and then produce his own evidence which may include witnesses that are examined on his behalf. The prosecution will then have the right of reply on the whole case.[17]

[16] Section 186 of the Criminal Procedure Code [17] Section 184 of the Criminal Procedure Code

At the end of the trial, if the Court finds the defendant not guilty, the Court shall record an order of acquittal. If the Court finds otherwise or if the defendant entered a plea of guilty, the Court shall pass sentence in accordance with the law. [18]

Sentencing

The types of sentences in Brunei Darussalam are: i) Death Penalty: The most serious punishment in Brunei Darussalam is the death penalty. In sentencing hearings dealing with the death penalty, there must be 2 judges present and both these judges must agree with the sentencing decision. Death penalties are not imposed on pregnant women who would get life imprisonment instead.

ii) Life imprisonment: The defendant will be imprisonment for as long as he shall live.

iii) Whipping: There is also whipping in Brunei Darussalam, usually a maximum of 24 whips for an adult and a maximum of 18 whips for a defendant below the age of 18.[19] Women, men above 50 years old and those that are imposed the death penalty are exempted from whipping.[20]

iv) Fines: Fines are imposed according to the relevant written law. If that does not exist, the court will decide on the appropriate amount.

v) Pay compensation: On top of the above punishments, the Court can order the defendant to pay compensation if it is satisfied that the defendant can afford to pay such amount imposed. He will be imposed imprisonment or further imprisonment on default of payment. [21]

POST-TRIAL PROCEDURE (APPEALS)

If an appeal is made from the Magistrates Court, the appeal will be heard by the High Court. Any party can make an appeal against a judgment or sentence, be it the prosecution or the defendant. Appeals made from the High Court are heard by the Court of Appeal and these are governed by the Criminal Procedure Code (Criminal Appeal Rules) 2002. A person shall commence his appeal by sending a notice of appeal to the Registrar within 14 days of the judgment or sentence made. He can at any time abandon his appeal after serving his notice of appeal by giving notice of abandonment to the Registrar. His appeal should then be dismissed.

CIVIL PROCEDURE

Civil proceedings are usually private matters between parties that relates to breach of contracts or for compensation. The civil procedure in Brunei Darussalam is governed by the Supreme Court Rules for the High Court and the Magistrates' Court Rules (Civil

[18] Section 181 of the Criminal Procedure Code [19] Section 257 of the Criminal Procedure Code [20] Section 258 of the Criminal Procedure Code [21] Section 382 of the Criminal Procedure Code

Procedure and Civil Appeals Procedure) for the Magistrate Courts. These rules mainly prescribe regulations for types of action, procedure, process, addresses and forms.

Procedure in the Magistrate Court

INTRODUCTION

Civil proceedings in the Magistrate Court would include a civil action, an order for payment of any sum or money or an order for doing or abstaining from doing any act or thing not enforceable through a mere fine or by imprisonment. All civil proceedings heard by the Magistrate Court are dealt with summarily.[22]

PRE-HEARING PROCEDURE

A person who wishes to institute civil proceedings in the Magistrate Court would need to register a written statement to the Clerk of the Court to be included in the Civil Cause Book. This written statement is often referred to as the "plaint" and it shall state the names and last known place of residence of the parties and also include a statement on the substance of the action intended to be brought. Upon doing so, he is also required to pay a prescribed fee to the Court. The magistrate has discretion to refuse the plaint if it appears that there is no cause of action. They would naturally refuse the plaint if the matter is outside their jurisdiction. Any person dissatisfied with the magistrate's decision in refusing his plaint is allowed to appeal against that decision as if it was an order of the magistrate.[23]

Once the magistrate registers the plaint, it shall next issue a summons for the defendant requiring him to attend before him at a certain time but normally not more than 7 days after the summons have been served on him. The defendant will also be required to file his written statement of defence in answer to the plaint against him.[24] However, if he decides to admit the claim wholly or partially, he can then sign a statement admitting the amount of the claim or part of the amount of the claim entered against him. If this is the case, the Clerk of the Court shall send a notice regarding this admission to the plaintiff who is then required to prove the aforesaid claim. The magistrate shall then upon proof of the signature of the party enter judgment for the admitted claim.[25]

The defendant will then pay into Court the sum of money in full satisfaction of the claim against him together with the costs incurred by the plaintiff up to the time of such payment and this payment should then be notified to the plaintiff. This payment shall then be paid out to the plaintiff without further delay.[26]

A plaintiff may also apply for the magistrate to make a judgment when no defence or counterclaim has been filed. Once satisfied that the plaint was served on the defendant and yet he did not appear in Court, the Court can then enter judgment for the plaintiff

[22] Rule 3 of the Magistrates' Court (Civil Procedure) Rules 2001 [23] Rule 13 of the Magistrates' Court (Civil Procedure) Rules 2001 [24] Rule 14 of the Magistrates' Court (Civil Procedure) Rules 2001 [25] Rule 38 of the Magistrates' Court (Civil Procedure) Rules 2001 [26] Rule 40 of the Magistrates' Court (Civil Procedure) Rules 2001

with costs. If the defendant manages to file a defence or counterclaim before judgment bas been entered, then a judgment in default cannot be made by the Court.[27]

PROCEDURE AT HEARING[28]

All hearings in the Magistrate Court are heard in public but the magistrate may still decide to hear the matter in the presence of the parties only. The persons permitted to address the Court in a civil proceeding are any party to the proceedings, any advocate and solicitor qualified and admitted under the Legal Profession Act and also any person permitted by the magistrate if he is satisfied that that person is not appearing for fee or reward.

If both the plaintiff and defendant are present at the hearing, the plaint would first be read out to the defendant who will then be required to make his defence. On hearing his defence, the magistrate shall then proceed with the case. During the hearing, the magistrate shall take into consideration any question of law raised, legal submissions made and the substance of the oral evidence given. The party on whom the burden of proof lies shall commence the case before the magistrate. Once he has closed his case, his opponent may adduce his own evidence. If he does not choose to do so, the initiating party shall address the magistrate for the second time and will sum up his evidence. The opponent is then given his right to reply. When the initiating party has concluded his case, the opponent can decide to call his own witnesses and he is free to open his own case, calls his own witnesses and in the end sums up not only on his own evidence but also on his own case. The initiating party will in turn have the right to reply to his opponent. [29]

On the conclusion of the hearing, the magistrate can deliver judgment either at the same or at a subsequent sitting. A certified copy of the judgment can also be delivered to the parties upon payment of a prescribed fee to the court.

However, in the case where only the defendant appears in court either on the day of the hearing or at any continuation the case, the claim or case shall be struck out by the magistrate but excluding any counter-claims that may have been made by the defendant against the plaintiff. But if the defendant admits to the cause of action, the magistrate may then proceed to give judgment, with or without costs, as if the plaintiff were present. Where there has been a counter claim, the magistrate, if satisfied that the counter claim has been served on the plaintiff, may proceed to hear the defendant's case and may give judgment on the evidence adduced by the defendant or may postpone the hearing on the counter claim. Such postponement will be notified to the plaintiff. The magistrate may also award costs to the defendant when the plaintiff fails to appear.

Where the defendant is the party that has failed to appear in court, the magistrate once satisfied with the proof of service on the defendant and that the defendant lacks sufficient excuse for his non attendance, can determine the case and enter judgment. That judgment

[27] Rule 41 of the Magistrates' Court (Civil Procedure) Rules 2001 [28] Part VIII of the Magistrates' Court (Civil Procedure) Rules 2001 [29] Rule 61 of the Magistrates' Court (Civil Procedure) Rules 2001

shall be as valid as if both parties had appeared before him. Otherwise, the magistrate can still adjourn the hearing to a convenient date to allow more time for the defendant.

APPEALS

For additional analytical, business and investment opportunities information,
please contact Global Investment & Business Center, USA
at (703) 370-8082. Fax: (703) 370-8083. E-mail: ibpusa3@gmail.com
Global Business and Investment Info Databank - www.ibpus.com

Any civil appeals are governed by the Magistrates' Courts (Civil Appeal) Rules 2001. Every notice of appeal will be lodged in the magistrates court within a month of the decision appealed from was made and shall be served on all other parties affected by the appeal.[30]

The contents of the notice of appeal should include the reference number of the proceedings, names of parties, date of decision appealed, grounds of appeal and be accompanied by a certified copy of the decision appealed against.[31]

Appeals shall be heard by one Judge of the High Court who may reserve for the consideration of the Court of Appeal ay question of law which may arise on the hearing of such an appeal.[32]

The Registrar will notify the parties the date and time of the appeal hearing. If the appellant fails to appear at the appeal hearing, the case shall then be struck out and the decision shall be affirmed. If the respondent appeared at that appeal where the appellant failed to do so, the appellant shall be ordered to pay the costs of the appeal. But if the respondent did not appear, the High Court will need to consequently decide on the costs of the appeal. [33]

However if the appellant appears and whether or not the respondent appears, the High Court shall proceed with the hearing and determination of the case and shall thereafter give judgment according to the merits of the case. During the hearing, the appellant is not allowed to argue on any other points that are separate from the reasons for appeal and those set forth in his notice of appeal. But the Judge may allow amendments to the notice of appeal if he feels that there are actually other grounds than was not mentioned that should be included and also if he feels that the statement of grounds of appeal is defective.[34]

Once the Judge decides on the appeal, the High Court shall certify the judgment made and notify it to the magistrates' court. The magistrates' court will then act upon the judgment either by making such orders that are necessary and amending its own records in accordance with the judgment. The magistrate shall then have the same jurisdiction and power to enforce the High Court's judgment as if he himself made it.

[30] Rule 4 of the Magistrates' Court (Civil Appeals Procedure) Rules 2001

[31] Rule 5 of the Magistrates' Court (Civil Appeals Procedure) Rules 2001 [32] Rule 11 of the Magistrates' Court (Civil Appeals Procedure) Rules 2001 [33] Rule 12 and 13 of the Magistrates' Court (Civil Appeals Procedure) Rules 2001 [34] Rule 15 of the Magistrates' Court (Civil Appeals Procedure) Rules 2001

PROCEDURE IN THE HIGH COURT

INTRODUCTION

High Court Proceedings are initiated by writ, originating summons, originating motion or petition.[35]

There are certain proceedings that **must** be initiated by a writ and these are those relating to claims for relief or remedy for any tort (other than trespass to land), relating to an allegation of fraud, claims for damages for breach of duty (whether duty exists by virtue of a contract or of a provision made by any written law), claims for breach of promise of marriage and also relating to infringement of a patent.

Any applications that are made to a High Court Judge under any written law must be initiated by originating summons. There are also some proceedings that may be begun either by writ or by originating summons where the plaintiff can choose which is more appropriate for him. Such proceedings include those where the sole or principal question at issue is the construction of any written law, of any instrument made under any written law or of any deed, will contract or other document and also where there is unlikely to be any substantial dispute of fact in those proceedings.

PRE-HEARING PROCEDURE

Writ of Summons

All writs prior to them being issued must be indorsed with a statement of the nature of the claim made or the relief or remedy required in the action begun or a statement of the amount claimed in respect of a debt demand. It should also state that further proceedings will be stayed if the defendant pays the amount claimed to the plaintiff or the Court within a certain time limit. The Plaintiff upon presenting a writ for sealing and to be served must leave with the Registrar the original writ along with as many copies of it to be served on the defendant or defendants. The Registrar shall then assign a serial number to the writ and shall sign, seal and date the writ which shall deem the writ to be issued. [36]

Originating Summons

An originating summons must include the questions the plaintiff seeks the determination or direction of the High Court or a concise statement of the relief or remedy claimed in the proceedings with sufficient particulars to identify the cause or causes of action in respect of that claim. Similar to the process in writ of summons, the Registrar will assign a serial number to the originating summons and it will be signed, sealed and dated and thereupon issued. [37]

Originating Motion and Petition No originating motion can be made *ex parte* and without previous notice to the affected parties. However if the Court is satisfied that there will be a delay in proceedings, it may make an order *ex parte* on terms such as costs or otherwise. (Any affected party may apply to the Court to set that order aside). The notice of a motion must include a concise statement of the nature of the claim made or the relief or remedy required. The plaintiff can serve a notice of motion on the defendant together with the writ of summons or originating summons or at any time after service of such writ or summons whether or not the defendant has entered on appearance in the action.[38]

Petitions must also include a concise statement on the nature of the claim sought and the names of the persons the petition should be served with. The petition should be served on the defendant not less than 7 days before the day the Registrar has fixed to be the day and time for the hearing of the petition.[39]

Similar to writ of summons and originating summons, originating motion and petitions shall also be assigned by the Registrar a serial number and be signed, sealed and dated before it is deemed to be issued.

Service of Process[40]

All writs, originating summons to which an appearance by the defendant is required, an originating summons, notices of originating motion and petitions must be served personally on each defendant.

A plaintiff must serve a statement of claim to the defendant either when the writ or notice of writ is served on the defendant or at any time after the service of the writ or notice of writ but it must be before the expiration of 14 days after the defendant enters an appearance. Thereafter, the defendant who has entered an appearance and intends to defend himself must serve a defence on the plaintiff not more than 14 days either after the time that has been limited for him to appear or after the statement of claim is served on him, whichever is the later. Next, the plaintiff who has been served the defence must serve a reply back to the defendant. If the plaintiff was also served a counter claim from the defendant and he intends to defend it, should also serve a defence on the defendant along with the reply. In each of the pleadings served, they must contain a statement setting out summarily the material facts on which the party pleading relies for his claim or defence.[41] In particular, he must plead specifically what his claim is in relation to, for instance, performance, release, statutes of limitation, fraud or any fact showing illegality and stat that the opposite party cannot claim or defend on it. This information must always be included to avoid taking the opposite party by surprise.

It is possible for the plaintiff or the defendant to apply to the Court by summons for an order that the action be tried without pleadings or further pleadings. If the Court is satisfied that the issues in dispute can be defined without pleadings or further pleadings, then it shall direct the parties to prepare a statement of the issues in dispute or if the parties are unable to agree on such a statement, the Court may settle the statement itself.

[38] Order 8 of the Supreme Court Rules [39] Order 9 of the Supreme Court Rules [40] Order 10 of the Supreme Court Rules [41] Rule 6, Order 8 of the Supreme Court Rules

Cases involving libel, slander, breach of promise of marriage and allegations of fraud does not apply in this type of action.

Where the plaintiff fails to serve a statement of claim on the defendant, the defendant may, after the expiration of the period for him to appear apply for the Court to dismiss the action.[42] If the claim relates to a liquidated demand and if the defendant fails to serve a defence, then the plaintiff may enter a final judgment against the defendant for a sum not exceeding what is claimed in the writ and also for costs.

Entering of appearance

A defendant to an action that was begun by writ may appear in the action and defend the claim either by a solicitor or by himself. Where the defendant is a body corporate, they may not enter an appearance at the action and can only be defended by a solicitor. Entering an appearance entails completing the requisite documents, namely a memorandum of appearance and sending it along with a copy of it to the Registry.[43] A memorandum of appearance basically requests the Registry to enter an appearance for the defendant or defendants specified in the memorandum. It must specify the address of the defendant's place of residence or the business address if his solicitor.

Where the defendant fails to enter an appearance, the plaintiff may after the time limited for appearing has expired, enter final judgment against that defendant for a sum not exceeding the amount claimed by the writ and for costs and proceed with the action against other defendants, if there are any.[44] He may enter an interlocutory judgment in the case of claims for unliquidated damages.

Preparing for trial[45]

A cause or matter may be tried before a Judge or the Registrar of the Supreme Court. Notice of trial may be given by the plaintiff or the other party at any time after a reply has been delivered or after the time for delivery of a reply has expired. At least 14 days before the date for trial has been fixed, the defendant shall identify to the plaintiff those documents that are central to his case that he wishes to be included in the trial bundle. At least 2 days before the trial, the plaintiff shall have 2 bundles consisting of one copy of the following documents: a) witness statements that have been exchanged including expert's reports; b) the defendant's documents that he wishes to be included in the bundle; and c) a note agreed by the parties giving a summary of the issues involved, a summary of the propositions of law, the list of authorities to be cited and a chronology of relevant events.

A pre-trial conference may also be held at any time after the commencement of proceedings, and the Court may direct the parties to attend such a conference to discuss matters relating to the action.[46] Points to consider at this pre-trial conference would

[42] Rule 1, Order 19 [43] Rule 1, Order 12 [44] Order 13 [45] Order 34 [46] Order 34A

include any possibility of settlement, the need for the parties to furnish the Court with further information as the Court would require and the Court can also give directions as it appears necessary or desirable for securing a just, expeditious and economic disposal of the action. The parties can agree to settle at any time during the pre-trial conference on all or some of the matters in dispute. The Court can then enter judgment and make an order to give effect to that settlement.

PROCEDURE AT HEARING

At the trial, the Judge will first give directions as to which party may begin the proceedings and prescribe the orders of speeches at the trial. If the defendant decides not to adduce any evidence, the plaintiff may at the close of his case make a second speech closing his case and thereafter the defendant shall make a speech in closing his case. If the defendant does decide to adduce evidence, ha may do so at the closing of the plaintiff's case. At the close of the defendant's case, the plaintiff may make a speech in reply. Rules on evidence are prescribed under Order 38 of the rules.

Where a judgment has been given for damages and there is no provision made by the judgment in how damages are to be assessed, then the damages shall be assessed by the Registrar.[47] The Court may also make an award of provisional damages if the plaintiff has made a claim for one.[48]

Every judgment after a hearing is delivered in open Court or in Chambers, either on the conclusion of the hearing or on a subsequent day of which such notice shall be given to the parties.[49] A Judge can also give judgment and his reasons, in writing at a later date by sending a copy of it to all parties to the proceedings. In this case, the original copy of the written judgment must be signed and filed. The proper officer of the Registrar must enter into the cause book a minute of every judgment or order given by the Court.

In the enforcement of a judgment for the payment of money (and not one for the payment of money into Court), it can be enforced through writ of seizure or sale, garnishee proceedings, charging orders, appointment of a receiver, and an order of committal.[50]

To avoid hearing

Payment into and out of court[51]

In any action for a debt or damages, any defendant may pay into Court a sum of money as the plaintiff claims. Within 14 days of the payment, the plaintiff may accept the money in satisfaction of that cause of action by giving such notice to the defendant.

Offer to settle[52]

Parties to any proceeding may also serve on any other person an offer to settle any one or more of the claim in the proceedings. These can be made at any time before the Court disposes of the matter.

Summary Judgment[53]

A plaintiff can apply to the Court for a summary judgment against the defendant on the ground that that defendant has no defence to the claim included in the writ. Claims relating to libel, slander, malicious prosecution, false imprisonment, seduction or breach of promise of marriage are excluded from this application.

Application for summary judgments must be made by summons supported by an affidavit verifying the facts on which the claim, or the part of the claim, to which the application relates to is based on and it should also state the plaintiff's belief that there is no defence to that claim or no defence except as to the amount of any damages. Thereafter, the Court may dismiss the plaintiff's application especially where the defendant had satisfied the Court that there is still an issue or question in dispute which ought for some reason to be tried. On the other hand, the Court may also give such judgment for the plaintiff against the defendant on that claim.

APPEALS

Any appeal from a decision of a Registrar shall lie to a Judge in Chambers.[54] The appeal shall be brought by serving a notice on every other party to the proceedings to attend an appeal hearing before a Judge on a day specified in the notice. Appeals from a Judge shall lie to the Court of Appeal.

An appeal to the Court of Appeal shall be by way of rehearing and must be brought by a notice of appeal. Every notice of appeal must be filed and served within one month from the date when such order was pronounced (in the case of an appeal from a Judge in Chambers), from the date of refusal (in the case of an appeal against the refusal of an application), and in all other cases, from the date on which the judgment or order appealed against was pronounced.

RECIPROCAL ENFORCEMENT OF FOREIGN JUDGMENTS AND FOREIGN MAINTENANCE ORDERS

Brunei Darussalam also has in force a Maintenance Orders Reciprocal Enforcement Act[55] and a Reciprocal Enforcement of Foreign Judgments Act.[56] The Maintenance Orders Act basically provides for the enforcement in Brunei Darussalam any maintenance orders made in reciprocating countries listed in the Schedule and also for maintenance order made in Brunei Darussalam to be enforced in the listed reciprocating countries. To date, the reciprocating countries are Malaysia, Singapore, Australia and Hong Kong Special

[52] Order 23 [53] Order 14 [54] Order 56 [55] CAP 175 of the Laws of Brunei [56] CAP 176 of the Laws of Brunei

Administrative Region of the People's Republic of China. Maintenance orders are those that provide for the periodical payment of money towards the maintenance of any persons the person paying is liable to maintain.

The Foreign Judgments Act makes provision for the enforcement in Brunei Darussalam any judgments given in foreign countries listed in the Schedule who will in turn also enforce judgments given in Brunei Darussalam. Judgment in this case means a judgment or order given or made by a court in any civil proceedings, judgment in any criminal proceedings for the payment of a sum of money in respect of compensation or damages to an injured party and an award in proceedings on arbitration.[57] The countries listed for the purposes of this Act as at now are only Malaysia and Singapore, through their respective High Courts.

LEGAL PROCEDURE IN THE SYARIAH COURTS

With regards to procedure in general, the Syariah Courts Act (Chapter 184) has stated that every Syariah Court in Brunei Darussalam shall have and use where necessary a seal of such form and format as may be approved by the Majlis[58]. The language that shall be used in the Syariah Courts shall be the Malay language though it may allow the use of any other language in the interest of justice[59]. However, the courts may choose for all documents or records of proceedings to be written in jawi or rumi script[60].

PROCEDURE IN CRIMINAL PROCEEDINGS

In pre-trial procedure, section 69(1) of the Religious Council and Kadis Courts Act (Chapter 77) has laid down some guidelines concerning charge. A charge shall be framed by the prosecutor or by the Court and which shall contain sufficient particulars of the offence alleged. However in practice, during the initial stage of the case, the prosecutor would normally frame the charge, whereas at the closing of the prosecution's case, it would be up to the Court (at the stage of a prima facie) to frame or amend a charge if it thinks it is not appropriate with the charge by the prosecution based on the evidence given in Court[61].

For procedure during trial, section 70 of the Religious Council and Kadis Court (Chapter 77) has outlined procedure for hearing. Section 70(1) of this Act says that any necessary sanction to prosecute shall be proved. This is in accordance with section 62 which mentioned that for any offence under section 182, 183, 185, 186, 187 or 190, no prosecution shall be instituted except by resolution of the Majlis Ugama Islam sanctioning such prosecution.

[57] Section 2 of the Reciprocal Enforcement of Foreign Judgments Act [58] Section 7(1) of the Syariah Courts Act (Chapter 184). [59] Section 7(2)(a) Ibid. [60] Section 7(2)(b) Ibid. [61] Haji Sawas Haji Jebat, *Prosedur Perbicaraan Di Mahkamah Kadi*, Jurnal Undang-Undang Syariah Brunei Darussalam, Januari-Jun 2002 Jilid 2 Bil.2, p.35.

Section 70(2) of the Act also stated that the accused shall be charged and if he pleads guilty he may be sentenced on such plea. Though it seems too simple, in practice however, the plea will only be accepted if it is made without any qualification and that the accused understood the charge made against him as well as consequences of the charge. In addition to that, section 175(1) of the Criminal Procedure Code (Chapter 7) is also practiced whereby a charge containing the particulars of the offence of which he is accused shall be framed and explained to him, and he shall be asked whether he is guilty of the offence charged or claims to be tried. And the court before recording the plea may hear the complainant and such other evidence as it considers necessary and shall ascertain that the accused understands the nature and consequences of his plea and intends to admit, without qualification, the offence alleged against him[62].

If an accused claims trial or refuses to plead, the prosecutor shall outline the facts to be proved and the relevant law and shall then call his witnesses[63]. As laid down in section 70(4), each witness shall be examined by the party calling him[64] and this shall be called his examination-in-chief[65]; be cross-examined thereafter by the party opposing him, which shall be called his cross-examination[66] and, such cross-examination may be directed to credibility[67]. Each witness may thereafter be re-examined on matters arising out of cross-examination by the party calling him[68], and such examination shall be called his re-examination[69]. Each witness have put to him at any time any question by the Court[70] and may have any further questions put to him or be recalled at any time, by leave of the Court[71]. For particulars on examination of witnesses and in ensuring the truth of syahadah syahid reference shall be made to the Syariah Courts Evidence Order, 2001[72].

After hearing the witnesses for the prosecution the Court shall either dismiss the case or call on the accused for his defence[73]. This section is to be read together with section 177(1) of the Criminal Procedure Code (Chapter 7):

"If upon taking all evidence referred to in section 176 and making such examination (if any) of the accused under section 220 as the Court considers necessary it finds that no case against the accused has been made out which, if unrebutted, would warrant his conviction, the Court may, subject to the provisions of section 186, record an order of acquittal.

If called on for his defence, the accused may address the Court and may then either give evidence or make a statement without being sworn or affirmed, in which case he shall not

[62] Section 175(2) of the Criminal Procedure Code (Chapter 7). [63] Section 70(3) of the Religious Council and Kadis Courts Act (Chapter 77). [64] Section 70(4)(a) Ibid. [65] Section 120(1) of the Syariah Courts Evidence Order, 2001(S 63/2001). [66] Section 120(2) Ibid. [67] Section 70(4)(b) of the Religious Council and Kadis Courts Act (Chapter 77). [68] Section 70(4)(c) Ibid. [69] Section 120(3) of the Syariah Courts Evidence Order, 2001(S 63/2001). [70] Section 70(4)(d) of the Religious Council and Kadis Courts Act (Chapter 77). [71] Section 70(4)(e) Ibid. [72] Chapters IX and IV respectively, (S 63/2001) [73] Section 70(5) of the Religious Council and Kadis Courts Act (Chapter 77).

be liable to be cross-examined, or may stand silent provided that if the accused gives evidence, he may be cross-examined, but not as to character or as to other offences not charged[74].

In doing so the accused may then call his witnesses[75]. He may sum up his case[76], and the prosecutor may reply generally[77]. As in any other Court, the Syariah Court, after considering the case shall then either convict or acquit the accused[78]. If the accused is convicted, the court may be informed of previous offences and shall have regard to any plea of leniency[79]. The Court shall then pass sentence according to law[80].

One important section in the Religious Council and Kadis Courts Act (Chapter 77) relating to criminal procedure is section 78 where it says that in matters of practice and procedure not expressly provided for in this Act or any rules made thereunder, the Court shall have regard to the avoidance of injustice and the convenient dispatch of business and may in criminal proceedings have regard to the practice and procedure obtaining in the civil courts.

PROCEDURE IN CIVIL PROCEEDINGS

For civil proceedings, provisions used are as mentioned in the Religious Council and Kadis Courts Act (Chapter 77) in section 80 until section 93; section 95 and section 96. In practice, the Emergency (Islamic Family Law) Order, 1999 (S 12/2000) as well as relevant provisions being used in the civil courts are also applied. This is to ensure that justice is served especially for those matters not provided for in the Act or any rules thereunder. Section 96 of the Religious Council and Kadis Courts (Chapter 77) states that:

"In matters of practice and procedure, not expressly provided for in this Act or any rules made thereunder, the Court may adopt such procedure as may seem proper for the avoidance of injustice and the disposal of the matters in issue between the parties, and may in particular, but without prejudice to the generality of the foregoing, adopt the practice and procedure for the time being in force in the Magistrates' Courts in civil proceedings."

LEGAL QUALIFICATIONS FOR SYARIAH LAWYERS

Section 25 of the Syariah Courts Act (Chapter 184) has specified who may be appointed as Syar'ie Prosecutor. His Majesty the Sultan and Yang Di-Pertuan may, on the advice of the President of the Majlis Ugama Islam and after consultation with the Majlis, appoint a person who is qualified to become Syariah High Court Judge, to be the Chief Syar'ie Prosecutor[26]. The Chief Syar'ie Prosecutor shall have powers exercisable at his discretion to commence and carry out any proceedings for an offence before a Syariah Court[27]; and he shall not be subject to the direction or control of any other person or authority[28].

His Majesty the Sultan and Yang Di-Pertuan may, on the advice of the President of the Majlis and after consultation with the Chief Syar'ie Prosecutor, appoint a fit and suitable persons from members of the public service to be Syar'ie Prosecutors who shall act under the supervision and direction of the Chief Syar'ie Prosecutor and may exercise all or any right and power vested in or exercisable by the Chief Syar'ie Prosecutor himself[29].

Whereas for Syar'ie Lawyers, section 27(1) of the Syariah Courts Act (Chapter 184) says that the Chief Syar'ie Judge may, on payment of the prescribed fee, admit a person who possesses sufficient knowledge about *Hukum Syara'* and suitable to become a Syar'ie Lawyer to represent the parties in any proceedings before any Syariah Court. Subsection

(2) of section 27 also states that no person other than a Syar'ie Lawyer shall have the right to appear as a *bil-khusumah* representative in any Syariah Court on behalf of any party to any proceeding before it.

Section 28 of the Syariah Courts Act (Chapter 184), the Chief Syar'ie Judge may, with the approval of His Majesty the Sultan and Yang Di-Pertuan, make Rules of Court to provide for the procedure, qualifications and fees for admission of Syar'ie Lawyers as well as regulate, control and supervise the conduct of Syar'ie Lawyers. By virtue of that section, the Syariah Courts (Syar'ie Lawyers) Rules, 2002 has been enacted which commences on the same date as the Syariah Courts Act (Chapter 184). Part II of this Rules talks about the Establishment of Syar'ie Lawyers Committee, Part III talks about Syar'ie Lawyers, Part IV on discipline, Part V on miscellaneous provisions; whereas fees and forms under this Rules can be found in the First and Second Schedule respectively.

Rule 9 talks about admission of Syar'ie Lawyers, which shall be made by the Chief Syar'ie Judge. Rule 10 stated that a person may be admitted to be Syar'ie Lawyers if he –

(a) (i) is a Muslim and has passed the final examination which leads to a bachelor's degree in Syariah from any university or any Islamic

[26] Section 25(1) of the Syariah Courts Act (Chapter 184). [27] Section 25(2) Ibid. [28] Section 25(3) Ibid. [29] Section 25(4) Ibid.

educational institution recognized by the Government of Brunei Darussalam;

(ii) is a Muslim advocate or solicitor enrolled under the Legal Profession Act (Chapter 132) who has passed the Syar'ie Lawyer Certificate examination;

(iii) has served as a Syar'ie Judge, Kadi or Syar'ie Prosecutor for a period of not less than 3 years; or

(iv) is a Muslim who has received professional training in Islamic judicial matters which is recognized by the Government of Brunei Darussalam or who specializes in *Hukum Syara'*;

(b) has attained the age of 21 years;
(c) is of good behavior and –
(i) has never been convicted in Brunei Darussalam or in any other place of any criminal offence which makes him unfit to become a Syar'ie Lawyer;
(ii) has never been adjudged a bankrupt; and

(iii) has never been disbarred, struck off or suspended in his capacity as a legal practitioner by whatever name called in any other country.

LEGAL EDUCATION

Presently, there is no law faculty at the University of Brunei Darussalam. Most of the lawyers practicing in Brunei are either qualified in England or Malaysia.

As stated earlier in Rule 10 of the Syariah Courts (Syar'ie Lawyers) Rules, 2002, a person may be admitted as Syar'ie Lawyers if he fulfills all the necessary requirements. Therefore, in its effort to produce qualified Islamic lawyers and legal practitioners in the Syariah Court, the University of Brunei Darussalam has offered a course in Diploma In Islamic Law and Legal Practice[30], which started its first session in 2000/2001. This course stresses upon the practical aspect especially in practicality, legal administration and their executions.

Objectives of this course are, among others, to give wider opportunity for law degree holders and legal practitioners in Brunei Darussalam, in Syariah or Civil to undertake a formal program in Islamic law; to give more exposure to law graduates in Islamic law and Administration; to produce qualified Islamic lawyers; and to minimizing government expenditure on sending students abroad by providing the course locally.

Subjects offered in the program includes the Islamic Legal System, Islamic Family Law, Syariah Political Science, Islamic Judiciary and Practice, Brunei Legal System, Islamic Law and Evidence, Islamic Criminal law, Islamic Law of Contract and Trade, Procedures in Criminal and Civil and Commercial Law.

NATIONAL DEVELOPMENT PLAN

The current National Development Plan 1996 - 2000 is the 7th in the series and primarily aims at giving an all-round enhancement to all facets of life of the people, with emphasis to economic diversification through the development of export-oriented non- oil based industries. The Government has allocated a total of $7.2 billion for this purpose, with social services taking the lion's share at $1.98 billion; Public Utilities, $1.58 billion; Transport and Communications, $1.4 billion; Industry and Commerce, $907.66 million; Public Buildings, $623.83 million; Security, $528.1 million; and Miscellaneous, $173.3 million.

COMMUNICATIONS

Airport

The present day Brunei International Airport, located at Berakas about fifteen minutes drive from Bandar Seri Begawan operates 24 hours a day, providing facilities for both regional and international air traffic. It has a 4000-metre runway that can accommodate any type of aircraft currently in service, including the 'Jumbo' 747s. Its passenger and cargo handling facilities can handle 1.5 million passengers and 50,000 tones of cargo a year. Equipped with the latest state-of the-art technology in surveillance and tracking, the airport boasts radar, flight and auxiliary data processing, 2,000-line, high-resolution color raster displays, simulation facilities, voice switching system, voice and data recording and VHF/UHF air-ground transmitters. The national air carrier is Royal Brunei Airlines founded in November 18, 1974.

Another airport, at Anduki near Seria, is used by the Brunei Shell Petroleum Company for its helicopter services.

Ports

The main Port is Muara, which is about 28 kilometers from Bandar Seri Begawan. The port can accommodate ships over 196 meters L.O.A. and take up to 7 or 8 vessels averaging 8,000 Gross Registered Tonnage {GRT} or a single ship of up to 30,000 {GRT} with a draught of not more than 9.5 meters.

Since 1973, the port has undergone extensive improvements. These include extensions to the wharf bringing the total length to 948 meters including 250 meters dedicated container wharf and 87 meters aggregate wharf. The overall storage space in the form of covered storage is 16,950 square meters, long storage warehouses 16,630 square meters and open storage space 5 hectares. Facilities for the dedicated container wharf covers an area of 92,034 square meters including 8,034 square meters covered areas.

Besides Muara Port, there are two smaller ports located one at Bandar Seri Begawan and one at Kuala Belait. The port at Bandar Seri Begawan is utilized by vessels under 93 meters LOA drawing less than 5 meters draught carrying conventional cargoes for direct deliveries and passenger launches plying between Bandar Seri Begawan, Limbang and Temburong. The wharf also accommodates various small government crafts. The port at Kuala Belait can accommodate vessels with draught of 4 meters which carries mainly general cargo for Kuala Belait and the Brunei Petroleum Shell Company.

Road

For additional analytical, business and investment opportunities information, please contact Global Investment & Business Center, USA at (703) 370-8082. Fax: (703) 370-8083. E-mail: ibpusa3@gmail.com Global Business and Investment Info Databank - www.ibpus.com

The road network in Brunei Darussalam is the primary means of movement for people, goods and services on land. It plays a vital role in the overall growth and development of the State. The network has been designed to integrate housing, commercial and industrial development. The Sultanate has constructed a good road network with various types of road throughout the country that includes highways, link roads, flyovers and round-abouts. A major road, which was completed in 1983, is a 28-kilometre highway linking Muara through Berakas and Jerudong to a point in Tutong, where it connects with the existing Bandar Seri Begawan-Tutong-Seria trunk road thus providing an alternative routes to these places.

An 11-km road between Sungai Teraban and Sungai Tujoh, makes the journey from Brunei Darussalam to Sarawak's Fourth Division such as Miri and other parts of Sarawak much easier.

The State had 2,525 kilometers (km) of roads, of which 2,328 km were covered with asphalt, 187 with pebbles, and 10 km with concrete. Of the total 1,514 km were in Brunei/Muara, 481 km in Belait, 400 km in Tutong and 130 km in Temburong district.

For additional analytical, business and investment opportunities information, please contact Global Investment & Business Center, USA at (703) 370-8082. Fax: (703) 370-8083. E-mail: ibpusa3@gmail.com Global Business and Investment Info Databank - www.ibpus.com

BRUNEI LABOR MARKET - STRATEGIC INFORMATION AND DEVELOPMENTS

BASIC INFORMATION

LABOUR DEPARTMENT

Ministry or Board Name	Ministry of Home Affairs
Telephone	2383006
e-mail address	info.buruh@buruh.gov.bn
website	Website http://labour.gov.bn/Theme/Home.aspx
Fax No	2383244
Address	Jabatan Buruh Jalan Menteri Besar BS3910 Negara Brunei Darussalam

The 2014 labor force estimate was 203,600 persons with an unemployment rate of 6.9 percent, according to the Brunei Darussalam Statistical Yearbook 2014 (latest data available), though unofficial estimates place the unemployment figures higher.

Brunei relies heavily on foreign labor in lower-skill and lower-paying positions, with approximately 120,000 guest workers brought in to fulfill specific contracts. The largest percentage of those work in construction, followed by wholesale and retail trade and then professional, technical, administrative and support services. Most unskilled laborers in Brunei are immigrants from Bangladesh, India, Indonesia, Malaysia, and the Philippines on renewable two-year contracts.

The skilled labor pool includes both foreign laborers on short-term visas and Bruneian citizens and permanent residents, who often are well educated but who often prefer to work for the government due to generous benefits such as bonuses, education allowances, interest-free loans, housing allowances. The IMF estimated in 2013 that approximately 56 percent of the total Brunei citizen workforce is employed in the public sector.

In 2014, the Ministry of Home Affairs implemented policies that limited the numbers of foreign labor quotas upon renewal, and revoked unused foreign labor quotas, in an effort to create more employment opportunities for Brunei citizens.

While Brunei law permits the formation of trade union federations, it forbids affiliation with international labor organizations unless there is consent from the Minister of Home Affairs and the Department of Labor. The government prohibits strikes, and the law makes no explicit provision for the right to collective bargaining. The law prohibits employers from discriminating against workers in connection with union activities, but it does not provide for reinstatement for dismissal related to union activity. Under the Trade Unions Act of 1961, unions must be registered with the government.

All workers, including civil servants other than those serving in the military and those working as prison guards or police officers, may form and join trade unions of their choice without previous authorization or excessive requirements. The only active union in the country, which is composed of Brunei Shell Petroleum workers, appears to have minimal activity in recent years.

Various domestic laws prohibit the employment of children under age 16. Parental consent and approval by the Labor Commission are required for those under age 18. Female workers under age 18 may not work at night or on offshore oil platforms. The Department of Labor, which is part of the Ministry of Home Affairs, effectively enforced laws related to the employment of children. There were no reports of violations of child labor laws.

The law does not set a minimum wage, but most employed citizens commanded good salaries. The public sector pay scale covers all workers in government jobs. Wages for employed foreign residents were wide ranging. Some foreign embassies set minimum wage requirements for their nationals working in the country.

Government data from 2014, the latest data available, indicated approximately 86,500 foreigners lived in the country temporarily. Foreign workers receive a mandatory brief on labor rights from the Department of Labor when they sign their contract. The government also protects the rights of foreign workers through inspections of facilities and a telephone hotline for worker complaints. Immigration law allows prison sentences and caning for workers who overstay their work permits, for workers who fall into irregular status due to their employers' negligence.

DEMOGRAPHIC TRENDS

The demographic features of Brunei include population density, ethnicity, education level, health of the populace, economic status, religious affiliations and other aspects of the population. Like neighbouring countries, Brunei is a Malay-dominated country. Many cultural and linguistic differences make Brunei Malays distinct from the larger Malay populations in nearby Malaysia and Indonesia, even though they are ethnically related and share the Muslim religion.

Brunei has a hereditary nobility with the title Pengiran these are, more often than not, related to the Sultan by blood. The Sultan can award to commoners the title Pehin, the equivalent of a life peerage awarded in the United Kingdom. The Sultan also can award his subjects the Dato, the equivalent of a knighthood in the United Kingdom, and Datin, the equivalent of a damehood.

Bruneians adhere to the practice of using complete full names with all titles, including the title Haji (for men) or Hajjah (for women) for those who have made the Haj pilgrimage to Mecca. Many Brunei Malay women wear the tudong, a traditional head covering. Men wear the songkok, a traditional Malay cap. Men who have completed the Haj wear a white songkok.

The requirements to attain Brunei citizenship include passing tests in Malay culture, customs and language. Stateless permanent residents of Brunei are given International Certificates of Identity, which allow them to travel overseas. The majority of Brunei's Chinese are permanent residents, and many are stateless.

Petroleum wealth allows the Brunei Government to provide the population with one of Asia's finest health care systems. The Brunei Medical and Health Department introduced the region's first government "flying doctor service" in early 1965. Malaria has been eradicated, and cholera is virtually nonexistent. There are three general hospitals--in Bandar Seri Begawan, Tutong, and Kuala Belait--and there are numerous health clinics throughout the country.

Education starts with preschool, followed by 6 years of primary education and up to 6 years of secondary education. Nine years of education are mandatory. Most of Brunei's college students attend universities and other institutions abroad, but approximately 2,542 study at the University of Brunei Darussalam. Opened in 1985, the university has a faculty of over 300 instructors and is located on a sprawling campus at Tungku, overlooking the South China Sea.

The official language is Malay, but English is widely understood and used in business. Other languages spoken are several Chinese dialects, Iban, and a number of native dialects. Islam is the official religion, but religious freedom is guaranteed under the constitution.

Total population (thousands)	Population aged 0-14 (%)	Population aged 15-64 (%)	Population aged 65+ (%)	
1950	48	36.4	58.7	4.9
1955	63	39.5	56.1	4.4
1960	80	42.1	53.8	4.1
1965	100	44.7	51.4	3.9
1970	125	41.1	55.0	3.8
1975	157	39.8	56.3	3.8
1980	189	38.7	58.4	3.0
1985	219	38.7	58.3	3.0
1990	252	35.4	61.8	2.8
1995	290	33.3	63.7	3.0
2000	327	30.3	66.7	2.9
2005	363	28.2	68.6	3.2
2010	399	26.2	70.2	3.6

STRUCTURE OF THE POPULATION

Structure of the population (20.06.2011) (Census) :

Age Group	Male	Female	Total	%
Total	203 149	190 223	393 372	100
0-4	15 678	14 653	30 331	7,71
5-9	17 269	16 365	33 634	8,55
10-14	18 448	17 015	35 463	9,02
15-19	17 948	17 013	34 961	8,89
20-24	19 950	18 257	38 207	9,71
25-29	20 749	18 445	39 194	9,96
30-34	19 322	17 619	36 941	9,39
35-39	17 329	16 423	33 752	8,58
40-44	15 262	14 819	30 081	7,65
45-49	12 836	11 754	24 590	6,25
50-54	10 318	9 458	19 776	5,03
55-59	7 170	6 872	14 042	3,57

For additional analytical, business and investment opportunities information, please contact Global Investment & Business Center, USA at (703) 370-8082. Fax: (703) 370-8083. E-mail: ibpusa3@gmail.com Global Business and Investment Info Databank - www.ibpus.com

60-64	4 160	4 354	8 514	2,16
65-69	2 583	2 501	5 084	1,29
70-74	1 833	2 079	3 912	0,99
75-79	1 195	1 398	2 593	0,66
80-84	701	703	1 404	0,36
85+	398	495	893	0,23

Age group	Male	Female	Total	Percent
0-14	51 395	48 033	99 428	25,28
15-64	145 044	135 014	280 058	71,19
65+	6 710	7 176	13 886	3,53

MEDIAN AGE

total: 27.5 years
male: 27.5 years
female: 27.8 years

POPULATION GROWTH RATE

100.785% (2008 est.)

NET MIGRATION RATE

2.74 migrant(s)/1,000 population

SEX RATIO

under 15 years: 1.06 male(s)/female
15-64 years: 1 male(s)/female
65 years and over: 0.93 male(s)/female
total population: 1.01 male(s)/female (2008 est.)
at birth: 1.05 male(s)/female

URBANIZATION

Urban population: 79% of total population

According to the latest figures, the current population of Brunei Darussalam is estimated to be roughly 400,000. This is considered very small by international standards, and together with a steadily declining population growth rate (as shown in the Figure 1 below) from 4.8 per cent in 1960 to 1.9 per cent in 2009, presents a constraint to Labor-intensive economic activities. In addition, the Labor market is also limited by government regulations on the immigration of foreign Labor. Although foreign Labor represents a significant proportion of the Labor force, work permits for foreigners are issued only for short periods of time and must continually be renewed.

Slowing down of the population growth rate can be attributed to the reduced fertility rate, as shown in Figure 2 below, from an average of 6.95 births per woman in 1960 to an average of 2.05

births per woman in 2009. The declining fertility trend in Brunei is part of a wider trend that is common across many developed and developing countries, and has been the subject of considerable debate. It is important to study the causes and possible implications of this fertility trends, as it may have a broader social and economic impact. One plausible explanation for the declining fertility trend is that increased female participation in the Labor force (which will be elaborated further in the next subsection) tends to be associated with delayed marriage and family planning decisions, and subsequently smaller families.

Another feature of the population is increased life expectancy, which has been made possible due to an improvement in health standards and medical facilities. According to World Bank (2011) estimates, the life expectancy at birth in Brunei for 2009 was 77.5 years, which is an increase from 62.2 years in 1960. Taken together with the steady decline in the population growth rate, these two factors would tend to contribute to an ageing population. In line with increased life expectancy and longer productive years of the population, the national retirement age has recently been increased from 55 to 60 years old, which also helps reduce the (actual) dependency ratio, or the pressure on the productive group of the population.

The dependency ratio is the age-population ratio of those typically not in the Labor force (the *dependent* part) and those typically in the Labor force (the *productive* part). In published international statistics, the *dependent* part usually includes those in the population under the age of 15 and over the age of 65, whilst the *productive* part makes up the remainder of the population in between 15-64. Estimates from the Asian Development Bank (2011, p. 140) show that the dependency ratio for Brunei declined from 62.7 in 1990 to 43.3 in 2010, which suggests an increase in the productive part of the population relative to the dependent part. However, the combined effects of reduced fertility rates and increased life expectancy provide

reasonable doubt as to whether this trend will continue much longer into the future, reflected in the foresight of policymakers in increasing the retirement age. Additional provisions and precautions might need to be taken beforehand as too high a dependency ratio can cause direct consequences such as increased government expenditures (e.g. on healthcare, social security and education), as well as many indirect consequences.

Against the background of these population and demographic changes, the next two subsections will focus on changes in the structure of the Labor market in terms of Labor force participation and unemployment.

LABOR FORCE PARTICIPATION

The Labor force participation rate is a measure of the proportion of an economy's working-age population that is economically active, i.e. either employed or unemployed but actively seeking and available for work. It provides an indication

of the relative supply of the Labor force that is available for the production of goods and services. Taken from previous census estimates, Figure 3 above demonstrates the breakdown of the Labor force by gender and age group, and gives a profile of the distribution of the economically active population in Brunei for 1991 and 2001.

Often for traditional reasons, female participation tends to predominantly lag behind male participation in the Labor force. However, as shown in Figure 3, female participation in the Labor force has increased between 1991 and 2001, particularly for those within the 15-54 age groups. Increased female Labor force participation is a growing trend that can be traced back to earlier (Census) estimates2, as a result of increased opportunities in education and the Labor market.

The estimates from the Brunei Darussalam Government indicate that the trend of increasing female participation rates in the Labor force has been slowing down in the years after 2001. In 2010, the overall Labor force participation rate for females (males) was estimated to be 58.0 per cent (76.4 per cent), compared to 57.3 per cent (78.2 per cent) in 2006. Nevertheless, the Census estimates shown here are the latest comprehensive figures that illustrate the breakdown of the Labor force participation rate, according to gender and age group. The data collection for the 2011 Census was recently conducted in mid-2011 and the publication of its results is forthcoming.

There is evidence suggestive of an overall increase in the Labor force participation rate in recent years. For example, the latest Brunei Darussalam Statistical Yearbook 2010 (Government of Brunei Darussalam, various years), shows a very slight increase in the overall Labor force participation rate from 67.9 per cent in 2001 to 68.0 per cent in 2010.

The decline in the Labor force participation above the age of 55 between 1991 and 2001 for both males and females as shown in Figure 3 can largely be attributed to previous legislation on the national retirement age of 55. Although it is unclear why the male Labor force participation rate was previously higher for those aged over 55 in 1991, it should be expected to increase in the years to come, in line with the recent change in legislation on the national retirement age, as previously stated.

Students are not considered economically active and this is reflected in the low participation rates for the 15-24 age-groups, as shown in Figure 3. Typically, students seek to obtain the skills and training that would improve their employment prospects. Young people who enter the Labor force without sufficient skills or relevant work experience may encounter employment difficulties.

UNEMPLOYMENT

Unemployment is a central concern of Labor market issues. The formal definition of an unemployed person is one who is not currently undertaking paid work but is able, willing and actively seeking work. Taken together with those who are employed, they make up the Labor force and are considered as part of the population that is economically active. The rest of the population are considered economically inactive, and include children, students, retirees, those who are unable to work such as disabled people, and those who choose not to undertake paid work such as housewives.

The Census data does not distinguish between part-time and full-time employment, incorrectly records unemployment for temporary residents despite legal inconsistencies regarding employment law involving temporary residentship and does not make seasonal adjustments to account for school leavers during the Census period. Nevertheless, the Census estimates shown here are the latest comprehensive figures that illustrate the breakdown of the unemployment rate, according to gender and age group. The data collection for the 2011 Census was recently conducted in mid-2011 and the publication

of its results is forthcoming.

5 There is evidence suggestive of a reduction in the overall unemployment rate since 2001. For example, the Brunei Darussalam Statistical Yearbook (Government of Brunei Darussalam, various years) shows a decrease in the unemployment rate from 7.2 per cent in 2001 to 2.7 per cent in 2010. The unemployment rates recorded were highest amongst young people, with each subsequent age group recording a lower rate. The estimates also show that females experience less unemployment compared to males in each age group. Whilst neither finding is too surprising,

the extent of youth unemployment is an area of concern with approximately 50 per cent of those in the 15-19 age group that are economically active unable to find work.

In a recent survey paper on unemployment issues in Brunei, Cheong & Lawrey (2009) note that, aside from the Population Census, Labor force statistics are also collected by the Labor Department through its list of registered job seekers6. With

following reasons: (a) firstly, job seekers may be employed, but looking for a better (paying) job, (b) secondly, not all the unemployed register with the Labor Department, (c) and thirdly, those who have registered with the Labor Department and have subsequently found work are under no obligation to inform the Labor Department and have their names removed from the list. Thus, there are disparities between the definition used by the Labor Department and the formal definition for unemployment, and hence may not be directly comparable to the Census data or international statistics.

According to the data cited by the Brunei Darussalam Statistical Yearbook (Government of Brunei Darussalam, Various Years), Brunei's unemployment rate for 2008 stood at 3.7 per cent. Unemployment figures tend to fluctuate throughout the year for a variety of demand-side or supply-side reasons.

Another form of unemployment is cyclical or demand-deficient unemployment, which occurs during periods of economic downturns or recessions.

a significant number of registered job seekers currently employed, only 65 per cent of the sample from their study can be formally classified as unemployed. This corresponds to an estimated overall unemployment rate of 2.2 per cent during their period of study in 20087. They find that the main cause of unemployment was frictional, with a majority of their sample having left work voluntarily or still looking for their first job. However, in contrast to typical frictional unemployment, they also find that 74 per cent of the unemployed from the sample had been without a job for more than 6 months. This long-term unemployment that is experienced is a more serious form of unemployment. In addition, they also alluded to the presence of structural unemployment with "*a significant mismatch between skills and desired employment*" (Cheong & Lawrey 2009, p. ix), which implies an inefficient allocation of Labor resources8. For local job seekers, they infer that the reservation wage, the lowest wage below which they would prefer to stay unemployed rather than employed, is higher than the market salary for the jobs which they are qualified for.

With limited available, reliable and up-to-date statistics on the Labor force, as described above, many issues with regards to unemployment remain unresolved and continue to pose many questions. The answers to such questions could be obtained with more frequent and comprehensive surveys, such as the internationally-accepted Labor Force Survey (LFS)9. In addition to Labor force participation and unemployment, other key indicators of the Labor market (KILM)10, a multi-functional research tool of the ILO, could also be collected to further examine the health of the Labor market on a more regular and comprehensive basis, such as the employment-to-population ratio, youth unemployment, long-term unemployment, time-related underemployment, employment in the informal sector, hours of work, part-time workers, educational attainment and illiteracy, hourly compensation costs, occupational wage and earning indices, Labor productivity, working poverty and income distribution. The benefit of employing the KILM would not just be to highlight the most current

For further details on the KILM, see http://www.ilo.org/kilm . In 2007, Brunei became an official member of the ILO, an agency of the United Nations. There are some disparities in the unemployment rate and the Labor force participation rate figures quoted by the International

Labor Organization (2010) compared to those described above within this section. The reasons for this are not immediately clear, but the general points discussed should still hold.

Unemployment can occur as a result of the demand side or supply side pressures of the Labor market, and the next two sections examine these features in the Brunei context.

LABOR DEMAND

The strategy highlighted above indicates that increased emphasis will be given to the wealth-producing secondary sector, rather than the wealth-consuming service or tertiary sector, to increase exports and reduce over-reliance on imported consumer and capital goods, which would increase the circular flow of income within the economy. This would entail an expansion in the share of total employment in the secondary sector, which stood at 19 per cent in 2001, as shown in Figure 5 below11. However, the disadvantage posed by the lack of economies of scale afforded by a relatively small domestic market and Labor force coupled with competitively-priced imported goods presents a major challenge to this objective.

The industrial sectors that were included in the calculation of this figure for the secondary industry were: Manufacturing; Electrical, Gas & Water Supply; Construction.

Nevertheless, there is some recent evidence suggesting that the expansion of the secondary sector may already be underway12.

According to the data cited by the International Monetary Fund (2011, p. 21), the share of private sector employment in secondary industry (i.e. Sawmilling & Timber Processing; Other Mining, Quarrying & Manufacturing; Construction) was 39 per cent in 2009. Using the same Census data that was used to construct Figure 5, the share of private sector employment in secondary industry in 2001 was 29 per cent (Government of Brunei Darussalam, 2005). However, different industrial sectors were categorized (c.f. footnote 11) and thus caution should be exercised before making direct comparisons and deriving conclusive statements.

The wealth generated from natural resources has allowed for good infrastructure development, the provision of public goods and a relatively high material standard of living for citizens, one negative side-effect has been the structural rigidities left in the Labor market.

The dominance of two major employers in the Labor market – the public sector and Brunei Shell Petroleum in the oil and gas sector are highlighted.The market power exerted by these dominant employers in the demand for Labor creates an imperfectly competitive13 Labor market – especially in the recruitment of the local Labor force. The public sector employed 42,000 out of 74,000, or 57 per cent, of the local Labor force in 2004 (Crosby 2007, p. 33). High wages and generous non-pecuniary benefits provided by the public sector can only be matched by the largest private employer. However, Haji Hashim (2010, p. 41) explains that despite considerable power in the Labor market, Brunei Shell Petroleum and other oil-related companies employ only approximately 4 per cent of Brunei Darussalam's total workforce, due to the capital-intensive nature of the oil and gas industry.

13 "Imperfect competition" in the Labor market is often compared to a monopsonistic employer in the traditional sense, that is, the sole employer in a Labor market. Traditional textbook monopsony is unrealistic, since employers compete with one another to some extent. However, in the theoretical spectrum between the polar opposites of perfect competition and monopsony, there lies a range of points where a degree of market power coexists with competition between employers. The most accurate descriptions of the Labor market that exhibit this would be

"oligopsony" or "monopsonistic competition". Oligopsony refers to a situation where employer market power persists despite competition with other employers, while monopsonistic competition refers to oligopsony with free entry, such that employer profits are driven to zero. Nevertheless, the description of the overall Labor market in Brunei would certainly lie closer to the monopsony than perfect competition on this theoretical spectrum, though this should vary by sector.

The unbalanced incentive structure created by the dominance of these major employers contributes to the weakness of the private sector: another unintended consequence. The rest of the private sector is largely unable to compete, as Haji Hashim (2010, p. 41) noted that "well-educated Bruneians shied away from these establishments and opted for the Government in their bid to secure a more reliable and sustained source of income", and Brunei is left with a relatively weak residual

local Labor force. From the latest publication of the Brunei Darussalam Statistical Yearbook 2010 (Government of Brunei Darussalam, Various Years), only 39,025 out of 121,158 employees in the private sector in 2009, or 32.2 per cent of employees, were classified as Brunei citizens or permanent residents, with the remainder of private sector employment filled by temporary residents. The majority of temporary residents or foreign Labor would be classified as unskilled or semi-skilled, as will be shown in the next section.

Nevertheless, the bulk of total employment – the sum of the local and immigrant Labor force – is provided by the private sector in Brunei Darussalam, with 59 per cent in 200114, as shown in Figure 6 below. Haji Hashim (2010, p. 40) explains however, that "more than 95 per cent of all establishments in the private sector are considered as micro, small and medium enterprises and a large proportion of them are actively concentrated in the services industry". From the latest Brunei Darussalam Statistical Yearbook 2010 (Government of Brunei Darussalam, various years), out of the 8,935 establishments listed in the private sector in 2009, only 14 companies employed 500 workers or more, which includes four companies in the construction sector that engage in short-term employment, as highlighted by Haji Hashim (2010, p. 41). This is indicative of the size, and hence strength, of the firms in the private sector. The relatively low wages afforded by the lack of scale presents a challenge for the private sector in attracting highly skilled local or foreign talent. The structural rigidities and lopsided incentive structure caused by an imperfectly competitive Labor market as described above are symptomatic of the unique structure of the Brunei economy. Haji Hashim (2010, p. 41) further explains that the existing size and structure of the non-oil private sector in Brunei Darussalam is indicative of the legacy of rentierism – where the economy has been solely dependent on income accrued from abroad for the sale of its main product from a "booming sector" and thereby has a relatively "neglected" non-oil sector.

14 A more recent calculation of government sector employment and private sector employment using data cited from the International Monetary Fund (2011, p. 20-21) would suggest that the private sector accounted for as much as 72 per cent of total employment in 2009. However, this calculation may not be completely accurate as it would entail using two different data sets. Nevertheless, the broad point remains that the private sector provides the largest share of total employment in Brunei.

The overall business environment in Brunei has recently been scrutinised in the latest Ease of Doing Business (EoDB) report (World Bank & International Finance Corporation, 2011). The findings are succinctly summarized in Figure 7 below, in a ranking of Doing Business topics relative to 183 countries worldwide. Although Brunei scores relatively well in some measures, such as Paying Taxes, Getting Electricity, Trading Across Borders & Resolving Insolvency, its performance is relatively poor in other measures, particularly in Enforcing Contracts, Starting a

For additional analytical, business and investment opportunities information, please contact Global Investment & Business Center, USA at (703) 370-8082. Fax: (703) 370-8083. E-mail: ibpusa3@gmail.com Global Business and Investment Info Databank - www.ibpus.com

Business, Getting Credit & Protecting Investors as shown. This translates to an overall rank of 83 out of 183 countries worldwide and represents a 29-rank improvement over the previous year, the second successive year Brunei has posted a rank-improvement since joining the EoDB study in 2007. The formation of the EoDB Steering Committee and Working Committee earlier in 2011 should allow and oversee a coordinated effort by relevant agencies and stakeholders towards undertaking reforms that would enable continual improvements in the future, not just in terms of the EoDB indicators, but to the underlying business and regulatory environment15. This in turn should lead to a more competitive and flourishing private sector which would contribute towards a correction of the previously stated imbalances in the incentive structure present in the Labor market.

An improvement to the underlying business and regulatory environment should not just rely on an improvement in terms of the *Doing Business* indicators, but on a broader scale. For example, the World Bank's *Enterprise Surveys,* a comprehensive firm-level survey, can also be conducted to complement the *Doing Business* study, in order to benchmark the quality of the business environment in Brunei.

The recommendations advocated to promote economic diversification by authors such as Crosby (2007), Bhaskaran (2007), Lawrey (2010), Haji Hashim (2010) and Duraman & Tharumarajah (2010) include, among others, a reduction in the size of

the public sector, selective privatization, a gradual reduction in public sector wages, increased Public-Private Partnerships (PPPs), the establishment of and partnership with large multinational corporations, and increased opportunities in the private sector through grants and other incentives to promote the development of small and medium enterprises (SMEs). This essentially entails the promotion of private sector-driven growth, which in turn would reduce the size of the public sector relative to the private sector and hence reduce the dependency of locals on government jobs through a correction of the unbalanced incentive structure present in the Labor market in Brunei. Some of these recommendations may be expensive or politically less feasible, but may prove to be necessary measures to correct the imbalances in the demand for Labor. A thorough assessment of each of these recommendations is required to ensure a conducive and competitive environment in the Labor market to spur economic diversification and development.

LABOR SUPPLY

The supply of Labor, which can be thought to be a function of what is produced through the education system and the country's immigration policy, should address the skill needs and desired demand requirements in the market for Labor. An educated and skilled workforce is often associated with higher Labor productivity levels, and is one that is able to compete in an increasingly globalised world. Another key element of the Long Term Development Plan

SPN21 aims to build on the success of the existing education structure, which has seen great improvements in literacy rates and basic education standards. The quality of Brunei's overall education system is reflected in a recent survey published by the Global Competitiveness Report 2011-2012 (World Economic Forum 2011, 444-445), in particular the quality of math and science education16.

16 In a survey question of the quality of the educational system which asks "how well does the educational system in your country meet the needs of a competitive economy?" on a scale of 1 (not well at all) to 7 (very well), Brunei posted a score of 4.6 (against a worldwide mean of 3.8), which placed it at a rank of 28 out of 142 countries worldwide, whereas in a survey question of the quality of math and science education which asks "how would you assess the quality of math

and science education in your country's schools?" on a scale of 1 (poor) to 7 (excellent), Brunei posted a score of 4.9 (against a worldwide mean of 3.9), which placed it at a rank of 25 out of 142 countries worldwide.

Highest Qualification Attainment (%) by Total Population, Brunei Citizens & Permanent Residents and Temporary Residents & Others in 1991 and 2001[17]

17 Vocational and Technical Education (VTE) is taken to be the type of education offering vocational and technical subjects. For the purposes of the 1991 Census, this includes: lower technical or vocational education certificate; passed OND or equivalent; passed HND or equivalent; teachers training certificate or diploma or other certificate or diploma. For the purposes of the 2001 Census, this includes: teachers training; nursing courses; vocational or technical. The Census estimates shown here are the latest comprehensive figures that illustrate the breakdown of educational attainment and hence skill structure of the entire population, according to citizenship status. The data collection for the 2011 Census was recently conducted in mid-2011 and the publication of its results is forthcoming.

According to Bhaskaran (2007, p. 18), the prevalence of government jobs and subsidies creates a set of incentives that do not propel workers to strive and compete, and so excel. He explains further that "if people are complacent because everything is provided for them, there will not be much urge to improve themselves – a lack of keenness to upgrade, hone their skills, keep upgrading etc." Although it should not be taken too literally here that *everything* has been provided for Bruneians, to the extent that there exists the presence of over-generous, non-targeted subsidies and the lack of performance-related pay or the lack of incentives to reward more difficult courses or subjects, the point about the existing incentive structure being skewed towards this outcome should still remain.

These trends in education would appear to continue beyond 2001, as calculated and shown in Figure 9 below. While there has been an overall increase in the percentage pass rates for primary level examinations (PCE) over the 2000 to 2008 period, the percentage pass rates have been relatively lower at the critical secondary examination level (BCGCE O Level) and have even declined slightly over the 1999 to 2008 period. The challenge for SPN21 is to produce an increase in the percentage of pass rates in the student population at BCGCE O Level and above, or their equivalent, without a compromise in the quality or standards of education[19].

For students who are able to and choose to continue along the academic track, there are many opportunities to further their education to tertiary level, at local and foreign institutions. Over the past decade, a greater number and variety of scholarships have been made available by various public or publicly-backed institutions[20], as well as the expansion and establishment of more local universities[21]. However, despite these incentives and opportunities, as well as the

In addition to government support, private firms in Brunei can also invest in further staff training and employee development. In one of the survey questions published by the Global Competitiveness Report 2011-2012 (World Economic Forum 2011, p. 449), which asks "to what extent do companies in your country invest in training and employee development?" on a scale of 1 (hardly at all) to 7 (to a great extent), Brunei posted a score of 4.1 (against a worldwide mean of 4.0) at a rank of 59 out of 142 countries worldwide.

However, the local availability and quality of specialized training and research services is still lacking in Brunei, which is reflected by the need for locals to seek further education or training overseas. In another survey question published by the Global Competitiveness Report 2011-2012 (World Economic Forum 2011, p. 448), which asks "in your country, to what extent are high-quality, specialized training services available?" on a scale of 1 (not available) to 7 (widely available), Brunei posted a low score of 3.2 (against a worldwide mean of 4.1) at a rank of 116 out of 142 countries

More recent data has not been immediately available to the author. Nevertheless, bolstering the vocational and technical education system is acknowledged as one of the focuses of SPN21, as highlighted in a recent Oxford Business Group Economic Update (Oxford Business Group, 2011). Several plans are afoot to improve the quantity and quality of vocational and technical institutions. This will in turn improve the quantity and quality of vocational and technical graduates to meet the demands of both the students and the national economy.

The relatively low pass rates seen at secondary level would not be alarming if there were a significant alternative, that is, a vocational track for example, for those who are not suited to the academic route. This is related to the problem noted earlier regarding the constraints of the existing institutional framework for the development of human capital. Bhaskaran (2007, p. 19) explains (in theoretical terms) that "... *people are distributed along a curve since there is a spectrum of abilities in any population. Consequently, every country needs a range of institutions which can develop each strata of ability to the maximum possible.*" He adds that "*We are not sure if Brunei has the full spectrum of educational institutions - vocational schools for those who are not academically inclined or those who start late.*" The reduction in the proportion of the local population with vocational and technical education qualifications between 1991 and 2001, as shown in Figures 8(c) & (d) from 8 per cent to 5 per cent appears to confirm this supposition, and is another area that SPN21 should seek to address22.

Another aspect of the education system that should be addressed by SPN21 is the issue of gender disparity, where despite equal opportunities there have been unequal outcomes. Figure 10 below shows the calculated enrolment ratio of females-to-males in various public examinations, with a greater disparity between males and females recorded at upper secondary level - BCGCE A Levels. The enrolment ratio of females-to-males is shown to be relatively stable at all education levels during this period, except in the case of BCGCE O Levels. At this public examination level, there has been an increase in the enrolment of males which is reflected by an improvement in the calculated enrolment ratio of females-to-males from 1.24 in 2003 to 1.06 in 200823. Similarly, Leete (2008) reported that while enrolment in primary and secondary schools was nearly equal, there is a marked contrast when it came to the tertiary level, which favoured females rather than males. This shows that the overall trend of gender disparity has continued to higher levels of education.

23 In the latest Brunei Darussalam Statistical Yearbook 2010 (Government of Brunei Darussalam, Various Years), the calculated enrolment ratio of females-to-males has remained relatively constant at PCE and BCGCE O Level for 2010 compared to 2008 with a ratio of 1.0 and 1.1 respectively, but a slight improvement can be seen overall at BCGCE A Level with the enrolment ratio of females to males at 1.44 in 2010 compared to 1.63 in 2008. This has been doubly brought about by an increase in male enrolment and a decline in female enrolment in 2010 compared to 2008.

The level at which this gender disparity starts to appear can be ascertained from Figure 11 below, which shows the ratio of females-to-males in terms of passes in public examinations. While this ratio is roughly unitary at primary and lower secondary level, it becomes clear that the disparity in gender attainment begins to appear at the critical secondary level examination – BCGCE O Level, with the calculated ratio remaining relatively stable at a level of 1.4 during this period. This is followed by an even greater disparity at BCGCE A Level, albeit at a level that is calculated to be in decline from 1.89 in 2003 to 1.68 in 200824. The causes for and effects of gender disparity in educational attainment warrant further study, as they can have an impact on the supply of the Labor force in an economy.

24 A further improvement in terms of gender disparity in education attainment at BCGCE A Level can be seen recently in the latest Brunei Darussalam Statistical Yearbook 2010 (Government of Brunei Darussalam, Various Years), with the pass ratio for females-to-males calculated to be 1.55 in 2010 compared to 1.68 in 2008, a somewhat marked deviation away from the trend shown in Figure 11. However, this appears to be driven by enrolment differences (described in footnote 25), rather than an improvement in performance by males or a decline in performance of females. It remains to be seen whether this is a one-off deviation of a promising trend towards gender equality in outcomes. However, the pass ratio of females-to-males has remained relatively constant at PCE and BCGCE O Level for 2010 compared to 2008 with a ratio of 1.0 and 1.4 respectively.

The increasing gender disparity in educational attainment may have other social effects as well. In a survey of Bruneian women, Anaman & Kassim (2003) confirmed the positive assortative mating model of search for marriage partners across a range of characteristics of husbands. They find that women tend to choose their partners mainly from their educational attainment groups and social class. Given the rapid advancement of women in Brunei over a number of years, both in terms of educational attainment and formal Labor market participation, as seen previously, this increased gender disparity reduces the probability of finding suitable marriage partners for educated women in Brunei under the model. As a result, it is plausible that highly educated women may find more suitable marriage partners overseas and decide to emigrate, even reneging on their scholarship contract agreements to serve the country25. This represents an outflow of valuable Labor resources or a "brain drain"26. In a separate hypothetical scenario, young women might opt not to pursue higher education if they anticipate that education might pose a barrier to marriage. These issues present another potential area for further research. To this end, Anaman & Kassim (2003) suggest that the immigration policy may need to be relaxed by making citizenship and naturalization laws easier for Bruneian women to marry foreign men and encourage more stable family units in Brunei, which they note will be an extension of privileges already given to local married men.

Of course, there may be other reasons for reneging on these contractual agreements that will be true for both males and females, such as better career prospects or better incentives elsewhere.

Brunei's performance on this score relative to other countries is relatively fair. In another survey question published by the Global Competitiveness Report 2011-2012 (World Economic Forum 2011, p. 448) which asks "does your country retain and attract talented people?" on a scale of 1 (no, the best and brightest normally leave to pursue opportunities in other countries) to 7 (yes, there are many opportunities for talented people within the country), Brunei posted a score of 4.0 (against a worldwide mean of 3.5) at a rank of 42 out of 142 countries worldwide.

The current immigration policy does not appear to be geared to the active recruitment of skilled foreign Labor, as shown in Figures 8(e) & (f), with the majority only possessing secondary education level qualifications. A more aggressive policy in attracting professionals and skilled Labor from overseas could be pursued, as practiced in fast-growing nations such as Singapore, to inject greater productivity into the Labor force. Whilst some might argue that the influx of skilled foreign Labor might crowd out local jobs, it can also create employment opportunities and spur economic growth, as evidenced in many other countries. However, a relaxation of immigration policy may also bring about a wider social and economic impact, and thus careful consideration must be paid to this. For example, Odihi (2003) surveys some specific socio-economic problems of low-income immigrant workers in Brunei, and considers suggestions to improve their welfare.

In addition, some immigrant workers tend to repatriate a large proportion of their income earned in Brunei back to their country of origin, which may be detrimental to the economy.

BRUNEI VISION 2035 -WAWASAN 2035

According to the latest figures, the current population of Brunei Darussalam is estimated to be roughly 400,000. This is considered very small by international standards, and together with a steadily declining population growth rate from 4.8 per cent in 1960 to 1.9 per cent in 2009, presents a constraint to labour-intensive economic activities. In addition, the labour market is also limited by government regulations on the immigration of foreign labour. Although foreign labour represents a significant proportion of the labour force, work permits for foreigners are issued only for short periods of time and must continually be renewed.

An important feature of the population is increased life expectancy, which has been made possible due to an improvement in health standards and medical facilities. According to World Bank (2011) estimates, the life expectancy at birth in Brunei for 2009 was 77.5 years, which is an increase from 62.2 years in 1960. Taken together with the steady decline in the population growth rate, these two factors would tend to contribute to an ageing population. In line with increased life expectancy and longer productive years of the population, the national retirement age has recently been increased from 55 to 60 years old, which also helps reduce the (actual) dependency ratio, or the pressure on the productive group of the population.

In its effort to stimulate economic growth, His Majesty's government is actively promoting the development of various target sectors through its five-year National Development Plans. These outline the distribution of government funding and the budget allocated for development in various sectors of the country.

The 9th National Development Plan (2007-2012) marks a strategic shift in the planning and implementation of development projects, as it is the first national development plan to have been formulated in line with the objectives of Brunei Darussalam's recently launched long-term development plan, better known as "Wawasan Brunei 2035", or "Brunei Vision 2035".

As mentioned in Wawasan Brunei 2035, the country's main employer – the public sector – can no longer absorb the growing labour force and the hydrocarbon sector employs less than 3% of the workforce, anyway. And, since the private sector is limited, it is difficult to create sufficient employment opportunities that require university education. Workers at those levels – namely legislators, professionals and administrative workers – account for only around 16% of total private sector employment (Figure 2.1.8), which is well below the levels observed in Malaysia, Singapore or the Philippines.

The economic imbalances in the labour market lead to the prevalence of safe government jobs with high wages and generous subsidies. The existence of such jobs blunts the incentive for students to make the effort to go on to tertiary education. Despite the growing number of scholarships available, the percentage of students who pass the final exam at secondary level remains relatively low, which points to a lack of interest in moving on to university.

Similarly, evidence that the reservation wage of local job seekers is above the market salary for the jobs for which they are qualified is a further indication that the existence of government jobs robs them of incentive (Razak, 2010). Tertiary enrolment rates could also be improved by making higher education more appealing. There could be a wider choice of courses and a part-time learning provision with people of all ages in mind. Furthermore, the expansion of vocational and technical schools would be a welcome step as it would provide an alternative to academic paths.

Public spending on university education should be also increased as part of the effort to improve enrolment rates in tertiary education. Public expenditure on education was only 3.3% of GDP in 2012, well below the ratios of 5% and over in Malaysia, Thailand and Viet Nam. Although public expenditure as a percentage of overall government expenditure has been rising, it also remains low at 16.9% when compared to Malaysia, Thailand and Viet Nam. Clearly, there is room to increase overall spending on education and to reallocate resources to tertiary education.

Wawasan Brunei 2035 or Brunei Vision 2035 aims to turn Brunei Darussalam into a nation widely recognized for:

·   the accomplishments of its well educated and highly-skilled people as measured by the highest international standard;

·   quality of life that is among the top 10 nations in the world; and

·   dynamic and sustainable economy with income per capita within the top countries in the world.

To accomplish the above goals, eight strategies have been identified as follows:

·   An education strategy that will prepare the youth for employment and achievement in a world that is increasingly competitive and knowledge-based.

·   An economic strategy that will create new employment for the people and expand business opportunities within Brunei through the promotion of investment, foreign and domestic, both in downstream industries as well as in economic clusters beyond the oil and gas industry.

·   A security strategy that will safeguard Brunei's political stability and sovereignty as a nation which links the defence and diplomatic capabilities and its capacity to respond to threats from disease and natural catastrophe.

·   An institutional development strategy that will enhance good governance in both the public and private sectors, high quality public services, modern and pragmatic legal and regulatory frameworks and efficient government procedures that entail a minimum of bureaucratic "red tape"

·   A local business development strategy that will enhance opportunities for local small and medium sized enterprises (SMEs) as well as enable Brunei Malays to achieve leadership in business and industry by developing greater competitive strength.

·   An infrastructure development strategy that will ensure continued investment by government and through public-private sector partnership in developing and maintaining world-class infrastructure with special emphasis placed on education, health and industry.

·   A social security strategy that ensures that, as the nation prospers, all citizens are properly cared for.

·   An environmental strategy that ensures the proper conservation of our natural environment and cultural habitat. It will provide health and safety in line with the highest international practices.

In order to realise the Brunei Vision 2035, the strategies listed above will need to be developed by both government and private bodies and implemented as a well-coordinated national strategy.

The labour force during the period of 2007-2010 grew at an average rate of 2.2 per cent per annum, from 184,800 persons in 2007 to 198,800 persons in 2010, while the unemployment rate showed a declining trend from 3.7 per cent in 2008 to 2.7 per cent in 2010

Job opportunities are expected to increase with the implementation of mega projects in the oil and gas sector. Indeed, this will also generate growth in other sectors and provide employment opportunities. Other efforts are also being implemented such as enhancing the employability of the local labour force through various education and training schemes.

Education plays an important role towards producing a highly skilled population, which can be a strong platform for eradicating poverty and in guaranteeing security for the people. Education also is a key element towards the development of an individual's personal potential. In line with such role and purpose, one of the strategic thrusts identified under the RKN10 is therefore to produce an educated and highly skilled population.

The efforts to maximise productivity will not be an easy task and will require integrated commitment from all parties. This includes continuing substantial investment in human resource and investment in research and innovation and by supporting the use of latest technologies. In realising this theme, RKN10 will thus focus on speeding up the rate of economic growth. High economic growth will help the nation to increase income and accelerate development. It will also create numerous job opportunities for its citizens and residents and will enable the private sector to become more active. Sustainable high growth rates can be achieved through continuous improvement in productivity in the public and private sectors, and through existing and new industries. The increase in productivity will help reduce costs, produce better quality of work and consequently increase output. In this challenging era of globalisation, and in realising the need for efforts that are more effective and relevant, RKN10 will give priority to exploring approaches for increasing productivity through the use of knowledge and innovation. This strategy is aligned with international practices in developed and fast growing economies aimed at achieving high and sustainable productivity and increasing their competitiveness in the fast changing global market. It is feared that if the level of knowledge and innovativeness within the country is low, we may be left far behind other countries that have been vigorously implementing such activities. The concept of knowledge and innovation emphasised in RKN10 focuses on the generation of high productivity through increasing knowledge, skills and competency of the workforce in strategic areas; increasing research activities that have high commercial value; and instilling the culture of innova

In realising this theme, RKN10 will thus focus on speeding up the rate of economic growth. High economic growth will help the nation to increase income and accelerate development. It will also create numerous job opportunities for its citizens and residents and will enable the private sector to become more active.

Sustainable high growth rates can be achieved through continuous improvement in productivity in the public and private sectors, and through existing and new industries. The increase in productivity will help reduce costs, produce better quality of work and consequently increase output.

The efforts to maximise productivity will not be an easy task and will require integrated commitment from all parties. This includes continuing substantial investment in human resource and investment in research and innovation and by supporting the use of latest technologies.

In this challenging era of globalisation, and in realising the need for efforts that are more effective and relevant, RKN10 will give priority to exploring approaches for increasing productivity through the use of knowledge and innovation. This strategy is aligned with international practices in developed and fast growing economies aimed at achieving high and sustainable productivity and increasing their competitiveness in the fast changing global market. It is feared that if the level of knowledge and innovativeness within the country is low, we may be left far behind other countries that have been vigorously implementing such activities.

The concept of knowledge and innovation emphasised in RKN10 focuses on the generation of high productivity through increasing knowledge, skills and competency of the workforce in strategic areas; increasing research activities that have high commercial value; and instilling the culture of innovation creativity among the local youth. All of these will contribute to economic growth, particularly through the establishment of high value-added industries.

A highly skilled and competent workforce equipped with the latest technology will not only be able to increase their productivity but will also make the nation more competitive in the global market. Research activities that have a high commercial

A highly skilled and competent workforce equipped with the latest technology will not only be able to increase their productivity but will also make the nation more competitive in the global market.

Research activities that have a high commercial value will not only be able to boost productivity but is also a strategy that can support the diversification into high value-added non-oil and gas industries. Nevertheless, efforts in commercialising researches are expected to face numerous challenges as they are dependent on external factors.

Therefore, it is essential for the public sector to work in partnership with higher learning institutions and to get commitment from the private sector to be actively engaged in research and development (R&D). A more conducive environment for research will be put in place to further encourage research activities which can produce commercially viable output.

Having highly innovative and creative youths is also an important basis for the development of a knowledge-based economy. The outcome of innovation and creativity can be converted into intellectual property that will enhance the nation's ability to compete in the global market. The contribution to the economy can be doubled if the locals are also equipped with entrepreneurial skills and talents.

PROFESSIONAL AND HIGHLY SKILLED WORKFORCE

The provision of retraining and delivery of skills among the work force will further be reinforced as a means towards placing the economy in a higher value chain. Under the Human Resource Development (HRD) Fund that will continue to be provided under the RKN10, several programmes and academic-enhancement schemes as well as the provision of training and placements will continue to be delivered and strengthened. This is to ensure that the human resource pool in this country possesses 'up-to-date' skills and can adapt accordingly to any changes and needs of the economy.

The introduction of the Technical and Vocational Education Scholarship Scheme (BPTV) at the local private institutions on 15th July 2011 provides opportunities for local school leavers who have completed their 'O' and 'A' levels or its equivalent to pursue higher education.

For employees in the private sector, the Human Capacity Building Scheme in the Private Sector (PSTS) has been introduced to enable them to upgrade their academic qualifications and improve their professionalism so that they become more capable and more competitive in the labour market. In addition, through the Training and Employment Scheme (SLP), local school leavers will be given skills training and work experiences in various fields to enable them to enter the labour market more easily.

Meanwhile, programmes under the In-Service Training for the public sector employees will also continue to be made available to ensure improvements in the quality of its workforce.

Lifelong learning is the process of increasing the knowledge and skills of an individual in a continous manner, either in a formal or informal setting. This is very much in line with today's world which is becoming more challenging and is constantly changing. In this respect, efforts to encourage the local population, particularly those in the labour force, to continue acquiring knowledge and upgrading their skills will be implemented to ensure a continuous increase in productivity, either in the public or private sectors.

Some of the efforts that have been taken to encourage all levels of the population to continue their education outside the formal system include improving and increasing the provision of special classes for continuing education. Skills courses will also continue to be provided and expanded by various ministries and private institutions in order to produce competitive students and workforce, as well as to increase opportunities for employment.

EDUCATION AND EMPLOYMENT

The provision of retraining and delivery of skills among the work force will further be reinforced as a means towards placing the economy in a higher value chain. Under the Human Resource Development (HRD) Fund that will continue to be provided under the RKN10, several programmes and academic-enhancement schemes as well as the provision of training and placements will continue to be delivered and strengthened. This is to ensure that the human resource pool in this country possesses 'up-to-date' skills and can adapt accordingly to any changes and needs of the economy.

The introduction of the Technical and Vocational Education Scholarship Scheme (BPTV) at the local private institutions on 15th July 2011 provides opportunities for local school leavers who have completed their 'O' and 'A' levels or its equivalent to pursue higher education.

For employees in the private sector, the Human Capacity Building Scheme in the Private Sector (PSTS) has been introduced to enable them to upgrade their academic qualifications and improve their professionalism so that they become more capable and more competitive in the labour market. In addition, through the Training and Employment Scheme (SLP), local school leavers will be given skills training and work experiences in various fields to enable them to enter the labour market more easily.

Meanwhile, programmes under the In-Service Training for the public sector employees will also continue to be made available to ensure improvements in the quality of its workforce.

The government will continue its efforts to implement policies that can create a well-educated and highly skilled population, which is key to the development of a sustainable economy. The government also encourages strong private sector involvement and contribution towards such efforts.

Through all of this, the population will be nurtured from an early stage to become part of a society that is visionary, positive minded, dedicated, well educated, highly skilled, innovative as well as productive.

New approaches and programmes need to be explored and prepared, not only by the government but also through close collaboration with, and with integrated efforts from, various agencies to provide learning facilities, the use of research activities and technological advances in generating high and sustainable productivity as well as an economy that is based on knowledge.

The factors outlined herein aim to prepare the nation in facing future development challenges. It will also enable the country to grow and develop at par with regional and global economies which are constantly becoming more competitive and are fast advancing.

LABOR MARKET DEVELOPMENT TRENDS

As in any market, the forces of demand and supply jointly determine the price and quantity in the market for Labor, or in this case, the wage rate and the number of people employed, respectively. However, there are fundamental differences that distinguish the Labor market from other markets, such as the market for goods. Although most markets correspond to an equilibrium level without excess surplus or demand, even a perfectly competitive or a highly functional Labor market is expected to have a persistent level of unemployment. A perfectly competitive Labor market facilitates the easy movement of people and skills to their most productive use, thus minimizing frictional unemployment, with a low natural rate of unemployment. Departures from this theoretical outcome are common, as imperfections and rigidities can exist on both sides of the Labor market. Nevertheless, the concept of "equilibrium" in the Labor market that should be strived for needs to be viewed in this sense. The discussion in the preceding two sections has highlighted a variety of issues and challenges that need to be addressed on both the demand and supply sides of the Labor market in order to deliver the economic growth and development desired for the Long Term

Development Plan.

Long Term Development Plan - Wawasan 2035 has highlighted that an increased emphasis will be paid to downstream industries as well as in economic clusters beyond the oil and gas industry. This in turn places a greater importance on employment in the secondary sector – a challenge that needs to be met by Labor force supply. In addition, the promotion of private sector driven growth has also been advocated to aid economic diversification, partly through the creation of a better underlying business and regulatory environment. According to a survey in the recent Global Competitiveness Report (World Economic Forum 2011, p. 128), the five most problematic factors for doing business in Brunei (in rank order) are: restrictive Labor regulations; poor work ethic in the national Labor force; inefficient government bureaucracy; access to financing; and an inadequately educated workforce. This suggests that there is a close association between the reduction of barriers to doing business effectively and the creation of a better functioning Labor market in Brunei. A more vibrant private sector will reduce the reliance of locals on government jobs, and will eventually also shift the onus onto the private sector to address employment needs based on the market through a correction of the imbalances in the incentive structure.

This desired demand for Labor can be met by supply either through the education system or immigration policy. As discussed in Section 4, *Wawasan 2035* has placed particular emphasis on the new education strategy, or SPN21, to produce a competitive and educated Labor force. This would assist the prevention of more serious forms of unemployment. Young people who are unable to progress along the academic, vocational or technical track after secondary level education and drop out of the education system to enter the Labor market may find it difficult to gain employment without sufficient skills that employers look for. This may lead to a prolonged period of youth unemployment, unless they accept low-skilled jobs, undergo further training or re-enter the education system to enhance their skill set. Otherwise, the prospect of long-term unemployment looms. Those in long-term unemployment may eventually drop out of the Labor force, which will lower the

Labor force participation rate and represent a waste of productive potential. Furthermore, a greater proportion of boys compared to girls struggle to continue and drop out of the academic track after lower secondary level, which may suggest that there is a gender preference for boys to favour the vocational or technical route beyond lower secondary education. A lack of opportunities in vocational and technical fields would result in a large proportion of low-skilled local males in the Labor force. However, further improvements in vocational, technical and tertiary education attainment beyond current levels, should not be seen as an end in itself, but as a means towards better employment and an educated Labor force. The possible unintended consequences of an over-generous education policy is to create graduate unemployment, where too many people are qualified in too few available jobs, or over-education, where people work in jobs where they are over qualified, both of which represent a waste of valuable resources. Thus, further research should look into whether either scenario is observed in Brunei. The scholarships and opportunities provided for higher education need to be closely tailored to fit the employer requirements in the public sector and more importantly, in the private sector as well, to minimise or eliminate structural unemployment. Aside from education policy, the demand for Labor can also be addressed through immigration policy: via a more active recruitment of professionals or skilled foreign Labor to supplement the supply of Labor. With the aforementioned slowdown in population growth rates and falling fertility rates, a reassessment of existing immigration policy may be necessary in order to meet the goals that have been set out in *Wawasan 2035*.

In addition to adjustments on the demand and supply side of the Labor market, improvements can also be made to the infrastructure with regard to the availability, collection and dissemination of information to reduce cost, time and effort for employers to search for employees, and vice versa, to aid a highly functional and flexible Labor market. This includes the collection of more up-to-date data regarding employment issues, as well as better coordination between education providers, employers and other stakeholders to assess specific Labor demand requirements and focus on the challenge of meeting skill needs. This would ensure

a minimization of frictional unemployment, and lower the natural rate of unemployment. Further improvements to Labor market flexibility can be achieved through an assessment of employee needs that can enable further improvements to Labor force participation, and enhance the economy's productive capacity.

Furthermore, it should also be noted that other external factors can also influence the Brunei Labor market, even more so with the increased economic integration that comes with globalization. These external influences can be magnified domestically in Brunei because of its small size, and can bring about both positive and negative effects. A relevant example of this is the proposed establishment of the Asean Economic Community (AEC) by 2015 (ASEAN Secretariat, 2009), which aims to transform Asean into a region with free movement of goods, services, investment, skilled Labor, and freer flow of capital through the development and implementation of Mutual Recognition Agreements (MRAs). The establishment of the AEC has the potential to transform the economic climate of all countries in the region, including Brunei. This should enable greater market access that can supplement Brunei's small domestic market, as well as improve the competitiveness and productivity of Labor with the freer movement of skilled Labor. However, globalization, can also bring about threats and challenges from emerging economies such as Vietnam, India, China and Brazil, which will come in many forms including into the goods and Labor markets. Owing to its relatively small size, Brunei may not respond as easily to external opportunities brought about by globalization, yet competition from outside producers may bring about larger negative consequences, as a result of having a relatively open economy which is heavily dependent on foreign workers and products.

Finally, it is also important to highlight the available trends in Labor productivity, a metric that can objectively measure the (economic) performance and quality of the Labor force, in the Brunei economy. The OECD (2001, p. 11) defines productivity as "a ratio of a volume measure of output to a volume measure of input use". Labor productivity can be measured in a variety of ways. Whilst volume measures of output are normally gross domestic product (GDP) or gross value added (GVA) expressed at constant prices, i.e. adjusted for inflation, the three most commonly used measures of input are: hours worked; workforce jobs; and the number of people in employment. Based on GDP at constant prices and the number of employed people, Anaman (2003) has calculated a continued decline in Labor productivity and zero or negative real GDP growth rates between 1991 and 2001, which he attributes to the result of a decline in real wage per worker, despite an increase in total employment levels27. However, the measurement of output and productivity in non-market activities, such as government or in non-governmental organizations, may not be strictly correct in these terms, and thus a more complex methodology or enhanced data requirements is necessary. To this end, statisticians and researchers can follow the accepted guidelines set out by the OECD (2001) to build a more comprehensive measurement of all levels of productivity related to economic activities, which would constitute core indicators for the analysis of economic growth. Nevertheless, the declining trends observed in Labor productivity and real wage per worker observed by Anaman (2003) are indicative of a poor allocation of Labor resources, where Labor is not employed in its most productive use, or declining Labor performance in economic terms. This is an area of concern that needs to be addressed through improvements to Labor market flexibility and/or in human capital investments that would enable the economic progress necessary to achieve *Wawasan 2035*.

Using the same measurement of Labor productivity, which can be calculated by dividing real GDP at 2000 prices by the total number of employed workers in an economy, figures from the latest Brunei Darussalam Statistical Yearbook 2010 (Government of Brunei Darussalam, various years) suggest that Labor productivity in real terms has continued to decline throughout the 2006 to 2010 period

WORKER RIGHTS[1]

FREEDOM OF ASSOCIATION AND THE RIGHT TO COLLECTIVE BARGAINING

The law provides for the right of workers to form and join independent unions, but it prohibits strikes and does not provide for collective bargaining. The law prohibits employers from discriminating against workers in connection with union activities, but it does not provide for reinstatement for dismissal related to union activity.

By law unions must be registered with the government under the same process as other organizations (see section 2.b., "Freedom of Association"). While the law permits the formation of trade union federations for most professions, it forbids affiliation with international labor organizations unless the minister of home affairs and its Department of Labor provides consent. The law requires officers of trade unions to be "bona fide" (without explanation), which has been interpreted as allowing broad discretion to reject officers, and that such officers have been

---

[1] US Department of States Report

employed in the trade for at least two years. Unions are subject to laws limiting freedom of assembly, which require a government permit for public gatherings of 10 or more persons and approval by the minister of home affairs (see section 2.b.). By law the general penalty for violating laws on unions and other organizations is a fine up to BND 10,000 ($7,280), imprisonment for up to two years, or both. Penalties were sufficient to deter violations. Data on government enforcement efforts were not available.

There were no active unions or worker organizations in the country. The collective agreement for the only known union in recent history, the Brunei Oilfield Workers Union, expired "years ago due to lack of interest" according to the government, an assessment that was reportedly confirmed in a visit by the International Labor Organization. There were NGOs involved in labor issues, such as wages, contracts, and working conditions. These NGOs largely operated openly in cooperation with relevant government agencies, but they reported avoiding confrontation with the government and engaged in self-censorship.

PROHIBITION OF FORCED OR COMPULSORY LABOR

The law prohibits all forms of forced or compulsory labor. Conviction for forced labor could lead to penalties, including fines of up to one million BND ($728,000), imprisonment for a period of four to 30 years, and caning, but most labor disputes were settled out of court and the penalties were seldom applied.

The government did not investigate any cases of debt bondage or forced labor compelled through threats of deportation, although these practices continued to occur. The heads of Specialist Trafficking Units within the police continued to meet regularly to coordinate antitrafficking policy and implement the national action plan to combat trafficking, including for forced labor.

All employment agencies must be endorsed by the government and undergo government vetting and training before operating. Employment agencies must apply to the Department of Labor for permission to recruit foreign workers. Once hired foreign nationals must sign an approved contract before a government official. The Department of Labor continued some efforts to enforce licensing requirements for labor recruitment agencies.

The government did not always effectively enforce the law and forced labor occurred. Some of the approximately 100,000 foreign migrant workers in the country faced involuntary servitude, debt bondage, non-payment of wages, passport confiscation, abusive employers, and/or confinement to the home. Female migrant workers, who made up most of the domestic workers in the country, were particularly vulnerable to forced labor. Although it is illegal for employers to withhold wages from domestic workers, some employers, notably domestic and construction workers, did so to recoup labor broker or recruitment fees or to compel continued service by workers. Foreign workers could take legal action against employers for non-payment of wages, usually done so outside of court, and were often, but not always, successful.

Although the government forbade wage deductions by employers to repay in-country agencies or sponsors and mandated that employees receive their full salaries, many migrant workers arrived in debt bondage to actors outside the country. Although prohibited by law, retention of migrant workers' travel documents by employers or agencies remained a common practice.

Also see the Department of State's *Trafficking in Persons Report* at www.state.gov/j/tip/rls/tiprpt/.

PROHIBITION OF CHILD LABOR AND MINIMUM AGE FOR EMPLOYMENT

Various domestic laws prohibit the employment of children under age 16. Parental consent and approval by the Labor Commission are required in order for those under 18 to work. Female workers under 18 may not work at night or on offshore oil platforms. The Department of Labor, which is part of the Ministry of Home Affairs, effectively enforced child labor laws. Penalties for child labor violations include a fine not exceeding BND 2,000 ($1,460), imprisonment of up to two years, or both, and were sufficient to deter violations. There was no list of hazardous occupations prohibited for children. There were no reports of violations of child labor laws.

DISCRIMINATION WITH RESPECT TO EMPLOYMENT AND OCCUPATION

The law does not explicitly prohibit discrimination with respect to employment and occupation. There is no law requiring equal pay for equal work. The law limits employment in certain government positions and the military based on ethnic origin (see section 6). Many foreign workers had their wages established based on national origin.

Some professions were designated as women's professions, and men noted discrimination during hiring. Many public and private employers showed hiring biases against foreign workers, particularly in key sectors such as oil and gas. Some LGBTI job applicants faced discrimination and often were asked directly about their sexual identity.

ACCEPTABLE CONDITIONS OF WORK

The law does not set a minimum wage for the private sector. Wages were set by contract between the employee and employer, and were sometimes calculated based on national origin. Published reports calculated the average monthly compensation in the private sector to be BND 1,830 ($1,330) per worker. In the public sector, which employed the majority of citizens, salaries followed a scale determined by job, responsibility, qualifications, and time in service. There was no established poverty line.

The standard workweek for most government agencies and many private companies is Monday through Thursday and Saturday, with Friday and Sunday off, allowing for two rest periods of 24 hours each week. The law provides for paid annual holidays, overtime for work in excess of 48 hours per week, and double time for work performed on legal holidays. The law also stipulates an employee may not work more than 72 hours of overtime per month. Government regulations establish occupational health and safety standards. Individuals were encouraged to report violations of health and safety standards, but the law does not explicitly protect the right to remove oneself from a hazardous workplace.

Immigration law allows prison sentences and caning for foreign workers who overstay their work permits, for workers who fall into irregular status due to their employers' negligence, for illegal immigrants seeking work, and for foreign workers employed by companies other than their initial sponsor. The government enforced this law with regular immigration sweeps. There were reports of foreigner workers being deported in lieu of caning/imprisonment.

The Department of Labor inspected working conditions both on a routine basis and in response to complaints. There were approximately 40 labor inspectors in the Labor Department, which was adequate to conduct mandated inspections. The government usually moved quickly to investigate allegations of labor law violations, and employers faced criminal and civil penalties, although the focus was primarily on illegal workers rather than worker protection. The Labor

**For additional analytical, business and investment opportunities information,
please contact Global Investment & Business Center, USA
at (703) 370-8082. Fax: (703) 370-8083. E-mail: ibpusa3@gmail.com
Global Business and Investment Info Databank - www.ibpus.com**

Department has the power to terminate the licenses of abusive employers and revoke their foreign labor quotas, and it did so occasionally.

The commissioner of the Department of Labor is responsible for protecting foreign workers' rights. Foreign laborers (predominantly Filipinos, Malaysians, Indonesians, and Bangladeshis) dominated most low-wage professions, such as domestic workers, construction, maintenance, retail, and restaurants.

The government prosecuted employers who employed illegal immigrants or did not properly process workers' documents. When grievances could not be resolved, regulations require employers to pay for the repatriation of the foreign workers and all outstanding wages. Although the practice is illegal, some employers held employee passports and restricted employee activities during non-work hours, particularly for low-skilled workers and household staff (see section 7.b.).

Most reported violations of labor law not involving foreign workers' status were resolved through government mediation by the Department of Labor. The majority of abuse cases were settled out of court through agreements under which the employer paid financial compensation to the worker. Employers who violate laws regarding conditions of service, including pay, working hours, leave, and holidays, may be fined BND 800 ($580) for a first offense and for further offenses BND 1,600 ($1,160), imprisoned for one year, or both. Observers did not indicate whether the penalties for violations of wage, hour, and health and safety standards were sufficient to deter violations.

The government sought to enforce labor, health, and safety regulations effectively. Enforcement in sectors employing low-skilled labor, such as construction or maintenance, however, was weak. This was especially the case for foreign laborers at construction sites, where wage arrears and inadequate safety and living conditions were reported. Laws regarding working hours were frequently not observed for either citizen or foreign workers.

Many employed citizens commanded good salaries with numerous allowances, but complaints about low wages were common, especially in entry-level positions. The government found that local employees in the private sector had an average monthly compensation rate of BND 2,257 ($1,640), compared with BND 1,565 ($1,140) for foreign workers. Wages for employed foreign residents were wide ranging. Some foreign embassies negotiated agreements with the Brunei government covering minimum wage requirement for their nationals working in the country.

PRINCIPAL LAWS AND REGULATIONS

EMPLOYMENT ORDER, 2009

The Employment Order, 2009, which came into operation on 3rd September 2009, is the main legislation governing the terms and conditions of employment in Brunei Darussalam. It covers all persons who are employed under a contract of service, which may be written or implied but excludes seamen, domestic servants, and any person employed in a managerial, executive or confidential position. Civil servants and all employees of statutory bodies are also excluded from this Order.

· For a shift worker, the rest day can be a continuous period of 30 hours.

For additional analytical, business and investment opportunities information, please contact Global Investment & Business Center, USA at (703) 370-8082. Fax: (703) 370-8083. E-mail: ibpusa3@gmail.com Global Business and Investment Info Databank - www.ibpus.com

14 days outpatient sick leave per year and 60 days hospitlization leave (including the 14 days outpatient sick leave) provided he satisfies the following conditions:-

The Employment Order, 2009, sets out the minimum terms and conditions of employment. You are encouraged to provide better terms and conditions than those stipulated, so as to attract and retain valued employees in an increasingly global labour market. These should be clearly set out in your company policies and made known to all employees.

Must have worked for at least 6 months;

Has obtained a medical certificate from the company doctor. If no such doctor is appointed, from a government doctor or a doctor employed by any of the approved hospitals; and

Must inform employer of the sick leave within 48 hours.

WORKMEN'S COMPENSATION ACT, 1957

The main aim of this act is to compensate an injured worker for the loss of earning capacity as a result of an injury arising out of and in the course of employment.

WORKPLACE SAFETY AND HEALTH ORDER, 2009

The Workplace, Safety and Health Order was fully enforced on 1st August 2013. It is an order relating to the safety, health and welfare of persons at work in workplaces.

This Order shall apply to all workplaces including:-

· Any workplace wholly or partly owned or occupied by the government;

· Any premises in which any building operation or any construction work carried on by or on behalf of the Government.

EMPLOYMENT AGENCIES ORDER, 2004

The Employment Agencies Order, 2004 was fully enforced on 1st January 2012. This Order is designed to regulate the employment agency activities within Brunei Darussalam through:

· Registering and licensing of all employment agencies;

· Monitoring of employment agency activities;

· Receiving and addressing complaints from the public that are related to employment agencies;

· Conducting investigations on employment agency matters; and

· Taking appropriate actions when necessary in order to enforce the Order.

It is aimed at preventing:-

· Human / labour trafficking

· Forgery of documents and signatures

· Irresponsible and unscrupulous employment agencies

Employment Agencies Order, 2004 aimed towards the protection of employers and employees.

EMPLOYMENT INFORMATION ACT, 1974

This is an Act to provide for the collection of information regarding employed persons in the private sectors. The annual census will be conducted by the Department of Labour in October (every year) to collect detailed information of the employer's/ employees', wages, earnings and hours of work in the private sectors and shall be submitted on or before the 30th November every year.

Employment Agency License or *Lesen Agensi Pekejaan* (LAP) is used to identify and recognise an employment agency, which have been registered and licensed by the Department of Labour.

There are three categories of licence issued;

CONTRACT OF SERVICE

· A contract of service creates an employer and an employee relationship between the two parties.

· It shall be in writing and signed by both parties (subject to *Section 10 of Employment Order, 2009).*

· The agreed terms and conditions of employment cannot be less favourable than the Employment Order,2009.

1) Category A – For bringing in and processing domestic workers only (such as maids);

2) Category B – For bringing in and processing workers in the private sectors only, and

3) Category C – Combination of Category A & B

Under the provision of Employment Information Act 1974, Chapter 99, Section 3(1), all employers must fill in the Annual Census of Employer's/Employees' Wages, Earnings and Hours of Work and all forms must be returned before or on 30TH NOVEMBER of the Census Year. Appropriate actions will be taken for late submission of forms.

TERMS OF EMPLOYMENT (MINIMUM TERMS PROVIDED BY THE LAW)

The employer is required to include the following particulars in writing in the contract of service:-

The name of employers or group of employers and place of employment.

The name and place of origin of the employee.

Where possible, the names and address of the next of kin of the employee.

The nature of employment.

The duration of employment and the method of calculation.

The appropriate period of notice to be given by the party wishing to terminate the contract of service.

The rates of salary and the method of calculation, the manner and times of payment of salary.

The measures to be taken to provide the welfare of the employee.

The conditions of repatriation, if the employee is not a citizen of Brunei Darussalam.

Any special conditions of the contract of service.

It is an offence under Employment Information Act 1974, Chapter 99, Section 8, for any employer, who without any lawful excuse, wilfully refuses or neglects to furnish, or wilfully gives a false answer to any question necessary for obtaining any information or particulars required the particulars or information required in this form within the time allowed, shall be guilty of an offence and will be fined TWO THOUSAND FIVE HUNDRED DOLLARS [BND 2,500.00] and serve a jail term of Six [6] months, and in the event of a continuing offence, a further fine of FIFTY DOLLARS [BND 50.00] per day will be incurred during which the offence continues.

TERMINATION OF CONTRACT

A termination of contract may occur when:-

Survey and Statistics Counter

· The work specified in the contract has been completed or when a date specified in the contract for the expiry of the contract has been reached.

· Either party has decided to end the contract with appropriate notice in accordance with terms of the contract.

· There has been a breach of contract and the other party wishes to terminate the contract.

SOCIAL SECURITY SYSTEM

OLD AGE, DISABILITY, AND SURVIVORS

REGULATORY FRAMEWORK

First and current laws: 1955 (old-age and disability pensions), with 1984 (universal pension) amendment; 1992 (employees' trust fund); and 2009 (supplementary pension scheme), implemented in 2010.

Type of program: Provident fund, supplementary defined contribution scheme, and universal old-age and disability pension system.

COVERAGE

Provident fund: Employees up to age 60 who are citizens or permanent residents of Brunei, including government civil servants who began service on or after January 1, 1993. (Civil servants who began service before January 1, 1993, are covered by the government pension scheme.)

Voluntary coverage for persons aged 60 or older and self-employed persons.

Exclusions: Foreign workers.

Special systems for armed forces personnel, police force personnel, and prison wardens.

Supplementary pension: Public- and private-sector employees aged 18 to 59 who are citizens or permanent residents of Brunei.

Voluntary coverage for self-employed persons.

Exclusions: Employees covered under the public service pension scheme.

Universal old-age and disability pension: All residents of Brunei.

SOURCE OF FUNDS

INSURED PERSON

Provident fund: 5% of monthly earnings that exceed B$80. (Additional voluntary contributions are permitted.)

There are no maximum earnings used to calculate contributions.

Supplementary pension: 3.5% of monthly earnings (3% for the insured's account and 0.5% for survivor benefits). Additional voluntary contributions are permitted.

There are no minimum or maximum earnings used to calculate contributions.

Universal old-age and disability pension: None.

SELF-EMPLOYED PERSON

Provident fund: Voluntary contributions only.

There are no minimum or maximum declared earnings used to calculate contributions.

Supplementary pension: B$17.50 a month.

Universal old-age and disability pension: None.

EMPLOYER

Provident fund: 5% of monthly payroll (3% for the insured's account and 0.5% for survivor benefits). Additional voluntary contributions are permitted.

There are no minimum or maximum earnings used to calculate contributions.

Supplementary pension: 3.5% of monthly payroll.

The minimum earnings used to calculate contributions is B$500.

The maximum earnings used to calculate contributions is B$2,800.

Universal old-age pension: None.

GOVERNMENT

Provident fund: None.

Supplementary pension: Any deficit and supplements the employee contribution for employees earning less than B$500; B$17.50 a month for self-employed persons in the informal sector.

The government pays B$30 for each month the insured was a provident fund member before January 1, 2010, regardless of the insured's salary. If the insured was younger than age 25 when he or she joined the provident fund, the contribution is calculated from age 25.

Universal old-age and disability pension: The total cost.

QUALIFYING CONDITIONS

OLD-AGE BENEFIT

Provident fund: Age 60. Retirement is not necessary.

Early withdrawal: Age 50.

Drawdown payment: Fund members with at least B$40,000 in their individual account or who have been provident fund members for at least 10 years may draw down funds from their account to build or purchase a house for personal residence.

A lump sum is paid to members at any age if emigrating permanently from the country.

Supplementary pension: Age 60 with at least 35 years of continuous contributions.

Insured persons who do not meet the contribution requirements at retirement age may receive a lump-sum benefit.

(The government pays retroactive contributions for those who joined the provident fund scheme before January 1, 2010.)

The pension may not be drawn down before retirement.

Universal old-age pension: Age 60 and a resident of Brunei. Persons born in Brunei must have at least 10 years of residence immediately before claiming the pension; persons born outside Brunei must have lived in Brunei for at least 30 years immediately before claiming the pension.

DISABILITY BENEFIT

Provident fund: The fund member must be unable to work as the result of a physical or mental disability. The Medical Board assesses the degree of disability.

Universal disability pension: The insured must be unable to work, have resided in Brunei in the 10 years immediately before the disability began, and receive suitable medical treatment and rehabilitation.

Survivor benefit (provident fund): Paid to the next of kin or named survivors.

Survivor pension (supplementary pension): Paid to a widow and children younger than age 21 if the insured had continuous contributions until death.

The widow's portion of the survivor pension ceases on remarriage and is paid to eligible orphans.

OLD-AGE BENEFITS

OLD-AGE BENEFIT

Old-age benefit (provident fund): A lump sum is paid of total employee and employer contributions plus interest.

Early withdrawal: Fund members may draw down 25% of accumulated assets.

Drawdown payment: The fund member may draw down up to 45% of accumulated assets in the individual account only once before age 55.

Interest rate adjustment: Set by the government annually according to the financial health of the fund, interest rates on savings accounts, and inflation rates.

Supplementary pension: At least B$150 a month is paid for up to 20 years.

If the insured did not meet the supplementary pension contribution requirements at retirement age, a lump-sum of the supplementary scheme account balance is paid.

Universal old-age pension: B$250 a month is paid.

Benefit adjustment: The pension is adjusted on an ad hoc basis.

PERMANENT DISABILITY BENEFITS

DISABILITY BENEFIT

Disability benefit (provident fund): A lump sum is paid of total employee and employer contributions plus interest.

Interest rate adjustment: Set by the government annually according to the financial health of the fund, interest rates on savings accounts, and inflation rates.

Universal disability pension: B$250 a month is paid.

Benefit adjustment: The pension is adjusted on an ad hoc basis.

SURVIVOR BENEFITS

Survivor benefit (provident fund): A lump sum is paid of total employee and employer contributions plus interest.

Interest rate adjustment: Set by the government annually according to the financial health of the fund, interest rates on savings accounts, and inflation rates.

Survivor benefit (supplementary pension): If the deceased died before the normal retirement age, eligible survivors share a total of up to $400 a month for 15 years from the date of death.

If the deceased was aged 60 to 75, eligible survivors share a monthly amount based on the supplementary scheme account balance until the deceased would have been aged 75.

If the deceased was older than age 75, a lump-sum of the supplementary scheme account balance is paid.

ADMINISTRATIVE ORGANIZATION

Employees' Trust Fund Department (http://www.etf.gov.bn) of the Ministry of Finance, under the supervision of the Employees' Trust Fund Board, administers the contributions and benefits and the investment of funds for the provident fund.

The Ministry of Finance administers the supplementary pension.

Department of Community Development of the Ministry of Culture, Youth, and Sports (http://www.belia-sukan.gov.bn) administers the universal benefit program.

SICKNESS AND MATERNITY

REGULATORY FRAMEWORK

The government provides all residents of Brunei with access to medical benefits, including outpatient and inpatient care provided by registered physicians and in approved hospitals.

Ministry of Health (http://www.moh.gov.bn) registers physicians and approves hospitals that provide services to residents.

WORK INJURY

REGULATORY FRAMEWORK

First and current law: 1957 (workmen's compensation).

Type of program: Employer-liability system.

COVERAGE

All employees who are citizens or permanent residents of Brunei.

Exclusions: Household workers, self-employed persons, security personnel, and home-based workers.

SOURCE OF FUNDS

Insured person: None.

Self-employed person: Not applicable.

Employer: Provides benefits directly to employees.

Government: None.

QUALIFYING CONDITIONS

Work injury benefits: There is no minimum qualifying period.

TEMPORARY DISABILITY BENEFITS

A monthly benefit of 66.7% of the employee's average monthly earnings in the 6 months before the disability began is paid.

The maximum monthly benefit is B$130.

The benefit is paid after a 4-day waiting period for up to 5 years. If the disability lasts more than 14 days, the benefit is paid retroactively for the first 4 days.

For additional analytical, business and investment opportunities information,
please contact Global Investment & Business Center, USA
at (703) 370-8082. Fax: (703) 370-8083. E-mail: ibpusa3@gmail.com
Global Business and Investment Info Databank - www.ibpus.com

PERMANENT DISABILITY BENEFITS

Permanent disability benefit: A lump sum of 48 times the employee's average monthly earnings in the 6 months before the disability began is paid.

The maximum benefit is B$9,600.

Constant-attendance supplement (total permanent disability): A lump sum of 25% of the total permanent disability benefit is paid if the insured requires the constant attendance of others to perform daily functions.

Partial disability: A lump sum of the total permanent disability benefit multiplied by the assessed percentage of disability is paid, according to a schedule.

If temporary disability benefits are paid for more than 6 months before the determination of total or partial permanent disability, the amount of temporary disability benefits paid after the 6-month period are deducted from the permanent disability benefit.

WORKERS' MEDICAL BENEFITS

The employer pays for the examination and treatment of the insured by a registered physician and in approved hospitals.

SURVIVOR BENEFITS

Survivor benefit: A lump sum of 36 times the insured's average monthly earnings in the last 6 months before death is paid.

The maximum benefit is B$7,200.

Eligible survivors are dependent members of the deceased's family, including the spouse, children, parents, and brothers and sisters.

In the absence of eligible survivors, the employer must pay for the insured's funeral.

ADMINISTRATIVE ORGANIZATION

Workmen's Compensation, Health and Safety Section, of the Department of Labour (http://www.labour.gov.bn) enforces the law. The Department of Labour is part of the Ministry of Home Affairs.

Individual employers must pay compensation directly to employees or dependent survivors.

An arbitrator settles disputes regarding the determination and provision of benefits.

PRACTICAL REGULATIONS

FOREIGN WORKERS LICENSE APPLICATION PROCEDURE

Company License Application

Admission procedure application form New License, Additional and Renewal currently is:

Implement the counter by the Assistant Labour Inspector (ALI)
The application form is received subsequently after applicants are interviewed
For new application, inspection of the place of business / company will be carried out within a week of receiving application
For additional application / renewal, inspection is the instruction of the Secretariat of License

Documents Required For Application of New Company License:

1. Copy of applicant's Smart Identity Card

2. Copy of business partner's Smart Identity Card / Passport

3. Copy of Registration of Company Section 16 & 17 / Form 'X'

4. Copy of Tenancy Agreement:
    • Office/ Place of Business
    • Worker's Accommodation

5. Layout of Office/ Place of Business/ Worker's Accommodation

6. 3R Sized Photos:
    • Office (front, back, right, left and side view of the office)
    • Place of Business (front of the building, including signage, back and inside building)
    • Project site Worker's Accommodation

7. A) If the applicant is a Main Contractor, please attach a copy of a valid (duration) Project Award documents specifying the following items:
    • Name of Project
    • Project Address
    • Principal
    • Work Schedule and Job Specification
    • Project Value
    • Commencement Date of Project
    • Completion Date of Project
    • Main Contract
    • Verification Court Stamp for non-Government Projects

    B) If the applicant is a Sub- Contractor, please attach a copy of relevant documents including:
    • Sub-contract agreement specifying Name of Main Contractor; Name of Sub Contractor; Project Value Sub Contracted out
    • Contract from Principal to Main Contractor (as specified in 7(A))

    C) If the applicant has projects as Main Contractor and Sub-Contractor, please attach documents as specified in 7(A) and 7(B)

8. Copy of Documents from government agencies such as:
    • Contractor and Supplier Registration Certificate from Ministry of Development
    • Permit to carry out construction projects from the competent authority such as Land Department and District Office

9. List of local workers employed in the company

10. If the applicant possesses other foreign worker recruitment licenses or own other companies, pleases specify:
   • List of companies owned by the applicant
   • Type of business activities
   • Copy of the Company Registration

11. Other relevant documents.

Reminder:
• Applicants must complete the application form
• Applicants must attach the required documents
• Any incomplete applications will not be accepted

DOMESIC WORKERS

NEW APPLICATION FOR DOMESTIC HELPER LICENSE

For citizen of Brunei Darussalam or Permanent Residents Application:

Valid copies of the applicant's and his/her spouse's identity cards.
Completed financial details form (BUR300)
Copies of the applicant's latest salary slips.
A copy of birth certificate and/or identity card for children or other family members living in the same household.
Authorization letter from the Government of His Majesty the Sultan and Yang Di-Pertuan or Brunei Darussalam for Government Housing or Tenancy Agreement (if applicable).
Copy of Registration of Companies or Form X of the Applicant and/or his/her spouse (whom holds ownership of the business).
Copy of authorization letter for pensioners.
Other income details (if any) such as Tenancy Agreement for businesses/ residence.
Copies of spouse's latest salary slips (if needed to support applicant).
Copy of Doctor's verification letter for the Application for sick or other special needs family members (if applicable)
A copy of mother/father/mother-in-law/father-in-law identity card if the application of this licence is intended for the case of the mentioned (Kebenaran Khas).
For the position of driver, please include a copy of the vehicle Bluecard and children's daily school routine schedule/timetable and/or other activities.

Additional Documents For Foreign Citizen Application

A copy of the contract of service or offer letter from the Government of His Majesty the Sultan and Yang DI-Pertuan of Brunei Darussalam.
A copy of the contract of service between the applicant and the employer endorsed by the Commissioner or Labour.
Approved Work Pass Recommendation (BUR500/555) by the Department of Labour.

RENEWAL APPLICATION FOR DOMESTIC HELPER LICENSE

BORANG MEMBAHARUI LESEN AMAH BUR 302.png

For citizen of Brunei Darussalam or Permanent Residents Application:

Original Domestic Helper License.
Valid copies of the applicant's and his/her spouse's identity cards.
Copies of the applicant's latest salary slips.
Copy of authorization letter for pensioners.
A copy of identity card for family members where applicable (Kebenaran Khas)
Copies of spouse's latest salary slips.
A copy of birth certificate and/or identity card for children or other family members living in the same household.

Additional Documents For Foreign Citizen Application:

A Copy of the contract of service or offer letter from the Government of His Majesty the Sultan and Yang Di-Pertuan of Brunei Darussalam
A Copy of the contract of service between the applicant and the employer endorsed by the Commissioner of Labour.
Approved Work Pass Recommendation (BUR500/555) by the Department of Labour.

APPLICATION FOR ADDITIONAL LICENSE FOR DOMESTIC WORKERS

For citizen of Brunei Darussalam or Permanent Residents Application:

Original Domestic Helper License.
Valid copies of the applicant's and his/her spouse's identity cards.
Copies of the applicant's latest salary slips.
Completed financial details form (BUR300).
Letter explaining reason's for additional.
Copy of authorization letter for pensioners.
A copy of identity card for family members where applicable (Kebenaran Khas).
Copies of spouse's latest salary slips.
A copy of birth certificate and/or identity card for children or other family members living in the same household.

ADDITIONAL DOCUMENTS FOR FOREIGN CITIZEN APPLICATION:

A Copy of the contract of service or offer letter from the Government of His Majesty the Sultan and Yang Di-Pertuan of Brunei Darussalam
A Copy of the contract of service between the applicant and the employer endorsed by the Commissioner of Labour.
Approved Work Pass Recommendation (BUR500/555) by the Department of Labour.
* Bold : Mandatory

Reminder:
• When submitting BUR302A, please attach the original copy of the licence for endorsement.
• Applicant must complete this application form.
• Applicant is required to attach all the prerequisite documents as stated above.
• Any incomplete application form will not be accepted.

WORK PASS RECOMMENDATION APPLICATION PROCEDURE

Submitted application is subject to the following items:
Meets the conditions prescribed application
Foreign workers have applied for qualification or work experience relevant to the position applied for

Position applied for can not be filled by local children

Ensure their transition opportunities skills of foreign workers to local children in a way that truth is eliminated and replaced by locals

One branch control in the influx of foreign workers to always meet the requirements of the State

BUR500.pdf Work Pass Recommendation (New)

Required Documents:

    1.   4 sets of BUR 500 form (1 original and 3 copies). All copies must bear original signature and company's stamp.

    2.   Worker's personal information form complete with passport photo..

    3.   Valid copy of the worker's passport page with personal information (including date of birth and passport expiry date).

    4.   Copy of Foreign Worker Recruitment License with a validity period of at least 3 months from the date of submitting this application (with banker's   guarantee stamp if applicable).

    5.   Security deposit stamp for cash deposit (if not using a bank guarantee).

    6.   Copy of miscellaneous license (if applicable).

    7.   For companies in construction sector, kindly submit a copy of ongoing project document ('project awards'). If the project is a sub-contract, a copy of
        the project award given to the main-contractor must be attached. Project documents must be complete and clearly show the company's name as main-   con/ sub-con, value & duration of the project including the commencement date and completion date of the project.

    8.   For the position of 'driver' – kindly submit a copy of the worker's driving license and copy of the blue card of the vehicle (one vehicle per w orker) under
        the company's name and also permit stamp from the Land Transport Department (If applicable).

    9.   For the position in the category of staff – kindly attach a copy of the relevant or equivalent qualifications with position applied for.

    10.   Copy of Job Order with a Licensed Employment Agency.

    11.   Recommendation/ Authorization letter from relevant agencies where applicable such as the Ministry of Education, Ministry of Health, Ministry of
        Finance and others.

Reminder*:

•   Applicant must complete the BUR500 form and must be submitted by Licensed Employment Agency Only.

•   All required documents must be attached together.

•   Any query regarding application status will only be entertained after the estimated date of result (as stated in the receipt given upon submission of application)

For additional analytical, business and investment opportunities information,
please contact Global Investment & Business Center, USA
at (703) 370-8082. Fax: (703) 370-8083. E-mail: ibpusa3@gmail.com
Global Business and Investment Info Databank - www.ibpus.com

• The department will not be responsible in cases where application is rejected due to non-availability of quota (in the foreign worker recruitment license).
    Employers are advised to make sure that labour quota usage is up to date. Where a worker has been repatriated to country of origin, kindly inform the
    department by submitting employment pass cancellation.

• This application form may be photocopied on condition pages 1 and 2 are printed back-to-back.

*Failure to comply with this reminder will result in application to be rejected.

Required Documents :

1.   4 sets of BUR 500 form (1 original and 3 copies). All copies must bear original signature and company stamp
2.   A copy of previous BUR 500/ BUR 555 form
3.   A copy of worker's passport with valid/ latest sponsor stamp
4.   Copy of Foreign Worker Recruitment License with a validity period of at least 3 months from the date of submitting this application (with banker's guarantee
        stamp if applicable)
5.   Copy of miscellaneous license (if applicable)
6.   For the position of driver, kindly submit a copy of the worker's driving license and copy of the blue card of the vehicle (one vehicle per worker) under the
        company's name and also permit stamp from the Land Transport Department (If applicable).
7.   A copy of current/ ongoing Project Awards (If applicable).
8.   If the Project Awards is a sub-contracted project, a copy of the Project Awards given to Main-Con must be attached.

Reminder*:
• Applicant must complete the BUR555 form.
• All required documents must be attached together.
• Any query regarding application status will only be entertained after the estimated date of result (as stated in the receipt given upon submission of application)
• This application form may be photocopied on condition pages 1 and 2 are printed back-to-back.

*Failure to comply with this reminder will result in application to be rejected.

For additional analytical, business and investment opportunities information, please contact Global Investment & Business Center, USA
at (703) 370-8082. Fax: (703) 370-8083. E-mail: ibpusa3@gmail.com
Global Business and Investment Info Databank - www.ibpus.com

IMPORTANT LAWS AND REGULATIONS AFFECTING LABOR MARKER AND EMPLOYMENT

BRUNEI LABOR LAW

AN ACT TO AMEND AND CONSOLIDATE THE LAW RELATING TO LABOUR

PART I LABOUR DEPARTMENT

Chapter I Preliminary and Interpretation

CITATION.

1. This Act may be cited as the Labour Act.

INTERPRETATION.

2. In this Act, unless the context otherwise requires —

"agreement" means an oral engagement to work entered into in accordance with the provisions of this Act;

"apprentice" means any person of either sex who has contracted to serve an employer and to learn and be taught any business, trade manufacture, undertaking, calling or employment in which workers are employed;

"child" means a person under the age of 14 years;

"confinement" means the delivery of a child;

"contract" means a written engagement to work entered into in accordance with the provisions of this Act;

"dependant" means the wife or wives of a worker, and his children, step-children and lawfully adopted children who are unmarried and under the age of 16 years and any aged or incapacitated relative whom the Commissioner is satisfied is wholly dependant upon and living with the worker;

"domestic servant" means any house, stable or garden servant or car driver habitually employed in, or in connection with, the domestic services of any public or private dwelling-house, eating house, club or institution;

"employer" includes the Government of Brunei and any person or body of persons, corporate or unincorporate, and the legal personal representative of a deceased employer who or which enters into any agreement or contract with any worker and the duly authorised agent or manager of such person or body of persons and, where any person (hereinafter referred to as the principal) in the course of or for the purposes of his trade or business enters into any agreement or contract with any person (hereinafter referred to as the contractor) for the execution by or under the contractor of the whole or any part of any work undertaken by the principal, the principal shall, in respect only of any liability for the payment of wages remaining unpaid for a period not exceeding 3 months, be held to be the employer;

"family" means the wife or wives of a worker, and his children, stepchildren and lawfully adopted children who are unmarried and under the age of 14 years;

"Health Officer" means the Director of Medical Services and includes any officer to whom, by writing under his hand, he delegates the exercise or performance of all or any of the powers or duties conferred or imposed on the Health Officer by this Act to the extent of the powers or duties so delegated;

"immigrant worker" means any worker who is normally resident outside Brunei Darussalam who has come to Brunei Darussalam for the purpose of performing work in Brunei Darussalam;

"industrial undertaking" means —

(a) mines, quarries and other works for the extraction of minerals from the earth;

(b) industries in which articles are manufactured, altered, cleaned, repaired, ornamented, finished, adapted for sale, broken up or demolished, or in which materials are

transformed, including ship buildings, and the generation, transformation and transmission of electricity and motive power of any kind;

(c) construction, reconstruction, maintenance, repair, alteration, or demolition of any building, railway, tramway, harbour, dock, pier, canal, inland waterway, road, tunnel bridge, viaduct, sewer, drain, well, telegraphic or telephonic installation, electrical undertaking, gaswork, waterworks or other work of construction, as well as the preparation for or laying the foundation of any such work or structure;

(d) transport of passengers or goods by road or rail, or inland waterway, including the handling of goods at dock, quays, wharves, and warehouses, but excluding transport by hand:

Provided that if, having regard to the nature of the work involved in any occupation which forms part of the industrial undertaking, His Majesty the Sultan and Yang Di-Pertuan in Council considers that such occupation should be excluded from the provisions of this Act relating to industrial occupations, he may declare, by order, that employment in such occupation shall be deemed not to be employment in an industrial undertaking for the purpose of this Act:

Provided further that any undertaking of which a part only is an industrial undertaking shall not for that reason alone be deemed to be an industrial undertaking;

"mine" includes any undertaking whether public or private for the extraction of any substance from under the surface of the earth;

"place of employment" means any place where work is carried on by or on behalf of any employer;

"rate of pay", "rate of wages" and "wage rate" each means the total amount of money including allowances to which a worker is entitled under his contract of service for working either for a period of time stated or implied in his contract or for the performance of each completed piece or task of work, but does not include —

(i) additional payments in respect of overtime work;

(ii) additional payments by way of bonus;

(iii) allowances for travelling or food;

(iv) such additional payments or allowances made by reason of the special nature of work performed, as the Commissioner may approve:

Provided that in the case of a worker employed on piece rates, the ordinary rate of pay shall be calculated by dividing the period of 14 days immediately preceding the day on which the rate of pay is required to be calculated by the number of days on which such worker actually worked during such period;

"recruit," with its grammatical variations and cognate expressions, means to procure, engage, hire or supply or undertake or attempt to procure, engage, hire or supply workers for the purpose of being employed by the recruiter or by any other person, where such worker does not spontaneously offer his services at the place of employment or at a public employment office or at an office conducted by an employers' organisation and supervised by the Government;

"repatriation" means the return of a worker to his country of domicile or origin and includes the return to his house of a worker who has been brought to a place of employment by an employer from any other place within Brunei Darussalam;

"shift worker" means a worker who is engaged in work which by reason of its nature requires to be carried on continuously by a succession of shifts or any other work which the Commissioner has by notice published in the *Gazette* declared to be shift work for the purpose of this definition;

"ship" includes any vessel or boat of any nature whatsoever, engaged in navigation whether publicly or privately owned but does not include a ship of war;

"wages" means all remuneration which is payable to a worker for work done in respect of his agreement or contract but does not include —

(i) the value of any house accommodation or the supply of any food, fuel, light or water or medical attendance, or of any amenity or services excluded by general or special order of the State Secretary published in the *Gazette*;

(ii) any contribution paid by the employer on his own account to any pension fund or provident fund;

(iii) any travelling allowance or the value of any travelling concession;

(iv) any sum payable to the worker to defray special expenses entailed on him by the nature of his employment; or

(v) any gratuity payable on discharge or retirement;

"woman" means a female of the age of 18 years or upwards;

"worker" means a labourer, servant in husbandry, journeyman, artificer, handicraftsman, miner or other person engaged in manual labour or in recruiting such or in supervising in person any workman in and throughout the performance of his work, who has entered into and works under an agreement or contract with an employer, and includes an immigrant worker and any person, other than clerical staff, employed in the operation or maintenance of mechanically propelled vehicles used for transport of passengers or goods for hire or for commercial purposes, but does not include an apprentice or seaman engaged on ships articles;

"worker-recruiter" means a person who, being employed as a worker, is authorised in writing by this employer to recruit, but who does not receive any remuneration or other advantage for such recruiting;

"young person" means a person who has ceased to be a child but who is under the age of 18 years.

Chapter II Officers

COMMISSIONER OF LABOUR AND OTHER OFFICERS.

3. (1) His Majesty may, by notification in the *Gazette,* appoint by name or by office an officer to be styled the Commissioner of Labour, hereinafter referred to as the Commissioner, and also appoint one or more officers to be styled Deputy Commissioner of Labour or Assistant Commissioner of Labour and such other officers as may be necessary for carrying out the provisions of this Act, who, subject to such limitations as His Majesty in Council may by rule prescribe, may perform all duties imposed and exercise all powers conferred on the Commissioner by this Act.

(2) If any employer is dissatisfied with any decision or order of a Deputy Commissioner of Labour or an Assistant Commissioner of Labour made or given by virtue of the provisions of the preceding subsection, he may appeal from such decision or order to the Commissioner within 14 days of the date of such decision or order being communicated to him.

(3) If any employer is dissatisfied with any decision or order made or given by the Commissioner either original or by virtue of the preceding subsection, he may appeal from such decision or order to the Minister within 14 days of the date of such decision or order being communicated to him.

GOVERNMENT INSPECTIONS.

4. (1) The Commissioner or Health Officer may enter at all reasonable times upon any place of employment and into any house accommodation provided by an employer for workers, and put questions concerning the workers to the employer or to any person who may be in charge of them or to the workers themselves, and the employer or such person, or any such worker, shall be legally bound to answer such questions truly to the best of his ability.

(2) If the Commissioner or Health Officer has reasonable ground for suspecting that any offence has been committed against a worker, and whenever any complaint of personal ill-usage or breach of any of the

provisions of this Act is made to the Commissioner or Health Officer, the Commissioner or Health Officer, as the case may be, may forthwith remove, or cause to be removed, such worker from the place of employment where he is employed for further inquiry into the matter.

(3) The Commissioner or Health Officer may by order in writing require any employer to take within a reasonable time in the circumstances such steps as he considers necessary with a view to remedying defects observed in plant, layout, working methods, supervision medical or sanitary provision or other matters at any place or employment which he may have reasonable cause to believe constitute a threat to the health or safety of the workers.

ACCIDENTS TO BE NOTIFIED.

5. (1) Whenever an accident caused by machinery results in loss of life or grievous hurt to any worker the employer shall forthwith notify the Commissioner who shall at the earliest opportunity cause an examination to be made as to the cause of such accident:

Provided that a notice served by the employer on the Commissioner under the provisions of section 13 of the Workmen's Compensation Act (Chapter 74), shall, if it is therein stated that the accident was caused by machinery, be deemed to be notification for the purposes of this subsection.

(2) Where an examination of any machinery is required by virtue of the provisions of subsection (1), no alteration shall be made to that machinery until such examination has been carried out.

(3) In this section "machinery" means any engine, electrical machinery, powerplant, boiler, sawmill, gasometer, gas-holder, generator, gearing and appliances for transmission of power and all appurtenances of any of the above, but does not include machinery driven by manual power, machinery for driving any vehicle or marine machinery.

INSPECTION OF DOCUMENTS SUBSTANCES ETC.

6. The Commissioner or Health Officer may —

(a) call for and examine all contracts, registers, books of account and other documents concerning any workers or relating to their employment; and

(b) take or remove for purposes of analysis samples of materials and substances used or handled, subject to the employer or his representative being notified of any samples or substances taken or removed for such purposes.

POWER OF SUMMONS AND INSTITUTION OF PROCEEDINGS.

7. (1) Whenever the Commissioner has reasonable grounds for suspicion that any offence under this Act or any rule made thereunder has been committed or wishes to inquire into any matter concerning disputes as to wages, wrongful termination of agreement or contract, misconduct, food, medical attendance, death, mining usage and mining complaint, Government inspection, sanitation or any other matter relating to employer and worker dealt with under the provisions of

For additional analytical, business and investment opportunities information,
please contact Global Investment & Business Center, USA
at (703) 370-8082. Fax: (703) 370-8083. E-mail: ibpusa3@gmail.com
Global Business and Investment Info Databank - www.ibpus.com

this Act or any rule made thereunder, the Commissioner may summon any person who he has reason to believe can give information respecting the subject-matter of the enquiry, and the person so summoned shall be legally bound to attend at the time and place specified in the summons and to answer truthfully all questions which the Commissioner may put to him.

(2) If the Commissioner is of the opinion that an offence has been committed or that any complaint is well founded he may institute such proceedings criminal or civil for and in the name of the worker as he shall deem necessary in the circumstances.

PENALTIES.

8. (1) Any employer or other person who wilfully obstructs or impedes any entry, inquiry or investigation made under this Act or wilfully obstructs the service of, or obedience to, any summons and any person summoned who neglects to attend as required in such summons, and any person who commits in that connection any offence described in Chapter X of the Penal Code (Chapter 22) shall be punished as provided in Chapter X of the Penal Code (Chapter 22).

(2) Any employer who contravenes or fails to comply with any order of the Commissioner or Health Officer made under section 4 or fails to report an accident, or alters, or causes, or permits to be altered any machinery, in contravention of the provisions of section 5 shall be guilty of an offence: Penalty, a fine of $1,500 and in default thereof imprisonment for 6 months.

CHAPTER III RULES

Power to make rules.

9. (1) His Majesty in Council may from time to time make rules generally for carrying out the provisions of this Part.

(2) Without prejudice to the generality of the foregoing such rules may provide for any matter which by this Part is to be, or may be, prescribed.

(3) Any such rule may provide a penalty for the breach or contravention thereof not exceeding a fine of $600 or in default thereof imprisonment for a term not exceeding 3 months.

PART II AGREEMENTS AND CONTRACTS

Chapter IV Agreements

TERMS OF AGREEMENT.

10. (1) An agreement may be entered into for any period not exceeding one month or for any number of days' work not exceeding 26 or for the performance by a worker for an employer of any specified piece of work capable of being completed within one month from the commencement of the work. Every agreement shall, subject to any stipulation to the contrary, terminate on the last day of the period agreed upon or upon the completion of the specified number of days' work or piece of work, as the case may be:

Provided that each party to an agreement for a period not exceeding one month shall on the termination of such agreement in the manner aforesaid be conclusively presumed to have entered into a fresh agreement upon the same terms and conditions as those of the agreement so terminated unless notice has been given previously by either party to such agreement in accordance with the provisions of section 12.

(2) In the absence of proof to the contrary every agreement shall be presumed to be for a period of one month.

GUARANTEED WEEK.

11. In the case of a worker employed on an agreement for a period of a week or more and paid according to the number of days' work performed, an employer shall provide work suitable to the capacity of such worker for not less than 5½ days in every week with the exception of prescribed holidays and Fridays (or such other rest day as may be substituted for a Friday by agreement between the employer and the worker, entered into not less than 3 days before the rest is taken) and if he is unable or fails to provide such work on such number of days whereon the worker presents himself for work and is fit to work the employer shall nevertheless be bound to pay to the worker in respect of each of such days, wages at not less than his usual rate of pay, including cost of living allowance, if any, or if the worker is on piece rates at not less than the average of his previous week's earnings or if he has not been working, at the average rate during the last full week's work earned by a similar class of worker engaged on similar work:

Provided that if such day is a work day, other than a Saturday, the employer shall pay at a rate as if a whole day's work had been performed.

TERMINATION OF AGREEMENT BY NOTICE.

12. (1) Either party to an agreement for a period of time may terminate such agreement on the expiration of due notice given by him to the other party of his intention so to do; the length of the notice to be given shall, unless otherwise stipulated by the terms of the agreement, be equal to the period of the agreement to be terminated:

Provided that in no case shall it be necessary to give notice exceeding in length one month or in the case of domestic servants 14 days.

(2) Such notice may be either oral or written and may be given at any time and the day on which notice is given shall be included in the period of the notice.

TERMINATION OF AGREEMENT WITHOUT NOTICE BY EITHER PARTY.

13. Either party to an agreement may terminate the same without notice upon payment to the other party of a sum equal to the amount of wages which would have accrued to the worker during the period of the notice required by section 12.

DISMISSAL BY THE EMPLOYER WITHOUT NOTICE.

14. An employer shall not dismiss a worker employed without notice except in the following circumstances —

(a) where the worker is guilty of misconduct, whether in the course of his duties or not, inconsistent with the fulfilment of the express or implied conditions of his agreement;

(b) for wilful disobedience to lawful orders given by the employer;

(c) for lack of the skill which the worker expressly or implicitly warrants himself to posses;

(d) for habitual or substantial neglect of his duties;

(e) for absence from work without leave from the employer or absence without other reasonable excuse.

CANCELLATION OF AGREEMENT BY COMMISSIONER.

15. An agreement may be cancelled by an order of the Commissioner if the worker is subject to ill-usage in person or property and the Commissioner may by such order award the worker reasonable compensation.

CAPACITY TO ENTER INTO AN AGREEMENT.

16. Notwithstanding anything contained in any written law any young person shall be capable of entering into an agreement.

PENALTIES.

17. (1) Every employer who fails to make payment in accordance with the provisions of section 11 or contravenes the provisions of section 14 shall be guilty of an offence: Penalty, a fine of $1,500 or in default thereof imprisonment for 6 months.

(2) A court may in any proceedings under this section order the payment of such wages as are found due by an employer together with such sum or sums for damages, costs, and expenses as it shall deem fit.

Chapter V Contracts

Certain contracts excluded.

18. This Chapter and any rules made thereunder do not apply to contracts of apprenticeship.

CONTRACTS TO BE IN WRITING.

19. (1) When an engagement with a worker —

(a) is made for a period exceeding one month or a number of working days exceeding 26;

(b) is made or the performance of a specified piece of work for an employer, incapable of being completed within one month from the commencement of the work;

(c) stipulates conditions of employment which differ materially from those customary in the district of employment for similar work, the engagement shall be in writing and shall be signed by both parties:

Provided that a worker unable to sign may indicate his consent by affixing thereto the impression of his thumb.

(2) If the omission to make in writing any contract, which is required by this section, is due to the wilful act or negligence of the employer, the worker shall, without prejudice to any right he may have to sue for damages for breach of contract be entitled to apply to the Commissioner for cancellation of the contract.

CONTENTS OF CONTRACT.

20. Every contract shall contain in clear and unambiguous terms all that may be necessary to define the rights and obligations of the parties thereto and without prejudice to the generality of the foregoing shall in all cases include the following particulars —

(a) the name of the employer or group of employers and, where practicable, of the undertaking and the place of employment;

(b) the name of the worker, the place of engagement and the place of origin of the worker, and any other particulars necessary for his identification;

(c) where possible the names and addresses of the next of kin of the worker;

(d) the nature of the employment;

(e) the duration of the employment and the method of calculating this duration;

(f) the appropriate period of notice to be given by the party wishing to terminate the contract, due regard being had to the provisions of section 27 and to the fact that such provisions refer to an equitable settlement of monetary and other question;

(g) the rates of wages and method of calculation thereof, the manner and periodicity of payment of wages, the advances of wages, if any, and the manner of repayment of any such advances;

(h) the measures to be taken to provide for the welfare of the worker and any dependant who may accompany him under the terms of the contract;

(i) the conditions of repatriation; and

(j) any special conditions of the contract.

CONTRACT NOT ORDINARILY BINDING ON FAMILY DEPENDANTS.

21. No contract shall be deemed to be binding on the family or dependants of the worker, unless it contains an express provision to that effect.

ATTESTATION OF CONTRACTS.

22. (1) Every contract shall be presented for attestation to the Commissioner.

(2) Before attesting any such contract the Commissioner shall —

(a) ascertain that the worker has freely consented to the contract and that his consent has not been obtained by coercion or undue influence or as the result of misrepresentation or mistake; and

(b) satisfy himself that —

(i) the contract is in due legal form;

(ii) the terms of the contract are in accordance with the requirements of this Act;

(iii) the worker has fully understood the terms of the contract before signing it or otherwise indicating his assent;

(iv) the provisions relating to medical examination set out in section 23 have been complied with; and

(v) the worker declares himself not bound by any previous engagement.

(3) The Commissioner may refuse to attest any contract in respect of which he is not satisfied in regard to any of the matters specified in subsection (2) of this section, and any contract which the Commissioner has refused to attest shall have no further validity.

(4) A contract which has not been presented to the Commissioner for attestation shall only be enforceable as an agreement under the provisions of Chapter IV of this Part, but each of the parties shall be entitled to have it presented for attestation at any time prior to the expiry of the period for which it was made.

(5) If the omission to present the contract for attestation was due to the wilful act or the negligence of either party the other party shall be entitled to apply to the Commissioner for the cancellation of the contract.

(6) 4 copies of every contract attested under the provisions of this Chapter shall be attested including the original. One copy shall be delivered to the employer, one to the worker or in the case of a gang to one of their

number, one to the Assistant Commissioner in the district of employment and the original shall be retained by the Commissioner who shall keep a record of all such contracts.

(7) Notwithstanding the other provisions of this section, the Commissioner may, in his discretion, approve a standard form of contract to be used by any particular person or firm and when such approved form of contract is used individual attestation by the Commissioner shall not be necessary, but the employer shall render to the Commissioner a quarterly return of all persons newly employed during each quarter under such approved form of contract together with a certificate that the terms and conditions thereof were read over to and understood by the worker before he signed such contract.

MEDICAL EXAMINATIONS.

23. (1) Every worker who enters into a contract shall be medically examined at the expense of the employer.

(2) As a general rule the worker shall be medically examined and a medical certificate issued before the attestation of the contract.

(3) Where it has not been possible for the worker to be medically examined before the attestation of the contract, the Commissioner when attesting the contract shall endorse it to that effect and the worker shall be examined at the earliest opportunity.

(4) The Commissioner may, by endorsement on the contract, exempt from the requirement of medical examination workers entering into contracts for —

(a) employment in agricultural undertakings not employing more than such number of workers as may be prescribed;

(b) employment in the vicinity of workers, homes —

(i) in agricultural work;

(ii) in non-agricultural work which the Commissioner is satisfied is not a dangerous character or likely to be injurious to the health of the workers.

CAPACITY TO ENTER INTO A CONTRACT.

24. (1) A person whose apparent age is less than 16 years shall not be capable of entering into contract.

(2) Notwithstanding anything contained in any written law a person whose apparent age exceeds 16 years but is less than 18 years shall be capable of entering into a contract for employment in an occupation approved by the Commissioner as not being injurious to the moral and physical development of non-adults.

MAXIMUM DURATION OF CONTRACTS.

25. (1) *(a)* the maximum duration that may be stipulated or implied in any contract involving a journey within Brunei Darussalam and the Malaysian territories of Sarawak and Sabah from the place of recruitment to the place of employment, shall in no case exceed 12 months if the worker is not accompanied by his family;

(b) the maximum duration which may be stipulated or implied in any contract involving a journey other than a journey referred to in the preceding subsection from the place of recruitment to the place of employment shall in no case exceed 2 years if the worker is not accompanied by his family or 3 years if the worker is accompanied by his family.

(2) The Commissioner may, after consultation with any employers' and workers' organisations, representative of the interests concerned, exclude from the application of this section contracts entered into between employers and literate workers whose freedom of choice in employment is satisfactorily safeguarded; such exclusion may apply generally, or to the workers in any specified industry of undertaking or to special groups of workers.

TRANSFER TO OTHER EMPLOYMENT.

26. (1) The transfer of any contract from one employer to another shall be subject to the consent of the worker and the endorsement of the transfer upon the contract by the Commissioner.

(2) Before endorsing the transfer upon the contract the Commissioner —

(a) shall ascertain that the worker has freely consented to the transfer and that his consent has not been obtained by coercion or undue influence or as the result of misrepresentation or mistake; and

(b) in any case in which by such transfer the worker —

(i) will change his form of employment from one the subject of an exemption made under the provisions of subsection (4) of section 23; or

(ii) will be subject to such change in conditions as in the opinion of the Commissioner renders such a course advisable, may require the worker to be medically examined or re-examined as the case may be.

TERMINATION OF CONTRACT.

27. (1) A contract shall be terminated —

(a) by the expiry of the period for which it was made; or

(b) by the death of the employer or worker before the expiry of the period for which it was made.

(2) The termination of a contract by the death of the worker shall be without prejudice to the legal claims of any person entitled thereto.

(3) If the employer is unable to fulfil a contract or if owing to sickness or accident the worker is unable to fulfil the contract, the contract may be terminated with the consent of the Commissioner subject to conditions safeguarding the right of the worker to wages earned, any deferred pay due to him, any compensation due to him in respect of accident or disease, and his right to repatriation.

(4) A contract may be terminated by agreement between the parties with the consent of the Commissioner subject to conditions safeguarding the worker from the loss of his right to repatriation unless the agreement for the termination of the contract otherwise provides and to the Commissioner being satisfied —

(a) that the worker has freely consented to the termination and that his consent has not been obtained by coercion or undue influence or as the result of misrepresentation or mistake; and

 (b) that all monetary liabilities between the parties have been settled.

(5) A contract other than a contract to perform some specific work without reference to time, may be terminated by either party giving to the other, notice of such termination in accordance with the terms of the contract; the minimum requirements of which shall be —

(a) where the duration is for more than one month the period of notice shall be not less than 14 days and may be given only after the expiry of the first month of employment; or

(b) where the duration is for one month or less the period of notice shall be not less than 7 days:

Provided that except where the Commissioner in his discretion shall otherwise permit the period of notice stipulated in the contract shall not exceed one month:

Provided further that an equitable settlement of monetary and other conditions including the question of repatriation shall be agreed upon between the worker and the employer and in default of such agreement either party may refer the matter to the Commissioner who shall make such order, including the award of any subsistence expenses reasonably incurred pending such order, as may be just and equitable.

CANCELLATION OF CONTRACT BY COMMISSIONER.

28. A contract may be cancelled by an order of the Commissioner if the worker is subject to ill-usage in person or property and in such event the Commissioner may award the worker reasonable compensation.

DURATION OF RE-ENGAGEMENT CONTRACTS.

29. (1) The maximum duration that may be stipulated in any re-engagement contract on the expiry of the period for which the original contract was made shall be three-quarters of that prescribed in section 25 but in no case exceeding one year.

(2) Where the duration to be stipulated in any re-engagement contract, together with the period already served under the expired contract, involves the separation of any worker from his family for more than the respective periods prescribed in section 25 the worker shall not begin the service stipulated in the re-engagement contract until he has had the opportunity to return home at the employer's expense:

Provided that the Commissioner may grant exemption from this provision whenever its application is impracticable or undesirable.

PROVISIONS APPLICABLE TO RE-ENGAGEMENT CONTRACTS.

30. Except as provided in section 29 all the provisions of the preceding sections of this Chapter shall apply to re-engagement contracts:

Provided that the Commissioner may in his discretion exempt such contracts from the provisions of section 22 relating to attestation and of section 23 relating to medical examination subject to such terms and conditions as may be prescribed.

SUMMARY OF CHAPTER TO BE BROUGHT TO NOTICE OF WORKERS.

31. (1) The Commissioner shall, where necessary, cause concise summaries of this Chapter to be printed in Malay and in a language known to the workers and shall make such summaries available to the employer and workers concerned.

(2) Where necessary, the employer shall be required by the Commissioner to post such summaries in a language known to the workers in conspicuous places at the place of employment.

CONTRACTS FOR SERVICE OUTSIDE BRUNEI DARUSSALAM.

32. Where a contract made in Brunei Darussalam relates to employment in another territory (in this section referred to as the territory of employment) —

(a) the attestation of the contract required by section 22 shall take place before the worker leaves Brunei Darussalam;

(b) the measures required by subsection (6) of section 22 shall be taken by the Commissioner in Brunei Darussalam;

(c) the medical examination required by section 23 shall take place at the latest at the place of departure of the worker from Brunei Darussalam;

(d) a person whose apparent age is less than either the minimum age prescribed in section 24 or the minimum age of capacity for entering into a contract allowed by the law of the territory of employment if such minimum age is higher than that prescribed in section 24 shall not be capable of entering into a contract;

(e) the contract shall contain a proviso that it is not transferable unless such transfer is endorsed on the contract by a public officer of the territory of employment;

(f) the duration stipulated in the contract shall not exceed either the maximum period prescribed in section 25 or the maximum period prescribed by the law of the territory of employment whichever is the less;

(g) if the laws of the territory of employment are substantially the same as this Chapter the conditions under which the contract is subject to termination and any question of exemption from liability for repatriation shall be determined by the law of the territory of employment;

(h) if the laws of the territory of employment differ from the laws of Brunei in respect to repatriation the Commissioner may require such deposit or security from the employer as he deems necessary and such deposit or security may be used to defray the costs of repatriation at the discretion of the Commissioner;

(i) the Commissioner shall co-operate with the appropriate authority of the territory of employment to ensure the application of the provisions of subsection (2) of section 98;

(j) the period of service stipulated in any re-engagement contract shall not exceed either the maximum period allowed by the provisions of section 30 or if the maximum period allowed by the law of the territory of employment is less, then such lesser period.

EXTRATERRITORIAL CONTRACTS FOR EMPLOYMENT IN BRUNEI DARUSSALAM.

33. When a contract made in another territory (in this section referred to as the territory of origin) relates to employment in Brunei Darussalam —

(a) if such territory of origin has enacted laws substantially the same as this Chapter and all the provisions of such laws have been complied with prior to worker leaving such territory of origin, then —

(i) the endorsement of a transfer on a contract shall be made by the Commissioner as provided in section 26;

(ii) the conditions under which the contract is subject to termination shall be determined by the provisions of this Act and any rules made thereunder;

(iii) if the employer fails to fulfil his obligations in respect of repatriation the said obligations may be discharged by the Commissioner as provided in section 96 and such expenses may be recovered from the employer as a debt due to the Government;

(iv) the authority which may exempt the employer from liability for repatriation expenses and exercise any other powers conferred upon a competent authority in the territory of origin shall be the Commissioner;

(v) the Commissioner shall co-operate with the appropriate authority of the territory of origin to ensure the application of the provisions of subsection (2) of section 98;

(vi) the duration stipulated in any re-engagement contract shall not exceed either the maximum period allowed by the law of the territory of origin, which ever is less;

(b) If such territory has not enacted laws substantially the same as this Chapter or has not complied with any provisions of the law in respect of any contract then the whole of the provisions of this Chapter or such portion thereof as has not been complied with shall be complied with immediately upon the arrival of the worker in Brunei Darussalam and thereafter the provisions of this Chapter shall be deemed to apply *mutatis mutandis* as if such contract had been entered into in Brunei Darussalam.

PENALTIES.

34. Any employer who fails to comply with any order made by the Commissioner in pursuance of the provisions of this Chapter or who makes with a worker a contract contrary to the provisions of this Chapter shall be guilty of an offence: Penalty, a fine of $1,500 and imprisonment for 6 months.

Chapter VI Contracts of Apprenticeship

CONTRACTS OF APPRENTICESHIP OF YOUNG PERSONS UNDER 16.

35. (1) The parent, or in the case of an orphan the guardian, of a young person under the age of 16 years may, with the consent of such person, execute a written contract of apprenticeship, apprenticing such person to an employer to train him or have him trained systematically for a prescribed trade or employment for any period not exceeding 5 years.

(2) Whenever any young person under the age of 16 years is without known parent or guardian, the Commissioner may authorise the apprenticeship of such young person and may appoint some fit and proper person to execute the written contract of apprenticeship and act generally as guardian of such young person.

CONTRACTS OF APPRENTICESHIP OF YOUNG PERSONS OVER 16.

36. Any young person above the age of 16 years or any person above the age of 18 years not being under any contract of apprenticeship may apprentice himself for any period not exceeding 5 years to an employer in any prescribed trade or employment.

ASSIGNMENT.

37. Every contract of apprenticeship may with the consent of the parties thereto be assigned.

ATTESTATION.

38. Every contract of apprenticeship and every assignment thereof shall be in writing and no such contract shall be valid unless attested by and made with the approval of Commissioner certified in writing under his hand on the contract of apprenticeship or assignment.

DUTIES OF ATTESTING OFFICER.

39. Before attesting any contract of apprenticeship the Commissioner shall satisfy himself —

(a) that the employer is a fit and proper person and able and having facilities sufficient to instruct the apprentice in the trade or employment;

(b) that the apprentice has consented to such contract and that his consent has not been obtained by coercion, or undue influence or as the result of misrepresentation or mistake;

(c) that the apprentice has been medically examined and certified by a registered medical practitioner to be physically and mentally fit to be employed and trained in the trade or employment specified in such contract;

(d) that the parties to such contract have fully understood the terms of the contract before signing it or otherwise indicating assent;

(e) that provision has been made in such contract as to how any remuneration in cash or otherwise due to the apprentice shall be determined and as to the scale of increase in remuneration during the course of the apprenticeship;

(f) that provision has been made in such contract for payment of such remuneration to the apprentice during illness and during holidays;

(g) that the terms of such contract are in accordance with any rules made under the provisions of this Part.

CERTIFICATE OF SERVICE ON DISCHARGE.

40. (1) Whenever for any reason including the completion of his contract of apprenticeship an apprentice ceases to be employed by an employer it shall be the duty of the employer to supply the apprentice with a statement in the prescribed form setting forth the service of the apprentice.

(2) The employer shall forward a copy of such statement to the Commissioner, who shall endorse a note thereof on every copy of the contract of apprenticeship submitted to him for that purpose by any of the parties to such contract.

RETENTION OF APPRENTICES AFTER EXPIRY OF CONTRACTS.

41. If any person with whom an apprentice has been placed retains such apprentice in his service after the stipulated period of service has expired

without any agreement between the parties for the payment of wages, the apprentice shall be entitled to recover from the person so retaining him wages at the ordinary current rate payable for service similar to that performed by such apprentice.

SUSPENSION AND DISCHARGE.

42. (1) In any case where an apprentice so misconducts himself or proves himself to be so incapable that if he were an employee other than an apprentice it would be reasonable for his employer to discharge him, the employer may suspend him and apply forthwith to the Commissioner for leave to discharge him.

(2) The Commissioner shall enquire into the circumstances and where such leave is granted the employer shall be entitled to discharge the apprentice as from the date on which he was suspended and as from such date the contract of apprenticeship shall be deemed to be cancelled.

(3) Where such leave is refused the Commissioner may make such order as he thinks fit with respect to payment of wages to the apprentice in respect of the period of his suspension. If no such order is made, the employer shall pay to the apprentice all wages that would have been payable to him in respect of such period had he not been suspended.

(4) If the employer, notwithstanding that leave to discharge the apprentice has been refused by the Commissioner, discharges the apprentice, such discharge shall for all purposes be conclusive proof of a breach by the employer of the contract of apprenticeship.

(5) Where an employer, without proceeding in accordance with the foregoing provisions of this section, discharges or purports to discharge an apprentice, or, having suspended him does not within 3 days thereafter make application as aforesaid for leave to discharge him, the apprentice within 7 days after such discharge or within 10 days after such suspension, as the case may be, may apply to the Commissioner for relief from such discharge or suspension and thereupon the provisions of the section shall apply in like manner as if the employer had proceeded in accordance with subsection (1) of this section.

(6) The Commissioner may fix an amount that shall be payable to the apprentice as damages for breach of the contract of apprenticeship in the event of the employer discharging him contrary to the provisions of this section. Such amount shall be in addition to the amount of wages payable in respect of the period of suspension.

(7) Any person aggrieved by any decision or order of the Commissioner under this section may appeal against such decision or order to a magistrate who may hear and determine such appeal either in open court or in chambers as he may think fit and may make such order as to costs as he may think fit.

PENALTIES.

43. Any employer who fails to comply with any order made by the Commissioner in pursuance of the provisions of this Chapter or makes a contract of apprenticeship contrary to the provisions of this Chapter shall be guilty of an offence: Penalty, a fine of $1,500 or in default thereof imprisonment for a term of 6 months.

Chapter VII **Rules**

Power to make rules.

44. (1) His Majesty in Council may from time to time make rules generally for carrying out the provisions of this Part.

(2) Without prejudice to the generality of the foregoing power such rules may —

(a) provide for any matter which by this Part is to be or may be prescribed;

(b) prescribed the form of contracts of apprenticeship and the terms and conditions upon which such contracts may be lawfully entered into, and the duties and obligations of apprentices and their employers;

(c) provide for the registration of contracts of apprenticeship;

(d) stipulate the number of apprentices who may be apprenticed during a specified period in any specified trade or employment;

(e) stipulate the conditions governing the entry of young persons under the age of 16 years into apprenticeship;

(f) prescribed the mutual rights and obligations of employer and apprentice;

(g) provide for the supervision to be established over apprenticeship, particularly with a view to ensuring that the regulations governing apprenticeship and the terms of any contract of apprenticeship are observed, that the training is satisfactory and that there is reasonable uniformity in the conditions of apprenticeship;

(h) provide for the holding of examinations of apprentices on the expiry of the period of apprenticeship and where necessary in the course of apprenticeship; and for determining the methods of organising such examinations and for the issue of certificates based on the results thereof;

(i) prescribe the fees to be paid and by whom payable for attestations, endorsements or registrations effected or any acts required to be done in pursuance of the provisions of this Part or of any rules made thereunder.

(3) Any such rule may provide a penalty for the breach or contravention thereof not exceeding a fine of $600 or in default thereof imprisonment for a term not exceeding 3 months.

PART III ECRUITING OF WORKERS

Chapter VIII **Recruiting**

Exemptions.

45. The Minister may, by notification in the *Gazette,* except in respect of recruiting by professional recruiters, exempt from the provisions of this Part —

(a) the recruiting of workers by or on behalf of employers who do not employ more than such number of workers as shall from time to time be fixed by such notification;

(b) the recruiting of workers within a specified area or a specified distance from the place of employment; or

(c) the recruiting of personal or domestic servants.

PUBLIC OFFICERS ETC.

46. Public officers shall not recruit for private undertaking either directly or indirectly except when the recruited workers are to be employed on works of public utility for the execution of which private undertakings are acting as contractors for a public authority.

PERSONS WHO RECRUIT TO BE LICENSED.

47. (1) Subject to the provisions of subsection (6) of this section, no person shall recruit workers unless he is licensed in that behalf under the provisions of this Part or unless he has obtained a licence to recruit issued by a territory under laws substantially the same as this Part and has produced such licence to the Commissioner who may, on being satisfied in accordance with the provisions of the next succeeding subsection, countersign the same and such licence shall thereupon be deemed to be licence issued under the provisions of this Part.

(2) Every person desirous of obtaining a licence under this section shall apply to the Commissioner who may in his discretion issue a licence —

(a) if he is satisfied that the applicant is a fit and proper person to be granted a licence;

(b) if any security prescribed has been furnished; and

(c) if he is satisfied that adequate provision has been made for safeguarding the health and welfare of the workers to be recruited; and

(d) if he is satisfied that the person is proposing to recruit for a public department or authority or for a specified employer or association of employers.

(3) A licence shall be subject to such conditions as may be endorsed thereon, and shall not be transferable.

(4) No licence shall be issued for a period exceeding one year, but if the Commissioner is satisfied that the conditions on which it was granted have been complied with he may renew such licence for such period not exceeding one year as he may think fit.

For additional analytical, business and investment opportunities information,
please contact Global Investment & Business Center, USA
at (703) 370-8082. Fax: (703) 370-8083. E-mail: ibpusa3@gmail.com
Global Business and Investment Info Databank - www.ibpus.com

(5) The Commissioner may cancel any licence in any case where the licensee has been convicted of an offence under this Part or the rules made thereunder or has not complied with the conditions under which it was granted or is guilty of conduct which in the opinion of the Commissioner renders him no longer a fit and proper person to hold a licence; and the Commissioner may suspend any licence pending the decision of the court or the making of any enquiry which he shall consider necessary.

(6) His Majesty in Council may by rules made hereunder and subject to such conditions as he may therein prescribe exempt worker-recruiters from the provisions of this section.

NON-ADULTS NOT TO BE RECRUITED.

48. Persons under the age of 16 years shall not be recruited:

Provided that young persons under that age may be recruited with the consent of their parents or guardians for employment upon light work in an occupation approved by the Commissioner.

FAMILY NOT DEEMED RECRUITED.

49. The recruiting of the head of a family shall not be deemed to involve the recruiting of any member of his family.

EXAMINATION OF WORKERS.

50. (1) Every recruited worker shall —

(a) be brought before the Commissioner or officer in charge of an administrative district;

(b)

be medically examined at the expense of the recruiter or employer,

as nearly as may be convenient to the place of recruitment and in accordance with rules made under this Part.

(2) The Commissioner or officer before whom any recruited worker is brought shall satisfy himself that the provisions of this Part and the rules made thereunder have been observed and that the worker has not been subject to illegal pressure or recruited by misrepresentation or mistake.

EXPENSES OF WORKER OR BURIAL OF WORKER DURING JOURNEY.

51. (1) The expenses of the journey of recruited workers and their dependants to the place of employment, including all the expenses incurred for their protection during the journey, shall be borne and transport and necessaries for the journey shall be provided by the recruiter(not being a worker recruiter) or employer to a standard and on conditions in accordance with rules made under this Part.

(2) In the event of the death of any recruited worker or of any dependant occurring during any journey to the place of employment from the place of recruitment the recruiter shall provide decent burial and pay the reasonable expenses of burial.

RETURN OF WORKERS.

52. A recruited worker who —

(a) becomes incapacitated by sickness or accident during the journey to his place of employment;

(b) is found on medical examination to be unfit for employment;

(c) is not engaged after being recruited for a reason for which he is not responsible; or

(d) is found by the Commissioner or officer in charge of an administrative district to have been recruited by illegal misrepresentation or mistake, and the dependants of such recruited worker, and any dependant of a recruited worker who dies during the journey to the place of employment, shall be returned to their place of origin, or place of engagement if the latter be nearer to the place of employment and the laws of the place of engagement permit, at the expense of the recruiter or employer in accordance with rules made under this Part.

WORKERS RECRUITERS.

53. The provisions of this Part and the rules made thereunder shall, unless otherwise expressly provided, apply to worker-recruiters as if they were licensees:

Provided that worker-recruiters shall recruit only in such areas as may be specified by the Commissioner and shall not make advances of wages to recruited workers.

EXTRATERRITORIAL RECRUITING.

54. (1) Any person acting or proposing to act as a recruiter in a territory of origin outside Brunei Darussalam for the purpose of recruiting workers for employment in Brunei Darussalam shall, before leaving Brunei Darussalam to do so, first obtain a licence under this Part, and thereafter, if such territory provides in its laws provisions substantially the same as this Part, shall also obtain such licence as may be required under such laws and shall comply with all laws of such territory relating to recruiting and shall in any event, whether required by such laws or not, fulfil all the obligations of this Part of this Act as if the same were written into the laws of such territory and its provisions, where possible, shall be observed both prior to the departure of the worker from the territory of recruitment as well as upon arrival in Brunei Darussalam.

(2) Any agreement or contract of employment entered into with a worker arising from a contravention of the provisions of the last preceding subsection may be declared void by the Commissioner and thereupon any such worker and his family may be repatriated by the Commissioner and all costs of such repatriation shall be recovered from any security or borne by the offending recruiter or employer and may be recovered as a debt due to the Government.

PENALTIES.

55. Any person who recruits or attempts to recruit any person contrary to the provisions of this Chapter or contravenes or fails to comply with any of the provisions of this Chapter or any special conditions to which his licence is subject, shall be guilty of an offence: Penalty, a fine of $1,500 and imprisonment for 6 months.

Chapter IX **Rules**

Power to make rules.

56. (1) His Majesty in Council may, by notification in the *Gazette,* make rules not inconsistent with this part for the purpose of giving effect thereto or to any of the provisions of the Recruiting of Indigenous Workers Convention 1936 and without prejudice to the generality of the foregoing power, he may by rule provide for —

(a) the manner and form in which applications shall be made for licences, the particulars to be furnished upon every such application, the conditions under which any licence may be issued, the form of licences, the fees payable therefore, and particulars to be set forth therein;

(b) the security to be furnished by applicants for licences;

(c) the records to be kept by licensees;

(d) the remuneration to be paid to the agents of licensees;

(e) the prohibition of recruiting within any specified area;

(f) the supervision of worker-recruiters;

(g) the documents to be given to the recruited workers by licensees;

(h) the conditions under which recruited workers may be accompanied by dependants;

(i) the provision of necessaries and transport for recruited workers and dependants from the place of recruitment to the place of employment and the conditions applicable to the journey;

(j) the amount of wages which may be paid in advance to recruited workers and the conditions under which advances of wages may be made;

(k) the fees to be paid and by whom payable for any licences issued, attestations, endorsements or registrations effected or any other acts required to be done in pursuance of the provisions of this Act or any rules made thereunder;

(l) the establishment of a fund or other method to make provision for securing the payment of any expenses of recruitment or transport of workers upon such terms and conditions and subject to such control as he deems necessary and for providing that any such fund may be administered in conjunction with any fund established under paragraph *(c)* of subsection (2) of section 121;

(m) anything which by this Part is to be or may be prescribed, or as to which rules are to be made.

(2) Any such rule may provide a penalty for the breach or contravention thereof not exceeding a fine of $1,500 or in default thereof imprisonment for a term not exceeding 6 months.

PART IV CONDITIONS OF EMPLOYMENT

Chapter X Special Places of Employment

APPLICATION.

57. (1) This Chapter and any rule made thereunder shall apply only to the places of employment in respect of which a declaration is made in accordance with subsection (2).

(2) His Majesty in Council may by notification in the *Gazette,* declare that the provisions of this Chapter or of such sections thereof as may be specified in such notification shall apply to any place of employment either generally or specifically and be complied with by employer of the workers thereon or therein.

NAME TO BE PAINTED ON NOTICE BOARD AND DISPLAYED.

58. Every employer shall cause to be erected and exhibited in a conspicuous place at the place of employment a notice board on which shall be painted in easily legible characters, the name of the place of employment and the name and address of the person responsible for its management and, if the employer is a company, the situation of the registered office of the company.

REGISTER OF WORKERS.

59. Every employer shall keep a register of all workers in his employment in the prescribed form.

HOUSING, WATER SUPPLY AND SANITATION.

60. (1) Every employer shall provide and maintain —

(a) sufficient and hygienic house accommodation;

(b) a sufficient supply of wholesome water; and

(c) sufficient and proper sanitary arrangements,

for every worker who resides on the place of employment and for such other employees who reside on the place of employment. Such house accommodation, water supply and sanitary arrangements shall conform to such requirements and standards of health and hygiene as may be prescribed.

(2) No employer shall house any worker or other person in a building the state of which or the surroundings of which are, in the opinion of the Commissioner or Health Officer, such as to endanger the health of such worker or other person and should it appear to the Commissioner or Health Officer that the accommodation provided is likely, by reason of its site, construction, size, or otherwise, to endanger the health of any worker or of any person, the Commissioner may serve the employer with an order in writing requiring him to remove, alter, enlarge or reconstruct such accommodation within a reasonable time to be stated in such order; and such order may also, if necessary, declare that no worker or other person shall be permitted to occupy any building the subject of such order pending removal, alteration, enlargement or reconstruction.

(3) Should it appear to the Commissioner that accommodation ought to be provided for non-resident workers owing to their having no adequate or suitable housing of their own or by reason of the distance of their houses from the place of employment he may forbid the employment of such workers until such accommodations has been provided.

SURROUNDINGS OF HOUSING TO BE KEPT CLEAN.

61. A space of not less than 100 feet round any housing area shall be kept clear of jungle and secondary growth and the employer shall cause such space to be kept in a clean and sanitary condition and all refuse and excreta in or near the housing to be collected and buried or burned and shall detail a sufficient number of workers daily to carry out these duties.

REGULAR INSPECTION OF HOUSING.

62. (1) Every employer shall cause all housing to be visited and inspected not less than once a week by some responsible person who shall report to the employer if the housing is not kept clean or any refuse or excreta is allowed to accumulate in the neighbourhood of the housing and the employer shall make such arrangements as may be necessary for the cleaning of the housing and surroundings and for the removal of any refuse or excreta which may have accumulated.

(2) In any case where the Commissioner or Health Officer considers that visits, inspections or other duties prescribed by subsection (1) are not satisfactorily carried out he may notify the employer accordingly, specifying the matters in respect whereof he is not satisfied, and the employer shall thereupon make such further or other arrangements, whether by substituting a different person to perform the said duties or otherwise, as the Commissioner or Health Officer may require.

SEPARATE HOUSE ACCOMMODATION TO BE PROVIDED FOR EACH RACE.

63. On every place of employment upon which the workers employed and residing are not all of one race the employer shall, if the Commissioner so directs, provide separate house accommodation for the workers of each race.

AGRICULTURAL ALLOTMENTS.

64. (1) Every employer shall set aside land suitable for allotments for the use of resident workers who have worked and resided on such place of employment for not less than 6 consecutive months and who have dependants.

(2) The area of the land so set a side shall ordinarily be not less than one sixteenth of an acre for each such worker and such area shall be cleared and made available for cultivation at the expense of the employer:

Provided that if the employer shall satisfy the Commissioner that any worker has failed to make proper use of the area so set aside the employer shall be relieved of his duty as aforesaid in respect of such worker.

(3) The Commissioner may for good and sufficient reason by writing under his hand exempt any employer or class of employer from compliance with this section on such terms and conditions and for such period as to him may seem fit.

MEDICAL CARE AND TREATMENT.

65. (1) At every place of employment the employer shall provide for all workers such medical attention and treatment with medicines of good quality, first aid equipment and appliances for the transportation of sick or injured workers as may be prescribed.

For additional analytical, business and investment opportunities information,
please contact Global Investment & Business Center, USA
at (703) 370-8082. Fax: (703) 370-8083. E-mail: ibpusa3@gmail.com
Global Business and Investment Info Databank - www.ibpus.com

(2) Every employer shall take or cause to be taken, for treatment with as little delay as possible every worker injured or falling ill during the course of his employment and every resident worker and resident dependant on a place of employment requiring medical attention at a hospital or dispensary to the hospital or dispensary maintained for the workers at such place of employment or, if there is no such hospital or dispensary, to the nearest hospital or dispensary maintained by the Government or approved by the Commissioner and shall also provide any treatment necessary therefor.

(3) The cost of maintenance and treatment of a worker and of his dependants residing on the place of employment in or at any hospital or dispensary to which the worker or his dependant is sent by the employer shall be borne or paid by the employer as long as the worker remains in his employment:

Provided that if the employer continues to pay to the worker wages or part wages amounting to not less than half his usual wages he may recover by deduction from the wages of such worker the cost of such maintenance in hospital at such rate as may be prescribed.

(4) Where any such worker or dependant has been admitted to a Government hospital or dispensary, the cost of maintenance and treatment at such rate as may from time to time be prescribed and, in the event of the death of such worker or dependant in such hospital, any reasonable burial expenses incurred shall be recoverable from the employer at the suit of the Medical Officer in Charge.

BURIAL OF DECEASED WORKERS OR DEPENDANTS.

66. The employer shall provide decent interment for any worker resident on a place of employment and for any dependant dying during the employment of such worker unless a relative or friend undertakes such duty.

HOSPITAL MAINTAINED BY EMPLOYERS.

67. (1) The Commissioner may at any time having regard to the situation of any place of employment and the number of workers employed and resident thereon, by order in writing, require any employer to construct within a reasonable time to be stated in such order, and thereafter to maintain at his own expense, a hospital on or in the immediate neighbourhood of any place of employment upon which workers are employed by him with accommodation for such number of patients as may be stated in such order, of if there is already a hospital maintained by such employer to enlarge or add to such hospital so as to provide accommodation for a further number of patients as stated in the order; and may further require him to employ a duly registered medical practitioner to reside at and have charge of such hospital or any hospital maintained by such employer and to provide such medical practitioner with fit and proper house accommodation to the satisfaction of the Commissioner.

(2) If 2 or more such places of employment are so situated that the required accommodation for patients from such places of employment can be conveniently provided in one hospital the Commissioner may, instead of ordering each employer to construct and maintain a separate hospital, order all the employers concerned to construct within a reasonable time to be stated in such order, and thereafter to maintain at their own expense one hospital hereinafter called a "group hospital" for all such places of employment with accommodation for such number of patients as may be stated in the order or if there is already a hospital erected and maintained jointly by 2 or more employers (whether constructed in pursuance of the provisions of this section

or not) may order them to enlarge or add to such hospital so as to provide accommodation for such further number of patients

in their employment as may be stated in the order; and may further require such employers to employ a duly registered medical practitioner to take charge of such group hospital and to provide such medical practitioner with fit and proper house accommodation to the satisfaction of the Commissioner.

(3) Every employer referred to in the preceding subsection shall be responsible for the due maintenance of the group hospital as the case may be and for the provision of the staff, equipment, diet and medicines and for the observance of any rules made under this Part for the inspection and management of the hospital and the furnishing of any returns required as if the hospital were provided and maintained solely by him.

APPROVAL OF PLACE OF EMPLOYMENT AND PROHIBITION OF EMPLOYMENT OF WORKERS WHERE ARRANGEMENTS ARE INADEQUATE.

68. (1) Every person intending —

(a) to employ resident workers at a place of employment where workers have not hitherto been employed or have not been employed within the preceding 12 months; or

(b) to increase the number of workers already employed on a place of employment so that the existing arrangement would not conform to the prescribed requirements and standards of health and hygiene, shall give notice in writing of such intention to the Commissioner.

(2) If the Commissioner at any time has reason to believe that the arrangements made for the residence and employment of workers on any place of employment where it is intended that workers shall live or be employed or where workers are living or employed are from any cause inadequate for the residence and employment of such workers or of additional workers or that the health or conditions of workers living or employed on any place of employment is from any cause unsatisfactory, he may by order served on the employer prohibit the residence or employment, or both, of workers or of additional workers on such place and it shall thereupon be unlawful for any person to employ or permit to reside on such place any workers or dependants, or any workers or dependants other than those who were residing or employed thereon before the issue of such order, as the case may be.

(3) The Commissioner may, upon being satisfied that adequate arrangements have been made for the residence and employment of the workers or of additional workers on such place of employment or that the health and condition of the workers living or employed thereon have become satisfactory, rescind the order made under subsection (2) of this section, and thereupon it shall be lawful for the employer to employ workers or additional workers as the case may be on such place of employment.

PENALTIES.

69. Every employer who —

(a) contravenes or fails to comply with any of the provisions of section 58, 59, or 64 shall be guilty of an offence: Penalty, a fine of $600 or in default thereof imprisonment for 3 months;

(b) contravenes or fails to comply with the provisions of section 60, 61, 62, 63, 65, 66, 67 or 68 shall be guilty of an offence: Penalty, a fine of $1,500 and imprisonment for 6 months;

(c) contravenes or fails to comply with any order or requirements of the Commissioner or the Health Officer made under this Chapter shall be guilty of an offence: Penalty, a fine of $600 or imprisonment for 3 months.

Chapter XI Special Provisions Relating to the Employment of Women, Young Persons and Children

APPLICATION.

70. Nothing in this Chapter or in any rule made thereunder shall apply to an industrial or other undertaking or trade or to any ship in which only members of the same family are employed, unless such employment by its nature or the circumstances in which it is carried on is dangerous to the life, health or morals of the persons employed therein.

DETERMINATION OF AGE.

71. The age of any person may, where the birth of such person has not been registered or the registration thereof cannot be traced, be enquired into and determined by the Commissioner and the age so determined shall be conclusive for the purposes of this Act.

CERTAIN RESTRICTION ON EMPLOYMENT OF CHILDREN.

72. No child shall be employed in any industrial undertaking:

Provided that His Majesty in Council may by notification in the *Gazette* permit the employment of children in any specified industrial undertaking or in any specified occupation which forms part of any specified industrial undertaking.

POWER TO PROHIBIT EMPLOYMENT OF CHILDREN IN OTHER SPECIFIED WAYS.

73. His Majesty in Council may by notification in the *Gazette* prohibit the employment of any child, or prescribe the terms and conditions on which children may be employed, in any specified trade undertaking or in any specified occupation which forms part of any specified trade or undertaking.

NIGHT WORK OF YOUNG PERSONS IN INDUSTRY.

74. (1) Young persons shall not be employed or work during the night in any industrial undertaking except as hereinafter provided.

(2) For the purpose of this section "night" means a period of at least 12 consecutive hours —

(a) in the case of young persons under the age of 16 years this period shall include the interval between 10 o'clock in the evening and 6 o'clock in the morning;

(b) in the case of young persons who have attained the age of 16 years this period shall include an interval to be prescribed of at least 7 consecutive hours falling between 10 o'clock in the

evening and 7 o'clock in the morning. Different intervals may be prescribed for different areas, industrial undertakings or branches of industrial undertakings:

Provided that before an interval beginning after 11 o'clock in the evening is prescribed the employers' and workers' organisations concerned, if any, shall be consulted.

(3) For the purposes of apprenticeship or vocational training the Commissioner may authorise the employment during the night of young persons who have attained the age of 16 years, under such conditions as he may impose.

(4) Every employer shall grant to young persons, employed during the night by virtue of the preceding subsection, a rest period of at least 13 consecutive hours between 2 working periods.

(5) The provisions of this section shall not apply to employment during the night of young persons who have attained the age of 16 years, in an emergency which could not have been controlled or foreseen, which is not of a periodical character and which interferes with the normal working of the industrial undertaking.

FEMALES NOT TO BE EMPLOYED AT NIGHT IN INDUSTRY.

75. (1) No female shall be employed during the night in any industrial undertaking.

(2) For the purpose of this section "night" means a period of at least 11 consecutive hours including an interval to be prescribed of at least 7 consecutive hours falling between 10 o'clock in the evening and 7 o'clock in the morning. Different intervals may be prescribed for different areas, industrial undertakings or branches of industrial undertakings:

Provided that before an interval beginning after 11 o'clock in the evening is prescribed the employers' and workers' organisations concerned, if any, shall be consulted.

(3) The provisions of this section shall not apply —

(a) in an emergency which could not have been controlled or foreseen, which is not of a periodical character and which interferes with the normal working of the industrial undertaking;

(b) where the work is connected with raw materials or materials in course of treatment which are subject to rapid deterioration and work during the night is necessary to preserve such materials from certain loss;

(c) to a woman holding a responsible position of a managerial or technical character; and

(d) to a woman employed in health and welfare services who is not ordinarily engaged in manual work.

EMERGENCIES.

76. In any serious emergency when the public interest demands it the Minister may by notification in the *Gazette* suspend the operation of sections 74 and 75 in so far as they affect young persons who have attained the age of 16 years and women.

REGISTER OF YOUNG PERSONS EMPLOYED IN INDUSTRIAL UNDERTAKINGS.

77. Where young persons are employed in any industrial undertakings a register of the young persons so employed, containing particulars of their ages and of the dates on which they enter or leave the service of their employer, shall be kept by such employer and shall at all times be open to inspection by the Commissioner.

RESTRICTION ON EMPLOYMENT OF FEMALES AND YOUNG PERSONS UNDERGROUND.

78. (1) No young person under the age of 16 years shall be employed on underground work in any mine.

(2) No female shall be employed on underground work in any mine except in the following circumstances —

(a) a woman holding a position of management who does not perform manual work;

(b) a woman engaged in health or welfare services;

(c) a woman who in the course of her studies spends a period of training in the underground parts of a mine; or

(d) a woman who may for any other reason have to enter the underground parts of a mine for the purpose of non-manual occupation.

RESTRICTION ON EMPLOYMENT OF CHILDREN IN SHIPS.

79. No child shall be employed in any ship except a ship approved by the Commissioner as a school or training ship.

RESTRICTION ON EMPLOYMENT OF YOUNG PERSONS IN SHIPS.

80. No young person shall be employed on work as a trimmer or stoker in any ship unless prior written approval for such employment has been given by the Commissioner.

REGISTER OF YOUNG PERSONS EMPLOYED IN SHIPS.

81. Every master of a ship shall, if young persons are employed therein, keep a register of such persons containing particulars of their ages and of the dates on which they become or cease to be members of the crew and the register so kept shall be open to inspection by the Commissioner.

MEDICAL CERTIFICATE.

82. (1) The employment of any child or young person on any ship shall be conditional on the production of a medical certificate attesting fitness for such work signed by a duly registered medical practitioner.

(2) The continued employment at sea of any such child or young person shall be subject to the repetition of such medical examination at intervals of not more than one year and the production,

after each such examination, of a further medical certificate attesting fitness for such work. Should a medical certificate expire in the course of a voyage it shall remain in force until the end of the said voyage.

MATERNITY BENEFITS.

83. (1) Every female worker shall be entitled to abstain from work during periods 4 weeks each before and after confinement and in respect of such periods, hereinafter jointly referred to as "benefit period," to receive from her employer maternity benefit to be calculated in accordance with the provisions of the succeeding subsections of this section.

(2) A female worker who has worked for the employer from whom she claims maternity benefit on not less than 180 days within the period of one year immediately preceding the notice required under section 87 shall be paid maternity benefit during the benefit period at such rate as may be prescribed.

(3) A female worker who has worked for the employer from whom she claims such maternity benefit on not less than 90 days within the period of 6 calendar months immediately preceding the date of the notice required under section 87 shall be paid maternity benefit during the benefit period at such rate as may be prescribed.

(4) A female worker who has worked in her employment on any day during the period of 4 weeks immediately preceding her confinement shall not be entitled to any maternity benefit for that day or that part of that period which precedes that day.

(5) No employer shall knowingly employ a worker at any time during the period of 4 weeks immediately following her confinement.

PAYMENTS TO INCLUDE REST DAYS AND HOLIDAYS.

84. Subject to the provisions of subsection (4) of section 83, payments made under subsections (2) and (3) of section 83 shall be made for every day of the benefit period including Sundays or other agreed rest days prescribed holidays.

PAYMENT OF MATERNITY BENEFIT.

85. The amount of the maternity benefit shall be payable in 2 instalments; the first for the period up to and including the day of confinement to be paid within 7 days after the birth of the child and the second for the period after confinement to be paid within 7 days after the end of that period; and shall not be payable in advance.

DEATH DURING BENEFIT.

86. If a female worker dies during the benefit period the maternity benefit shall be payable only for the days up to and including the day of her death.

NOTICE OF CONFINEMENT.

87. (1) A female worker may prior to her confinement give notice to her employer that she expects to be confined within one month from the date of such notice.

(2) A female worker who has been confined shall within 7 days of her confinement give notice to her employer of the date on which she was confined.

(3) Any female worker who omits to give notice as required by subsection (2) shall forfeit her claim for any maternity benefit to which she is entitled unless she was prevented by any sufficient cause from the giving of such notice.

PERMISSION FOR ABSENCE TO BE GIVEN BY EMPLOYER.

88. The employer shall, on receipt of a notice from a female worker under section 87, or on the fact of the confinement of a female worker otherwise coming to his knowledge, permit such worker to absent herself from work until the expiry of 4 weeks after the day of her confinement.

FORFEITURE OF BENEFIT.

89. If a female worker for any other employer after she has been permitted by her employer to absent herself under section 88 such worker shall forfeit her claim to the payment of any maternity benefit to which she would have been entitled.

APPOINTMENT OF NOMINEE.

90. (1) A female worker who gives notice under section 87 may in such notice nominate some other person to whom her maternity benefit may be paid on her behalf and any payment of any maternity benefit made to the person so nominated shall, for the purpose of this Chapter, be deemed to be payment to the worker who nominated such person.

(2) If a female worker entitled to maternity benefit under the provisions of this Chapter dies during the period for which she is entitled to such benefit the employer shall pay the amount of maternity benefit due to the person nominated or, if there is no such person, to the legal representative to such person as is approved by the Commissioner.

NOTICE OF TERMINATION OF EMPLOYMENT.

91. When a female worker absents herself from work in accordance with the provisions of this Chapter her employer shall not give her notice of termination of employment during such absence or so that the notice will expire during such absence.

BENEFIT UNAFFECTED BY NOTICE OF TERMINATION IN SPECIFIED CIRCUMSTANCES.

92. (1) No notice of termination of employment given without sufficient cause by an employer to a female worker within a period of 3 months before her confinement shall have the effect of depriving her of any maternity benefit which but for such notice she would have been eligible to receive under this Chapter.

(2) If any question arises as to whether any notice of termination of employment given under subsection (1) of this section was or was not given for sufficient cause it shall be referred to the Commissioner for decision.

CLAIM FROM ONE EMPLOYER.

93. Nothing contained in section 83 shall be construed as entitling any female worker to claim maternity benefit from more than one employer in respect of the same confinement.

CONTRACTING OUT.

94. Any agreement or contract whereby a female worker relinquishes any right under this Chapter shall be null and void in so far as it purports to deprive her of that right or to remove or reduce the liability of any employer to pay maternity benefit under this Chapter.

PENALTIES.

95. Any employer who contravenes or fails to comply with any of the provisions of this Chapter, or any person who makes an entry in a register, required to be kept under the provisions of section 77 or 81, which he knows or has reason to believe to be false shall be guilty of an offence: Penalty, a fine of $1,500 or in default thereof imprisonment for 6 months.

Chapter XII Repatriation

RIGHTS AND OBLIGATIONS OF WORKER AND EMPLOYER IN RESPECT OF REPATRIATION.

96. (1) Every worker who is a party to an agreement or contract under this Act and who has been brought to the place of employment by an employer or by any person acting on behalf of the employer shall have the right to be repatriated at the expense of the employer to his place of origin or to the place of engagement, if the latter be nearer to the place of employment and the laws of the place of engagement permit, in the following cases —

(a) on the termination of the agreement or contract by expiry of the period for which it was made;

(b) on the termination of the agreement or contract by reason of the inability of the employer to fulfil the agreement or contract;

(c) on the termination of the agreement or contract by reason of inability of the worker to fulfil the agreement or contract owing to sickness or accident;

(d) on the termination of the agreement or contract by notice but in the case of a contract subject to the provisions of the particular contract and Chapter V of this Act;

(e) on the cancellation of the agreement or contract under section 15 or 28;

(f) on the termination of the agreement or contract by agreement between the parties, unless the Commissioner otherwise decides.

(2) Every immigrant worker who is ordered to leave Brunei Darussalam under or in accordance with any provision of any written law for the time being in force relating to immigration shall be repatriated at the expense of the employer to his place of origin or to the place of engagement, if the latter be nearer to the place of employment and the laws of the place of engagement permit.

(3) Where any dependant of the worker has been brought to the place of employment by the employer or by any person acting on behalf of the employer such dependant shall be repatriated at the expense of the employer whenever the worker is repatriated or in the event of his death.

(4) The expenses of repatriation shall include —

(a) travelling and subsistence expenses during the journey;

(b) subsistence expenses during the period if any, between the date of termination of the agreement or contract and the date of repatriation; and

(c) provision of decent interment and the payment of the reasonable expenses of burial in the event of death of a worker occurring during the course of, or pending, repatriation.

(5)

The employer shall not be liable for subsistence expenses in respect of any period during which the repatriation of the worker has been delayed —

(a) by the worker's own choice; or *(b)* for reasons of *force majeure,* when the employer has been able during the said period to use the services of the worker at the rate of wages stipulated in the expired contract.

(6) If the employer fails to fulfil his obligation in respect of repatriation the said obligation shall be discharged by or under directions of the Commissioner and any sums so expended may be recovered from the employer or employers by civil suit as a debt due to the Government.

EXEMPTION FROM OBLIGATION TO REPATRIATE.

97. The Commissioner may exempt the employer from liability for repatriation expenses in the following cases —

(a) when the Commissioner is satisfied —

(i) that the worker by a declaration before the Commissioner has signified that he does not wish to repatriation; and

(ii) that the worker has been settled at his request or with his consent at or near the place of employment;

(b) when the Commissioner is satisfied that the worker by his own choice has failed to exercise his right of repatriation before the expiry of 6 months from the date of termination of the agreement or contract;

(c) when the liability of the employer has been provided for under any of the provisions of any Fund established under paragraph (c) of subsection (2) of section 121;

(d) when the agreement or contract has been terminated otherwise than by reason of the inability of the worker to fulfil the agreement or contract owing to sickness or accident and the Commissioner is satisfied —

(i) that in fixing the rates of wages proper allowance has been made for the payment of repatriation expenses by the worker; and

For additional analytical, business and investment opportunities information,
please contact Global Investment & Business Center, USA
at (703) 370-8082. Fax: (703) 370-8083. E-mail: ibpusa3@gmail.com
Global Business and Investment Info Databank - www.ibpus.com

(ii) that suitable arrangements have been made by means of a system of deferred pay or otherwise to ensure that the worker has the funds necessary for the payment of such expenses.

EMPLOYER TO PROVIDE TRANSPORT.

98. (1) The employer shall whenever possible provide transport for workers who are being repatriated.

(2) The Commissioner shall take all necessary measures to ensure and may give such directions to the employer or to any person acting on behalf of the employer as will ensure —

(a) that all vehicles or vessels used for transport of workers are suitable for such transport, are in good sanitary condition and are not overcrowded;

(b) that when it is necessary to break the journey for the night suitable accommodation is provided for the workers;

(c) that when the workers have to make long journeys on foot the length of the daily journey is compatible with the maintenance of their health and strength; and

(d) that in the case of long journeys suitable arrangements are made for medical assistance and for the welfare of the workers.

(3) When the workers have to make long journeys in groups they shall be convoyed by a responsible person to be approved by the Commissioner.

PENALTIES.

99. Any employer who fails to comply with the direction given to him by the Commissioner in pursuance of the provisions of section 98 shall be guilty of an offence: Penalty, a fine of $600 or in default thereof imprisonment for 3 months.

Chapter XIII Domestic Service

Domestic servants.

100. His Majesty in Council may from time to time make rules applying all or any of the provisions of this Act to all domestic servants or to any group, class or number of domestic servants and make rules not inconsistent with any of the provisions of this Act to provide generally for the engagement, repatriation and working conditions of domestic servants.

Chapter XIV General Provisions Relating to Agreements and Contracts

WORKER NOT LIABLE FOR DEFAULT OF ANOTHER.

101. No worker shall be bound in or by virtue of any agreement or contract under this Act to answer for the debt, default or miscarriage of another person.

LIABILITY OF WORKER FOR ADVANCES.

102. (1) An advance of wages to worker or to a person in consideration of his taking up employment as a worker shall not without the previous permission of the Commissioner exceed an amount equivalent to the wages earned by the worker during the previous month or if he has been employed for that period the wages he is likely to earn during one month or an amount authorised by rule under Chapter IX.

(2) No worker shall be held to be liable for the amount of any advance made to him by his employer which exceeds the amount authorised under subsection (1).

(3) No worker shall be held to be liable for the amount of any moneys expended on his behalf prior to his arrival in Brunei Darussalam in consideration of his engagement to work within Brunei Darussalam, other than an advance of wages as authorised by rule under Chapter IX.

(4) Any advance of wages may be recovered in instalments by deduction from wages in such manner as may be prescribed.

PRESCRIBED HOLIDAYS.

103. Holidays may be prescribed for workers. Such holidays may be fixed having regard to the religion and customs of workers.

DAYS AND HOURS OF WORK.

104. Subject to any provisions to the contrary contained in his contract —

(a) no worker other than a shift worker shall be required to work on a prescribed holiday or on more than 6 days in one week or for more than 6 consecutive hours without a break, or for more than 8 hours a day of actual work:

Provided that any worker on a prescribed holiday or for more than 8 hours in any day, or for more than 6 consecutive hours in the case of accident, actual or threatened, or in case of urgent work to be done to machinery, or in case of an interruption of work which it was impossible to foresee and which is not of a recurring character, but only in so far as may be necessary to avoid serious interference with the ordinary working of the undertaking concerned;

(b) if any worker works for and at the request of his employer on a prescribed holiday or on a Friday (or other agreed rest day substituted for a Friday by agreement between the employer and the worker entered into not less than 3 days before such rest day is taken) or for more than 8 hours in any day he shall be paid wages for such extra work at the following rates —

(i) on prescribed holidays, at a rate of not less than double his ordinary rate of pay, but in such case wages shall not be payable under the provisions of section 103;

(ii) on Friday or other rest days, at a rate of not less than one and a half times his ordinary rate of pay; and

(iii) for overtime in excess of 8 hours in any one day for workers other than those paid on piece work or shift work, at a rate of not less than one and a half times his ordinary rate of pay;

(c) a shift worker may be required by his employer to work for any number of hours not exceeding 56 in any one week and not exceeding 12 in any one day:

Provided that where a shift worker is required to work for more than 48 hours in any one week, the average number of hours for which he may be required to work in that week and the next preceding and next succeeding week shall not, except with the approval of the Commissioner, exceed 48 hours;

(d) the provisions of this section shall not apply to workers engaged in work which by its nature involves long and regular hours of inactive or standby employment; and

(e) for the purposes of this section the Commissioner, in the event of any dispute, may, and shall if so required by either party to the dispute, decide whether or not any worker is a shift worker.

TASK WORK.

105. (1) An employer and a worker may agree to the assignment of a task to be performed by the worker as equivalent to work for a day of 8 hours and the performance of such task shall, for the purposes of this Act, be equivalent to working for a day.

(2) Nothing in this Chapter contained shall prevent any employer from agreeing with any worker in his employment that the wages of such worker shall be paid at an agreed rate in accordance with the amount of work done and not by the day.

WORKING BOARD.

106. Every employer shall keep in some conspicuous position on the place of employment, so that it shall be readily accessible to the workers there employed, a Working Board on which, at intervals not exceeding 2 days, in a language understood by the workers shall be shown —

(a) the wage rate, whether by day, hour, piece, task or otherwise of each worker;

(b) the amount earned, including overtime payments each day by each worker;

(c) the amount of any deductions made from the earnings of each worker:

Provided that if any record, check roll or other document maintained by an employer as part of the routine of the place of employment gives the particulars required to be shown on a Working Board or required to be shown in a register or registers in accordance with the provisions of section 59 and that such record, check roll or other document is readily accessible to all of the workers employed by him, such record, check roll or other document may, to the corresponding extent, be maintained in place of and be treated as a Working Board for the purposes of this section.

PERIOD FOR WHICH WAGES PAYABLE.

107. Unless the agreement or contract otherwise stipulates, and subject to the provisions of section 104, wages shall only be payable for days actually worked, for prescribed holidays, for days other than Sundays or other rest days on which through no fault of the worker no work is provided by the employer and for time spent in attending before any court if such court certifies that his attendance was necessary for the ends of public justice.

PAYMENT OF WAGES.

For additional analytical, business and investment opportunities information,
please contact Global Investment & Business Center, USA
at (703) 370-8082. Fax: (703) 370-8083. E-mail: ibpusa3@gmail.com
Global Business and Investment Info Databank - www.ibpus.com

108. (1) The wages of a worker payable monthly shall be paid not later than 10 days after the expiration of the period in respect of which they are due.

(2) All wages due to a worker whose agreement or contract is terminated by expiry of the period for which it was made shall be paid to him on the day on which such agreement or contract terminates.

(3) All wages due to a worker whose agreement or contract is terminated by his employer shall be paid to him on the day on which such agreement or contract is terminated or if this is not possible, on the first day, not being a rest day or prescribed holiday, after the day on which such agreement or contract is terminated.

(4) All wages due to a worker who terminates his agreement or contract with his employer after he has given due notice to such employer as required under section 12 or 27 shall be paid to him on the day on which such agreement or contract is terminated.

(5) If a worker terminates his agreement or contract without giving notice to his employer as required by section 12 or by the terms of any contract or if the required notice having been given the worker terminates his agreement or contract without waiting for the expiry of such notice, all wages due shall be paid to him before the expiry of the tenth day after the day on which he terminates his agreement or contract:

Provided that the employer may, subject to any order made by a court or the Commissioner to the contrary, deduct from the wages due to the worker such sum as the worker is liable to pay in lieu of notice according to the provisions of section 13 or the terms of his contract, if any.

PAYMENT THROUGH OVERSEER OR IN SHOPS ETC. PROHIBITED.

109. (1) No wages shall be paid to any worker —

(a) through the agency of any overseer; or

(b) at or within any shop or store; or

(c) at any place or premises where intoxicating liquors are sold, except with the prior approval of the Commissioner.

(2) The payment of wages where made in cash shall be made on a working day only and at or near the work place, except as may be otherwise prescribed or provided for by collective agreement, arbitration award or where other arrangements known to the workers concerned are considered more appropriate.

WAGES TO BE PAID IN LEGAL TENDER.

110. Except where otherwise expressly prescribed the entire amount of the wages earned by, or payable to, any worker in respect of any work done by him shall be actually paid to him in legal tender and every payment of, or on account of, and such wages made in any other form shall be illegal, null and void.

AGREEMENTS AND CONTRACTS TO PAY WAGES OTHERWISE THAN IN LEGAL TENDER ILLEGAL.

111. In all agreements and contracts for the employment of any worker or for the performance by any worker of any work, the wages of such worker shall be made payable in legal tender and not otherwise and in any agreement or contract the whole or any part of such wages shall be made payable in any other manner such agreement or contract shall be illegal, null and void.

STIPULATION AS TO PLACE AND MANNER OF SPENDING WAGES ILLEGAL.

112. No employer shall impose in any agreement or contract for the employment of any worker any terms as to the place at which, or the manner in which, or the person with whom, any wages paid to the worker are to be expended and every agreement or contract between an employer and a worker containing such terms shall be illegal, null and void.

DEDUCTIONS AND WORKERS' RIGHT TO RECOVER WAGES.

113. (1) No deductions shall be made by an employer from the wages of a worker otherwise than in accordance with the provisions of this Act or of any other written law.

(2) The following deductions may be made from the wages of a worker —

(a) deductions made at the request in writing of the worker in respect of the payment to any superannuation scheme lawfully established for the benefit of the worker and approved by the Commissioner;

(b) deductions made at the request in writing of the worker for the purpose of remittance by the employer to a specified member of the family of the worker;

(c) deductions of any overpayment made during the immediately preceding 3 months by the employer to the worker by the employer's mistake;

(d) deductions for the recovery of advances made in accordance with the provisions of subsection (4) of section 102 and for the cost of maintenance in hospital of the workers or any dependant incurred pursuant to the provisions of subsection (3) of section 65;

(e) deductions for goods and services (including dwelling-houses) provided for the benefit of and with the consent of, the worker and approved by the Commissioner; and

(f) with the consent of the worker and subject to the approval of the Commissioner deductions for damage to or loss of goods entrusted to a worker for custody if such damage or loss is directly attributable to his neglect or default.

(3) The total of any deductions made under this section from the wages of a worker in respect of any one month shall not exceed 50% of the wages earned by the worker during that period.

(4) Every worker shall be entitled to recover in the courts of Brunei Darussalam so much of his wages exclusive of sums lawfully deducted in accordance with the provisions of this Act or any rules made thereunder as shall not have been actually paid to him in legal tender.

INTEREST ON ADVANCES FORBIDDEN.

114. No employer shall make any deduction by way of discount, interest or any similar charge on account of any advance of wages made to any worker.

DEDUCTIONS FOR FINES ETC.

115. Except where otherwise expressly permitted by the provisions of this Act or any rule made thereunder no employer shall make any deduction or make any agreement or contract with a worker for any deduction from wages to be paid by the employer to the worker or for any payment to the employer by the worker for or in respect of any fine, or of bad or negligent work or of injury to the materials or other property of the employer.

REMUNERATION OTHER THAN WAGES.

116. Nothing in this Chapter or in any rule made thereunder shall render illegal an agreement or contract with a worker for giving to him food, a dwelling place or other allowances or privileges in addition to money wages as a remuneration for his services but so that no employer shall give to a worker any intoxicating liquor by way of such remuneration:

Provided that such legal allowances are with the consent of the worker and approved by the Commissioner, both as to suitability for the personal use and benefit of the worker and his family and the monetary value attributed to such allowances.

EMPLOYER'S SHOP.

117. (1) Nothing in this Chapter or in any rule made thereunder shall prevent an employer with the approval in writing of the Commissioner, which may at any time be revoked, from establishing a shop for the sale of rice and provisions generally to his workers at prices to be approved by the Commissioner and marked or exhibited in such manner as he may require but such employer shall not compel any worker to purchase rice or such provisions at such shop.

(2) No employer shall trade with any worker or establish or keep a shop on any place of employment otherwise than in accordance with the preceding subsection.

(3) No person employed on any place of employment as an assistant or overseer shall traffic with any worker employed under or together with him or shall such person be either directly or indirectly financially concerned in the management of any shop wheresoever it be situated which is used or maintained for the purpose of supplying commodities of any kind whatsoever to those employed under or together with such person:

Provided that nothing in this subsection shall prevent the establishment, under the law for the time being in force relating to societies or co-operative societies, of any co-operative society.

EMPLOYMENT OF IMMIGRANT WORKERS.

118. (1) No person shall knowingly employ any immigrant worker unless he has obtained a licence from the Commissioner to do so in such form and subject to such conditions as may be prescribed unless such worker has been brought before the Commissioner for the purpose of subsection (2) of section 50:

Provided that where an immigrant worker is found at any premises or place and is in possession of any tools or other implements or is engaged in any activity which may give rise to the inference that he is doing any work, the occupier of such premises or place shall, until the contrary is proved, be presumed to have employed him knowing that he is an immigrant worker.

(2) In subsection (1), "occupier", in relation to any premises or place, includes —

(a) the person having the charge, management or control of either the whole or part of the premises or place, either on his own account or as an agent; and

(b) a contractor who is carrying out building operations or construction works at the premises or place on behalf of some other person.

[S 25/90]

(3) Any employer who contravenes the provisions of subsection (1) and any immigrant worker found working for such an employer shall each be guilty of an offence: Penalty, a fine of $10,000 and imprisonment for a term of not less than 6 months and not more than 3 years.

(4) In subsection (3), "employer" includes a person who has entered into an engagement for money or money's worth for another person to work where —

(a) that other person is already under an agreement or contract with an employer (as defined in section 2) and in respect of whom a licence has been contained by such employer from the Commissioner under subsection (1); or

(b) the work is at piece rates or on commission, whether or not as the result of an arrangement with an employer (as defined in section 2).

EXEMPTION OF EMPLOYER IF NOT ACTUAL OFFENDER.

119. (1) When an employer is charged with an offence against this Chapter or any rule made thereunder he shall be entitled, upon information duly laid by him, to have any other person whom he charges as the actual offender brought before the court at the time appointed for hearing the charge and if, after the commission of the offence has been proved, the employer shall prove to the satisfaction of the court that he has used due diligence to enforce the provisions of this Chapter and that the said other person has committed the offence in question without his knowledge, consent or connivance, the said other person shall be liable to be summarily convicted of such offence and in such case the employer shall be exempt from any penalty.

(2) When it appears to the Commissioner at the time of discovering an offence that the employer has used due diligence to comply with the provisions of this Chapter or any rule made thereunder and that the person who committed the offence did so without knowledge, consent or connivance of the employer, then the Commissioner may proceed against that person in the first instance without first proceeding against the employer.

PENALTIES.

120. Any employer who —

(a) requires any worker to work on any occasion or under any circumstances in which it is unlawful for him to require such worker to work; or

(b) fails to pay wages in accordance with the provisions of this Chapter; or

(c) give any remuneration for services contrary to the provisions of this Chapter, or makes any deduction from the wages of any worker or receives any payment from any worker contrary to the provisions of this Chapter; or

(d) trades with his worker or keeps a shop otherwise than in accordance with the provisions of this Chapter; or

(e) contravenes or fails to comply with any order of the Commissioner made under this Chapter, and any person employed on a place of employment who contravenes the provisions of subsection (3) of section 117 shall be guilty of an offence: Penalty, a fine of $1,500 or in default thereof imprisonment for 6 months.

CHAPTER XV RULES

Power to make rules.

121. (1) His Majesty in Council may from time to time make rules generally for carrying out the provisions of this Part.

(2) Without prejudice to the generality of the foregoing power such rules may —

(a) provide for any matter which by this Part is to be or may be prescribed;

(b) prescribe in respect of place of employment to which Chapter X has been applied —

(i) the form and siting of latrines and the arrangements to be made for disposal of night soil;

(ii) the steps to be taken for the control of malaria, including the administration of prophylactics;

(iii) the steps to be taken for the protection and adequacy of the water supply; and (iv) the requirements for inspection and management of hospitals;

(c) provide for the establishment of a fund or other method of securing the discharge of any liabilities and the expenses of repatriation of workers upon such terms and conditions and subject to such control as he deems necessary and for the administration of such a fund in conjunction with any fund established under the provisions of paragraph *(l)* of subsection (1) of section 56;

(d) prescribe the fees to be paid and by whom payable for any licences issued, attestations, endorsements or registration effected or any other acts required to be done in pursuance of the provisions of this Act or any rules made thereunder.

(3) Any rule may provide a penalty for the breach or contravention thereof not exceeding a fine of $600 or in default thereof imprisonment for a term not exceeding 3 months.

PART V PROCEDURE AND SAVINGS

Chapter XVI **Procedure**

Costs of proceedings.

122. No court fees shall be chargeable in the first instance on any proceeding commenced by a worker, or by the Commissioner on his behalf, against his employer under this Act; but in case a conviction shall be had or judgement given against the employer, the same shall be paid by the employer, together with the general costs of the proceeding.

CONVICTIONS AND PENALTIES.

123. (1) Subject to any special provisions to the contrary contained in the Act, all convictions and penalties for offences under this Act may be had and recovered before a Court of a Magistrate on complaint by any person aggrieved or by the Commissioner or any person authorised by him in that behalf.

(2) Any such Court may, notwithstanding anything contained in any written law to the contrary, impose the full punishment prescribed by this Act.

RIGHT OF HEARING.

124. The Commissioner and any officer authorised by him in writing shall have the right to appear and be heard before any Court in any proceedings under this Act instituted by him.

PUBLIC SERVANTS.

125. For the purposes of this Act and of the Penal Code (Chapter 22), the Commissioner and all officers duly appointed or authorised under this Act shall be deemed to be public servants.

PUBLIC PLACE.

126. For the purposes of sections 159 and 510 of the Penal Code (Chapter 22), every state, factory, mine or place of employment in which 10 or more workers are employed shall be deemed to be a public place.

ENACTMENT NO BAR TO CIVIL SUIT.

127. Nothing in this Act shall operate to prevent any employer or worker from enforcing their respective civil rights and remedies for any breach or non-performance of an agreement or contract by any suit in Court in any case which proceedings are not instituted or if instituted are not proceeded with to judgement and satisfaction under this Act.

ONUS OF PROOF.

128. In all proceedings under this Act the onus of proving that he is not the employer or the person whose duty it is under this Act or under any rule made thereunder to do or abstain from doing anything shall be on the person who alleges that he is not the employer or other person as the case may be.

SERVICE OF SUMMONS.

129. (1) A summons issued by the Commissioner in accordance with section 6 may be served on any person by delivering or tendering to him a copy thereof signed by the Commissioner:

Provided that —

(a) if the person to be summoned has an agent authorised to accept service of the summons on his behalf, service on such agent shall be sufficient;

(b) if the person to be summoned cannot be found and has no agent authorised to accept service of the summons on his behalf, service on any adult male member (not being a servant) of the family of the person to be summoned who is residing with him shall be sufficient.

(2) When such summons as aforesaid is addressed to a company it may be served —

(a) by leaving a copy thereof signed by the Commissioner, at the registered office, if any, of the company; or

(b) by sending such copy by post in a letter addressed to the company at its principal office, whether such office is situated within Brunei Darussalam or elsewhere; or

(c) by delivering such copy to any director, secretary or other principal officer of the company.

(3) When the serving officer delivers or tenders a copy of the summons to the person to be summoned or to any agent or other person to be summoned or to an agent or other person on his behalf, he shall require the signature of the person to whom the copy is so delivered or tendered to an acknowledgement of service endorsed on the original summons.

(4) If —

(a) such person refuses or is unable to sign the acknowledgement; or

(b) the serving officer cannot find the person to be summoned and there is no agent empowered to accept service of the summons on his behalf nor any other person on whom the service can be made,

the serving officer shall affix a copy of the summons on the outdoor of the house in which the person to be summoned ordinarily resides and then return the original to the Commissioner with a return endorsed thereon or annexed thereto stating that he has so affixed the copy and the circumstances under which he did so.

(5) The serving officer shall, in all cases in which the summons has been served under subsection (3) of this section endorse or annex, or cause to be endorsed or annexed, on or to the original summons a return stating the time when and the manner in which the summons was served.

(6) When the summons is returned under subsection (4) of this section, the Commissioner shall, if the return under that subsection has not been verified by the affidavit of the serving officer, and may if it has been so verified, examine the serving officer on affirmation touching his proceedings and may make such further enquiry in the matter as he thinks fit and shall either declare that the summons has been duly served or order such service as he thinks fit.

(7) When the Commissioner is satisfied that there is reason to believe that the person to be summoned is keeping out of the way for the purpose of avoiding service or that for any other reason cannot be served in the ordinary way, the Commissioner may order the summons to be served by affixing a copy thereof in some conspicuous place or near the office of the Commissioner and also upon some conspicuous part of the house, if any, in which the person to be summoned is known to have resided, or in such other manner as the Commissioner thinks fit.

(8) The service substituted by order of the Commissioner shall be as effectual as if it had been made personally on the person to be summoned.

(9) Whenever service is substituted by order of the Commissioner, the Commissioner shall fix such time for the appearance of the person to be summoned as the case may require.

(10) Any order or notice in writing made or issued by the Commissioner or the Health Officer in the exercise of powers conferred by this Act may be served as if the same were a summons, and the provisions of this section, other than subsection (9) of this section, shall apply to the service of any such order or notice.

APPLICATION OF FINES.

130. When under this Act any court imposes a fine the court may, if it thinks fit, direct that the whole or any part of such fine or sum when recovered by paid to the aggrieved party.

Chapter XVII **Savings**

Existing Acts not affected.

131. Nothing in this Act shall operate to relieve any employer of any duty or liability imposed upon him by the provisions of any other Act for the time being in force or to limit any powers given to any Government officer by any such Act.

EXISTING AGREEMENTS ETC. NOT AFFECTED.

132. All agreements and contracts entered into between any employer and any worker, valid and in force on the date of the commencement of this Act shall continue to be in force after such date and, subject to the express provisions contained in any such agreement or contract, the parties thereto shall be subject to and entitled to the benefit of the provisions of this Act.

EMPLOYMENT ORDER, 2009

In exercise of the power conferred by Article 83(3) of the Constitution of

Brunei Darussalam, His Majesty the Sultan and Yang Di-Pertuan hereby makes

the following Order

PART I PRELIMINARY

Citation and long title.

1. (1) This Order may be cited as the Employment Order, 2009.

(2) The long title of this Order is "An Order relating to employment and for matters connected therewith or incidental thereto".

Interpretation.

2. In this Order, unless the context otherwise require

"apprentice" means any person who has contracted to serve an employer and to learn and to be taught any business, trade, manufacture, undertaking, calling or employment in which employees are employed;

"Assistant Commissioner" means an Assistant Commissioner of Labour appointed under section 3(1);

"authorised officer" means any person appointed as such under section 5;

"basic rate of pay" means the total amount of money (including salary adjustments and increments) to which an employee is entitled under his contract of service either for working for a period of time, that is, for one hour, one day, one week, one month or for such other period as may be stated or implied in his contract of service, or for each completed piece or task of work but does not include

(a} additional payments by way of overtime payments;

{b} additional payments by way of bonus payments or annual salary supplements;

(c) any sum paid to the employee to reimburse him for special expenses incurred by him in the course of his employment; fd} productivity incentive payments; and (e/ any allowance however described;

"child" means a person who has not attained the age of 15 years; "collective agreement" means an agreement relating the regulation of the relations of employers and employees;

"commencement of this Order" means the date of commencement of the

main substantive provisions of this Order; "Commissioner" means the Commissioner of Labour appointed under section 3(1);

"confinement" means the delivery of a child; "contract of service" means, subject to section 10, any agreement, whether in writing or oral and whether express or implied, whereby one person

agrees to employ another as an employee and that other agrees to serve him as an employee, and includes a contract of apprenticeship; "contractor" means any person who contracts with a principal to supply

labour or to carry out the whole or any part of any work undertaken by the principal in the course of or for the purposes of the principal's trade or business;

"day" means a period of 24 hours beginning at midnight; "dependant" means the following members of an employee's family

(a) the wife; *(b/* the husband;

(c) the father;

(d) the mother; and

(e) any child and any adopted child, living with or dependent on him;

"Deputy Commissioner" means a Deputy Commissioner of Labour appointed under section 3(1);

"domestic worker" means any house, stable or garden worker or motor vehicle driver employed in, or in connection with the domestic services of, any private premises and not in connection with any trade, business or profession carried on by the employer in such premises;

"employee" means a person who has entered into or who works under a contract of service with an employer, and includes a workman and any public officer or employee of the Government included in a category, class or description of such officers or employees declared by the Minister, with the approval of His Majesty the Sultan and Yang Di-Pertuan, to be employees for the purposes of this Order or any Part thereof; but does not include any seaman, domestic worker or any person employed in a managerial, executive or confidential position or any person belonging to any other class of person whom the Minister, with the approval of His Majesty the Sultan and Yang Di-Pertuan, may by notification published in the *Gazette,* declare not to be employees for the purposes of this Order;

"employer" means any person who employs another person under a contract of service and includes-

fa} the Government, in respect of such categories, classes or descriptions of public officers or employees of the Government as are declared by the Minister, with the approval of His Majesty the Sultan and Yang Di-Pertuan, to be employees for the purposes of this Order;

(b) any statutory body;

(cj the duly authorised agent or manager of the employer;

(d} the person who owns or is carrying on or for the time being responsible for the management of the profession, business, trade or work in which the employee is engaged;

"gross rate of pay" means the total amount of money including allowances to which an employee is entitled under his contract of service either for working for a period of time, that is, for one hour, one day, one week, one month or for such other period as may be stated or implied in his contract of service, or for each completed piece or task of work but does not include

(a} additional payments by way of overtime payments;

(b) additional payments by way of bonus payments or annual salary supplements;

(d) productivity incentive payments; and

(e) travelling, food or housing allowances:

(c) any sum paid to the employee to reimburse him for special expenses incurred by him in the course of his employment;

Provided that in the case of employee on piece rates, the ordinary rate of pay shall be calculated by dividing the period of 14 days immediately preceding the day on which the rate of pay is required to be calculated by the number of days on which such employee actually worked during such period;

"health officer" means the Director-General of Health Services, and includes any officer to whom he has delegated the exercise or performance of any power or duty conferred or imposed on him by this Order to the extent of the power or duty so delegated;

"hours of work" means the time during which an employee is at the disposal of the employer and is not free to dispose of his own time and movements, exclusive of any intervals allowed for rest and meals;

"immigrant employee" means any employee who is normally resident outside Brunei Darussalam who has come to Brunei Darussalam for the purpose of performing work in Brunei Darussalam;

"industrial undertaking" means

(a) mines, quarries and other works for the extraction of minerals from the earth;

(b) industries in which articles are manufactured, assembled altered, cleaned, repaired, ornamented, finished, adapted for sale, broken up or demolished, or in which materials are transformed, including ship-building and the generation, transformation and transmission of electricity and motive power of any kind;

(c) the construction, reconstruction, maintenance, repair, alteration or demolition of any building, railway, tramway, harbour, dock, pier, canal, inland waterway, road, tunnel, bridge, viaduct, sewer, drain, well, telegraphic or telephonic installation, electrical undertaking, gaswork, waterworks or other work of construction, as well as the preparation for or the laying of the foundation of any such work or structure;

(d) the transport of passengers or goods by road, rail sea, air or inland waterway, including the handling of goods at docks, quays, wharves, warehouses and airports, but excluding transport by hand:

Provided that if, having regard to the nature of the work involved in any occupation which forms part of the industrial undertaking, His Majesty

the Sultan and Yang Di-Pertuan considers that such occupation should be excluded from the provisions of this Order relating to industrial undertakings, he may declare by order published in the *Gazette* that employment in such occupation shall be deemed not to be employment in an industrial undertaking for the purposes of this Order:

Provided further that any undertaking of which a part only is an industrial undertaking shall not for that reason alone be deemed to be an industrial undertaking;

"licence" means a licence granted under this Order;

"medical practitioner" means a medical practitioner registered under the Medical Practitioners and Dentists Act (Chapter 112);

"mine" includes any undertaking, whether public or private, for the extraction of any substance from under the surface of the earth;

"Minister" means the Minister of Home Affairs;

"overtime" means the number of hours worked in any one day or in any one week in excess of the limits specified in Part VII;

"place of employment" means any place where work is carried on, for or on behalf of an employer, by an employee;

"principal" means any person who, in the course of or for the purposes of his profession, business, trade or work, contracts with a contractor for the supply of labour or for execution by the contractor of the whole or any part of any work undertaken by the principal;

"public holiday" means the days specified in the Third Schedule;

"repatriation" means the return of an employee to his country of domicile or origin, and includes the return to his house of an employee who has been brought to a place of employment by an employer from any other place within Brunei Darussalam;

"salary" means all remuneration including allowances payable to an employee in respect of work done under his contract of service, but does not include

(a) the value of any accommodation or the supply of any food, fuel, electricity, water or medical attendance, or of any amenity or service excluded by order of the Minister published in the Gazette;

(b) any contribution paid by the employer on his own account to any pension fund or provident fund;

(c) any travelling allowance or the value of any travelling concession;

(dJ any sum paid to the employee to reimburse him for special expenses incurred by him in the course of his employment;

(e) any gratuity payable on discharge or retirement; and

{f) any retrenchment benefit payable on retrenchment;

"shift work" means work which by reason of its nature requires to be carried on continuously by 2 or more shifts;

"sub-contractor" means any person who contracts with a contractor for the supply of labour or for the execution by the sub-contractor of the whole or any part of any work undertaken by the contractor for his principal, and includes any person who contracts with a sub-contractor to supply labour or to carry out the whole or any part of any work undertaken by the sub-contractor for a contractor;

"sub-contractor for labour" means any person who contracts with a contractor or sub-contractor to supply the labour required for the execution of the whole or any part of any work a contractor or sub-contractor has contracted to carry out for a principal or contractor, as the case may be;

"workman" means

(aJ any person who has entered into a contract of service with an employer in pursuance of which he is engaged in manual labour, including any artisan or apprentice, but excluding any seaman or domestic worker;

(bJ any person, other than clerical staff, employed in the operation or maintenance of mechanically-propelled vehicles used for the transport of passengers for hire or for commercial purposes;

(cJ any person employed partly for manual labour and partly for the purpose of supervising in person any workman in and throughout the performance of his work:

Provided that when any person is employed by any one employer partly as a workman and partly in some other capacity or capacities, that person shall be deemed for the purposes of this Order to be a workman unless it can be established that the time during which he has been required to work as a workman in any one salary period as defined in

Part IV has on no occasion amounted to or exceeded one-half of the total time during which he has been required to work in such salary period;

{d) any other person specified in the First Schedule;

{e) any person whom the Minister may, by notification published in the *Gazette,* declare to be a workman for the purposes of this Order.

"young person" means a person who has attained the age of 15 years but who has not attained the age of 18 years.

Appointment of officers.

3. (1) His Majesty the Sultan and Yang Di-Pertuan may appoint a Commissioner of Labour and such number of Deputy Commissioners of Labour, Assistant Commissioners of Labour and other officers as may be necessary for the purpose of carrying into effect the provisions of this Order.

(2) The Commissioner shall have the general responsibility of all matters to which this Order relates.

Delegation of powers and appeals.

4. (1) The Commissioner may delegate the exercise of any power or the performance of any duty conferred or imposed on him by this Order to a Deputy Commissioner, Assistant Commissioners or to such other person as he may think fit.

(2) A delegation under subsection [1] may be made subject to such conditions as may be determined by the Commissioner in the instrument of delegation.

(3) The power of delegation under subsection (1) shall only be exercised by the Commissioner personally.

(4) If any employer is dissatisfied with any decision or order of a Deputy Commissioner or an Assistant Commissioner made or given by virtue of the provisions of subsections (1) and (2), he may appeal from such decision or order to the Commissioner within 14 days of the date of the decision or order being communicated to him.

(5) If any employer is dissatisfied with any decision or order made or given by the Commissioner under any provision of this Order or by virtue of subsection (4), he may appeal from such decision or order to the Minister within 14 days of the date of the decision or order being communicated to him, and the decision of the Minister shall be final.

5. The Minister may, with the approval of His Majesty the Sultan and Yang Di-Pertuan, appoint such number of authorised officers to carry into effect any specific provisions of this Order or of any regulations made thereunder.

Effect of Order on other written laws.

6. Nothing in this Order shall be construed

{a) to relieve any person who has entered into a contract of service, either as an employee or as the employer, of any duty or liability imposed upon him;

{b) to limit any power which may be exercised by any public officer; or

(c) to limit any right conferred upon any person referred to in paragraph {a),

under or by virtue of any other written law.

PART II CONTRACTS OF SERVICE

Certain contracts excluded.

7. This Part does not apply to contracts of apprenticeship.

Minister may prohibit employment other than under contract of service.

8. (1) The Minister may, by order published in the *Gazette,* prohibit the employment or contracting of any person or class of person to carry out work in any occupation in any agricultural or industrial undertaking, constructional work, statutory body, the Government or any other trade, business or place of work, unless under a contract of service entered into with

(a) the principal or owner of that agricultural or industrial undertaking, constructional work, trade, business or place of work; or

(b) the statutory body or the Government.

(2) Upon the commencement of any such order, the person or class of person employed or contracted to carry out any such work shall be deemed to be an employee or employees and

{a} the principal or owner of that agricultural or industrial undertaking, constructional work, trade, business or place of work; or

{b) the statutory body or the Government,

shall be deemed to be the employer for the purposes of such provisions of this Order and of any other written law as may be specified in such order.

(3) Notwithstanding subsection (1], Minister may, by order published in the *Gazette,* approve the employment of any person or class of person by such other person or class of person (not being the principal or owner) as he may specify, subject to such conditions as he may impose.

(4) Any person who contravenes any order made under this section is guilty of an offence.

Contractual age.

9. (1) A person who has not attained the age of 16 years shall not be capable of entering into a contract of service.

(2) Notwithstanding anything contained in any other written law, a person who has attained the age of 16 years but who has not attained the age of 18 years shall be capable of entering into a contract of service in an occupation approved by the Commissioner as not being injurious to the moral and physical development of youths.

Contract of service to be in writing and to include provision for termination.

10. (1) A contract of service for

(a) a specified period of time exceeding one month; or

{b) the performance of a specified piece of work, where the time reasonably required for the completion of the work exceeds or may exceed one month,

shall be in writing and signed by both parties:

Provided that an employee unable to sign may indicate his consent by affixing his thumbprint thereto.

(2) Every contract of service shall set out the manner in which the contract of service may be terminated by either party in accordance with this Part.

Contents of contract of service.

11. Every contract of service shall clearly define the rights and obligations of the parties thereto, and without prejudice to the generality thereof shall include the following particulars

(a) the name of the employer or group of employers and, where practicable, the undertaking and place of employment;

(b) the name and place of origin of the employee, his place of engagement and any other particulars necessary for his identification;

(c) where possible, the names and addresses of the next of kin of the employee;

(d) the nature of employment;

(e) the duration of employment and the method of calculation thereof;

(f) the appropriate period of notice to be given by the party wishing to terminate the contract of service, due regard being had to sections 24, 25 and 26 and to the fact that such provisions refer to an equitable settlement of monetary and other questions;

(g) the rates of salary and the method of calculation thereof, the manner and times of payment of salary, the advances of salary, if any, and the manner of repayment of any such advances;

(h) the measures to be taken to provide for the welfare of the employee and any dependant who may accompany him under the terms of the contract of service;

(i) the conditions of repatriation, if the employee is not a citizen of Brunei Darussalam; and

(j) any special conditions of the contract of service.

Illegal terms of contract of service.

12. Every term of a contract of service, whether made before or after the commencement of this Order, which provides a condition of service which is less favourable to an employee than any of the conditions of service prescribed by this Order shall be illegal and not valid to the extent that it is so less favourable.

Contract of service not ordinarily binding on dependants.

13. No contract of service shall be binding on the dependants of an employee, unless it contains an express provision to that effect.

Maximum duration of contracts of service.

14. (1) The duration which may be stipulated or implied in any contract of service involving a journey from the place of recruitment to the place of employment shall not exceed 2 years if the employee is not accompanied by his dependants, or shall not exceed 3 years if the employee is accompanied by his dependants.

(2) The Commissioner may, after consultation with any employers' and employees' organisations and representatives of the interests concerned, exempt from the application of this section

contracts of service entered into between employers and literate employees whose freedom of choice in employment is in the opinion of the Commissioner satisfactorily safeguarded.

[3] The exemption under subsection (2) may apply generally, or to employees in any specified industry or undertaking or to special groups of employees.

Forms of contract of service.

15. (1) The Commissioner may approve a standard form of contract of service to be used by any person.

(2) Every employer shall furnish the Commissioner with a quarterly report of all persons newly-employed during each quarter under the approved form of contract of service, together with a certificate to indicate that the conditions thereof were read over to and understood by the employee before he signed it.

Medical examinations.

16. [1] Every employee who enters into a contract of service shall be medically examined by a medical practitioner at the expense of the employer.

Termination by Commissioner of contract of service.

17. A contract of service may be terminated by the Commissioner if the employee has been mistreated in person or property, and in such event the Commissioner may order the employer to award the employee reasonable compensation for such mistreatment.

Termination by employee threatened by danger.

18. An employee may terminate his contract of service with his employer without notice where he or his dependant is immediately threatened by danger to the person by violence or disease such as the employee did not by his contract of service undertake to run.

When contract of service deemed to be breached by employer and employee.

19. (1) An employer shall be deemed to be in breach of his contract of service with the employee if he fails to pay his salary in accordance with this Order.

[2] An employee shall be deemed to be in breach of his contract of service with the employer if he has been continuously absent from work for more than 2 days

(a) without prior leave from his employer or without reasonable excuse; or

(b) without informing or attempting to inform his employer of the reason for the absence.

Liability on breach of contract of service.

20. Subject to any provision in the contract of service to the contrary for the payment of a greater sum, the party who is in breach of the contract of service shall be liable to pay to the other party a

For additional analytical, business and investment opportunities information,
please contact Global Investment & Business Center, USA
at (703) 370-8082. Fax: (703) 370-8083. E-mail: ibpusa3@gmail.com
Global Business and Investment Info Databank - www.ibpus.com

sum equal to the amount he would have been liable to pay under section 23 had he terminated the contract of service without notice or with insufficient notice.

Termination of contract of service.

21. (1) A contract of service for a specified period of time or for the performance of a specified piece of work shall, unless otherwise terminated in accordance with this Part, terminate when the period of time for which such contract of service was made has expired or when the piece of work specified in such contract of service has been completed.

(2) A contract of service for an unspecified period of time shall continue in force until terminated in accordance with this Part.

Notice of termination of contract of service.

22. (1) Either party to a contract of service may at any time give to the other party notice of his intention to terminate the contract of service.

(2) The length of such notice shall be determined by the contract of service or, in the absence of any provision, in accordance with subsection (3).

(3) Subject to subsection (2), the notice to terminate a contract of service shall be not less than

(a) one day's notice, if the employee has been employed for less than 26 weeks;

(b) one week's notice, if the employee has been employed for at least 26 weeks but less than 2 years;

(c) 2 week's notice, if the employee has been employed for at least 2 years but less than 5 years;

(d) 4 week's notice, if the employee has been employed for at least 5 years.

(4) This section does not prevent either party from waiving his right to notice on any occasion.

(5) The notice to terminate shall be in writing and may be given at any time, and the day on which the notice is given shall be included in calculating the period of the notice.

Termination of contract of service without notice.

23. (1) Either party to a contract of service may terminate the contract of service without notice or, if notice has already been given in accordance with section 22, without waiting for the expiry of that notice, by paying to the other party a sum equal to the amount of salary at the gross rate of pay which would have accrued to the employee during the period of the notice and in the case of a monthly-rated employee where the period of the notice is less than a month, the amount payable for any one day shall be the gross rate of pay for one day's work.

(2) Either party to a contract of service may terminate the contract of service without notice in the event of any wilful breach by the other party of a condition of the contract of service.

Transfer to other employment.

24. (1) The transfer of any contract of service from one employer to another shall be subject to the consent of the employee and the endorsement of the transfer on the contract of service by the Commissioner.

(2) Before endorsing the contract of service, the Commissioner

{a} shall ascertain that the employee has consented to the transfer, and that his consent has not been obtained by coercion, undue influence or as the result of misrepresentation or mistake; and

{b} may require the employee to be medically examined or re

examined, as the case may be, by a medical practitioner in any case in which by such transfer the employee

(i) will change his form of employment; or

(ii) will be subject to such change in conditions of his employment as in the opinion of the Commissioner renders the examination advisable.

Change of employer.

25. (1) If by or under any written law, whether enacted before or after the commencement of this Order, a contract of employment between any body corporate and an employee is modified and some other body corporate is substituted as the employer, the employee's period of employment at the time when the modification takes effect shall count as a period of employment with such other body corporate and the change of employer shall not break the continuity of the period of employment.

(2) If on the death of an employer the employee is taken into the employment of the personal representatives or trustees of the deceased, the employee's period of employment at the time of the death shall count as a period of employment with the employer's personal representatives or trustees, and the death of the employer shall not break the continuity of the period of employment.

(3) If there is a change in the partners, personal representatives or trustees who employ any person, the employee's period of employment at the time of the change shall count as a period of employment with the partners, personal

representatives or trustees after the change, and the change shall not break the continuity of the period of employment.

Misconduct of employee.

26. (1) An employer may after due inquiry dismiss without notice an employee employed by him on the grounds of misconduct inconsistent with the fulfilment of the express or implied conditions of his service except that instead of dismissing an employee an employer may

(a} instantly down-grade the employee; or

(b} instantly suspend him from work without payment of salary for a period not exceeding one week.

(2) Notwithstanding subsection (1), where an employee considers that he has been dismissed without just cause or excuse by his employer, he may, within one month of the dismissal, make representations in writing to the Minister to be reinstated in his former employment.

(3) The Minister may, before making a decision on any such representations, by writing under his hand request the Commissioner to inquire into the dismissal and report whether in his opinion the dismissal is without just cause or excuse.

(4) If, after considering the report made by the Commissioner under subsection (3), the Minister is satisfied that the employee has been dismissed without just cause or excuse, he may, notwithstanding any rule of law or agreement to the contrary

(a} direct the employer to reinstate the employee in his former employment and to pay the employee an amount that is equivalent to the salaries that the employee would have earned had he not been dismissed by the employer; or

(b} direct the employer to pay such amount of salaries as compensation as may be determined by the Minister,

and the employer shall comply with the direction of the Minister.

(5) The decision of the Minister on any representation made under this section shall be final and shall not be challenged in any court.

(6) Any direction of the Minister under subsection (4) shall operate as a bar to any action for damages by the employee in any court in respect of the wrongful dismissaL

(8) Where any amount to be paid by an employer under subsection {4} is not paid in accordance with the direction of the Minister and the employer has been convicted of an offence under subsection 17). the amount or so much thereof as remains unpaid shall be recoverable by the court as if it were a fine and the amount so recoverable shall be paid to the employee entitled to payment under the direction of the Minister.

(9) For the purpose of an inquiry under subsection (1), the employer may suspend the employee from work for a period not exceeding one week but shall pay him not less than one-half of his salary for such period.

(10) If the inquiry does not disclose any misconduct on the part of the employee, the employer shall forthwith restore to the employee the full amount of the salary so withheld.

Offences.

27. Any employer who

(a} fails to comply with any order or requirement made by the Commissioner in pursuance of the provisions of this Part; or

For additional analytical, business and investment opportunities information,
please contact Global Investment & Business Center, USA
at (703) 370-8082. Fax: (703) 370-8083. E-mail: ibpusa3@gmail.com
Global Business and Investment Info Databank - www.ibpus.com

(b) enters into a contract of service contrary to any provision of this Part,

is guilty of an offence and liable on conviction to a fine not exceeding $3,000, imprisonment for a term not exceeding one year or both.

PART III CONTRACTS OF APPRENTICESHIP

Contracts of apprenticeship of persons under age 16.

28. (1) The parent or guardian of a person who has not attained the age of 16 years may, with his consent, enter into a written contract of apprenticeship, apprenticing him to an employer to train him or to have him trained systematically for an agreed trade or employment for a period not exceeding 5 years.

(2) Whenever any person who has not attained the age of 16 years is without a known parent or guardian, the Commissioner may authorise his apprenticeship, and may appoint any fit and proper person to sign the contract of apprenticeship and act generally as his guardian.

Contracts of apprenticeship of persons age 16 and above.

29. Any person who has attained the age of 16 years and any person who is above the age of 18 years, not being under any contract of apprenticeship, may apprentice himself to an employer in any agreed trade or employment for a period not exceeding 5 years.

Assignment.

30. Every contract of apprenticeship may, with the consent of the parties thereto, be assigned.

Attestation.

31. Every contract of apprenticeship and any assignment thereof shall be in writing and no such contract shall be valid unless made with the approval of and attested by the Commissioner in writing on the contract of apprenticeship or assignment (as the case may be).

Duties of Commissioner as attesting officer.

32. Before attesting any contract of apprenticeship, the Commissioner shall satisfy himself

(a) that the employer is a fit, able and proper person and has facilities sufficient to instruct the apprentice in the agreed trade or employment;

(b) that the apprentice has consented to such contract and that his consent has not been obtained by coercion, undue influence or as the result of misrepresentation or mistake;

(c) that the apprentice has been medically examined and certified by

a medical practitioner to be physically and mentally fit to be employed and

trained in the agreed trade or employment;

{d) that the parties to such contract have fully understood the terms of the contract before signing it, or otherwise indicating assent;

{e) that provision has been made in such contract as to how any remuneration in cash or otherwise due to the apprentice shall be

(f) that provision has been made in such contract for payment of such remuneration to the apprentice during illness and during holidays;

(g} that the terms of such contract are in accordance with the provisions of this Part.

Certificate of service on discharge.

33. (1) Whenever for any reason, including the completion of his contract of apprenticeship, an apprentice ceases to be employed by the employer, the employer shall supply the apprentice with a statement, in such form as the Commissioner may determine, setting forth the service of the apprentice.

(2) The employer shall forward a copy of such statement to the Commissioner, who shall endorse a note of the service on the contract of apprenticeship.

Retention of apprentices after expiry of contracts.

34. If any person to whom an apprentice has been apprenticed retains him in his service after the agreed period of apprenticeship has expired without any arrangement between them for the payment of salary, the apprentice shall be entitled to recover from him salary at the current rate payable for services similar to that performed by such apprentice.

Suspension and discharge.

35. (1) In any case where an apprentice so misconducts himself or proves himself to be so incapable that, if he were an employee other than an apprentice, it would have been reasonable for his employer to discharge him, the employer may suspend the apprentice and apply to the Commissioner for leave to discharge him.

(2) The Commissioner shall enquire into the circumstances and where he grants such leave the employer shall be entitled to discharge the apprentice as from the date on which he was suspended and as from such date the contract of apprenticeship shall be deemed to be terminated.

(3) Where such leave is refused, the Commissioner may make such order as he thinks fit with respect to payment to be made to the apprentice in respect of the period of his suspension.

(4) If no such order is made, the employer shall pay to the apprentice all the salary that would have been payable to him in respect of such period as if he had not been suspended.

(5) If the employer, notwithstanding that leave to discharge the apprentice has been refused by the Commissioner, discharges the apprentice, such discharge shall for all purposes be deemed to be a breach by the employer of the contract of apprenticeship.

(6) Where an employer

{a) without proceeding in accordance with subsections (1), (2), (3), (4) and (5), discharges or purports to discharge an apprentice; or

(b) having suspended him, does not within 3 days thereafter make application under subsection (1) for leave to discharge him,

the apprentice may, within 7 days after such discharge or purported discharge or within 10 days after such suspension (as the case may be) apply to the Commissioner for relief from such discharge, purported discharge or suspension and thereupon the provisions of this section shall apply in like manner as if the employer had proceeded in accordance with subsection (1).

(7) The Commissioner may fix an amount that shall be payable to the apprentice as damages for breach or deemed breach of the contract of apprenticeship if the employer discharges him contrary to the provisions of this section, and such amount shall be in addition to the amount of salary payable in respect of the period of suspension.

Offences.

36. Any employer who

{a) fails to comply with any order made by the Commissioner under this Part; or

(b) enters into a contract of apprenticeship contrary to the provisions of this Part,

is guilty of an offence and liable on conviction to a fine not exceeding $1,500, imprisonment for a term not exceeding 6 months or both.

PART IV PAYMENT OF SALARIES

Fixation of salary period.

37. Ill An employer may fix periods, which for the purpose of this Order shall be called salary periods, in respect of which salary earned shall be payable.

(2) No salary period shall exceed one month.

(3) In the absence of a salary period so fixed, the salary period shall be deemed to be one month.

Computation of salary for incomplete month's work.

38. (1) If a monthly-rated employee has not completed a whole month of service because

(a} he commenced employment after the first day of the month;

(b) his employment was terminated before the end of the month; or

(c) he took leave of absence without pay for one or more days of the month,

the salary due to him for that month shall be calculated in accordance with the

following formula-

Monthly gross rate of pay Number of days on which the the employee is required to	X	Number of days the employee actually worked in that month.

work in that month

(2) In calculating the number of days actually worked by an employee in a month under subsection (1), any day on which an employee is required to work for 5 hours or less under his contract of service shall be regarded as half a day.

Time of payment.

39. (1) Salary earned by an employee under a contract of service, other than additional payments for overtime work, shall be paid before the expiry of the 7th. day after the last day of the salary period in respect of which the salary is payable.

!2) Additional payments for overtime work shall be paid not later than 14 days after the last day of the salary period during which the overtime work was performed.

(3) The total salary due to an employee on completion of his contract of service shall be paid to him on completion of the contract.

Payment on termination by employee.

40. (1) Subject to the provisions of this Order, the total salary due to an employee who terminates his contract of service with his employer under section 26, or after giving prior notice to the employer as required under section 22, shall be paid to him on the day on which the contract of service is terminated.

(2) Subject to the provisions of this Order, the total salary due to an employee who

{a) terminates his contract of service without giving prior notice to his employer as required under section 22; or

{b) has already given prior notice under section 22, but the employee terminates his contract of service without waiting for the expiry of the notice,

shall be paid to him not later than 7 days after the day on which the contract of service is terminated.

(3) The employer may, subject to any order made by a court or the Commissioner to the contrary, deduct from the salary due to the employee such sum as the employee is liable to pay in lieu of prior notice under section 23(1).

Payment on dismissal or termination by employer.

For additional analytical, business and investment opportunities information,
please contact Global Investment & Business Center, USA
at (703) 370-8082. Fax: (703) 370-8083. E-mail: ibpusa3@gmail.com
Global Business and Investment Info Databank - www.ibpus.com

41. Subject to the provisions of this Order, the salary and any other sum due to an employee who has been dismissed or whose contract of service has been terminated by his employer shall be paid on the day of dismissal or termination, as the case may be, or, if this is not possible, within 3 days thereafter, not including rest days and public holidays.

Payment to be made during working hours.

42. (1) Payment of salary shall be made on a working day and during working hours at the place of work or at any other place agreed to between the employer and the employee.

Salaries not due for absence from work through imprisonment etc.

43. Salary shall not be payable to or recoverable by an employee from his employer in respect of {a) the term of any sentence of imprisonment undergone by him; {b) any period spent by him in lawful custody; {c) any period spent by him in going to or returning from prison or any other place of lawful custody;

{d) any period spent by him in going to, attending before or returning from, a court, otherwise than as a witness on his employer's behalf.

No unauthorised deductions to be made.

44. No deductions other than deductions authorised under the provisions of this Order shall be made by an employer from the salary of an employee unless they are required to be made by order of a court or other authority competent to make such order.

Authorised deductions.

45. (1) The following deductions may be made from the salary of an employee

{a) deductions for absence from work;

(b) deductions for damage to or loss of goods expressly entrusted to an employee for custody or for loss of money for which an employee is required to account, where the damage or loss is directly attributable to his neglect or default;

{c) deductions for the actual cost of meals supplied by the employer at the request of the employee;

(d) deductions for house accommodation supplied by the employer;

(e) deductions for such amenities and services supplied by the employer as the Commissioner may authorise;

(f) deductions for recovery of advances or loans or for adjustment of over-payments of salary;

(g) deductions for income tax payable by the employee;

(h) deductions of contributions payable by an employer on behalf of an employee under and in accordance with the provisions of the Tabung Amanah Pekerja Act (Chapter 167);

(i) deductions made at the request of the employee for the purpose of a superannuation scheme or provident fund or any other scheme which is lawfully established for the benefit of the employee and is approved by the Commissioner;

(j) deductions made with the written consent of the employee and paid by the employer to any co-operative society registered under any written law in respect of subscriptions, entrance fees, instalments of loans, interest and other dues payable by the employee to such society; and

(k) any other deductions which may be approved by the Minister.

(2) For the purposes of subsection *(l)(e)*, "services" does not include the supply of tools and raw materials required for the purposes of employment.

Deductions for absence.

46. (1) Deductions may be made under section *45(1)(a)* only on account of the absence of an employee from the place where, by the terms of his employment, he is required to work, the absence being for the whole or any part of the period during which he is so required to work.

(2) The amount of any deduction referred to in subsection (ll shall in no case bear to the salary payable at the gross rate of pay to the employee in respect of the salary period for which the deduction is made a larger proportion than the period for which he was absent bears to the total period, within such salary period, during which he was required to work by the terms of his employment, and in the case of a monthly-rated employee the amount of deduction in respect of any one day shall be the gross rate of pay for one day's work.

(3) Ifany employee absents himself from work otherwise than as provided by this Order or by his contract of service, the employer may, subject to any order which may be made by a court or by the Commissioner on complaint of either

Deductions for damages or loss.

47. (1) A deduction under section 45(l)(b} shall not exceed the amount of the damage or loss caused to the employer by the neglect or default of the employee and, except with the approval of the Commissioner, shall in no case exceed onequarter of one month's salary and shall not be made until the employee has been given an opportunity of showing cause against the deduction.

(2) All such deductions and all realisations thereof shall be recorded in a register to be kept by the employer in such form as the Commissioner may determine.

Deductions for accommodation, amenity and service.

48. A deduction under sections 45(1)(d) or *(e)* shall not be made from the salary of an employee unless the house accommodation, amenity or service has been accepted by him, as a term of employment or otherwise, and the deduction shall not exceed an amount equivalent to the value of the house accommodation, amenity or service supplied and, in the case of a deduction under section 45(1)(e}, shall be subject to such conditions as the Commissioner may impose.

Recovery of advances and loans.

49. (1) The recovery of an advance of money made to an employee before the commencement of a contract of service shall begin from the first payment of salary in respect of a completed salary period, but no recovery shall be made of any such advance made for travelling expenses.

(2) Advances may be recovered in instalments by deductions from salary spread over not more than 12 months.

(3) No instalment under subsection (2) shall exceed one-quarter of the salary due for the salary period in respect of which the deduction is made.

(4) Loans may be recovered in instalments by deductions from salary.

(5) No instalment under subsection (4) shall exceed one-quarter of the salary due for the salary period in respect of which the deduction is made.

Deductions not to exceed 50 per cent of salary.

50. (1) The total amount of all deductions made from the salary of an employee by an employer in any one salary period, other than deductions under sections 45(1){a}, {(}, {g} or {j}, shall not exceed 50 per cent of the salary payable to the employee in respect of that period.

(2) Subsection (1) shall not apply to deductions made from the last salary due to an employee on termination of his contract of service or on completion of his contract of service.

Priority of salary **to other debts.**

51. (1) This section shall apply to all workmen and to other employees who are in receipt of a salary not exceeding $1,600 a month (excluding overtime payments, bonus payments, annual salary supplements, productivity incentive payments and any allowance however described) or such other amount as may be prescribed by the Minister.

(2) When, on the application of a person holding a mortgage, charge or lien or of a person who has obtained a judgment or decree, the property of an employer is sold, or any money due to the employer is garnished, the court ordering the sale or garnishment shall not distribute the proceeds of the sale or the money to the person entitled thereto unless the court has ascertained and paid the salary due to all the employees employed by that employer and to all employees engaged by a contractor or sub-contractor and working for that employer.

(3 J This section shall only apply

{a} to property on which those employees were or are working;

{b} where the property sold was or is the produce of the work of those employees;

{c} where the property sold is movable property used or being used by those employees in the course of their work; or

{d) to money due to the employer in respect of work done by those employees.

j4) The amount payable to each such employee under subsection [2] shall not exceed 5 months' salary.

[5] For the purpose of ascertaining the amount due to any employee under subsection (2), the court may refer the matter to the Commissioner with a request that he holds an inquiry into the matter and forwards his findings in respect thereof to the court, and the Commissioner shall thereupon comply with any such request.

(6) For the purposes of any inquiry under subsection (5), the Commissioner shall have all the powers conferred upon him by section 124.

(7) For the purposes of this section, "employees" includes sub-contractors for labour and "salary" includes money due to a sub-contractor for labour.

Offence.

52. Any employer who fails to pay the salary of an employee in accordance with the provisions of this Part is guilty of an offence.

PART V PRINCIPALS AND CONTRACTORS

Liability of principals and contractors for salary.

53. (1) Where a principal in the course of his trade or business

(a) contracts with a contractor for

(i) the supply of labour; or

(ii) the execution by or under the contractor, of the whole or any part of any work undertaken by the principal; and

(b) any salary is due to any workman by the contractor or any subcontractor under the contractor, for labour supplied or for work done in the course of the execution of such work,

the principal, the contractor and any such sub-contractor, not being the employer, shall be jointly and severally liable with the employer to pay the workman as if the workman had been immediately employed by him.

(2) Where salary is claimed from the principal, this Order, with the exception of section 51, shall apply as if a reference to the principal were substituted for the reference to the employer, except that salary claimed shall be calculated with reference to the salary of the workman under the employer by whom he was immediately employed.

(3) No principal, contractor or sub-contractor, not being the employer, shall be jointly and severally liable to any workman under subsections (1) or (2) for more than the salary earned in one month for the work done by the employer.

(4) In the case of a contract of service for constructional work, the principal shall not be liable for the payment of salary under subsections (1) or (2) unless he is also a constructional contractor.

(5) The workman shall institute proceedings for the recovery of his salary within 60 days or such longer period as the Commissioner may allow from the date on which the salary became due for payment in accordance with the provisions for the payment of salary in Part IV.

(6) A claim for salary under this section shall be made in the manner provided for in Part XVI.

(7) Nothing in this section shall prevent any principal, contractor or subcontractor, not being the employer, who, as the result of a claim made under this section, has paid any salary to a workman from instituting civil proceedings for the recovery of the amount of that salary so paid from the employer of that workman.

(8) Nothing in this section shall be construed so as to prevent a workman from recovering salary under this Order from his employer instead of the principal, contractor or sub-contractor.

(9) The reference to principal in this section shall include the Government and a statutory body.

Registration of contractors and sub-contractors.

54. (1) The Minister may, by notification published in the *Gazette,* require all contractors and sub-contractors to be registered with the Commissioner and thereafter no person shall act as a contractor or a sub-contractor unless he is so registered.

(2) Every application for such registration shall be in such form as the Commissioner may determine.

(3) Every person so registered under this section as a contractor or subcontractor shall be deemed to be the employer of the workmen employed by him.

(4) Every contractor or sub-contractor who has been so registered and who changes the name under which he carries on business shall, within 7 days of the change of name, apply in writing to the Commissioner for re-registration and cancellation of the previous registration.

(5) The Commissioner may effect the registration of any person under this section and may cancel any such registration.

(6) The Minister may, with the approval of His Majesty the Sultan and Yang Di-Pertuan, make regulations to prescribe the requirements and conditions for registration of a contractor or sub-contractor under this section.

(7) Any person who contravenes this section is guilty of an offence.

PART VI TRUCK SYSTEM

Agreements to pay salary otherwise than in legal tender illegal.

55. The salary of an employee shall be payable in legal tender and not otherwise and if in any contract of service the whole or any part of the salary is made payable in any other manner the contract of service shall be illegal and invalid.

Agreements as to place and manner etc. of spending salary illegal.

56. No contract of service shall contain any terms as to the place at which, or the manner in which, or the person with whom, any salary paid to the employee is to be expended and every contract of service containing such terms shall be illegal and invalid.

Salary to be paid entirely in legal tender.

57. Except where otherwise expressly permitted by the prov1s10ns of this Order, the entire amount of the salary earned by, or payable to, any employee in respect of any work done by him shall be actually paid to him in legal tender, and every payment of, or on account of, any such salary made in any other form shall be illegal and invalid.

Recovery of salary not paid in legal tender.

58. Every employee shall be entitled to recover in any court or before the Commissioner, acting under section 124, so much of his salary exclusive of sums lawfully deducted in accordance with the provisions of this Order as has not been actually paid to him in legal tender.

Payment of salary through bank.

59. (1) Nothing in sections 55 or 57 shall render illegal any payment of salary by an employer to an employee in accordance with the employee's written approval in either of the following ways

{a) payment into an account at a bank in Brunei Darussalam holding a licence granted under the Banking Order, 2006 (S 45/06), a licence being an account in the name of the employee or an account in the name of the employee jointly with one or more other persons;

{b) payment by cheque made payable to or to the order of the employee.

(2) Where the salary or part thereof has been paid in either of the ways set out in subsection (1), section 58 shall not operate to give a right of recovery of so much of the salary as have been so paid.

(3) The employee may at any time withdraw his approval under subsection (1) by notice in writing given to the employer.

(4) Such notice shall take effect 14 days from the date on which it was served on the employer.

(5) The approval of the employee to the mode of payment of his salary under subsection (1) shall not be unreasonably withheld, or if granted and notwithstanding subsection (3) shall not be unreasonably withdrawn, by the employee.

(6) Any dispute as to whether an employee has unreasonably withheld or withdrawn his approval to the mode of payment of his salary under subsection (1) shall be referred to the Commissioner, whose decision shall be final.

Remuneration other than salary.

60. Nothing in this Part shall render illegal a contract of service with an employee for giving to him food, accommodation and other privileges in addition to money as remuneration for his services,

but no employer shall to a workman any noxious drugs or intoxicating liquor by way of remuneration.

Shops and canteens.

61. (1) Nothing in this Part shall prevent the employer from establishing *or* permitting to be established a shop *or* a canteen for the sale of foodstuffs, provisions, meals or refreshments; but no workman shall be compelled by any

(2) No employer shall establish or keep or permit to be established or kept, a shop or canteen on any place of employment for the sale of foodstuffs, provisions, meals or refreshments to his workmen otherwise than in accordance with subsection (1 J.

Offences.

62. Any employer who

{a} enters into any contract of service or gives any remuneration for services which is contrary to the provisions of this Part or is declared by this Part to be illegal; or

{b} receives any payment from any employee contrary to the provisions of this Part or who contravenes section 61{2},

is guilty of an offence and liable on conviction to a fine not exceeding $1,000, and for a second or subsequent offence to a fine not exceeding $2,000, imprisonment for a term not exceeding one year or both.

PART VII REST DAYS, HOURS OF WORK, HOLIDAYS AND OTHER CONDITIONS OF SERVICE

Rest days.

63. {1) Every employee shall be allowed, in each week, a rest day of one whole day which shall be Sunday or such other day as the employer may determine.

(2! The employer may substitute any continuous period of 30 hours as a rest day for an employee engaged in shift work.

(3) Where in any week a continuous period of 30 hours commencing at any time before 6.00 p.m. on a Sunday is substituted as a rest day for an employee engaged in shift work, such rest day shall be deemed to have been granted within that week notwithstanding that the period of 30 hours ends after that week.

(4) Where the rest days of an employee are determined by the employer, the employer shall, before the commencement of the month in which the rest days fall, prepare or cause to be prepared a roster of t~ e days appointed to be rest days therein.

Work on rest day.

64. !ll Subject to section 65(2L no employee shall be compelled to work on a rest day unless he is engaged in work which by reason of its nature requires to be carried on continuously by a succession of shifts.

(2) In the event of any dispute, the Commissioner may decide whether or not an employee is engaged in work which by reason of its nature requires to be carried on continuously by a succession of shifts.

!3) Any employee who at his own request works on a rest day or a public holiday shall be paid for that day

(a) if the period of work does not exceed one-half of his normal hours of work, a sum at the basic rate of pay for half a day's work;

(b) if the period of work is more than one-half but does not exceed his normal hours of work, a sum of the basic rate of pay for one day's work;

(c) if the period of work exceeds his normal hours of work for one day

(i) a sum at the basic rate of pay for one day's work; and

(ii) a sum at the rate of not less than one and one-half times his hourly basic rate of pay for each hour or part thereof that the period of work exceeds his normal hours of work for one day.

(4) Any employee who at the request of his employer works on a rest day or a public holiday shall be paid for that day

(a) if the period of work does not exceed one-half of his normal hours of work, a sum at the basic rate of pay for one day's work;

(b) if the period of work is more than one-half but does not exceed his normal hours of work, a sum at the basic rate of pay for 2 days' work;

(c) if the period of work exceeds his normal hours of work for one day

(i) a sum at the basic rate of pay for 2 days, work; and

(ii) a sum at the rate of not less than one and one-half times his hourly basic rate of pay for each hour or part thereof that the period of work exceeds his normal hours of work for one day.

(5) In this section

(a} "hourly basic rate of pay" of an employee is to be calculated in the same manner as for the purpose of calculating payment due to an employee under section 65 for working overtime;

{b) [11]"normal hours of work" means the number of hours of work (not exceeding the limits applicable to an employee under sections 65 or 67, as the case may be) that is agreed between an employer and an employee to be the usual hours of work per day; or in the absence of any such agreement, shall be deemed to be 8 hours a day.

(6) Subsection (3) shall not apply to any employee who is employed by the Government or a statutory body in any of the essential services as defined in section 3(3) of the Internal Security Act (Chapter 133) for the purposes of that section, but any such employee who at the request of his employer works on a rest day or part thereof shall be given a day or part of a day off, as the case may be, in substitution for such a rest day or part thereof.

Hours of work.

65. (1) Except as hereinafter provided, an employee shall not be required under his contract of service to work for

fa} more than 6 consecutive hours without a period of leisure;

(b) more than 8 hours in one day or for more than 44 hours in one week:

Provided that

(i) an employee who is engaged in work which must be carried on continuously may be required to work for 8 consecutive hours, inclusive of a period or periods of not less than 45 minutes in the aggregate, during which he shall have the opportunity to have a meal;

(ii) where under a contract of service, the number of hours of work on one or more days of the week is less than 8, the limit of 8 hours may be exceeded on the remaining days of the week, but no employee shall be required to work for more than 9 hours in one day or 44 hours in one week;

(iii) where under a contract of service, the number of days on which the employee is required to work in a week is not more than 5 days, the limit of 8 hours in one day may be exceeded, but no employee shall be required to work for more than 9 hours in one day or 44 hours in one week; and

[iv) where under a contract of service, the number of hours of work in every alternate week is less than 44, the limit of 44 hours in one week may be exceeded in the other week, but no employee shall be required to work for more than 48 hours in one week or for more than 88 hours in any continuous period of 2 weeks.

[2] An employee may be required by his employer to exceed the limit of

hours set out in subsection (1) and to work on a rest day or a public holiday, in the case of

{aj an accident, actual or threatened;

{bj any work, the performance of which is essential to the life of the community;

{cj any work which is essential for defence or security;

{dj any urgent work to be done to any machinery or plant;

{ej any interruption of work which was impossible to foresee;

{fJ work to be performed by employees in any industrial undertaking essential to the economy of Brunei Darussalam or in any of the essential services as defined in section 3(3) of the Internal Security Act (Chapter 133) for the purposes of that section.

(3) In the event of any dispute, the Commissioner shall have the power to decide whether or not the employer was justified in calling upon the employee to work in the circumstances specified in subsection 2*{fJ*.

(4) If an employee at the request of the employer works

{aj for more than 8 hours in one day, except as provided in paragraphs (ii) and (iii) of the proviso to subsection (1), or for more than 9 hours in one day in any case specified in those paragraphs; or

{bJ for more than 44 hours in one week, except as provided in paragraph (iv) of the proviso to subsection (1), or for more than 48 hours in any one week or more than 88 hours in any continuous period of 2 weeks in any case specified in that paragraph,

he shall be paid for such extra work at the rate of not less than one and one-half of his hourly basic rate of pay, irrespective of the basis on which his rate of pay is fixed.

(5} An employee shall not be permitted to work overtime for more than 72 hours a month.

(6) For the purpose of calculating the payment due for overtime to an employee, his hourly basic rate of salary shall be calculated in accordance with the following formula

(aj in the case of a person employed on a monthly rate of pay

12 X the employee's monthly basic rate of salary 52 X 44 hours; and

(bj in the case of a person employed on piece rates-

the total weekly salary at the basic rate of salary received the total number of hours worked in the week.

(7) The Minister may, with the approval of His Majesty the Sultan and Yang Di-Pertuan, make regulations for the purpose of calculating the payment due for overtime to an employee employed on piece rates.

(8) Except in the circumstances described in subsection (2), an employee shall not be permitted to work for more than 12 hours in any one day.

(9) This section does not apply to employees engaged in the fire and rescue service or in any work which by its nature involves long hours of inactive or stand-by employment.

Task work.

66. Nothing in this Part shall prevent any employer from agreeing with any employee that the salary of the employee shall be paid at an agreed rate in accordance with the specific amount of work required to be performed, instead of by the basic daily rate or by piece rate.

Shift workers **etc.**

67. (1) Notwithstanding section 65(1), an employee who is engaged under his contract of service in regular shift work or who has otherwise consented in writing to work in accordance with the hours of work specified in this section, may be required to work for more than 6 consecutive hours, for more than 8 hours in any one day or for more than 44 hours in any one week, but the average number of hours worked over any continuous period of 3 weeks shall not exceed 44 hours per week.

(2) No consent given by an employee under this section shall be valid unless fa} this section and section 65 have been explained to him; and

fb} he has been informed of [i) the times at which the hours of work begin and end;

(ii) the number of working days in each week; and

(iii) the weekly rest day.

[3) An employee to whom this section applies shall not be permitted to work for more than 12 hours in any one day.

[4) Section 65(4) does not apply to any employee to whom this section applies, but any such employee who, at the request of his employer, works for more than an average of 44 hours per week over any continuous period of 3 weeks, shall be paid for such extra work in accordance with section 65(4).

Interpretation of week for purposes of sections 63, 65 and 67.

68. For the purposes of sections 63, 65 and 67, "week" shall mean a continuous period of 7 days commencing at midnight on Sunday.

Power to exempt.

69. (1) The Commissioner may, after considering the operational needs of the employer and the health and safety of any employee or class of employee, by order in writing exempt an employee or any class of employee from sections 65(1), (5) and (8) and section 67(3), subject to such conditions as the Commissioner thinks fit.

(2) The Commissioner may, after considering the operational needs of an employer and the interests of any employee or class of employee, by order in writing, direct that the entitlement to be paid for extra work under sections 64(3), 64(4), 65(4), 67(4) or 70(4) shall not apply to that employee or class of employee, subject to such conditions as the Commissioner thinks fit.

(3) Where the Commissioner

{a} exempts any employee or class of employee from sections 65(1), (5) and (8} or section 67(3}; or

{bj directs that the entitlement to be paid for extra work under

sections 64(3), 64(4), 65(4), 67(4) or 70(4) shall not apply to any employee or

class of employee,

the employer shall display the order or a copy thereof conspicuously in the place where the employee or class of employee is employed.

Holidays.

70. (1) Every employee shall be entitled to a paid holiday at his gross rate of pay on every public holiday that falls during the time that he is employed:

Provided that

{a} by agreement between the employer and the employee, any other day or days may be substituted for any one or more public holidays;

{bj if any public holiday falls on a rest day, the working day next following that rest day shall be a paid holiday; and

{cj if any public holiday falls on a day when the employee is not required to work under his contract of service, the employer may either pay the employee for that holiday at his gross rate of pay or give the employee a day off in substitution for that holiday.

(2) Notwithstanding subsection (1), no employee shall be entitled to holiday pay for any public holiday which falls on a day when the employee is on leave of absence without pay granted by the employer at the request of the employee.

(3) An employee who absents himself from work on the working day immediately preceding or immediately succeeding a public holiday or on any day substituted therefor under subsection (1), without the prior approval of his employer or without reasonable excuse, shall not be entitled to any holiday pay for that public holiday.

(4) Notwithstanding subsection (1), any employee may be required by his employer to work on any holiday to which he would otherwise be entitled under that subsection, and in such event he shall be paid an extra day's salary at the basic rate of pay for one day's work, in addition to the gross rate of pay for that

day and to a travelling allowance, if payable to him under the contract of service with his employer, for one day.

(5) No employee shall be entitled under subsection (4) to receive double any housing allowance or food allowance.

(6) Subsection (4) does not apply to an employee who is employed in the public service or in any of the essential services as defined in section 3(3) of the Internal Security Act (Chapter 133) for the purposes of that section, but any such employee may, notwithstanding subsection (1), be required by his employer to work on a holiday or part thereof to which he would otherwise be certified under that subsection, and in any such case he shall be given a day or part of a day off, as the case may be, in substitution for the holiday or part thereof.

(7) For the purposes of this section, if any public holiday falls on a half working day, the gross or basic rate of pay payable shall be that of a full working day.

Annual leave.

71. (1) An employee who has served an employer for a period of not less than 3 months shall be entitled to

(a) paid annual leave of 7 days in respect of the first 12 months of continuous service with the same employer; and

(b) an additional one day's annual leave for every subsequent 12 months of continuous service with the same employer,

subject to a maximum of 14 days of such leave, which shall be in addition to the rest days, public holidays and sick leave to which the employee is entitled under sections 63, 70 and 72 respectively.

(2) An employee who has served an employer for a period of not less than 3 months but who has not completed 12 months of continuous service in any year shall be entitled to annual leave in proportion to the number of completed months of service in that year.

(3) In calculating the proportionate annual leave under subsection [2), any fraction of a day which is less than one-half of a day shall be disregarded and where the fraction of the day is one-half or more it shall be regarded as one day.

(4) Where an employee is granted leave of absence without pay by the employer at the request of the employee, the period of the leave shall be disregarded for the purpose of computing continuous service under this section.

(5) An employee shall forfeit his entitlement to annual leave if he absents himself from work without the permission of the employer or without reasonable excuse for more than 20 per cent of the number of working days in the months or year, as the case may be, in which his entitlement to such leave accrues.

(6) The employer shall grant and the employee shall take such annual leave not later than 12 months after the end of every 12 months continuous service and any employee who fails to take that leave by the end of such period shall thereupon cease to be entitled thereto.

(7} The employer shall pay the employee his gross rate of pay for every day of such annual leave and if an employee has been dismissed otherwise than for misconduct before he has taken that leave, the employer shall pay him his gross rate of pay in respect of every day of that leave.

(8) The Minister may, with the approval of His Majesty the Sultan and Yang Di-Pertuan, by notification published in the *Gazette,* fix the periods when and prescribe the manner in which, annual leave shall be granted to employees in different types of employment or in different classes of industry.

Sick leave.

72. PI Any employee who has served an employer for a period of not less than 6 months shall, after undergoing a medical examination at the expense of the employer by a medical practitioner be entitled to paid sick leave not exceeding in the aggregate

(a) 14 days in each year if no hospitalisation is necessary; or

(b) 60 days in each year if hospitalisation is necessary,

as may be certified by the medical practitioner.

(2} Notwithstanding subsection (1), if an employee is hospitalised for less than 46 days in any one year, his entitlement to paid sick leave for that year shall not exceed the aggregate of 14 days plus the number of days on which he was hospitalised.

(3) If an employee is certified by the medical practitioner to be ill enough to need to be hospitalised but is not hospitalised, the employee shall be deemed to be hospitalised for the purposes of this section.

(4) An employee who absents himself on sick leave

(a) which is not certified by a medical practitioner; or

(b) which is certified by a medical practitioner, but without him informing or attempting to inform his employer of such sick leave within 48 hours of its commencement,

shall be deemed to absent himself from work without the permission of his employer and without reasonable excuse for the days on which he is so absent from work.

j5J The employer shall pay the employee for every day of such sick leave

(a} where no hospitalisation is necessary, at the gross rate of pay excluding any allowance payable in respect of shift work; and

(b) where hospitalisation is necessary, at the gross rate of pay.

(6) Notwithstanding subsection (5), no employee shall be entitled to paid sick leave

(a} on a rest day or on a public holiday to which he is entitled under sections 63 or 70;

(b) on any day of paid annual leave;

(c) on a day when he is not required to work under his contract of service; or

(d) on a day when he is on leave of absence without pay granted by the employer at his request.

(7) No employee shall be entitled to paid sick leave for the period during which he is receiving compensation for temporary incapacity under paragraph 3 of the Third Schedule to the Workmen's Compensation Act (Chapter 74).

Payment of retrenchment benefit.

73. No employee, who has been in continuous service with an employer for less than 5 years, shall be entitled to any retrenchment benefit on the termination of his service by the employer on the ground of redundancy or by reason of any re-organisation of the employer's profession, business, trade or work.

Retirement benefit.

74. No employee, who has been in continuous service with an employer for less than 5 years, shall be entitled to any retirement benefit other than the sums

Payment of annual salary supplement or other variable payment.

75. (1) Where a contract of service or collective agreement made before the commencement of this Order provides for the payment by the employer of any annual salary supplement, annual bonus or annual salary increase, such payments shall continue to be payable by the employer until the employer and his employees or a trade union representing his employees have negotiated and agreed to vary such payments.

(2) An employer and his employees or a trade union representing his employees may negotiate for and agree to a variable payment based on the trading results, productivity or on any other criteria agreed upon by the parties concerned.

(3) Where an employer has not paid any annual salary supplement prior to the commencement of this Order, any contract of service or collective agreement made on or after such commencement between the employer and his employees or a trade union representing his employees shall not contain a provision for the payment of an annual salary supplement exceeding the equivalent of one and one-half month's salary of the employees.

(4) Any

(a) person who, or trade union of employees which, requests (whether orally or in writing) or invites negotiations for the payment by an employer of an annual salary supplement which is in excess of the amount specified in subsection (3); and

(b) employer who pays an annual salary supplement exceeding the amount specified in subsection (3),

is guilty of an offence.

(5) Notwithstanding that an annual salary supplement may be payable under subsections (1) or (3), an employer may, in the event of exceptionally poor business results for any year, invite the employees or a trade union representing his employees to negotiate for a lower quantum of annual salary supplement or for no annual salary supplement to be paid for that year.

Power of Minister to make recommendations for salary adjustments.

76. The Minister may make recommendations for salary adjustment and, upon the publication of such recommendations in the *Gazette,* the employer and his employees or a trade union representing his employees may negotiate based on such recommendations.

Interpretation for purposes of sections 75 and 76.

77. In sections 75 and 76

"annual salary supplement' means a single annual payment to employees that is supplemental to the total amount of annual salary earned by them, whether expressed as a percentage thereof or otherwise;

"salary" means the basic salary payable to an employee in respect of work done under his contract of service, but does not include any commission, overtime allowance or any other allowance payable to an employee;

"variable payment' means such payment, however expressed and whether paid annually or otherwise, which serves as an incentive to all employees to increase their productivity or as a reward for their contribution.

Power to suspend application of this Part.

78. The Minister may, with the approval of His Majesty the Sultan and Yang Di-Pertuan, by notification published in the *Gazette,* suspend the application of any of the provisions of this Part to any class of employee when the public interest so requires it.

Offences.

79. (1) Any employer who

{a} employs any person as an employee contrary to the provisions of this Part; or

{bj fails to pay any salary in accordance with the provisions of this Part,

is guilty of an offence and liable on conviction to a fine not exceeding $800, and for a second or subsequent offence to a fine not exceeding $1,600, imprisonment for a term not exceeding one year or both.

(2) This section does not apply where the terms of service under which a person is employed are provided for in a collective agreement entered into before the commencement of this Order and while the collective agreement remains in force.

(3} Notwithstanding subsection (1)

(a} an employer and his employees or a trade union representing his employees may negotiate for and agree to terms of service relating to leave more favourable than those contained in sections 71 and 72; and

For additional analytical, business and investment opportunities information,
please contact Global Investment & Business Center, USA
at (703) 370-8082. Fax: (703) 370-8083. E-mail: ibpusa3@gmail.com
Global Business and Investment Info Databank - www.ibpus.com

(b/ it shall not be an offence for an employer to grant to his employees terms of service relating to leave more favourable than those contained in sections 71 and 72.

PART VIII HEALTH, ACCOMMODATION AND MEDICAL CARE

Duty to provide accommodation and sanitary arrangements.

80. Every employer who undertakes to provide accommodation for workmen employed either by him or by some other person with whom he has entered into a contract of service, shall provide and maintain for those workmen and their dependants

(aJ sufficient and proper hygienic accommodation;

(bJ sufficient supply of wholesome water; and

(cJ sufficient and proper sanitary arrangements.

Buildings to conform with legal requirements.

81. (1) All accommodation provided shall be constructed in accordance with the provisions of any other written law.

(2) All such accommodation shall be maintained and kept in a sanitary condition in accordance with the provisions of any other written law.

First-aid equipment.

82. (1) At every place of employment where workmen are employed, the employer shall provide such first-aid equipment as the Commissioner may determine.

(2) The Commissioner may, having regard to the nature and circumstances of the work, in writing, exempt any employer from this section.

Medical care and treatment.

83. (1 J At every place of employment the employer shall provide for all workmen such medical attention and treatment with medicines of good quality, first aid equipment and appliances for the transportation of sick or injured workmen.

(2) Every employer shall take or cause to be taken, for treatment as soon as possible every workman injured or falling ill during the course of his employment and every resident workman and resident dependant on a place of employment requiring medical attention at a hospital or dispensary to the hospital or dispensary maintained for the workmen at such place of employment or, if there is no such hospital or dispensary, to the nearest hospital or dispensary maintained by the Government or approved by the Commissioner and shall also provide any treatment necessary therefor.

(3) The cost of maintenance and treatment of a workman and of his dependants residing on the place of employment in or at any hospital or dispensary to which the workman or his dependant is

sent by the employer shall be borne or paid by the employer as long as the workman remains in his employment:

Provided that if the employer continues to pay to the workman salary or part salary amounting to not less than half his usual salary, he may recover by deduction from the salary of such workman the cost of such maintenance in hospital.

(4) Where any such workman or dependant has been admitted to a Government hospital or dispensary, the cost of maintenance and treatment and, in the event of the death of such workman or dependant in such hospital, any reasonable burial expenses incurred, shall be recoverable from the employer at the suit of the medical practitioner in charge.

Burial of deceased workmen or dependants.

84. The employer shall provide decent interment for any workman resident on a place of employment and for any dependant dying during the employment of such workman unless a relative or friend undertakes such duty.

Hospital maintained by employers.

85. (1) The Commissioner may at any time having regard to the situation of any place of employment and the number of workmen employed and resident thereon, by order in writing, require any employer

fa) to construct within a reasonable time to be stated in such order, and thereafter to maintain at his own expense, a hospital on or in the immediate neighbourhood of any place of employment upon which workmen are employed by him with accommodation, for such number of patients as may be stated in such order; or

(bj if there is already a hospital maintained by such employer, to

enlarge or add to such hospital so as to provide accommodation for a

further number of patients as stated in the order,

and may further require him to employ a medical practitioner to reside at and have charge of such hospital or any hospital maintained by such employer and to provide such medical practitioner with fit and proper house accommodation to the satisfaction of the Commissioner.

(2) If 2 or more such places of employment are so situated that the required accommodation for patients from such places of employment can be conveniently provided in one hospital, the Commissioner may

fa} instead of ordering each employer to construct and maintain a separate hospital, order all the employers concerned to construct within a reasonable time to be stated in such order, and thereafter to maintain at their own expense one hospital, in this section referred to as a group hospital, for all such places of employment with accommodation for such number of patients as may be stated in the order; or

{b) if there is already a hospital erected and maintained jointly by 2 or more employers (whether constructed in pursuance of the provisions of this section or not), order them to enlarge or add to such hospital so as to provide accommodation for such further number of patients in their employment as may be stated in the order,

and may further require such employers to employ a medical practitioner to take charge of such group hospital and to provide such medical practitioner with fit and proper house accommodation to the satisfaction of the Commissioner.

(3) Every employer referred to in subsection (3) shall be responsible for the due maintenance of the group hospital as the case may be and for the provision of the staff, equipment, diet and medicines and for the observance of any regulations made under this Order for the inspection and management of the hospital and the furnishing of any returns required as if the hospital were provided and maintained solely by him.

Approval of place of employment and prohibition of employment of workmen where arrangements are inadequate.

86. (**1**) Every person intending to

(a)

employ resident workmen at a place of employment where workmen have not hitherto been employed or have not been employed within the preceding 12 months; or

(b) increase the number of workmen already employed on a place of employment so that the existing arrangement would not conform to any prescribed requirements and standards of health and hygiene,

shall give notice in writing of such intention to the Commissioner.

(2) If the Commissioner at any time has reason to believe that

(a) the arrangements made for the residence and employment of workmen on any place of employment where it is intended that workmen shall live or be employed or where workmen are living or employed are, from any cause, inadequate for the residence and employment of such workmen or of additional workmen; or

(b) that the health or condition of workmen living or employed on any place of employment is from any cause unsatisfactory, he may by order served on the employer prohibit the residence or employment, or both, of workmen or of additional workmen on such place and it shall thereupon be unlawful for any person to employ or permit to reside on such place any workmen or dependants, or any workmen or dependants other than those who were residing or employed thereon before the issue of such order, as the case may be.

[3] The Commissioner may, upon being satisfied that

(a) adequate arrangements have been made for the residence and employment of the workmen or of additional workmen on such place of employment; or

(b) that the health and condition of the workmen living or employed thereon have become satisfactory, rescind the order made under subsection (2), and thereupon it shall be lawful for the employer to employ workmen or additional workmen as the case may be on such place of employment.

87. Any person who contravenes or fails to comply with any of the provisions of this Part is guilty of an offence.

PART IX PART-TIME EMPLOYEES

Part-time employees.

88. (1) In this Part, "part-time employee" means an employee who is required under his contract of service with an employer to work for less than 30 hours a week.

(2) Notwithstanding subsection (1), the Minister may, with the approval of His Majesty the Sultan and Yang Di-Pertuan and by notification published in the *Gazette,* declare that any employee or class of employee is not to be regarded as a part-time employee for the purposes of this Part.

Minister may exclude or modify Order in relation to part-time employees.

89. The Minister may, with the approval of His Majesty the Sultan and Yang Di-Pertuan, by regulations exclude or modify any or all of the provisions of this Order in their application to any part-time employee or class of part-time employee.

PART X EMPLOYMENT OF WOMEN

Interpretation of benefit period.

90. In this Part, "benefit period" means the period referred to in section 91(2).

Length of benefit period.

91. (1) Subject to this section, every female employee shall be entitled to absent herself from work-

fa) during

(i) the period of 4 weeks immediately before her confinement; and

(ii) the period of 5 weeks immediately after her confinement;

{b) during a period of 9 weeks, as agreed to by her and her employer, commencing

(i) not earlier than 28 days immediately preceding the day of her confinement; and

(ii) not later than the day of her confinement.

(2) Subject to this section, every female employee shall be entitled to receive payment from her employer at her gross rate of pay for any of the following periods

{a) where subsection (l){a) applies, the period of 4 weeks referred to in subsection (l){a)(i] and the first 4 weeks of the period referred to in subsection (l){a)(ii);

{b) where subsection *(l){b)* applies, the first 8 weeks of the period referred to in subsection *(l){b).*

(3) A female employee who has served an employer for less than 180 days immediately preceding the day of her confinement shall not be entitled to any pay during the benefit period.

(4) Where a female employee has worked in her employment for any day during the benefit period before her confinement, she shall be entitled to receive in addition to her gross rate of pay for that day an amount that is equivalent to a day's pay at the gross rate of pay or to absent herself from work on another day at the end of the benefit period.

Claim from one employer only.

92. Nothing in this Part shall be deemed to entitle any female employee to claim any payment under this Part from more than one employer in respect of the same confinement.

Contracting out.

Any contract of service whereby a female employee relinquishes any right to maternity benefit under this Part shall not be valid in so far as it purports to deprive her of that right or to remove or reduce the liability of any employer to make any payment under this Part.

(1} A female employee shall, at least one week before absenting herself from work in accordance with section 91(1), give notice to her employer specifying the date of which she intends to commence absenting herself from work.

(2) A female employee who has been confined shall, as soon as practicable, inform her employer of the date on which she was confined.

(3) Any female employee who fails to give notice as required under subsection (1) or who fails to inform her employer as required under subsection (2) shall be entitled to only one-half of the amount of any payment to which she would otherwise be entitled under this Part, unless she was prevented by any sufficient cause from giving such notice or information.

(4) A female employee may at any time in writing nominate some other person to whom any payment to which she is entitled under this Part may be paid on her behalf; and any such payment made to the person so nominated shall for the purpose of this Order be deemed to be a payment to the female employee who nominated such other person.

When payment to be made.

95. (1) In the case of a female employee who is a daily-rated employee, the payment referred to in section 91 shall be paid in 2 instalments

(a} the first, for the period up to and including the day of confinement, to be paid within 7 days from the date of confinement; and

(b} the second, for the period after confinement, to be paid within 7 days from the end of that period.

(2) In the case of any other female employee, the payment shall be paid at such time as the salary earned by the employee under her contract of service is due to be paid to her.

Payments to include public holidays.

96. (1) The payment referred to in section 91 shall be paid for every day of the benefit period, including public holidays.

(2) Nothing in this section shall be construed to require an employer to pay to a female employee an extra day's salary for a public holiday which falls within the benefit period.

Payment of benefit on death of female employee before confinement.

97. (1) If a female employee, after giving notice to her employer under section 94(1), abstains from work in expectation of her confinement and dies from any cause before her confinement, the employer shall pay

(a) to the person nominated by her under section 94(4); or

(b) if there is no such person, to her personal representative,

a sum of money at the rate set out in section 91 from the date immediately following the last day on which she worked to the day immediately preceding the day of her death and, except in the circumstances mentioned in this subsection, no employer shall be liable to pay any sum in respect of a period exceeding 30 days.

(2) If a female employee dies from any cause on or after the day of her confinement and before any payment to which she is entitled has been paid to her, the employer shall pay

(a) to the person nominated by her under section 94(4); or

(b) if there is no such person, to her personal representative,

a sum of money to which she was on the date of her death entitled in respect of the period up to the day of her confinement and in respect of the period after her confinement up to the day immediately preceding the day of her death.

Dismissal during absence prohibited.

98. Subject to the provisions of this Part, when a female employee absents herself from work in accordance with the provisions of this Part it shall not be lawful for her employer to give her notice of dismissal during her absence or on such a day that the notice will expire during her absence.

Right to benefit unaffected by notice of dismissal in specified circumstances.

99. (1) No notice of dismissal given without sufficient cause by an employer to a female employee within a period of 3 months before her confinement shall have the effect of depriving her of any payment to which

(a} but for that notice, she would have been entitled; or

{b) she would, on or before the date of her confinement, have become entitled to, under this Part.

(2) If any question arises as to whether any notice of dismissal given under subsection i1) was or was not given for sufficient cause, it shall be referred to the Minister within 2 months from the date of the employee's confinement.

(3) Where the Minister is satisfied that the employee has been dismissed without sufficient cause, he may, notwithstanding any rule of law or agreement to the contrary

(a} direct the employer to reinstate the employee in her former employment and pay the employee an amount equal to the salary that she would have earned had she not been dismissed; or

(bJ direct the employer to pay such amount of salary as compensation as the Minister may consider just and equitable having regard to all the circumstances of the case,

and the employer shall comply with the direction of the Minister.

(4) The decision of the Minister under subsection (3) shall be final.

(5) Any direction of the Minister under subsection (3) shall operate as a bar to any action for damages by the employee in any court in respect of the dismissal without sufficient cause under subsection (1).

(6) An employer who fails to comply with a direction of the Minister under subsection (3) is guilty of an offence and liable on conviction to a fine not exceeding $5,000, imprisonment for a term not exceeding one year or both.

(7) Where any amount to be paid by an employer under subsection (3) is not paid in accordance with the direction of the Minister and the employer has been convicted of an offence under subsection (6), the amount or so much thereof as remains unpaid shall be recoverable by the court as if it were a fine and the amount so recoverable shall be paid to the employee entitled to payment under the direction of the Minister.

Employment after confinement.

100. Any employer who knowingly employs a female employee at any time during the period of 4 weeks immediately following her confinement is guilty of an offence.

Forfeiture of payment.

101. If a female employee works for any other employer after she has absented herself from work under the provisions of this Part, she shall forfeit her claim to any payment to which she is entitled under this Part and shall be liable to dismissaL

Offences.

102. Any employer who

(a) fails to pay his female employee in accordance with the provisions of this Part; or

(b) acts in contravention of section 98,

is guilty of an offence and liable on conviction to a fine not exceeding $1,000, imprisonment for a term not exceeding 6 months or both.

PART XI EMPLOYMENT OF CHILDREN AND YOUNG PERSONS

Restriction on employment of children.

103. (1) No person shall employ a child in an industrial undertaking or in an undertaking which is not an industrial undertaking, except as provided for in subsections (2) and (3).

(2) A child may be employed in an industrial undertaking in which only members of the same family are employed.

(3) A child who has attained the age of 14 years may be employed in light work suited to his capacity in an undertaking which is not in industrial undertaking.

(4) For the purposes of subsection (3), a certificate of a medical practitioner shall be conclusive on the question of whether any work is suited to the capacity of any particular child.

Restriction on employment of young persons.

104. (1) No young person shall be employed in any industrial undertaking which the Minister has declared under subsection (2) to be an industrial undertaking in which no young person shall be employed.

{2) The Minister may, with the approval of His Majesty the Sultan and Yang Di-Pertuan and by notification published in the *Gazette,* declare any industrial undertaking to be an industrial undertaking in which no young person shall be employed.

Conditions of employment.

105. The Minister may, with the approval of His Majesty the Sultan and Yang Di-Pertuan, prescribe the conditions upon which a child or young person may be employed in any industrial or an undertaking which is not an industrial undertaking.

Minimum rates of salary may be prescribed.

106. (1) If it is shown to the satisfaction of the Minister, upon the application of the Commissioner and after such inquiry as the Minister may think fit to direct, having regard to the nature of the work and the conditions of employment, that the salaries of children, young persons or both employed in any industry, for any particular work or in any area are insufficient, the Minister may, with the approval of His Majesty the Sultan and Yang Di-Pertuan and by order published in the

Gazette, prescribe minimum rates of salary to be paid to children, young persons or both in that industry, type of employment or area.

{2) Any person who contravenes any such order is guilty of an offence and liable on conviction to a fine not exceeding $1,000, imprisonment for a term not exceeding 6 months or both, and for a second or subsequent offence to a fine not exceeding $2,000, imprisonment for a term not exceeding 2 years or both.

Approved employment.

107. (1) Sections 103 and 104 do not apply to

(a) the employment of children and young persons

(i) in any work approved and supervised by the Ministry of Education, the Institute of Technical Education or any authorised government agency; and

(ii) carried on in any technical, vocational or industrial training school or institute; and

(b) the employment of young persons under any apprenticeship programme approved and supervised by the Institute of Technical Education or any authorised government agency.

(2) In this section

"authorised government agency" means any government agency authorised by the Ministry of Home Affairs;

"Institute of Technical Education" means the Institute of Technical Education established by the Ministry of Education.

Power of court in respect of children or young persons requiring care or protection.

108. A child or young person in respect of whom any of the offences mentioned in this Part has been committed may be brought before any court and that court, if satisfied that the child or young person is in need of care or protection, may exercise with respect to that child or young person all or any of the powers conferred by section 262 of the Criminal Procedure Code (Chapter 7) or by any other written law.

Regulations regulating employment.

109. The Minister may, with the approval of His Majesty the Sultan and Yang Di-Pertuan, make regulations to regulate the employment of children in any occupation and no child or young person shall be employed under any circumstances or under any conditions which may be prohibited by the Minister by such regulations.

Offences.

110. Ill Any

(a} person who employs a child or young person in contravention of the provisions of this Part or any of the regulations made thereunder;

(b) parent or guardian who knowingly or negligently suffers or permits any such employment,

is guilty of an offence and liable on conviction to a fine not exceeding $2,000, imprisonment for a term not exceeding 2 years or both.

(2) In the case where a child or young person suffers serious injury or death resulting from any breach of the provisions of this Part or any regulations made thereunder, the offender is guilty of an offence and liable on a further conviction to a fine not exceeding $2,000 and imprisonment for a term not exceeding 2 years.

Minister may apply Order to domestic workers.

111. The Minister may, with the approval of His Majesty the Sultan and Yang Di-Pertuan, make regulations applying all or any of the provisions of this Order with such modification as may be set out in the regulation to all domestic workers or to any group, class or number of domestic workers and to provide generally for the engagement, repatriation and working conditions of domestic workers.

PART XIII IMMIGRANT EMPLOYEES

Employment of immigrant employees.

112. (1) No person shall knowingly employ any immigrant employee unless he has obtained a licence from the Commissioner to do so in such form and subject to such conditions as the Commissioner may determine:

Provided that where an immigrant employee is found at any premises or place and is in possession of any tools or other implements or is engaged in any activity which may give rise to the inference that he is doing any work, the occupier of such premises or place shall, until the contrary is proved, be presumed to have employed him knowing that he is an immigrant employee.

(2) Any employer who contravenes the provisions of subsection (1) and any immigrant employee found working for such an employer are each guilty of an offence and liable on conviction to a fine of not less than $6,000 and not exceeding $10,000, imprisonment for a term of not less than 6 months or not more than 3 years or both.

(3) In this section

"construction work" means construction, reconstruction, maintenance, repair, alteration or demolition of any building, harbour, dock, pier, canal, sewer, drain, well telegraphic or telephonic installation, electrical undertaking, gasworks, waterworks or other work of construction, as well as the preparation for or laying the foundation of any such work or structure;

"employer" includes a person who has entered into an engagement for money or money's worth for another person to work where *(a)* that other person is already under a contract of service with an employer (as defined in section 2) and in respect of whom a licence has been obtained by such employer from the Commissioner under subsection (1); or

(b) that work is at piece rates or on commtsswn, whether or not as the result of an arrangement with an employer (as defined in section 2);

"occupier", in relation to any premises or place, includes

(a} the person having the charge, management or control of

either the whole or part of the premises or place, either on his own

account or as an agent; and

(b) a contractor who is carrying out building operations or construction works at the premises or place on behalf of some other person.

Prohibition on termination of local for immigrant employee.

113. No employer shall, without reasonable grounds, terminate the contract of service of a local employee for the purpose of employing an immigrant employee.

PART XIV REPATRIATION

Rights and obligations in respect of repatriation.

114. (1) Every immigrant employee who is a party to a contract of service under this Order and who has been brought to Brunei Darussalam by an employer or by any person acting on behalf of the employer shall have the right to be repatriated at the expense of the employer to his place of origin or to the place of engagement, if the latter be nearer to the place of employment and if the law of the place of engagement permits, in the following cases

(a) on the termination of the contract of service by expiry of the period for which it was made;

(b) on the termination of the contract of service by reason of the inability of the employer to fulfil the contract of service;

{cj on the termination of the contract of service by reason of the

inability of the employee to fulfil the contract of service owing to sickness

or accident;

{dj on the termination of the contract of service by notice and subject to the provisions of the particular contract of service and Part II;

{e) on the termination of the contract of service under section 17;

{fJ on the termination of the contract of service by agreement or contract between the parties, unless the Commissioner otherwise decides.

(2) Every immigrant employee who is ordered to leave Brunei Darussalam under or in accordance with any provision of any written law shall be repatriated at the expense of the employer to his place of origin or to the place of engagement, if the latter be nearer to the place of employment and if the law of the place of engagement so permits.

(3) Where any dependant of the immigrant employee has been brought to the place of employment by the employer or by any person acting on behalf of the employer, such dependant shall be repatriated at the expense of the employer whenever the employee is repatriated or in the event of his death.

(4) The expenses of repatriation shall include

{a} travelling and subsistence expenses during the journey;

{bj any subsistence expenses during the period between the date of termination of the contract of service and the date of repatriation; and

(cj provision for interment and the payment of the reasonable expenses of burial in the event of death of an employee occurring during the course of, or pending, repatriation.

(5) The employer shall not be liable for subsistence expenses in respect of any period during which the repatriation of the employee has been delayed

{aj by the employee's own choice; or

(bj for reason of *force majeure,* when the employer has been able during such period to use the services of the employee at the gross rate of pay stipulated in the expired contract of service.

(6) If the employer fails to fulfil his obligation in respect of repatriation, the obligation shall be discharged by or under direction of the Commissioner, and any sums so expended may be recovered from the employer by civil suit as a debt due to the Government.

Exemption from obligation to repatriate.

115. The Commissioner may exempt the employer from liability for repatriation expenses in the following cases

{a) when the Commissioner is satisfied that

(i) the employee, by a declaration before the Commissioner, has signified that he does not wish to be repatriated; and

(ii) the employee has been settled at his request or with his consent at or near the place of employment;

(b) when the Commissioner is satisfied that the employee, by his own choice, has failed to exercise his right of repatriation before the expiry of 6 months from the date of termination of the contract of service;

{c) when the liability of the employer has been provided for under any of the provisions of any fund established under section 152(3){i);

(d) when the contract of service has been terminated otherwise than by reason of the inability of the employee to fulfil the contract of service owing to sickness or accident and the Commissioner is satisfied that

(i) in fixing the rates of salary, proper allowance has been made for the payment of repatriation expenses by the employee; and

(ii) suitable arrangements have been made by means of a system of deferred pay or otherwise to ensure that the employee has the funds necessary for the payment of such expenses.

Employer to provide transport.

116. (1) The employer shall whenever possible provide transport for employees who are being repatriated.

(2) The Commissioner shall take all necessary measures to ensure and may give such directions to the employer or to any person acting on behalf of the employer to ensure that

{a) all vehicles or vessels to be used for transport of employees are suitable for such transport, in good sanitary condition and are not overcrowded;

(cJ when the employees have to make long journeys on foot, the length of the daily journey is compatible with the maintenance of their health and strength; and

(dj in the case of long journeys, suitable arrangements are made for medical assistance and for the welfare of the employees.

(3) When the employees have to make long journeys in groups, they shall be accompanied by a responsible person approved by the Commissioner.

Offence.

117. Any employer who fails to comply with the direction given to him by the Commissioner in pursuance of the provisions of section 116 is guilty of an offence and liable on conviction to a fine not exceeding $1,500 or in default thereof imprisonment for a term not exceeding 6 months.

PART XV INSPECTION

Powers of entry, inspection and enquiry.

118. The Commissioner and any authorised officer may

(aj enter and inspect, without previous notice at any hour of the day or night

(i) any place where he has reasonable cause to believe that any employee resides or is employed; or

(ii) any building occupied or used for any purpose connected with that employment; and

(bJ make any enquiry which he considers necessary in relation to any matter within the provisions of this Order.

Notice to employer of inspection.

119. On the occasion of an inspection or enquiry visit, the Commissioner and any authorised officer shall notify the employer or his representative of his presence unless he considers that such notification may be prejudicial to the performance of his duties.

Powers of Commissioner and authorised officers during inspection.

120. (1) In the course of an inspection or enquiry, the Commissioner or any authorised officer may

{a) examine orally any person whom he believes to be acquainted with the facts and circumstances of the employment of any person or any matter within the provisions of this Order, and to reduce into writing the answer given or statement made by that person; and such person shall be bound to answer truthfully all questions put to him; and the statement made by that person shall be read over to him, in the language in which he made it and, after correction, be signed by him or affixed with his thumb print, as the case may be;

{b) require the employer to

(i) produce before him all or any of the employees employed by him together with any contracts of service, books of account of salary, registers and other documents concerning the employees or their employment;

(ii) answer such questions relating thereto as he may think proper to ask;

{c) examine notices and all documents which are required to be kept under the provisions of this Order or any regulations made thereunder;

{d) make copies of, or make extracts from, the contract of service, books of account of salary, registers or other documents required to be produced under paragraph *{b);*

{e) take or remove for purposes of analysis samples of materials and substances used or handled by employees, except that the employer or his representative shall be notified of any such samples of materials or substances taken or removed for this purpose;

{f) take possession of the contracts of service, books of account of salary, registers and other documents relating to the employees or their employment where in his opinion

(i) the inspection, copying or the making of extracts from the contract of service, books of account of salary, registers or

For additional analytical, business and investment opportunities information,
please contact Global Investment & Business Center, USA
at (703) 370-8082. Fax: (703) 370-8083. E-mail: ibpusa3@gmail.com
Global Business and Investment Info Databank - www.ibpus.com

(ii) the contracts of service, book of account of salary, registers or other documents may be interfered with or destroyed unless he takes possession of them; or

(iii) the contracts of service, books of account of salary, registers or other documents may be needed as evidence in any legal proceedings under this Order;

(g) take or remove for the purposes of an enquiry any other document concerning the employees or their employment.

(2) No answer which a person is legally bound to give under subsection (1)(a) shall be proved against him in any criminal proceeding, except on a prosecution for giving false evidence by that answer.

(3) Notwithstanding subsection *(1)(b),* no employee shall be required to leave or to cease from performing any work on which he is engaged if his absence or cessation from such work would endanger life or property or seriously disrupt any operation being carried on by his employer.

(4) For the purpose of this section, the Commissioner and an authorised officer shall have the same powers of investigation as a police officer under Chapter XIII of the Criminal Procedure Code (Chapter 7).

Identification card to be produced.

121. (1) Every authorised officer, when exerc1smg any of his powers or performing any of his duties under this Order, shall declare his office and shall on demand produce to any person against whom he is taking action such identification card as the Commissioner may direct to be carried by an authorised officer.

(2) It shall not be an offence for any person to refuse to comply with any request, demand or order made or given by an authorised officer if such officer refuses on demand being made by that person to declare his office and produce his identification card.

Offences.

122. Any employer who, without reasonable excuse, the proof of which shall lie on him

(a} neglects or refuses to produce any contracts of service, books of account of salary, registers or other documents concerning any employee or relating to that employee's employment as required under section 120(1)(b};

(b} hinders or obstructs the Commissioner or any authorised officer in the exercise of the power under section 120(1); or

(c} makes to the Commissioner or an authorised officer exercising the power under section 120(1) a statement either orally or in writing which is false in a material particular,

is guilty of an offence and liable on conviction to a fine not exceeding $2,000, imprisonment for a term not exceeding one year or both.

PART XVI COMPLAINTS AND INQUIRIES

For additional analytical, business and investment opportunities information,
please contact Global Investment & Business Center, USA
at (703) 370-8082. Fax: (703) 370-8083. E-mail: ibpusa3@gmail.com
Global Business and Investment Info Databank - www.ibpus.com

Application of this Part.

123. This Part shall apply to all workmen and to other employees who are in receipt of a salary not exceeding $1,600 a month (excluding overtime payments, bonus payments, annual salary supplements, productivity incentive payments and any allowance however described) or such other amount as may be prescribed by the Minister.

Commissioner's power to inquire into complaints.

124. (1) The Commissioner may inquire into and decide any dispute between an employee and his employer or any person liable under the provisions of this Order to pay any salary due to the employee, where the dispute arises out of

(a} any term in the contract of service between the employee and his employer; or

(b} any of the provisions of this Order or any regulations made thereunder.

(2) In pursuance of that decision, the Commissioner may make an order in such form as he may determine, for the payment by either party of such sum of money as he considers just without limitation of the amount thereof.

(3) The power of the Commissioner under subsection (1) shall include the power to

(i) an employee against any person liable under section 53;

(ii) a sub-contractor for labour against a contractor or subcontractor for any sum which the sub-contractor for labour claims to be due to him in respect of any labour provided by him under his contract of service with the contractor or sub-contractor; and

{b} make such consequential orders as may be necessary to give effect to his decision.

Power of Commissioner to confirm or set aside decisions by employers.

125. (1) The Commissioner may inquire into and confirm or set aside any decision made by an employer under section 26(1) and may make such consequential orders as may be necessary to give effect to his decision.

(2) If the Commissioner sets aside any such decision, the consequential order against such employer shall be confined to payment of compensation in lieu of notice and other payments that the employee is entitled to as if no misconduct had been committed by the employee.

(3) The Commissioner shall not exercise his power under subsection (1) unless the employee has made a complaint to him under the provisions of this Part within 30 days from the date on which the decision made by his employer under section 26 was communicated to him either orally or in writing by the employer.

Procedure in Commissioner's inquiry.

126. The procedure for disposing of questions arising under sections 124 and 125 shall be as follows

fa} the complainant shall present a written statement or in person make a statement, to the Commissioner, of his complaint and of the remedy which he seeks;

{b) the Commissioner shall, as soon as practicable thereafter, examine the complainant on oath and shall record the substance of the complainant's statement in his case book;

(c) the Commissioner may make such inquiry as he thinks necessary to satisfy himself that the complaint discloses matters which in his opinion ought to be inquired into and may summon the person complained against, or if it appears to him without any inquiry that the complaint discloses matters which ought to be inquired into, he may forthwith summon the person complained against:

Provided that if the person complained against attends in person before the Commissioner it shall not be necessary to serve a summons upon him;

(d) when issuing a summons to the person complained against, the Commissioner shall

(i) give him notice of the nature of the complaint made against him and of the name of the complainant; and

Iii) inform him of the date, time and place at which he is required to attend, that he may bring with him any witnesses he may wish to call on his behalf and that he may apply to the Commissioner for summonses to such persons to appear as witnesses on his behalf;

(e) when the Commissioner issues a summons to a person complained against

(i) he shall inform the complainant of the date, time and place mentioned therein;

(iiJ he shall instruct the complainant to bring with him any witnesses he may wish to call on his behalf; and

(iii) he may, on the request of the complainant and subject to any conditions he may think fit to impose, issue summonses to such witnesses to appear on behalf of the complainant;

(f) when at any time before or during an inquiry the Commissioner has reason to believe that there is any person whose financial interests are likely to be affected by such decision as he may give on completion of the inquiry or who he has reason to believe have knowledge of the matters in issue or can give any evidence relevant thereto, he may summon any or all of such persons;

(g) the Commissioner shall, at the date, time and place appointed, examine on oath those persons summoned or otherwise present whose evidence he thinks is material to the matters in issue and shall then give his decision;

(h) if the person complained against or any person whose financial interests the Commissioner has reason to believe are likely to be affected

and who has been duly summoned to attend at the date1 time and place appointed in the summons, fails to attend, the Commissioner may hear and decide the complaint in the absence of such person notwithstanding that the interests of such person may be prejudicially affected by his decision;

(iJ in order to enable a court to enforce the decision of the Commissioner, the Commissioner shall embody his decision in an order in such form as he may determine.

Commissioner's record of inquiry.

127. (1) The Commissioner shall keep a case book in which he shall record the evidence of persons summoned or otherwise present and his decision and order in each matter in issue before him, and shall authenticate the record by attaching his signature thereto.

(2)

The record in such case book shall be sufficient evidence of the giving of any decision.

(3)

Any person interested in the decision or order shall be entitled to a copy of the record upon payment of the fee prescribed in the Second Schedule.

Joinder of several complaints in one complaint.

128. (1) Where it appears to the Commissioner in any proceedings under this Part that there are more than one employee having a common cause for complaint against the same employer or person liable, it shall not be necessary for each employee to make a separate complaint.

(2) The Commissioner may, if he thinks fit, permit one or more of the employees to make a complaint and to attend and act on behalf of and generally to represent the others, and the Commissioner may proceed to a decision on the joint complaint or complaints of each and all such employees:

Provided that where the Commissioner is of the opinion that the interests of the employer or person liable are likely to be prejudiced by the non-attendance of any employee, he shall require the personal attendance of such employee.

Prohibitory order by Commissioner to third party.

129. (1) Whenever the Commissioner

(aJ has made an order under sections 124 and 125 against an employer or any other person liable for the payment of any sum of money to any employee or sub-contractor for labour; and

{b} has reason to believe that there exists between such employer or that other person liable and any other person a contract of service in the course of the performance of which the employee or sub-contractor performed the work in respect of which the order was made,

the Commissioner may

(i) summon such other person; and

(ii) if after enquiry he is satisfied that such a contract of service exists, make an order in such form as he may determine, prohibiting such other person from paying to the employer or that other person liable and requiring him to pay to the Commissioner any money (not exceeding the amount found due to such employee or sub-contractor for labour) admitted by him to be owing to the employer or that other person liable in respect of such contract of service.

(2) However, where such other person admits to the Commissioner in writing that money is owing by him under the contract of service to the employer or that other person liable, he need not be summoned under subsection (1 J (i) and the Commissioner may make an order under subsection (1)(ii) in his absence.

(3) Where such other person is liable as a principal under section 53(1) to pay any salary due by the employer or that other person liable and where the money admitted by him to be owing to the employer or that other person liable is not sufficient to pay the whole of such salary, nothing in this section shall relieve him of his liability for the balance of such salary up to the amount for which he is liable under section 53(3).

(4) The payment of any money in pursuance of an order under subsection (1)(ii) shall be a discharge and payment up to the amount so paid of money due to the employer or that other person liable under the contract of service.

Service of summons.

130. (1 J Any summons issued by the Commissioner under this Part may be served by an Intermediate Court or any Court of a Magistrate, on behalf of the Commissioner, or in such other manner and by such person as the Commissioner may direct.

(2) No fee shall be charged by the Commissioner in respect of any such summons.

131. (1} Where an order has been made by the Commissioner under this Part and the person against whom it is made fails to comply therewith, the Commissioner may send a certified copy thereof to the registrar of the Intermediate Courts or to any Court of a Magistrate.

(2) The registrar or the Court of a Magistrate, as the case may be, shall cause the certified copy to be recorded and thereupon the order shall for all purposes be enforceable as a judgment of an Intermediate Court or of the Court of a Magistrate, as the case may be, notwithstanding that the order may, in respect of amount or value, be in excess of the ordinary jurisdiction of that court:

Provided that no sale of immovable property shall for the purposes of such enforcement be ordered, except by the High Court.

Submission by Commissioner to High Court on point of law.

132. (1) In any proceedings under this Part, the Commissioner may, if he thinks fit, submit any question of law for the decision of the High Court and if he does so, he shall decide the proceedings in conformity with such decision.

(2) An appeal by any person aggrieved shall lie to the Court of Appeal from any decision of the High Court under subsection (1).

Appeal against Commissioner's order to High Court.

133. (1) If any person whose financial interests are affected is dissatisfied with the decision or order of the Commissioner under sections 124, 125 or 129, he may appeal to the High Court.

!2} Subject to any Rules of Court made under section 25(1) of the Subordinate Courts Act (Chapter 6), the procedure in an appeal to the High Court shall be the procedure in a civil appeal from the Court of a Magistrate with such modifications as the circumstances may require.

Employee's remedy when employer about to abscond.

134. (1} If any employee complains to the Court of a Magistrate that he has reasonable grounds for believing that his employer, in order to evade payment of his salary due to him, is about to leave Brunei Darussalam, the court may summon such employer and direct him to show cause why he should not be required to give security by bond to remain in Brunei Darussalam until such salary is paid.

(2) If after hearing the evidence of the employer, the court decides that such bond shall be given, the court may order him to give security by bond in such sum as the court considers reasonable that he will not leave Brunei Darussalam until the court is satisfied that all the claims of such employee against him for salary have been paid or settled.

(3) If the employer fails to comply with the order to give security, he shall be detained in prison until arrangements have been made to the satisfaction of the court for settling the claims of the employee.

(4) However

(a} the employer shall be released at any time by the court

(il on security being furnished;

(ii) on payment of all or such part of the salary as the court considers reasonable; or

(iii) on the presentation of a bankruptcy petition by or against him; and

(b) the period of such detention shall not exceed 3 months.

(5) The bond to be given by an employer shall be a personal bond with one or more sureties, and the penalty for breach of the bond shall be fixed with due regard to the circumstances of the case and the means of the employer.

(6) If on or after a complaint by any employee under subsection (1) it appears to the court that there is good ground for believing that the employer has absconded, is absconding or is about to abscond, the court may issue a warrant for the arrest of the employer and he shall be detained in custody pending the hearing of the complaint unless he provides security to the satisfaction of the court.

(7) For the purposes of this section, a certificate signed by the Commissioner and issued to the court to the effect that the salary claimed has been paid or settled shall be sufficient evidence of the payment or settlement thereof.

For additional analytical, business and investment opportunities information, please contact Global Investment & Business Center, USA at (703) 370-8082. Fax: (703) 370-8083. E-mail: ibpusa3@gmail.com Global Business and Investment Info Databank - www.ibpus.com

Powers of Commissioner to investigate possible offences against Order.

135. [1] Whenever

(a} the Commissioner has reasonable grounds for suspecting that an offence against this Order has been committed;

{b) the Commissioner wishes to inquire into

(i) any matter dealt with by this Order;

(ii) any dispute as to such matter;

(iii) the death of or injury to an employee; or

(iv) any matter connected with the keeping of registers and other documents; or

{c) any person has complained to the Commissioner of any breach of any provision of this Order,

the Commissioner may summon any person who he has reason to believe can give information in respect of such offence or the subject-matter of such inquiry or complaint.

(2) If upon such inquiry the Commissioner considers that an offence has been committed, he may institute such criminal proceedings as he may think necessary.

(3) A summons issued under this section shall be in such form as the Commissioner may determine.

Examination on summons by Commissioner.

136. Any person summoned by the Commissioner under this Part shall attend at the date, time and place specified in the summons and to answer truthfully all questions which the Commissioner may put to him.

Right of employee to appear before Commissioner.

137. No employer shall prevent or attempt to prevent any employee from appearing before the Commissioner in pursuance of this Part.

Offences.

138. (1) Any person who fails to comply with any decision or order of the Commissioner made under sections 124 and 125 is guilty of an offence and liable on conviction to a fine not exceeding $5,000 and, in the case of a continuing offence, to a fine not exceeding $100 for each day the offence continues after conviction.

(2) Any person who

(a) wilfully obstructs the service of, or obedience to, any summons;

For additional analytical, business and investment opportunities information,
please contact Global Investment & Business Center, USA
at (703) 370-8082. Fax: (703) 370-8083. E-mail: ibpusa3@gmail.com
Global Business and Investment Info Databank - www.ibpus.com

(b) neglects to attend as required in such summons;

(c) commits, in respect of any inquiry or complaint, any offence referred to in Chapter X of the Penal Code (Chapter 22),

shall be punished as provided in that Chapter.

PART XVII GENERAL

Cost of proceedings.

139. No court fees shall be chargeable in the first instance on any proceedings commenced by an employee or by the Commissioner on his behalf, against his employer under this Order but, in case of a conviction or judgment against the employer, the court fees and the general costs of the proceedings shall be paid by the employer.

Application of fines.

140. When under this Order any court imposes a fine or enforces the payment of any sum secured by a recognisance or bond, the court may, if it thinks fit, direct that the whole or any part of such fine or sum when recovered be paid to the party complaining, or where the offence was committed by an employer in respect of a liability to pay money to an employee, that employee.

Service of summons.

141. (1) A summons issued by the Commissioner under Part XVI may be served on any person by delivering or tendering to him a copy thereof signed by the Commissioner:

Provided that

(a) if the person to be summoned has an agent authorised to accept service of the summons on his behalf, service on such agent shall be sufficient;

(b) if the person to be summoned cannot be found and has no agent authorised to accept service of the summons on his behalf, service on any

(2) When the summons is addressed to a limited company/ it may be served

{a} by leaving a copy thereof, signed by the Commissioner, at the registered office of that company;

{b) by sending such copy by registered post in a letter addressed to the company at its principal office, whether such office is within Brunei Darussalam or elsewhere; or

{c} by delivering such copy to any director1 secretary or other principal office of the company.

(3) When the person serving such summons delivers or tenders a copy of the summons to the person to be summoned or to an agent or other person on his behalf, he shall require the signature of the person to whom the copy is so delivered or tendered to sign an acknowledgement of service endorsed on the original summons.

\4) If

{a} such person refuses or is unable to sign the acknowledgment; or

{b} the person serving such summons cannot find the person to be summoned and there is no agent authorised to accept service of the summons on his behalf nor any other person on whom the service can be made,

the person serving such summons shall affix a copy of the summons on the outer door of the residence in which the person to be summoned ordinarily resides and then return the original to the Commissioner with a return endorsed thereon or annexed thereto stating that he has so affixed the copy and the circumstances under which he did so.

[5] The person serving such summons shall, in all cases in which the summons has been served under subsection I3L endorse or annex, or cause to be endorsed or annexed, on or to the original summons a return stating the time when and the manner in which the summons was served.

(6) When the summons is returned to the Commissioner under subsection [4], the Commissioner shall, if the return under that subsection has not been verified by an affidavit of the person serving the summons1 and mayl if it has been so verified, examine the person serving the summonses on oath touching the manner of service and may make such further enquiry in the matter as he thinks

fit and shall either declare that the summons has been duly served or order such other service as he thinks fit.

(7) When the Commissioner is satisfied that there is reason to believe that the person to be summoned is avoiding service or that for any other reason cannot be served in the ordinary way, the Commissioner may order the summons to be served by affixing a copy thereof in some conspicuous part of the house residence which the person to be summoned is known to have last resided, or in such other manner as the Commissioner thinks fit, or may order the substitution for the service of the notice by advertisement in the *Gazette* and in any local newspaper as the Commissioner may think fit.

(8) The service substituted by order of the Commissioner under subsection (7) shall be as effectual as if it had been served personally on the person to be summoned.

(9) Whenever service is substituted by order of the Commissioner, he shall fix such time for the appearance of the person to be summoned as the case may require.

(10) Any order or notice in writing made or issued by the Commissioner or other officer in the exercise of powers conferred by this Order may be served as if the order or notice were a summons, and the provisions of this section, other than subsection (1), shall apply to the service of any such order or notice.

Civil proceedings not barred.

142. Nothing in this Order shall operate to prevent any employer or employee from enforcing his civil rights and remedies for any breach or non-performance of a contract of service by any proceedings in court in any case in which proceedings are not instituted or, if instituted, are not proceeded with to judgment, under this Order.

Right to hearing.

143. The Commissioner and any officer authorised by him in writing shall have the right to appear and be heard before any court in any proceedings instituted by him under this Order or any regulations made thereunder.

Onus of proof.

144. In all proceedings under this Order, the onus of proving that he is not the employer or the person whose duty it is under this Order or under any regulations made thereunder to do or abstain from doing anything shall be on the Public servants.

145. For the purposes of this Order and of the Penal Code (Chapter 22), the Commissioner and all other officers appointed or authorised under this Order shall be deemed to be public servants within the meaning of the Penal Code.

Place of employment deemed to be public place.

146. For the purposes of sections 159 and 510 of the Penal Code (Chapter 22), every place of employment shall be deemed to be a public place.

Power to compound offences.

147. (1) The Commissioner or a Deputy Commissioner may compound any offence against this Order or any regulations made thereunder which is prescribed as a compoundable offence by making a written offer to compound to and by collecting from the person reasonably suspected of having committed that offence a sum not exceeding $1,000.

(2) An offer to compound pursuant to subsection (1) may be made at any time after the offence has been committed, but before any prosecution for it has been instituted, and where the amount specified in the offer is not paid within the time specified in the offer or within such extended period as the Commissioner or a Deputy Commissioner may grant, prosecution for the offence may be instituted at any time thereafter against the person to whom the offer was made.

(3) Where an offence has been compounded under subsection (2)

{a) no prosecution shall thereafter be instituted in respect of the offence against the person to whom the offer to compound was made; and

{b) any book, register or document seized in connection with the offence shall be released immediately.

General penalty for offences not otherwise provided for.

148. Any person who is guilty of any breach of or of any offence against this Order or any regulations made thereunder, for which no penalty is provided, is liable on conviction to a fine not exceeding $3,000, imprisonment for a term not exceeding one year or both.

Offences committed by bodies corporate.

149. (1) Where an offence against this Order which has been committed by a body corporate is proved to have been committed with the consent or connivance of, or to be attributable to any neglect on the part of, a director, manager, secretary or other similar officer of that body, or of any person purporting to act in any such capacity, he, as well as the body corporate, is also guilty of the offence and liable to be proceeded against and punished accordingly.

(2) In relation to a body corporate whose affairs are managed by its members, "director", in subsection (1), means any member of that body corporate.

Existing laws not affected.

Nothing in this Order shall operate to relieve any employer of any duty or liability imposed upon him by the provisions of any other written law or to limit any powers given to any public officer by any such written law.

Amendment of Schedules.

The Minister may, with the approval of His Majesty the Sultan and Yang Di-Pertuan and by order published in the *Gazette,* amend the Schedules.

Regulations.

152. (1) The Minister may, with the approval of His Majesty the Sultan and Yang Di-Pertuan, make regulations which are necessary or expedient for giving effect to and carrying out the provisions of this Order, including the prescription of fees and of any other thing required to be or which may be prescribed under this Order, and for the due administration thereof.

(2) Such regulations may include such incidental, consequential and supplementary provisions as the Minister considers necessary or expedient.

(3) In particular and without prejudice to the generality of subsection (1), such regulations may

{a} prescribe the circumstances and conditions under which women may be employed as employees or may work at night;

{b} require registers and records to be maintained and prescribe the form and contents thereof and the manner in which they shall be displayed;

{c} regulate the method of collecting statistics either in connection with or independently of any other department of Government, the staff to be employed in connection therewith, the duties to be performed and the publications, if any, to be issued;

(d) prescribe the forms in which, the times and places at and the manner in which particulars or information shall be furnished, and the manner in which they same shall be authenticated;

(eJ exempt from the obligation to furnish particulars or information under this Order, either wholly or to the prescribed extent, and either unconditionally or subject to the prescribed conditions, any employer or class of employer;

(f) prescribe the form of any register, summons or order required to be kept, issued or made under this Order;

(g) to prescribe the offences which may be compounded and the manner and procedure thereof;

(h) prescribe the fees payable for filing of claims under section 124 and for copies of notes of evidence and decisions recorded under section 127(1);

(i) provide for the establishment of a fund or other method of securing the discharge of any liabilities and the expenses of repatriation of employees upon such conditions and subject to such control as the Minister considers necessary and for the administration of such a fund;

(j) prescribe penalties for any contravention or failure to comply with any of the provisions of the regulations made under this section; except that no such penalty shall exceed $1,000 in the case of a first offence or $2,000 in the case of a second or subsequent offence under the same regulation within one year.

Repeals.
153. The following written laws are repealed
the Labour Act (Chapter 93);
the Labour (Domestic Servants) Rules (R2 of Chapter 93);
the Labour (Maternity Benefits) Rules (R3 of Chapter 93);
the Labour (Public Holidays) Rules (R4 of Chapter 93);
the Labour (Payment of Wages by Cheque) Rules (R7 of Chapter 93);
the Labour (Special Places of Employment) Notification (N1 of Chapter 93);
the Labour (Restriction on Employment of Children) Notification (N2 of Chapter 93).

Savings.

154. (1) All agreements and contracts (by whatsoever name so called) entered into between an employer and an employee, valid on the commencement of this Order, shall continue to be in force after such commencement and, subject to any provision contained in any such agreement or contract, the parties thereto shall be subject to, and entitled to the benefit of, the provisions of this Order.

(2) Any licence, document, endorsement, exemption or certificate prepared, made, issued or granted under the Labour Act (Chapter 93) (repealed by this Order) shall, so far as it is not inconsistent with any provision of this Order and except as otherwise expressly provided in this Order or in any other written law, continue and be deemed to have been prepared, made, issued or granted under the corresponding provisions of this Order and shall have effect accordingly.

(3) All subsidiary legislation not repealed by section 153 and all appointments made and any thing done under the Labour Act (Chapter 93) (repealed by this Order) and in force immediately prior to the commencement of this Order shall, so far as it is not inconsistent with the provisions of this Order, continue in force as if made or done under this Order until they are amended, repealed or revoked under this Order.

SCHEDULES

FIRST SCHEDULE (section 2)

OTHER WORKMEN Bus conductor. Lorry attendant. Bus, lorry, van and taxi drivers. Motorboat and speedboat drivers. Bus inspector. Goldsmith and silversmith employed in the premises of the employer. Tailor and dressmaker employed in the premises of the employer. Harbour-craft crew. All workmen employed on piece rates in the premises of the employer.

for copy of record of decision or order made under section 127(1) $0.50 per page

THIRD SCHEDULE (section 2) PUBLIC **HOLIDAYS**
    1st. January (New Year's Day)
    First day of Hjjriah
    Chinese New Year
    23rd. February (National Day of Brunei Darussalam)
    Maulud Prophet Mohammad's birthday
    15th. July (His Majesty the Sultan and Yang Di-Pertuan's birthday)
7. First day of Ramadh~n
    Anniversary of the revelation of the Quran
    Hari Raya Aidilfitri
    Hari Raya Aidiladha
    25th. December (Christmas Day)
Made this 13th. day of Ramadan, 1430 Hijriah corresponding to the 3rd. day of September, 2009 at Our Istana Nurul Iman, Bandar Seri Begawan, Brunei Darussalam.
    HIS MAJESTY THE SULTAN AND YANG DI-PERTUAN BRUNEI DARUSSALAM

LABOUR (PUBLIC CONTRACTS) RULES

Citation.

1. These Rules may be cited as the Labour (Public Contracts)Rules.

Interpretation.

2. In these Rules, unless the context otherwise requires —

"Government" means the Government of Brunei Darussalam andincludes such Public Authorities, Municipal Boards or local authorities as theMinister may from time to time specify;

"Public contract" means any contract which fulfils the followingconditions —

(a) that one party to the contract is the Government or has enteredinto the contract with assistant from the Government by way of grant, loan,subsidy, licence, guarantee or other similar form of assistance;

(b) that the execution of the contract involves —

(i) the expenditure of Government funds; and

(ii) the employment of workers by the other party to the contract;

(c) that the contract is a contract for —

(i) the construction, alteration, repair or demolition of public works;or

(ii) the manufacture, assembly, handling or shipment of materials,supplies or equipment; or

(iii) the performance or supply of services;

(d) that the contract is awarded by a duly authorised officer of the Government; and

(e) that the contract involves the expenditure of Government fundsof an amount of not less than $10,000.

Terms and condition of public contracts set out in the Schedule.

3. There shall be implied in every public contract entered into on or after the commencement of these Rules the terms and conditions set out in the Schedule hereto and it shall be the duty of every contractor who enters into any such contract to observe and comply with such terms and conditions in the execution of such contract.

SCHEDULE TERMS AND CONDITIONS

1. The contractor shall, in respect of the workers employed in theexecution of a public contract, pay rates of wages and observe hours andconditions of work not less favourable than those established for work of thesame character in the trade or industry concerned in the district where the workis carried out by any written law or by collective agreement or other recognised machinery of negotiation or arbitration between employers andtrade unions representatives respectively of substantial proportions of theemployers and workers engaged in the trade or industry in such district(hereinafter referred to as "established rates and conditions").

2. In the absence of established rates and conditions in the trade orindustry in the district, the contractor shall observe established rates andconditions in other districts where the trade or industry is carried on undersimilar general circumstances.

3. In the absence of any established rates and conditions as defined in paragraphs 1 and 2 of this schedule the contractor shall pay rates of wages and observe hours and conditions of work which are not less favourable than the general level of wages, hours and conditions observed by other employers whose general circumstances in the trade or industry in which the contractor is engaged are similar.

4. Before being allowed to tender for any public contract thecontractor shall certify that to the best of his knowledge and belief the wages,hours of work and conditions of work of all workers employed by him in the tradeor industry in which he is offering himself as a contractor are fair andreasonable having regards to the provisions of this Schedule.

5. In the event of any differences or dispute arising (as to whatwages ought to be paid, or what hours or other working conditions ought to beobserved in accordance with the provisions of this Schedule, it shall, if not otherwise disposed of, be referred by the Commissioner of Labour toan independent tribunal, for decision. In arriving at its decision the tribunal,in the absence of any established rates and conditions in the trade or industryconcerned as specified in paragraph 1 of this Schedule, shall have regard to anyagreement, custom practice or award that may be brought to its notice relatingto the wages, hours or conditions of work of persons employed in a capacitysimilar to that of the persons to whom the difference or dispute relates intrades or industries carried on under similar general circumstances.

6. A sub-contractor shall be bound in all cases to conform to theconditions of the main contract and the main contractor shall be responsible forthe observance of all contract conditions on the part of sub-contractors.

7. Contractors and sub-contractors shall recognise the freedom oftheir workers to be members of registered trade unions.

8. The Commissioner of Labour may require any contractor concerned in the execution of a public contract to file a certificate —

(i) showing the rates of wages and hours of work of the various classes orworkers employed in the execution of the public contract;

(ii) whether any wages in respect of the said work remain in arrears;and

(iii) that all the conditions of work of the public contract have been dulycomplied with.

9. The contractor shall also from time to time furnish to theCommissioner of Labour such further detailed information and evidence as theCommissioner may deem necessary in order to satisfy himself that the conditionsof this Schedule have been complied with.

10. In the event of default being made in payment of any money inrespect of wages of any worker employed on the public contract or in respect ofany money due to such worker under any law relating to Workmen'sCompensation and if a claim thereafter is filed in the office of theCommissioner of Labour and proof thereof satisfactory to the Commissioner isfurnished, the Commissioner may, failing payment, by the contractor arrange for the payment of such claim out of the monies at any time payableunder the said contract and the amount so paid shall be deemed payment to thecontractor.

11. Any contractor or sub-contractor who is found to be in breach ofthe conditions of this Schedule shall cease to be awarded contracts for suchperiod as the Minister may determine after consultation with the Commissioner ofLabour and duly authorised officer of the Government by whom the contract wasawarded.

STRATEGIC BUSINESS AND LEGAL INFORMATION

Brunei Darussalam is still very much dependent on revenues from crude oil and natural gas to finance its development programs. Aside from this, Brunei Darussalam also receives income from rents, royalties, corporate tax and dividends. Due to the non-renewable nature of oil and gas, economic diversification has been in Brunei Darussalam's national development agenda. In the current Seventh national Development Plan, 1996-2000, the government has allocated more than $7.2 billion for the implementation of various projects and programs.

Brunei Darussalam is the third largest oil producer in Southeast Asia and it produced 163,000 barrels per day. It is also the fourth largest producer of liquefied natural gas in the world.

Brunei Darussalam is the third largest oil producer in Southeast Asia and it produced 163,000 barrels per day. It is also the fourth largest producer of liquefied natural gas in the world.
National Development Plan 1996 – 2000

Brunei welcomes foreign investment. Foreign investors are invited to actively participate in the current economic diversification programme of the country. The programme hinges on the development of the private sector. The Ministry of Industry and Primary Resources was formed in 1989 with the responsibility of promoting and facilitating industrial development in Brunei Darussalam. Brunei Darussalam offers all investors security, stability, continuity, confidence and competitiveness.

Competitive investment incentives are ready and available for investors throughout the business cycle of start up, growth, maturity and expansion. The Investment Incentive Act which was enacted in 1975 provides tax advantages at start up and ongoing incentives throughout growth and expansion that are comparable if not better than those offered by other countries in the region.

The Investment Incentives Act makes provision for encouraging the establishment and development of industrial and other economic enterprises, for economic expansion and incidental purposes.

Investment incentive benefits vary from one program to other. Amongst the benefits are:

- Exemption from income tax;
- Exemption from taxes on imported duties on machinery, equipment, component parts, accessories or building structures;
- Exemption from taxes on imported raw material not available or produced in Brunei Darussalam intended for the production of the pioneer products;
- Carry forward of losses and allowances.

This Act provides tax relief for a company which is granted pioneer status.

- Companies awarded pioneer status are exempted from corporate tax, tax import of raw materials and capital goods for a period ranging from 2 to 5 years, depending on fixed capital expenditure with possible extension at the discretion of the relevant authorities.

- Enterprises which are given expansion certificates are given tax relief for a period between 3 to 5 years.
- Approved foreign loans can be exempted from paying the 20% withholding tax for interest paid to non-resident lenders.

Brunei Darussalam is flexible towards foreign equity requirements. 100% foreign equity can be considered for export-oriented industries with the exception of industries based on local resources, industries related to national food security and car dealership whereby some level of local participation is required.
Industrial activities are classified into four categories:

- Industries related to national food security
- Industries for local market
- Industries based on local resources
- Industries for export market

Industrial policies including manpower, ownership, government support and facilities remain open and flexible for all categories of industrial activities. Brunei Darussalam maintains a realistic approach where a variety of arrangements are feasible. Policies relating to ownership allow for full foreign ownership, majority foreign ownership and minority foreign ownership, as per the type of industry and situation.
Only activities relating to national food security and those based on local resources require some level of local participation. Industries for the local market not related to national food security and industries for total export can be totally foreign owned. Overall, in Brunei Darussalam, any industrial enterprise will be considered.
The Investment Incentives Order 2001 expanded the tax holidays avaiable to investors.
Examples include:

- Corporate tax relief of up to 5 years for companies that invest B$500,000 to B$2.5 million in approved ventures
- 8-years tax relief for investing more than B$2.5 million
- An 11-year tax break if the venture is located in a high-tech industrial park.

INVESTMENT AND BUSINESS CLIMATE

Brunei Darussalam has enormous business potential that is yet to be exploited. The country has the advantage of peace and political stability, which is favourable for business activities.
Foreign investments are always welcome in Brunei and foreign investors are invited to actively engage in the current economic diversification programme.

The Ministry of Industry and Primary Resources, which was established in 1989, is the main government agency that promotes and facilitates investment, business and trade activities in the country.
Competitive investment incentives are ready and available for investors throughout the business cycle of start up, growth, maturity and expansion.
The Investment Incentive Act enacted in 1975 provides tax advantages at start up and ongoing incentives throughout growth and expansion that are comparable if not better than those offered by other countries in the region.

WHY INVEST IN BRUNEI DARUSSALAM?
¨ Brunei Darussalam is a stable and prosperous country that offers not only excellent

For additional analytical, business and investment opportunities information,
please contact Global Investment & Business Center, USA
at (703) 370-8082. Fax: (703) 370-8083. E-mail: ibpusa3@gmail.com
Global Business and Investment Info Databank - www.ibpus.com

infrastructure but also a strategic location within the Asean group of countries.
¨ No personal income tax is imposed in Brunei. Businesses are also not imposed sales tax, payroll, manufacturing and export tax. Approved foreign investors can enjoy a company tax holiday of up to eight years.

¨ The regulations relating to foreign participation in equity are flexible. In many instances there can be 100% foreign ownership.

¨ Approval for foreign workers, ranging from labourers to managers, can be secured.
¨ The cost of utilities is among the lowest in the region.
¨ The local market, while relatively small, is lucrative and most overseas investors will encounter little or no competition.

¨ The living conditions in Brunei Darussalam are among the best and most secure in the region
¨ On top of all, His Majesty's Government genuinely welcomes foreign investment in almost any enterprise and will ensure that you receive speedy, efficient and practical assistance on all your inquiries.

SUPPORTIVE ENVIRONMENT

Brunei Darussalam offers vast land and a variety of facilities throughout all four districts in the country. The majority of the 12 industrial sites presently developed are ready and available for occupation. Large expanses for agroforestry and aquaculture are also available. Rental terms and tenancy agreements are competitive and the sites offer a range of facilities, infrastructure and resources. Brunei Darussalam gives priority to ensuring the stability of the natural environment. As such, all sites are free from pollution and are ecologically well balanced. The government's philosophy is sustainable development. Therefore, all polluting industries are banned and one of the continuing criteria for engaging any industry's participation is the impact on the environment.

INFRASTRUCTURE

The country's infrastructure is well developed and ready to cater for the needs of the new and vigorous economic activities under the current economic diversification programme. The country's two main ports, at Muara and Kuala Belait, offer direct shipping to Hong Kong, Singapore and several other Asian destinations. Muara, the deep-water port situated 29 kilometres from the capital was opened in 1973 and has since been considerably developed. It has 12,542 sq. metres of transit sheds. Container yards have been increased in size and a container freight station handles unstuffing operations. Meanwhile, Pulau Muara Besar is being developed as a centre for dockyard, ship salvaging and for other related industries. The recently expanded Brunei International Airport in Bandar Seri Begawan can now handle 1.5 million passengers and 50,000 tonnes of cargo a year. The 2,000 kilometre road network serving the entire country is being expanded and modernised. A main highway runs the entire length of the country's coastline. It conveniently links Muara, the port of entry at one end, to Belait, the oil producing district at the western end of the state.

ECONOMY

The economy of the country is dominated by the oil and gas and liquefied natural gas industries and Government expenditure patterns. The country's exports consist of three major commodities namely crude oil, petroleum products and liquefied natural gas. Exports are destined mainly for Japan, the United States and Asean countries. The second most important industry is the construction industry. This is directly the result of increased investment by the Government in development and infrastructure projects within the five-year National Development Plans. Brunei Darussalam has entered a new phase of development in its drive towards economic diversification from dependence on the oil and liquefied natural gas-based economy. Official statistics showed that exports during the 1996 to 2000 period increased from B$3,682.1 million in 1996 to B$6,733.5 million in 2000, while imports declined from B$3,513.6 million to B$1,907.8 million. This trend has increased the balance of trade from B$168.9 million in 1996 to B$3289.0 million in 2000. In the current 8th National Development Plan, which is the last phase of Brunei's 20-year National Development Programme, the government is allocating a total of B$1.1 billion for commerce and industry. The Brunei International Financial Centre (BIFC) set up in 2000, is another effort undertaken by the government to diversify the country's economy. Brunei Darussalam has the potential to become an international financial centre and has the capability to provide similar facilities as those available in other successful financial centres. Brunei has political stability, modern infrastructure and up-to-date international communications system. Seven bills have been passed to govern the establishment and supervision of BIFC. These include the International Business Companies Order 2000, International Limited Partnership Order 2000, International Banking order 2000, International Trust Order 2000, Registered Agents and Trust Licensing order 2000, Money Laundering Order 2000 and Criminal Conduct (Recovery of Proceed) Order 2000. The BIFC also plans to establish international Islamic banks in Brunei whose legal framework has been provided under the International Banking Order 2000. The establishment of the international Islamic banks is in line with the national aspirations of encouraging the development of Islamic finance and also of making the Sultanate as a regional and international Islamic financial centre.

INDUSTRIES

Industrial activities are classified into four categories:

1. Industries related to national food security
2. Industries for local market
3. Industries based on local resources
4. Industries for export market

FLEXIBLE POLICIES

Industrial policies including manpower, ownership, government support and facilities remain open and flexible for all categories of industrial activities. Brunei Darussalam maintains a realistic approach where a variety of arrangements are feasible. Policies relating to ownership allow for full foreign ownership, majority foreign ownership and minority foreign ownership, as per type of industry and situation. Only activities relating to national food security and industries for total export can be totally foreign owned. Overall, in Brunei Darussalam, any industrial enterprise will be considered.

FINANCE, BANK AND INSURANCE

Brunei Darussalam has no central bank, but the Ministry of Finance through the Treasury, the Currency Board and the Brunei Investment Agency exercises most of the functions of a central bank. Brunei Darussalam has not established a single monetary authority. All works related to finance are being carried out by three institutions.

· The Brunei Currency Board (BCB) is responsible for the circulation and management of currencies in the country.

· The Financial Institution Division (FID) is tasked with the issuing of licenses and regulations to financial institutions including the enforcement of minimum cash balance in accordance to specified rates for the interest of investors

· The Banks Association of Brunei determines the daily interest rates. However, there is also an indication that a single monetary authority may be established in the future to undertake these functions.

In 2000, it was recorded that there were 85 financial institutions including banks, financial companies, security companies, conventional insurance companies, Takaful companies, remittance companies and moneychangers. The existing nine commercial banks have established many branches from 29 in 1995 to 61 in 2000. The number of finance companies has also increased from three in 1996 to five in 2000. Security companies remain at two and the number of conventional insurance companies decreased from 22 in 1996 to 19 in 2000. This is the result of the merging of the branch and parent companies. The number of Takaful companies have risen from two in 1996 to three in 2000. In 1996 and 1997 there were 20 moneychangers operating in the country. The number increased to 33 in 1998 but has reduced to 24 in 2000. Remittance companies have also experienced the same trend as they increased from 16 in 1996 to 30 in 1998 but have reduced to 23 in 2000. The Brunei dollar is pegged to the Singapore dollar. The Ministry of Finance believes that the Monetary Authority of Singapore exercises sufficient caution and such a link will not have detrimental effects on the economies of either country.

CURRENCY

Currency matters are under the jurisdiction of the Brunei Currency Board (BCB) which manages and distributes currency notes and coins in the country with the main mission of ensuring the integrity of the currency issued to safeguard public interest. In September 2000, the money supply comprising currency in circulation and demand deposits amounted to B$2,295 million compared to B$3,366 million, B$2,430 million, B$2,493 million and B$2,727 million in 1996, 1997, 1998 and 1999 respectively.

FOREIGN EXCHANGE

There is no restriction in foreign exchange. Banks permit non-resident accounts to be maintained and there is no restriction on borrowing by non-residents.

TAXATION

Brunei Darussalam has no personal income tax. Sole proprietorship and partnership businesses are not subject to income tax. Only companies are subject to income tax and it is one of the lowest in the region. Moreover tax advantages at start-up and ongoing incentives throughout growth and expansion offer investors profitable conditions that are comparable if not better than those offered by other countries in the region.

COMPANY TAXATION

Companies are subject to tax on the following types of income: -
¨ Gains of profits from any trade, business or vocation,
¨ Dividends received from companies not previously assessed for tax in Brunei Darussalam

¨ Interest and discounts
¨ Rent, royalties, premiums and any other profits arising from properties.

There is no capital gains tax. However, where the Collector of Income Tax can establish that the gains form part of the normal trading activities, they become taxable as revenue gains.

a. Scope of Income Tax
A resident company in Brunei Darussalam is liable to income tax on its income derived from or accrued in Brunei Darussalam or received from overseas. A non-resident company is only taxed on its income arising in Brunei Darussalam.

b. Concept of Residence
A company, whether incorporated locally or overseas, is considered as resident in Brunei Darussalam for tax purposes if the control and management of its business is exercised in Brunei Darussalam. The control and management of a company is normally regarded as resident in Brunei Darussalam if, among other things, its directors' meetings are held in Brunei Darussalam. The profits of a company are subject to tax at the rate of 30%. Tax concession may be available. The profit or loss of a company as per its account is adjusted for income tax purposes to take into account certain allowable expenses, certain expenses prohibited from deduction, wear and tear allowances and any losses brought forward from previous years, in order to arrive at taxable profits.

TREATMENT OF DIVIDENDS

Dividends accruing in, derived from, or received in Brunei Darussalam by a corporation are included in taxable income, apart from dividends received from a corporation taxable in Brunei Darussalam which are excluded.No tax is deducted at source on dividends paid by a Brunei Darussalam corporation. Dividends received in Brunei Darussalam from United Kingdom or Commonwealth countries are grossed up in the tax computation and credit is claimed against the Brunei Darussalam tax liability for tax suffered either under the double tax treaty with the United Kingdom or the provision Commonwealth tax relief.
Any other dividends are included net in the tax computation and no foreign tax is available. Brunei Darussalam does not impose any withholding tax on dividends.

ALLOWABLE DEDUCTIONS

All expenses wholly or exclusively incurred in the production of taxable income are allowable as deduction for tax purposes.
These deductions include:
¨ Interest on borrowed money used in acquiring income
¨ Rent on land and buildings used in the trade or business
¨ Costs of repair of premises, plant and machinery
¨ Bad debts and specific doubtful debts, with any subsequent recovery being treated as income when received, and
¨ Employer's contribution to approved pensions or provident funds

DISALLOWABLE DEDUCTIONS

Expenses not allowed as deductions for tax purposes include:
¨ Expenses not wholly or exclusively incurred in acquiring income
¨ Domestic private expenses
¨ Any capital withdrawal or any sum used as capital

¨ Any capital used in improvement apart from replanting of plantation
¨ Any sum recoverable under an insurance or indemnity contract
¨ Rent or repair expenses not incurred in the earning of income
¨ Any income tax paid in Brunei Darussalam or in other countries and
¨ Payments to any unapproved pension or provident funds

Donations are not allowable but claimable if they are made to approved institutions.

ALLOWANCES FOR CAPITAL EXPENDITURE

Depreciation is not an allowable expense and is replaced by capital allowances for qualifying expenditure. The taxpayer is entitled to claim wear and tear allowances calculated as follows:

a. Industrial Buildings
An initial allowance of 10% is given in the year of expenditure, and an annual allowance of 2% of the qualifying expenditure is provided on a straight-line basis until the total expenditure is written off.

b. Machinery and Plant
An initial allowance of 20% of the cost is given in the year of expenditure together with annual allowances calculated on the reducing value of the assets. The rates prescribed by the Collector of Income Tax range from 3% to 25%, depending on the nature of the assets. Balancing allowances or charges are made on disposal of the industrial building machinery or plant. These adjustments cover the shortfall or excess of the tax written down value as compared to the sale proceeds. Any balancing charge is limited to tax allowances previously granted, and any surplus is considered a capital gain and therefore does not become part of chargeable income. Unabsorbed capital allowances can be carried forward indefinitely but must be set off against income from the same trade.

LOSS CARRYOVERS
Losses incurred by a company can be carried forward for six years for setoff against future income and can be carried back one year. There is no requirement regarding continuity of ownership of the company and also the loss set-off is not restricted to the same trade.

FOREIGN TAX RELIEF
A double taxation agreement exists with the United Kingdom and provides proportionate relief from Brunei Darussalam income tax upon any part of the income which has been or is liable to be charged with United Kingdom income tax.
Tax credits are only available for resident companies. Unilateral relief may be obtained on income arising from Commonwealth countries that provide reciprocal relief. However, the maximum relief cannot exceed half the Brunei Darussalam rate. This relief applies to both resident and non-resident companies.

STAMP DUTY
Stamp duties are levied on a variety of documents. Certain types of documents attract an ad valorem duty, whereas with other documents the duty varies with the nature of the documents.

PETROLEUM TAXES
Special legislation exists in respect of income tax from petroleum operations, which is taxable under the Income Tax (Petroleum) Act 1963 as amended.

For additional analytical, business and investment opportunities information,
please contact Global Investment & Business Center, USA
at (703) 370-8082. Fax: (703) 370-8083. E-mail: ibpusa3@gmail.com
Global Business and Investment Info Databank - www.ibpus.com

WITHHOLDING TAXES
Interest paid to non-resident companies under a charge, debenture or in the respect of a loan, is subject to withholding tax of 20%. There are no other withholding taxes.

ESTATE DUTY
Estate duty is levied on an estate of over $2 million at 3% flat rate for a person who has died on or after 15th December 1988.

IMPORT DUTY
In general, basic foodstuffs and goods for industrial use are exempted from import duties. Electrical equipment and appliances, timber products, photographic materials and equipment, furniture, motor vehicles and spare parts are levied minimum duties, while cosmetics and perfumes are subject to 30% duty. Cigarettes are dutiable items, but the rates are low compared with neighbouring countries.

BUSINESSES AND COMPANIES

Registration and Guidelines
In Brunei Darussalam a business may be set up under any of the following forms:
¨ Sole proprietorship
¨ Partnership
¨ Company (Private or Public Company)
¨ Branch of foreign company

All businesses must be registered with the Registrar of Companies and Business Names. The proposed name of business or companies must first of all be approved by the Registrar of Companies and Business Names. For each name proposed, a fee of $5.00 is imposed.

Sole Proprietorship
¨ Upon arrival, a business name certificate is issued and a fee of $30.00 is imposed
¨ At the moment, it is not subject to corporate tax
¨ Foreigners are not eligible to register

Partnership
¨ May consist of individuals, local companies and/or branches of foreign companies
¨ The maximum permitted number of partners is 20
¨ Upon approval, a business name certificate is issued and a fee of $30.00 is imposed
¨ Application by foreign individuals are subject to prior clearance by the Immigration Department, Economic Planning and Development Unit and the Labour Department before they are registered
¨ At the moment, it is not subject to corporate tax

Private Company
¨ May be limited by shares, guarantee or both by shares and guarantee or unlimited
¨ Must have at least two and not more than 50 shareholders
¨ Shareholders need not be Brunei citizens or residents.
¨ Restrict the right of members to transfer shares and prohibit any invitations to the public to subscribe for shares and debentures
¨ A subsidiary company may hold shares in its parent company
¨ Memorandum and Articles of Association must be filed with the Registrar of Companies and Business Names with other incorporation documents in the prescribed form
¨ Upon arrival, a Certificate of Incorporation will be issued and a fee of $25 is imposed
¨ The registration fees are based on a graduated scale on the authorised share capital of the

company
¨ No minimum share capital is required
¨ Private Companies are required to do the following:
1. Appoint auditors who are registered in Brunei Darussalam
2. Prepare a profit and loss account and balance sheet, accompanied by the Director's Report annually
3. Submit accounting data annually to the Economic Development and Planning Department of the Ministry of Finance
4. File annual returns, containing information on directors and shareholders
5. Keep the following records:
a. Minute Book of Members' Meetings
b. Minute Book of Director's Meetings
c. Minute Book of Manager's Meetings
d. Register of Members
e. Register of Directors and Managers
f. Register of Charges
¨ Subject to corporate tax of 30% of the gross yearly profit

PUBLIC COMPANY
¨ May be limited or unlimited
¨ May issue freely transferable shares to the public
¨ Must have at least seven shareholders
¨ Shareholders need not be Brunei citizens or residents
¨ Subsidiary company may hold shares in its parent companies
¨ Half the directors in the company must be either Brunei Citizens or ordinary residents in Brunei Darussalam.
¨ Memorandum and Articles of Association must be registered with other incorporation documents in the prescribed forms
¨ Upon approval, Registration of Companies Certificate will be issued and a fee of $25.00 is imposed
¨ The registration fees are based on a graduated scale on the authorised share capital of the company.
¨ No minimum share capital is required
¨ Public Companies are required to do the following:
1. Appoint auditors who are registered in Brunei Darussalam
2. Prepare each year's profit and loss account and balance sheet, accompanied by the Director's Report annually.
3. Submit accounting data annually to the Economic Development and Planning Department of the Ministry of Finance
4. File annual returns, containing information on directors and shareholders
5. Keep the following records:
a. Minute Book of Members' Meetings
b. Minute Book of Director's Meetings
c. Minute Book of Manager's Meetings
d. Register of Members
e. Register of Directors and Managers
f. Register of Charges
¨ Subject to corporate tax of 30% of the gross yearly profit.

BRANCH OF FOREIGN COMPANY
The following documents must be filed with the Registrar of Companies and Business Names.
a. A certified copy of the charter, statutes or Memorandum and Articles of Association or other instruments defining the constitution of the foreign company duly authenticated and, when

For additional analytical, business and investment opportunities information,
please contact Global Investment & Business Center, USA
at (703) 370-8082. Fax: (703) 370-8083. E-mail: ibpusa3@gmail.com
Global Business and Investment Info Databank - www.ibpus.com

necessary, with English translation.
b. A list of directors together with their particulars and the names and addresses of one or more persons residing in Brunei Darussalam authorised to accept notices on the company's behalf.

¨ Upon approval, a Certificate of Incorporation will be issued and a fee of $25 is imposed
¨ The registration fees are based on a graduated scale on the authorised share capital of the company.
¨ No minimum share capital is required
¨ Branch of foreign company is required to do the following:
1. Appoint auditors who are registered in Brunei Darussalam
2. Prepare each year's profit and loss account and balance sheet, accompanied by the Director's Report annually.
3. Submit accounting data annually to the Economic Development and Planning Department of the Ministry of Finance
4. File annual returns, containing information on directors and shareholders
5. Keep the following records:
a. Minute Book of Members' Meetings
b. Minute Book of Director's Meetings
c. Minute Book of Manager's Meetings
d. Register of Members
e. Register of Directors and Managers
f. Register of Charges
¨ Subject to corporate tax of 30% of the gross yearly profit.

REGISTRATION OF TRADEMARKS AND PATENTS
Trademarks are registrable provided the requirements laid down in the Trademarks Act (Cap 98) are satisfied. Once registered, they are viable for an initial period of seven years and renewable for a further period of 14 years.
Any person who obtains a grant of a patent in the UK or Malaysia or Singapore may apply to the Ministry of Law within three years of the date of issue of such grant to have the grant registered in Brunei Darussalam under the Invention Act (Cap 72). There is no specific legislation for copyright protection, but UK legislation would apply where necessary.

EMPLOYMENT REGULATIONS
All non-Brunei Darussalam citizens require a work permit which are valid for two years. Application must first be made to the Labour Department for a labour license. On the recommendation of the Labour Department, the Immigration Department will give permission for the workers to enter Brunei Darussalam. The Labour Department requires either a cash deposit or a banker's guarantee to cover the cost of a one-way airfare to the home country of an immigrant worker. An approved labour licence cannot be altered for at least six months after issue. Applications will not be accepted until the formation of a local company or branch of a foreign company has been officially approved and registered.

INDUSTRIAL RELATIONS
The Trade Disputes Act (Cap 129) accords to trade unions the customary immunities and protections in respect of facts done in furtherance of trade disputes. It prescribes procedures for conciliation and subject to the consent of the parties, arbitration in disputes where machinery within the industry concerned does not exist or has failed to achieve settlement. Trade unionism of either the employers or workers is extensively practiced in Brunei Darussalam. As has been already observed, the industrial structure consists almost entirely of small scale enterprises. This state of affairs and nature and cultural characteristics of the population are conductive to accommodation and a 'give and take attitude' rather than a confrontational attitude. Except in the oil industry, the system of collective bargaining has not emerged. Relations between employers

and employees are generally good. Existing labour laws have adequate provisions such as for termination of employment, medical care, maternity leave and compensation for disablement. Labour disputes are very rare. The Government has recently implemented the Workers' Provident Fund Enactment to cover workers both in the public and private sectors.

INTERNATIONAL RELATION AND TRADE DEVELOPMENT

In the perspectives of economic co-operation with foreign countries at the bilateral and multilateral levels, Brunei Darussalam seeks relevant agencies that can contribute to development and networking.

The areas of concern are:

¨ To facilitate investment into Brunei Darussalam
¨ To facilitate the development of trade
¨ To enhance human resources development and technology transfer, and
¨ To enhance bilateral, regional and multilateral economic cooperation

In pursuing these areas, mechanism for consultations and cooperation have been established through bilateral, regional and multilateral forum such as Association of Southeast Asian Nations (ASEAN), Asia Pacific Economic Cooperation (APEC), Organisation of Islamic Countries (OIC), European Union (EU), the Commonwealth, United Nation (UN) and the Non-Aligned Movement (NAM).

INVESTMENT PROMOTION

In the area of investment, Brunei Darussalam is currently engaged in a programme to improve its investment climate to create and enhance investment opportunities in Brunei Darussalam, both for local and foreign investors. The programme involves the establishment of bilateral trade investment treaties with foreign Government and Memorandums of Understanding (MoUs) between Brunei Darussalam's private sector and private sectors of other countries.

TRADE DEVELOPMENT

In the area of trade development, Brunei Darussalam is facilitating market opportunities to increase market access in the region as well as globally. Brunei Darussalam practices open multilateral trading system which are being pursued through regional and multilateral trading arrangements such as the ASEAN Free Trade Area (AFTA) and General Agreement of Trade and Tariffs (GATT). This open trade policy is consistent with Brunei Darussalam's efforts in pursuing outward looking economic policies that will assist the country in expanding its industrial and primary resource-based industries.

HUMAN RESOURCE DEVELOPMENT AND TECHNOLOGY TRANSFER

In the area of human resource development and technology transfer, there is a need to improve the technological capabilities of existing local industries, which are mainly small and medium scale enterprises. This is in view of the existing shortage of local manpower and thus the need to import foreign workers. The programmes are targeted towards the development of the mid-band occupational structure in which Brunei Darussalam has the advantage in view of cost factors such as the non-existence of income tax. Within the context of general economic cooperation, Brunei Darussalam will continue to enhance economic linkages with other countries in the region as well as outside the region.

THE INVESTMENT & TRADING ARM OF THE GOVERNMENT

Semaun Holdings Sdn Bhd

Semaun Holdings Sendirian Berhad, incorporated on 8th December 1994, is a private limited company that serves as an investment/trading arm of the Government with the purpose of accelerating industrial development in Brunei Darussalam through direct investment. Semaun Holdings is wholly owned by His Majesty's Government and plays an important role in supporting the economic diversification programmes in the country. The Chairman is the Honourable Minister of Industry and Primary Resources, Pehin Orang Kaya Setia Pahlawan Dato Seri Setia Haji Awang Abdul Rahman bin Dato Setia Haji Mohammad Taib, who is also the Chairman to the Industrial and Trade Development Council, a body entrusted with facilitating the industrialisation programme of Brunei Darussalam. The mission of Semaun Holdings is to spearhead industrial and commercial development through direct investment in key industrial sectors. Its primary objectives are:

¨ To accelerate and commercial development in Brunei Darussalam
¨ To generate industrial and commercial opportunities for active participation of citizens

Investment Philosophy

a. Local investment
First priority shall be given to investment in the country. Investment shall be in areas of strategic importance and NOT in direct competition with local companies
b. Overseas Capital
The Holdings may invest overseas in activities which reinforce the position of its local investment, preferably through strategic partnering with suitable local companies

Authorised Capital

BND 500 million (Five hundred million dollars)

Type of Investment

The Holdings shall invest through its
¨ Wholly owned operations
¨ Joint Venture Companies
¨ Equity Participation

Scope of Operation

The Holdings shall invest in business, trading and commercial enterprises including agriculture, fishery, forestry, industry and mining activities in Brunei Darussalam. Participation in investment related activities outside the country are also considered.
For more information please contact:
Semaun Holdings Sdn Bhd,
Office Unit No. 02, Block D,
Complex Yayasan Sultan Haji Hassanal Bolkiah,
Bandar Seri Begawan 2085,
Brunei Darussalam
Telephone no: (673) 223-2957 Fax : (673) 223-2956

TRAVEL TO BRUNEI

US STATE DEPARTMENT SUGGESTIONS

COUNTRY DESCRIPTION: Brunei (known formally as the State of Brunei Darussalam) is a small Islamic Sultanate on the north coast of the island of Borneo. The capital, Bandar Seri Begawan, is the only major city. Tourist facilities are good, and generally available.

ENTRY REQUIREMENTS: For information about entry requirements, travelers may consult the Consular Section of the Embassy of the State of Brunei Darussalam, Suite 300, 2600 Virginia Ave., N.W. Washington, D.C. 20037; tel. (202) 342-0159.

MEDICAL FACILITIES: Adequate public and private hospitals and medical services are available in Brunei. Medical care clinics do not require deposits usually, but insist upon payment in full at time of treatment, and may require proof of ability to pay prior to treating or discharging a foreigner. U.S. medical insurance is not always valid outside the United States, and may not be accepted by health providers in Brunei. Travelers may wish to check with their health insurance providers regarding whether their U.S. policy applies overseas. The Medicare/ Medicaid program does not provide payment of medical services outside the United States. Supplemental medical insurance with specific overseas coverage, including provision for medical evacuation may be useful. Travel agents or insurance providers often have information about such programs. Useful information on medical emergencies abroad is provided in the Department of State, Bureau of Consular Affairs' brochure *Medical Information for Americans Traveling Abroad*, available via our home page and autofax service. For additional health information, the international travelers hotline of the Centers for Disease Control and Prevention may be reached at 1-877-FYI-TRIP (1-877-394-8747), via the CDC autofax service at 1-888-CDC-FAXX (1-888-232-3299), or via the CDC home page on the Internet: http://www.cdc.gov.

INFORMATION ON CRIME: The crime rate in Brunei is low, and violent crime is rare. The loss or theft abroad of a U.S. passport should be reported immediately to the local police and to the U.S. Embassy. Useful information on guarding valuables and protecting personal security while traveling abroad is provided in the Department of State pamphlet, *A Safe Trip Abroad*. It is available from the Superintendent of Documents, U.S. Government Printing Office, Washington, D.C. 20402 or via the Internet at http://www.access.gpo.gov /su_docs.

CRIMINAL PENALTIES: While in a foreign country, a U.S. citizen is subject to that country's laws and regulations, which sometimes differ significantly from those in the United States and do not afford the protections available to the individual under U.S. law. Penalties for breaking the law can be more severe than in the United States for similar offenses. Persons violating the law, even unknowingly, may be expelled, arrested or imprisoned. The trafficking in and the illegal importation of controlled drugs are very serious offenses in Brunei. Brunei has a mandatory death penalty for many narcotics offenses. Under the current law, possession of heroin and morphine derivatives of more than 15 grams, and cannabis of more than 20 grams, carries the death sentence. Possession of lesser amounts carries a minimum twenty-year jail term and caning.

AVIATION OVERSIGHT: The U.S. Federal Aviation Administration (FAA) has assessed the Government of Brunei's Civil Aviation Authority as Category 1 - in compliance with international aviation safety standards for oversight of Brunei's air carrier operations. For further information, travelers may contact the Department of Transportation within the U.S. at 1-800-322-7873, or visit the FAA's Internet website at http://www.faa.gov/avr/iasa/index.htm. The U.S. Department of Defense (DOD) separately assesses some foreign air carriers for suitability as official providers of air services. For information regarding the DOD policy on specific carriers, travelers may contact DOD at 618-256-4801.

ROAD SAFETY: Roads are generally good and most vehicles are new and well-maintained. However, vehicular accidents are now one of the leading causes of death in Brunei. Possibly due to excessive speed, tropical torrential rains, or driver carelessness, Brunei suffers a very high traffic accident rate.

CUSTOMS INFORMATION: More detailed information concerning regulations and procedures governing items that may be brought into Brunei is available from the Embassy of the State of Brunei Darussalam in the United States.

Registration/Embassy Location: U.S. citizens living in or visiting Brunei are encouraged to register in person or via telephone with the U.S. Embassy in Bandar Seri Begawan and to obtain updated information on travel and security within the country. The U.S Embassy is located on the third floor, Teck Guan Plaza, Jalan Sultan, in the capital city of Bandar Seri Begawan. The mailing address is American Embassy PSC 470 (BSB), FPO AP, 96534; the telephone number is (673)(2) 229-670; the fax number is (673) (2) 225-293.

Brunei-Muara

On her state visit to Brunei in September of 1998, Her Majesty Queen Elizabeth II of Britain made a tour of the Kampung Ayer in the capital a part of her busy itinerary. Made up of numerous communities, and home to some 30,000 people, the Kampung Ayer ("Villages on Water") is certainly the most well-known of all attractions in the country.

Kampung Ayer has been around for a very long time. When Antonio Pigafetta visited the country in the mid-16th century; Kampung Ayer was already a well-established, "home to some 25,000 families," according to Pigafetta. It was the hub for governance, business and social life in Brunei at that time.

The Kampung Ayer of today retains many of its old-world features described by Pigafetta. Only now, its daily well being is overlooked by the chiefs of the many villages in the area. The Kampung has almost all the amenities available in other communities, such as schools, shops and mosques. The houses there are usually well equipped with the latest in modern technology.

For as low as $1, boatmen will ferry passengers along the breadth and length of the Brunei river.

River cruises aboard ferryboats can start at both ends of the Brunei river, one at the Muara side, at the Queen Elizabeth jetty (named after the reigning British queen after her first Brunei visit in 1972), and others at the various river boat taxi stations in the heart of town.

The journey from the other end of the river starts at Kota Batu, the 16th century capital. The upstream journey during the 10 miles per hour cruise passes an ancient landmark, the tomb of Brunei's fifth ruler, Sultan Bolkiah, the Singing Captain, under whose reign Brunei was a dominant power in the 15th century.

On one bank of the Brunei river is a newer relic, a British warship used dur-ing World War II, sheltered from the elements.

For additional analytical, business and investment opportunities information, please contact Global Investment & Business Center, USA at (703) 370-8082. Fax: (703) 370-8083. E-mail: ibpusa3@gmail.com Global Business and Investment Info Databank - www.ibpus.com

The ferry moves on to Kampong Ayer, the Venice of the East. During the 18th century, here lived the fisher-men, blacksmiths, kris (native sword) makers, brass artisans, nipa palm mat makers, pearl and oyster collectors, traders and goldsmiths.

A new Kampong Ayer has risen, settlements of concrete houses with glass windowpanes, and connected by cement bridges instead of the rickety, wooden catwalks.

Overlooking the old Kampong Ayer is the House of Twelve Roofs (Bum-bungan Dua Belas), built in 1906 and formerly the official home of the British resident. In the Kota Batu area on Jalan Residency is the Arts and Handicrafts Centre, where traditional arts and crafts have been revived.

But Kampung Ayer is only one of the many charms of Brunei that intrigue visitors to the country.

The Sultan Omar Ali Saifuddien Mosque in the heart of Bandar Seri Begawan continues to attract visitors fascinated by its majestic presence, and its role in the spiritual development of the Muslim citizens of the country. The mosque is practically synonymous with Brunei in general, and with the capital in particular.

Situated very close to the mosque is the public library with its attractive mural depicting Brunei's lifestyles in the 60s. The mural was done by one of Brunei's foremost artist, Pg Dato Hj Asmalee, formerly the director of Welfare, Youth and Sports, but now the country's ambassador to a neighbour-ing country.

Another landmark of the capital is the Yayasan Sultan Hj Hassanal Bolkiah commercial complex, across the road from the Sultan Omar Ah Saifuddien mosque. The newly estab-lished complex is the prime shopping centre in Brunei - four storeys of some of the premier big-name retailers in the region! There're outlets bran-dishing branded clothing, fast food, video games, books and many more. There's a supermarket in the Yayasan's west wing, and a food court on the east.

The Royal Regalia Building is a new addition to the attractions found in the capital. Within easy walking distance of all the hotels in the capital centre, the Royal Regalia Building houses artifacts used in royal cere-monies in the country. Foremost among the displays are the Royal Chariot, the gold and silver ceremonial armoury and the jewel-encrusted crowns used in coronation ceremonies.

Entrance is free, and visitors are expected to take off their shoes before entering. Opening hours are from 8.30am to 5.00pm daily except for Fridays, the Building opens from 9.00am until II.30am, and in the afternoon, from 2.30pm till 5.00pm.

Located next to the Royal Regalia Building is the Brunei History Centre. Drop by the centre and learn all about the genealogy and history of the sultans of Brunei, and members of the royal family. There is an exhibition area open to the public from 7.45 am to 12.l5pm, and l.30pm to 4.30pm daily except for Fridays.

Across the road from the Brunei Hotel, is what is known throughout Borneo as the 'tamu.' A 'tamu' is a congregation of vendors selling farm produce and general items. If you are lucky, you can find valuable bargains among the potpourri of metalware and handicraft hawked by some peddlers.

The main Chinese temple in the country lies within sight of the 'tamu.' Its elaborately designed roof and loud red color of its outer walls make the temple stand out from among the more staid schemes of nearby buildings.

A visit during one of the many festivals that is observed at this sanctum of Taoist beliefs would be a celebration of colors, spectacle and smell. Another place of worship that should not be missed by visitors to Brunei is the Church of St Andrew's. The church, possibly the oldest in Brunei, is designed like an English country parish, complete with bells in the let fry. It lies within walking distance of the Royal Regalia Building.

If you are staying in a hotel or Bandar Seri Begawan, why not pay the nightly foodstalls a visit? The stalls are located at a site in front of Sheraton Hotel, and serve a wide variety of hawker fare cheap! A dollar worth of the fried noodles is enough to fill you up.

Check out the local burgers. They're as delicious as those you'll find in established fast food outlets. Or try out 'Roti John'-the Malay version of the Big Mac. Ask for 'goreng pisang' (banana fritters), 'begedil' (potato balls), or 'popiah' (meat rolls), in your jaunts to the sweetmeat stalls.

Outside the capital center, a worthwhile place to visit is the Jame' Asr Hassanil Bolkiah Mosque in Kiarong, about six kilometers away. This is a beautiful sanctuary for communication with God, a personal bequest from His Majesty the Sultan of Brunei himself for the people of the country.

More than just a place of worship, the Jame' Asr is also a center for learning. Classes teaching Islamic religious principles and practices are held there regularly, as do religious lectures. And every Friday morning, the lobbies of its vast edifice are filled with children studying the Quran.

A visit to the mosque is usually part of the itinerary of package tours to Brunei, but if not, visitors can make the necessary arrangement with local tour operators. Visitors wishing to come inside the mosque need to report to the officers on duty, at the security counter on the ground floor.

Further on, you will find the Jerudong Park Playground. Situated some 20 kms to the west of the capital, JP as it is popularly called, is a must-go place for visitors to the country. It has been described as "Brunei's first high-tech wonderland for people of all ages."

There are many amusement rides at the Jerudong Park Playground to cater to everyone's need.

For those who like to live life on the edge, you would be pleased to know that JP has THREE (that's right, three) roller coasters, each with different degrees of thrills (or insanity factors if you want).

'Pusing Lagi' takes riders up a crest almost six storeys high, and then takes them down a steep incline, before twisting and turning at breakneck speed, so much so you will regret the 'Roti John' you just had.

'Boomerang' is for people who would rather go for diabolical twists and turns, while 'Pony Express' is a ride for those newly-initiated to roller-coasters.

Other popular rides include the 'Condor', a very fast merry-go-round that takes you up some five stores high, the 'Aladdin' (a mechanical 'flying carpet'), 'Flashdance' (no dancing experience required), and the wildly swinging 'Pirate Ship'.

There is also a bumper car arena, only for children and youngsters though, a video arcade and tracks for skateboarding and carting. For those who prefer something more sedate, also available are a 'Merry-Go-Round', certainly the most beautiful this side of London, and the 'Simulator Tour' (virtual reality rides into the fantastic and the exotic). Try the up-tower rides, where you are taken up a tower 15 stores high, and given a superb view of the park, and the surrounding area.

Situated next to the playground is the 20-acre Jerudong Park Gardens, which is well-known for its concert class auditorium. This was where Michael Jackson had his performances some years back, drawing a record 60,000 people to a colorful extravaganza the first time he performed.

Whitney Houston was another megastar who has had performed here, as well as Stevie ("I Just Called To Say I Love You) Wonder and the wonderful Seal ("Kissed By A Rose").

And if all that running and riding gives you an appetite, there's good food to be found in the eating area next to the parking lot. Almost anything you could crave for is available, ranging from the local hawker spreads to international fast food fare.   If you're not doing anything on a Friday morning or late afternoon, take the no.55 purple bus to the end of its line at Jerudong Beach. Jerudong Beach on Fridays, especially around 9.00-10.00am, is a hive of activity as fishermen start landing their catch and customers rush to avail themselves of the freshest fish possible. The people you'll get to meet there are among the friendliest in the country, easy with the smile and always ready for the idle chatter.

But the place is more than just an informal fish market. Local fruits hang prominently from many of the stalls, and food stalls sell take-outs to cater to hungry visitors. Swim in the calm, waveless waters of the man-made cove, or try your luck fishing, if that is what you want to do. Just go around people watching.

 And if you need to go back to town, just board the purple bus to make the return journey.

The Bukit Shabbandar Forest Park is just the place to put those hiking legs to use. About ten minutes drive from the Jerudong Park Playground, the park is hectares upon hectares of greenery, dissected by tracks and paths for hiking, jogging and biking. While hiking, you can partake the wonders of the local forests - the rich diversity of its plant life, the exquisite charms and colors of the insects and reptiles that live within, and the symphony in the singing of the birds. Bukit Shahbandar Forest Park is just one of the 11 forest reserves in the country. To the east of Bandar Seri Begawan, about 6 kms into the Kota Batu area, visitors will find the Brunei Museum exhibits artifacts that archive the history of Negara Brunei Darussalam, both ancient and the relatively recent.

Well made cannons and kettles with their dragon motifs and elaborate patterns recall the glory days of the country -when Brunei was an important political and mercantile power in the region with territories that stretched that stretched all the way from Luzon Island in the Philippines to the whole western Borneo island.

There are exhibits which depict the traditional lifestyles of the various communities in the country, plus displays on the local flora and fauna. The exhibit by the local petroleum company Brunei Shell, illustrates the history on the discovery of oil in the country, and the commodity's significant role in economy of Brunei.

The Museum is open every day except Mondays from 9.00am till 5.00pm. On Fridays however, there is a scheduled prayer break from 11.30am until 2.30pm.

For additional analytical, business and investment opportunities information,
please contact Global Investment & Business Center, USA
at (703) 370-8082. Fax: (703) 370-8083. E-mail: ibpusa3@gmail.com
Global Business and Investment Info Databank - www.ibpus.com

And situated downhill of the Brunei Museum is the Malay Technology Museum, which, as its name implies, houses the technological tools utilised by the Malays in ancient times.

A government booklet describes it as offering the "the visitor an intriguing insight into the lifestyle of the people of Brunei in by-gone eras". The Technology Museum is open daily, except Tuesdays, from 9.00 am till 5.00 pm. with a 3-hour midday prayer break on Fridays. Entrance is free.

There is an "Asean Square" in Persiaran Damuan which is located on a stretch between Jalan Tutong and the bank of the Brunei River about 4.5km from the capital. The "Asean Square" has on permanent display the work of a chosen sculptor themed Harmony in Diversity from each of the Asean member countries.

HOLIDAYS

Brunei Darussalam's vision is to promote the country as a unique tourist destination and gateway to tourism excellence in South East Asia. The objectives are to create international awareness of Brunei Darussalam as a holiday destination; to maximize earings of foreign exchange and make tourism as one of the main contributor to GDP. In addition, it will create employment opportunities.

The country offers a wide variety of attractive places to be visited and experienced. The rainforest and National Parks are rich in flora and fauna. Its most magnificent mosques, water village (traditional and historic houses on stilts), rich culture and Jerudong Theme Park are among the uniqueness of Brunei Darussalam.

The government is now actively promoting tourism as an important part of its economic diversification. It would like to see a target of 1 million-visitor arrival by the year 2000. From January to August 1999, the statistic recorded 405,532 visitors visited Brunei Darussalam.

National Day Celebration

The nation celebrates this joyous occasion on the 23rd of February and the people usually prepare themselves two months beforehand. Schoolchildren, private sector representatives and civil servants work hand-in-hand rehearsing their part in flash card displays and other colourful crowd formations. In addition mass prayers and reading of Surah Yaasin are held at mosques throughout the country.

Fasting Month (Ramadhan)

Ramadhan is a holy month for all Muslims. This marks the beginning of the period of fasting - abstinence from food, drink and other material comforts from dawn to dusk. During this month, religious activities are held at mosques and *suraus* throughout the country

Hari Raya Aidilfitri

Hari Raya is a time for celebration after the end of the fasting month of Ramadhan. In the early part of the first day, prayers are held at every mosque in the country. Families get together to seek forgiveness from the elders and loved ones. You will see Bruneians decked-out in their traditional garb visiting relatives and friends.

For additional analytical, business and investment opportunities information,
please contact Global Investment & Business Center, USA
at (703) 370-8082. Fax: (703) 370-8083. E-mail: ibpusa3@gmail.com
Global Business and Investment Info Databank - www.ibpus.com

Special festive dishes are made especially for Hari Raya including satay (beef, chicken or mutton kebabs), ketupat or lontong (rice cakes in coconut or banana leaves), rendang (spicy marinated beef) and other tantalizing cuisines. In these auspicious occassion Istana Nurul Iman was open to the public as well as to visitors for 3 days. This provides the nation and other visitors the opportunity to meet His Majesty and other members of the Royal Family, in order to wish them a Selamat Hari Raya Aidilfitri.

Royal Brunei Armed Forces Day

31st of May marks the commemoration of the Royal Brunei Armed Forces formation day. The occassion is celebrated with military parades, artillery displays, parachuting and exhibitions.

Hari Raya Aidiladha

This is also known as Hari Raya Korban. Sacrifices of goats and cows are practiced to commemorate the Islamic historical event of Prophet Ibrahim S.A.W. The meat is then distributed among relatives, friends and the less fortunates.

His Majesty the Sultan's Birthday

This is one of the most important events in the national calendar with activities and festivities taking place nationwide. Celebrated on 15th July, this event begins with mass prayer throughout the country. On this occassion, His Majesty the Sultan delivers a 'titah' or royal address followed by investiture ceremony held at the Istana Nurul Iman. The event is also marked with gatherings at the four districts where His Majesty meets and gets together with his subjects.

Birthday of the Prophet Muhammad

In Brunei Darussalam, this occasion is known as the Mauludin Nabi S.A.W. Muslims throughout the country honour this event. Readings from the Holy Koran - the Muslim Holy Book, and an address on Islam from officials of the Ministry of Religious Affairs marks the beginning of this auspicious occasion. His Majesty the Sultan also gives a royal address and with other members of the Royal family, leads a procession on foot through the main streets of Bandar Seri Begawan. Religious functions, lectures and other activities are also held to celebrate this important occasion nationwide.

Chinese New Year

Celebrated by the Chinese community, this festival lasts for two weeks. It begins with a reunion dinner on the eve of the Lunar New Year to encourage closer rapport between family members. For the next two week, families visit one another bringing with them oranges to symbolize longevity and good fortune. Traditional cookies and food are aplenty during this festivity. Unmarried young people and children will receive 'angpow' or little red packets with money inside, a symbolic gesture of good luck, wealth and health.

Christmas Day

Throughout the world, 25th of December marks Christmas day, a significant day for all Christians. Christmas is nevertheless a joyous and colourful celebration enjoyed by Christians throughout the country.

Teachers' Day

Teachers' Day is celebrated on every 23rd September in recognition of the good deeds of the teachers to the community, religion and the country. It is celebrated in commemoration of the birthday of the late Sultan Haji Omar 'Ali Saifuddien Saadul Khairi Waddien, the 28th Sultan of Brunei for his contribution in the field of education including religious education. On this occassion, three awards are given away namely, Meritorious Teacher's Award, Outstanding Teacher's Award and *"Guru Tua"* Award.

Public Service Day

The date 29th September is observed as the Public Service Day with the objective to uphold the aspiration of the Government of His Majesty the Sultan and Yang Di-Pertuan of Brunei Darussalam towards creating an efficient, clean, sincere and honest public service. The Public Service Day commemorates the promulgation of the first written Constitution in Brunei Darussalam. The Public Service Day is celebrated with the presentation of the meritorious service award to Ministries and Government Departments.

PUBLIC HOLIDAYS

1 January	New Year's Day
8 January	* Hari Raya Aidilfitri
5 February	Chinese New Year
23 February	National Day
16 Mac	* Hari Raya Aidiladha
6 April	Muslim Holy Month of Hijiriah
31 May	Royal Brunei Armed Forces Day
15 Jun	The Birthday of Prophet Muhammad S.A.W.
15 July	The Birthday of His Majesty Sultan Haji Hassanal Bolkiah Mu'izzaddin Waddaulah, Sultan and Yang Di-Pertuan of Brunei Darussalam
25 October	* Israk Mikraj
27 November	* First Day of Ramadhan (Muslim fasting month)
13 December	Anniversary of The Revelation of the Quran
25 December	Christmas
27 December	* Hari Raya Aidilfitri

BUSINESS CUSTOMS

Customs & Traditions:	Brunei Darussalam possess a long heritage of traditions and customs, behavioural traits and forms of address. Muslims observe religious rites and rituals, which is woven into the lifestyle of Bruneian Malays. Breach of Malay conduct can be liable to prosecution in Islamic courts.
Social Protocol for non-Muslims:	It is customary for Bruneians to eat with their fingers rather than use forks and spoons. Always use the right hand when eating. It is polite to accept even just a little food and drink when offered. When refusing anything that is being offered, it is polite to touch the plate lightly with the right hand . As the left hand is considered unclean, one should use one's right hand to

give and receive things.

Bruneians sit on the floor, especially when there's a fairly large gathering of people. It is considered feminine to sit on the floor with a woman's legs tucked to one side, and equally polite for men to sit with folded legs crossed at the ankles.

It's rude for anyone to sit on the floor with the legs stretched out in front, especially if someone is sitting in front.

It is considered impolite to eat or drink while walking about in public except at picnics or fairs.

During the Islamic fasting (Puasa) month, Muslims do not take any food from sunrise to sundown. It would be inconsiderate to eat and drink in their presence during this period.

It is not customary for Muslims to shake hands with members of the opposite sex. Public display of affection such as kissing and hugging are seen to be in bad taste. Casual physical contact with the opposite sex will make Muslims feel uncomfortable.

In the relationship between sexes, Islam enforces strict legislation. If a non-Muslim is found in the company of a Muslim of the opposite sex in a secluded place rather than where there are a lot of people, he/she could be persecuted.

If you are found committing 'khalwat' that is seen in a compromising position with a person of the opposite sex who is a Muslim, you could be deported.

When walking in front of people, especially the elderly and those senior in rank or position, it is a gesture of courtesy and respect for one to bend down slightly, as if one is bowing, except this time side way to the person or persons in front of whom one is passing. One of the arms should be positioned straight downwards along the side of the body.

Leaning on a table with someone seated on it especially if he/she is an official or colleague in an office is considered rude.

Resting one's feet on the table or chair is seen as overbearing. So is sitting on the table while speaking to another person who is seated behind it. To touch or pat someone, including children, on the head is regarded as extremely disrespectful.

The polite way of beckoning at someone is by using all four fingers of the right hand with the palm down and motioning them towards yourself. It is considered extremely impolite to beckon at someone with the index finger.

SUPPLEMENTS

IMPORTANT LAWS OF BRUNEI

ACT / ORDER	CHAPTER / NOTIFICATION NO.	DATE OF COMMENCEMENT	STATUS
ADMIRALTY JURISDICTION ACT [2000 Ed.]	CAP. 179	01-10-1996	
ADOPTION OF CHILDREN ORDER 2001	S 16/2001	26-03-2001	
AGRICULTURAL PESTS AND NOXIOUS PLANTS ACT [1984 Ed.]	CAP. 43	01-08-1971	
AIR NAVIGATION ACT [1984 Ed., Amended by S 21/97, S 41/00, S 42/00, Repealed by S 63/06 - Civil Aviation Order]	CAP. 113	01-03-1978	REPEALED w.e.f. 20-05-06
AIRPORT PASSENGER SERVICE CHARGE ACT [2000 Ed.]	CAP. 188	01-05-1999	
ANTI-TERRORISM (FINANCIAL AND OTHER MEASURES) ACT [2008 Ed.]	CAP. 197	14-06-2002	
ANTIQUITIES AND TREASURE TROVE ACT [2002 Ed.]	CAP. 31	01-01-1967	
APPLICATION OF LAWS ACT [2009 Ed.]	CAP. 2	25-04-1951	
ARBITRATION ACT [1999 Ed.]	CAP. 173	24-04-1994	
ARBITRATION ORDER, 2009	S 34/2009		not yet in force
ARMS AND EXPLOSIVES ACT [2002 Ed.]	CAP. 58	08-04-1927	
ASIAN DEVELOPMENT BANK ACT [2009 Ed.]	CAP. 201	25-04-2006	
AUDIT ACT [1986 Ed., Amended by S 39/03]	CAP. 152	01-01-1960	
AUTHORITY FOR INFO-COMMUNICATIONS TECHNOLOGY INDUSTRY OF BRUNEI DARUSSALAM ORDER 2001 [Amended by S 13/03, S 35/03]	S 39/2001	01-01-2003	
BANISHMENT ACT [1984 Ed.]	CAP. 20	31-12-1918	
BANKERS' BOOKS (EVIDENCE) ACT [1984 Ed., Amended by S 29/93, Repealed by S 13/06]	CAP. 107	17-04-1939	REPEALED w.e.f. 12-02-06
BANKING ACT [2002 Ed., Repealed by S 45/06 - Banking Order]	CAP. 95	01-01-1957	REPEALED w.e.f. 04-03-06
BANKING ORDER, 2006	S 45/2006	04-03-2006	
BANKRUPTCY ACT [1984 Ed., Amended by S 12/96, S 52/00]	CAP. 67	01-01-1957	
BILLS OF EXCHANGE ACT [1999 Ed.]	CAP. 172	03-05-1994	
BILLS OF SALE ACT [1984 Ed.]	CAP. 70	16-01-1958	
BIOLOGICAL WEAPONS ACT [1984 Ed.]	CAP. 87	11-04-1975	
BIRTHS AND DEATHS REGISTRATION ACT [1984 Ed.]	CAP. 79	01-01-1923	

BISHOP OF BORNEO (INCORPORATION) ACT [1984 Ed.]	CAP. 88	25-04-1951	
BRETTON WOODS AGREEMENT ACT [2000 Ed.]	CAP. 176	30-09-1995	
BROADCASTING ACT [2000 Ed., Corrigendum S 41/07]	CAP. 180	15-03-1997	
BRUNEI ECONOMIC DEVELOPMENT BOARD ACT [2003 Ed., Amended by S 11/03]	CAP. 104	11-04-1975	
BRUNEI FISHERY LIMITS ACT [1984 Ed., Amended by S 25/09]	CAP. 130	01-01-1983	
BRUNEI INVESTMENT AGENCY ACT [2002 Ed., Amended by S 14/03, S 64/04, S 15/08, S 78/08]	CAP. 137	01-07-1983	
BRUNEI MALAY SILVERSMITHS GUILD (INCORPORATION) ACT [1984 Ed.]	CAP. 115	15-07-1959	
BRUNEI NATIONAL ARCHIVES ACT [1984 Ed.]	CAP. 116	01-08-1981	
BRUNEI NATIONAL PETROLEUM COMPANY SENDIRIAN BERHAD ORDER 2002 [Amended by S 6/2003, S 12/2003]	S 6/2002	05-01-2002	
BRUNEI NATIONALITY ACT [2002 Ed., Amended by S 55/2002]	CAP. 15	01-01-1962	
BUFFALOES ACT [1984 Ed.]	CAP. 59	01-01-1909	
BURIAL GROUNDS ACT [1984 Ed.]	CAP. 49	01-01-1932	
BUSINESS NAMES ACT [1984 Ed., Amended by S 30/88]	CAP. 92	01-03-1958	
CENSORSHIP OF FILMS AND PUBLIC ENTERTAINMENTS ACT [2002 Ed.]	CAP. 69	21-08-1962	
CENSUS ACT [2003 Ed.]	CAP. 78	07-06-1947	
CENTRE FOR STRATEGIC AND POLICY STUDIES ORDER, 2006	S 64/2006	01-07-2006	
CHILD CARE CENTRES ORDER 2006	S 37/06	04-03-2006	
CHILDREN AND YOUNG PERSONS ORDER, 2006 [Corrigendum S 24/06, Amended by S 60/08]	S 9/2006		not yet in force
CHILDREN ORDER 2000 [Amended by S 84/00, S 48/03]	S 64/2000	01-09-2000	
CHINESE MARRIAGE ACT [1984 Ed., Amended by S 44/89]	CAP. 126	31-07-1955	
CIVIL AVIATION ORDER, 2006	S 63/2006	20-05-2006	
COIN (IMPORT AND EXPORT) ACT [1984 Ed.]	CAP. 33	01-01-1909	
COMMISSIONS OF ENQUIRY ACT [1984 Ed., Amended by S 35/05]]	CAP. 9	28-04-1962	
COMMISSIONERS FOR OATHS ACT [1999 Ed.]	CAP. 169	26-08-1993	
COMMON GAMING HOUSES ACT [2002 Ed., Amended by S 20/08]	CAP. 28	01-01-1921	
COMPANIES ACT [1984 Ed., Amended by S 26/98, S 23/99, S 69/01, S 10/03, S 45/06, S ...]	CAP. 39	01-01-1957	

96/08]			
COMPULSORY EDUCATION ORDER, 2007	S 56/2007	24-11-2007	
COMPUTER MISUSE ACT [2007 Ed.]	CAP. 194	21-06-2000	
CONSTITUTION OF BRUNEI DARUSSALAM [2004 Ed., Amended by S 14/06] Article 8A, 9(2), 9(4), 9(5) - suspended by S 15/06 w.e.f. 21/02/06	CONST. I	29-09-1959	
CONSTITUTION [FINANCIAL PROCEDURE] ORDER [2004 Ed., Amended by S 14/08, S 36/08]	CONST. III	01-01-1960	
CONSULAR RELATIONS ACT [1984 Ed.]	CAP. 118	01-01-1984	
CONTINENTAL SHELF PROCLAMATION [1984 Ed.]	SUP. II		
CONTRACTS ACT [1984 Ed., Amended by S 60/02]	CAP. 106	17-04-1939	
CO-OPERATIVE SOCIETIES ACT [1984 Ed.]	CAP. 84	01-07-1975	
COPYRIGHT ORDER 1999	S 14/2000	01-05-2000	
CRIMINAL CONDUCT (RECOVERY OF PROCEEDS) ORDER 2000 [Amended by S 30/07]	S 52/2000	01-07-2000	
CRIMINAL LAW (PREVENTIVE DETENTION) ACT [2008 Ed.]	CAP. 150	26-11-1984	
CRIMINAL PROCEDURE CODE [2001 Ed., Amended by S 63/02, GN 273/02, S 62/04, S 32/05, S 6/06, S 9/06, S 4/07]	CAP. 7	01-05-1952	S 6/06 & S 9/06 not yet in force
CRIMINALS REGISTRATION ORDER, 2008	S 42/2008	01-04-2008	
CURRENCY ACT [1984 Ed., Repealed by S 16/04 - Currency and Monetary Order]	CAP. 32	Please refer Act	REPEALED w.e.f. 01-02-04
CURRENCY AND MONETARY ORDER 2004 [Corrigendum S 71/04; Amended by S 59/05, S 39/07]	S 16/2004	01-02-2004	
CUSTOMS ACT [1984 Ed., Amended by S 23/89, S 82/00, S 52/01, S 39/06, Repealed by S 39/06 - Customs Order]	CAP. 36	01-01-1955	REPEALED w.e.f. 04-03-06
CUSTOMS ORDER, 2006 [Amended by S 98/08]	S 39/06	04-03-2006	
DANA PENGIRAN MUDA MAHKOTA AL-MUHTADEE BILLAH FOR ORPHANS ACT [2000 Ed.]	CAP. 185	25-08-1998	
DEBTORS ACT [2008 Ed.]	CAP. 195	16-10-2000	
DEFAMATION ACT [2000 Ed.]	CAP. 192	17-08-1999	
DESCRIPTION OF LAND (SURVEY PLANS) ACT [1984 Ed.]	CAP. 101	03-09-1962	
DEVELOPMENT FUND ACT [1984 Ed.]	CAP. 136	01-01-1960	
DIPLOMATIC PRIVILEGES (EXTENSION) ACT [1984 Ed.]	CAP. 85	02-12-1949	

DIPLOMATIC PRIVILEGES (VIENNA CONVENTION) ACT [1984 Ed.]	CAP. 117	01-09-1982	
DISAFFECTED AND DANGEROUS PERSONS ACT [1984 Ed.]	CAP. 111	29-07-1953	
DISASTER MANAGEMENT ORDER 2006	S 26/06	01-08-2006	
DISSOLUTION OF MARRIAGE ACT [1999 Ed.]	CAP. 165	29-04-1992	
DISTRESS ACT [2009 Ed.]	CAP. 199	16-10-2000	
DOGS ACT [1984 Ed., Amended by S 14/90]	CAP. 60	17-04-1939	
DRUG TRAFFICKING (RECOVERY OF PROCEEDS) ACT [2000 Ed., Amended by S 29/07]	CAP. 178	30-03-1996	
EDUCATION ORDER 2003 [Amended by S 86/06]	S 59/2003	20-12-2003	
EDUCATION (BRUNEI BOARD OF EXAMINATIONS) ACT [1984 Ed.]	CAP. 56	01-01-1975	
EDUCATION (NON-GOVERNMENT SCHOOLS) ACT [1984 Ed., Repealed by S 59/03 - Education Order]	CAP. 55	01-01-1953	REPEALED w.e.f. 20-12-03
ELECTION OFFENCES ACT [1984 Ed.]	CAP. 26	28-04-1962	
ELECTRICITY ACT [2003 Ed. Amended by S 68/05]	CAP. 71	05-03-1973	
ELECTRONIC TRANSACTION ACT [2008 Ed.]	CAP. 196	01-05-2001	except Part X
EMBLEMS AND NAMES (PREVENTION OF IMPROPER USE) ACT [1984 Ed.]	CAP. 94	18-01-1968	
EMERGENCY REGULATIONS ACT [1984 Ed.]	CAP. 21	21-02-1933	
EMPLOYMENT AGENCIES ORDER, 2004	S 84/2004	20-12-2004	
EMPLOYMENT INFORMATION ACT [1984 Ed.]	CAP. 99	15-05-1974	
EVIDENCE ACT [2002 Ed., Amended by S 1/06, S 13/06]	CAP. 108	17-04-1939	
EXCHANGE CONTROL ACT [1984 Ed., Repealed by S 70/00]	CAP. 141	01-01-1957	REPEALED w.e.f. 01-07-00
EXCISE ACT [1984 Ed., Repealed by S 40/06 - Excise Order]	CAP. 37	01-01-1925	REPEALED w.e.f. 04-03-06
EXCISE ORDER 2006	S 40/06	04-03-2006	
EXCLUSIVE ECONOMIC ZONE, Proclamation of	S 4/94	20-07-1993	
EXTRADITION (MALAYSIA AND SINGAPORE) ACT [1999 Ed.]	CAP. 154	19-05-84 [S] 01-11-83 [M]	
EXTRADITION ACT [1984 Ed., Repealed by S 10/06 - Extradition Order]	CAP. 8	09-12-1915	REPEALED w.e.f. 07-02-06
EXTRADITION ORDER 2006	S 10/06	07-02-2006	
FATAL ACCIDENTS AND PERSONAL INJURIES ACT [1999 Ed.]	CAP. 160	01-02-1991	

FINANCE COMPANIES ACT [2003 Ed., Amended by S 41/06]	CAP. 89	01-08-1973	
FINGERPRINTS ENACTMENT [Repealed by S 42/08 - Criminals Registration Order, 2008]	17 of 1956	01-01-1957	REPEALED w.e.f. 01-04-08
FIRE SERVICES ACT [2002 Ed., Amended by S 79/06] now become FIRE AND RESCUE w.e.f. 1/8/2006	CAP. 82	04-08-1966	
FISHERIES ACT [1984 Ed., Amended by S 20/02, Repealed by S 25/09 - Fisheries Order, 2009]	CAP. 61	05-03-1973	REPEALED w.e.f. 30-05-09
FISHERIES ORDER, 2009	S 25/2009	30-05-2009	
FOREST ACT [2002 Ed., Amended by S 47/07]	CAP. 46	30-10-1934	
GENEVA AND RED CROSS ACT [1984 Ed.]	CAP. 86	12-12-1938	
GENEVA CONVENTION ORDER, 2005	S 40/2005		not yet in force
GUARDIANSHIP OF INFANTS ACT [2000 Ed.]	CAP. 191	01-08-1999	
GURKHA RESERVE UNIT ACT [1984 Ed.]	CAP. 135	09-05-1981	
HALAL CERTIFICATE AND HALAL LABEL ORDER, 2005 [Amended by S 75/08]	S 39/2005	01-08-2008	
HALAL MEAT ACT [2000 Ed., Amended by GN 274/02]	CAP. 183	17-04-1999	
HIJACKING AND PROTECTION OF AIRCRAFT ORDER 2000	S 41/2000	24-05-2000	
HIRE PURCHASE ORDER, 2006	S 44/06	04-03-2006	
IMMIGRATION ACT [2006 Ed., Amended by S 34/07]	CAP. 17	01-07-1958	
INCOME TAX ACT [2003 Ed., Amended by S 51/08, S 52/08, S 13/09]	CAP. 35	31-12-1949	
INCOME TAX (PETROLEUM) ACT [2004 Ed.]	CAP. 119	18-12-1963	
INDUSTRIAL CO-ORDINATION ORDER 2001	S 44/2001	01-06-2001	
INDUSTRIAL DESIGNS ORDER 1999	S 7/2000	01-05-2000	
INFECTIOUS DISEASES ORDER 2003 [Amended by S 27/06]	S 34/2003	08-05-2003	
INSURANCE ORDER, 2006 [Amended by S 88/06, S 28/07, S 54/07]	S 48/2006	04-03-2006	
INTERMEDIATE COURTS ACT [1999 Ed., Amended by S 57/04, S 74/04, S 80/06]	CAP. 162	01-07-1991	
INTERNAL SECURITY ACT [2008 Ed.]	CAP. 133	01-04-1983	
INTERNATIONAL ARBITRATION ORDER, 2009	S 35/2009		not yet in force
INTERNATIONAL BANKING ORDER 2000 [Amended by S 9/01]	S 53/2000	01-07-2000	
INTERNATIONAL BUSINESS COMPANIES ORDER 2000 [Amended by S 37/03]	S 56/2000	01-07-2000	

INTERNATIONAL INSURANCE AND TAKAFUL ORDER 2002	S 43/2002	01-07-2002	
INTERNATIONAL LIMITED PARTNERSHIP ORDER 2000 [Amended by S 7/01]	S 45/2000	01-07-2000	
INTERNATIONAL TRUSTS ORDER 2000	S 55/2000	01-07-2000	
INTERNATIONALLY PROTECTED PERSONS ACT [1984 Ed.]	CAP. 16	08-07-1995	
INTERPRETATION AND GENERAL CLAUSES ACT [2006 Ed.]	CAP. 4	29-09-1959	
INTOXICATING SUBSTANCES ACT [1999 Ed., Amended by S 58/07]	CAP. 161	01-05-1992	
INVENTIONS ACT [1984 Ed., Amended by S 28/97]	CAP. 72	01-03-1952	
INVESTMENT INCENTIVES ACT [1984 Ed., Repealed by S 48/01 - Investment Incentives Order]	CAP. 97	01-05-1975	REPEALED w.e.f. 01-06-01
INVESTMENT INCENTIVES ORDER 2001	S 48/2001	01-06-2001	
ISLAMIC ADOPTION OF CHILDREN ORDER 2001	S 14/2001	26-03-2001	except section 3
ISLAMIC BANKING ACT [1999 Ed., Repealed by S 96/08 - Islamic Banking Order, 2008]	CAP. 168	02-12-1992	REPEALED w.e.f. 30-09-08
ISLAMIC BANKING ORDER, 2008	S 96/2008	30-09-2008	
ISLAMIC FAMILY LAW ORDER 1999 [Corrigenda S 42/04, Amended by S 17/05]	S 12/2000	26-03-2001	except section 3
KIDNAPPING ACT [1999 Ed.]	CAP. 164	22-02-1992	
KOLEJ UNIVERSITI PERGURUAN UGAMA SERI BEGAWAN ORDER, 2008	S 84/2008	30-08-2008	
LABOUR ACT [2002 Ed., Amended by GN 274/02, S 84/04]	CAP. 93	01-02-1955	
LAND ACQUISITION ACT [1984 Ed.]	CAP. 41	03-01-1949	
LAND CODE [1984 Ed., Amended by S 29/09]	CAP. 40	06-09-1909	
LAND CODE (STRATA) ACT [2000 Ed., Amended by S 28/09]	CAP. 189	01-07-2009	
LAW REFORM (CONTRIBUTORY NEGLIGENCE) ACT [1984 Ed., Repealed by S 4/91]	CAP. 53	25-04-1951	REPEALED w.e.f. 01-02-91
LAW REFORM (PERSONAL INJURIES) ACT [1984 Ed., Repealed by S 4/91]	CAP. 10	25-04-1951	REPEALED w.e.f. 01-02-91
LAW REVISION ACT [2001 Ed., Amended by S 93/00]	CAP. 1	01-01-1984	
LAYOUT DESIGNS ORDER 1999	S 8/2000	01-05-2000	
LEGAL PROFESSION ACT [2006 Ed.]	CAP. 132	01-01-1987	

LEGISLATIVE COUNCIL AND COUNCIL OF MINISTERS ACT (REMUNERATION AND PRIVILEGES) [1984 Ed., Amended by S 46/05, S 12/06]	CAP. 134	30-01-1965	
LEGITIMACY ORDER 2001	S 33/2001	21-04-2001	
LICENSED LAND SURVEYORS ACT [1984 Ed.]	CAP. 100	01-07-1980	
LIMITATION ACT [2000 Ed.]	CAP. 14	01-09-1991	
LUNACY ACT [1984 Ed.]	CAP. 48	09-07-1929	
MAINTENANCE ORDERS RECIPROCAL ENFORCEMENT ACT [2000 Ed.]	CAP. 175	25-02-1998	
MARITIME OFFENCES (SHIPS AND FIXED PLATFORMS) ORDER, 2007	S 61/2007	17-12-2007	
MARRIAGE ACT [1984 Ed., Amended by S 42/05]	CAP. 76	03-08-1948	
MARRIED WOMEN ACT [2000 Ed.]	CAP. 190	01-08-1999	
MEDICAL PRACTITIONERS AND DENTISTS ACT [1984 Ed., Amended by GN 273/02]	CAP. 112	29-07-1953	
MEDICINES ORDER, 2007	S 79/2007	01-01-2008	sec.1(2)(a) only
MERCHANDISE MARKS ACT [1984 Ed.]	CAP. 96	07-10-1953	
MERCHANT SHIPPING ACT [1984 Ed., Repealed by S 27/02 - Merchant Shipping Order]	CAP. 145	01-09-1984	REPEALED w.e.f. 16-05-02
MERCHANT SHIPPING ORDER, 2002 [Amended by S 23/09]	S 27/2002	16-05-2002	
MERCHANT SHIPPING (CIVIL LIABILITY AND COMPENSATION FOR OIL POLLUTION) ORDER, 2008	S 54/2008	17-04-2008	
MIDWIVES ACT [1984 Ed., Amended by S 47/02]	CAP. 139	01-01-1959	
MINING ACT [1984 Ed.]	CAP. 42	04-03-1920	
MINOR OFFENCES ACT [1984 Ed., Amended by S 26/90, S 43/98, S 89/06, S 82/08]	CAP. 30	29-07-1929	
MISCELLANEOUS LICENCES ACT [1984 Ed., Amended by S 43/08, S 85/08]	CAP. 127	01-01-1983	
MISUSE OF DRUGS ACT [2001 Ed., Amended by S 7/2002, GN 273/02, S 59/07, S 5/08]	CAP. 27	01-07-1978	
MONEY CHANGING AND REMITTANCE BUSINESS ACT [1999 Ed.]	CAP. 174	01-01-1995	
MONEY LAUNDERING ORDER 2000	S 44/2000	01-07-2000	
MONEYLENDERS ACT [1984 Ed., Amended by S 53/00, S 45/06]	CAP. 62	01-01-1922	
MONOPOLIES ACT [2003 Ed.]	CAP. 73	13-12-1932	
MOTOR VEHICLES INSURANCE (THIRD PARTY RISKS) ACT [1984 Ed., Amended by S 28/98, S 48/08 (corrig)]	CAP. 90	28-02-1950	

For additional analytical, business and investment opportunities information, please contact Global Investment & Business Center, USA at (703) 370-8082. Fax: (703) 370-8083. E-mail: ibpusa3@gmail.com Global Business and Investment Info Databank - www.ibpus.com

MUNICIPAL BOARDS ACT [1984 Ed.]	CAP. 57	01-01-1921	
MUTUAL ASSISTANCE IN CRIMINAL MATTERS ORDER, 2005	S 7/2005	01-01-2006	
MUTUAL FUNDS ORDER 2001	S 18/2001	01-01-2001	
NATIONAL BANK OF BRUNEI BERHAD; NATIONAL FINANCE SENDIRIAN BERHAD ACT [1999 Ed.]	CAP. 156	19-11-1986	
NATIONAL REGISTRATION ACT [2002 Ed.]	CAP. 19	01-03-1965	
NEWSPAPERS ACT [2002 Ed., Amended by S 36/05, S 86/08]	CAP. 105	01-01-1959	
NORTH BORNEO (DEFINITION BOUNDARIES) ORDER IN COUNCIL 1958 [1984 Ed.]	Sup. III		
NURSES REGISTRATION ACT [1984 Ed.]	CAP. 140	01-01-1968	
OATHS AND AFFIRMATIONS ACT [2001 Ed.]	CAP. 3	08-09-1958	
OFFENDERS (PROBATION AND COMMUNITY SERVICE) ORDER, 2006 [Amended by S 80/08]	S 6/2006		not yet in force
OFFICIAL SECRETS ACT [1988 Ed., Amended by S 52/05]	CAP. 153	02-01-1940	
OLD AGE AND DISABILITY PENSIONS ACT [1984 Ed., Amended by GN 273/02, GN 649/03, S 38/08]	CAP. 18	01-01-1955	
PASSPORTS ACT [1984 Ed., Amended by S 6/86, S 2/00, S 44/03, S 24/04, S 54/05, S 33/07]	CAP. 146	14-12-1983	
PATENTS ORDER, 1999	S 42/99		not yet in force
PAWNBROKERS ACT [1984 Ed., Repealed by S 41/05 - Pawnbrokers Order]	CAP. 63	01-01-1920	REPEALED w.e.f. 01-08-05
PAWNBROKERS ORDER 2002 [Amended by S 41/05]	S 60/2002	01-08-2005	
PENAL CODE [2001 Ed.]	CAP. 22	01-05-1952	
PENSIONS ACT [1984 Ed., Amended S 23/87, S 37/08]	CAP. 38	01-03-1959	
PERBADANAN TABUNG AMANAH ISLAM BRUNEI ACT [1999 Ed., Amended by S 15/03, S 29/04]	CAP. 163	29-09-1991	
PERSATUAN BULAN SABIT MERAH NEGARA BRUNEI DARUSSALAM (INCORPORATION) ACT [1999 Ed., Amended by S 40/05]	CAP. 159	28-11-1999	S 40/05 not yet in force
PETROLEUM MINING ACT [2002 Ed.]	CAP. 44	18-11-1963	
PETROLEUM (PIPE-LINES) ACT [1984 Ed.]	CAP. 45	04-03-1920	
PHARMACISTS REGISTRATION ORDER 2001	S 21/2001	01-07-2001	
POISONS ACT [1984 Ed., Amended by S 16/96, S 28/01]	CAP. 114	01-07-1957	
PORTS ACT [1984 Ed., Amended by S 17/88, S 26/02, S 18/05]	CAP. 144	01-01-1986	

POST OFFICE ACT [1984 Ed., Amended by S 17/97]	CAP. 52	01-05-1988	
POWERS OF ATTORNEY ACT [2002 Ed.]	CAP. 13	01-01-1922	
PRESERVATION OF BOOKS ACT [1984 Ed.]	CAP. 125	18-01-1967	
PREVENTION OF CORRUPTION ACT [2002 Ed.]	CAP. 131	01-01-1982	
PREVENTION OF POLLUTION OF THE SEA ORDER, 2005	S 18/2005	28-03-2005	
PRICE CONTROL ACT [2002 Ed.]	CAP. 142	13-03-1974	
PRIME MINISTER'S INCORPORATION ORDER 1984 [Amended the Constitution (Mentri Besar Incorporation) Order 1960 (S 55/60)]	S 5/84	01-01-1984	
PRISONS ACT [1984 Ed., Amended by S 12/89]	CAP. 51	01-07-1979	
PROBATE AND ADMINISTRATION ACT [1984 Ed.]	CAP. 11	01-02-1956	
PROTECTED AREAS AND PROTECTED PLACES ACT [1984 Ed.]	CAP. 147	01-12-1983	
PUBLIC ENTERTAINMENT ACT [2000 Ed.]	CAP. 181	01-06-1997	
PUBLIC HEALTH (FOOD) ACT [2000 Ed., Amended by S 73/00, S 64/02]	CAP. 182	01-01-2001	
PUBLIC OFFICERS (LIABILITIES) ACT [1984 Ed., Repealed by S 40/00]	CAP. 80	25-02-1929	REPEALED w.e.f. 24-05-00
PUBLIC ORDER ACT [2002 Ed., Amended by S 33/05]	CAP. 148	01-11-1983	
PUBLIC SERVICE COMMISSION ACT [1984 Ed.]	CAP. 83	01-01-1983	
QUARANTINE AND PREVENTION OF DISEASE ACT [1984 Ed., Repealed by S 34/03 - Infectious Diseases Order]	CAP. 47	09-08-1934	REPEALED w.e.f. 08-05-03
RECIPROCAL ENFORCEMENT OF FOREIGN JUDGMENTS ACT [2000 Ed.]	CAP. 177	27-03-1996	
REGISTERED AGENTS AND TRUSTEES LICENSING ORDER 2000	S 54/2000	01-07-2000	
REGISTRATION OF ADOPTIONS ACT [1984 Ed., Amended by S 15/01]	CAP. 123	01-01-1962	
REGISTRATION OF GUESTS ACT [1984 Ed.]	CAP. 122	01-07-1974	
REGISTRATION OF MARRIAGES ACT [2002 Ed.]	CAP. 124	01-01-1962	
RELIGIOUS COUNCIL AND KADIS COURTS ACT [1984 Ed., Amended by S 1/88, S 31/90, S 37/98, S 12/00, S 24/03, S 17/05, S 26/05]	CAP. 77	01-02-1956	
ROAD TRAFFIC ACT [2007 Ed., Amended by S 39/04, S 59/08]	CAP. 68	01-01-1956	S 39/04 not yet in force
ROYAL BRUNEI ARMED FORCES ACT [1984 Ed., Amended by S 2/06]	CAP. 149	01-01-1984	
ROYAL BRUNEI POLICE FORCE ACT [1984 Ed.]	CAP. 50	31-12-1983	

ROYAL ORDERS AND DECORATIONS [1984 Ed.]	Sup. V		
RUBBER DEALERS ACT [1984 Ed.]	CAP. 64	01-01-1921	
SALE OF GOODS ACT [1999 Ed.]	CAP. 170	03-05-1994	
SARAWAK (DEFINITION OF BOUNDARIES) ORDER IN COUNCIL 1958 [1984 Ed.]	Sup. IV		
SEAMEN'S UNEMPLOYMENT INDEMNITY ACT [1984 Ed.]	CAP. 75	02-10-1939	
SECOND-HAND DEALERS ACT [1984 Ed.]	CAP. 65	01-01-1934	
SECURITIES ORDER 2001 [Amended by S 33/02, S 43/05]	S 31/2001	01-03-2001	
SECURITY AGENCIES ACT [2000 Ed.]	CAP. 187	01-06-2000	
SEDITION ACT [1984 Ed., Amended by S 34/05]	CAP. 24	06-04-1948	
SMALL CLAIMS TRIBUNALS ORDER, 2006	S 81/2006		not yet in force
SOCIETIES ACT [1984 Ed., Repealed by S 1/05 - Societies Order]	CAP. 66	04-10-1948	REPEALED w.e.f. 04-01-05
SOCIETIES ORDER, 2005	S 1/2005	04-01-2005	
SPECIFIC RELIEF ACT [1984 Ed., Amended by S 59/04]	CAP. 109	17-04-1939	
STAMP ACT [2003 Ed.]	CAP. 34	01-01-1909	
STATISTICS ACT [1984 Ed.]	CAP. 81	01-08-1977	
STATUTORY DECLARATION ACT [1984 Ed.]	CAP. 12	11-01-1951	
STATUTORY FUNDS APPROPRIATION ENACTMENT 1959 [Amended by S 63/63, 7 of 1966, 19 of 1967, 4 of 1975, S 50/76, S 49/76, S 110/79, S 12/82, S 13/82, S 42/84, S 13/86, S 22/93, S 22/03, S 39/08]	9 of 1959	01-01-1960	
SUBORDINATE COURTS ACT [2001 Ed., Amended by S 56/04, S 73/04, S 9/06, S 60/08]	CAP. 6	01-01-1983	S 9/06 and S60/08 not yet in force
SUBSCRIPTION CONTROL ACT [1984 Ed.]	CAP. 91	15-12-1953	
SUCCESSION AND REGENCY PROCLAMATION 1959 [2004 Ed., Amended by S 16/06, S 78/06]	CONST. II	29-09-1959	
SUMMONSES AND WARRANTS (SPECIAL PROVISIONS) ACT [1999 Ed.]	CAP. 155	19-05-84 [S] 01-11-83 [M]	
SUNGAI LIANG AUTHORITY ACT [2009 Ed.]	CAP. 200	06-04-2007	
SUPREME COURT ACT [2001 Ed., Amended by S 55/04, S 61/04, S 72/04]	CAP. 5	16-09-1963	
SUPREME COURT (APPEALS TO PRIVY COUNCIL) ACT [1999 Ed., Amended by S 45/05]	CAP. 158	01-02-1990	
SUSTAINABILITY FUND ORDER, 2008	S 36/2008	11-03-2008	

- 244 -

SYARIAH COURTS ACT [2000 Ed., Amended by S 17/05]	CAP. 184	26-03-2001	
SYARIAH COURTS CIVIL PROCEDURE ORDER, 2005 [available in Malay text only] - PERINTAH ACARA MAL MAHKAMAH-MAHKAMAH SYARIAH, 2005	S 26/2005	06-04-2005	
SYARIAH COURTS EVIDENCE ORDER, 2001	S 63/2001	15-10-2001 except s.5	
SYARIAH FINANCIAL SUPERVISORY BOARD ORDER, 2006 [Amended by S 65/07]	S 5/2006	17-01-2006	
TABUNG AMANAH PEKERJA ACT [1999 Ed., Amended by S 9/99, S 9/00, S 16/03, S 2/07]	CAP. 167	01-01-1993	
TAKAFUL ORDER, 2008	S 100/2008	30-09-2008	
TELECOMMUNICATIONS ACT [1984 Ed. Repealed by S 38/01 - Telecommunication Order]	CAP. 54	01-12-1974	REPEALED w.e.f. 01-04-06
TELECOMMUNICATIONS ORDER 2001	S 38/2001	01-04-2006	
TELECOMMUNICATION SUCCESSOR COMPANY ORDER 2001 [Corrigendum S 25/06]	S 37/2001	01-04-2006	
TERRITORIAL WATERS OF BRUNEI ACT [2002 Ed.]	CAP. 138	10-02-1983	
TOBACCO ORDER 2005	S 49/2005	01-06-2008	
TOKYO CONVENTION ACT [2008 Ed.]	CAP. 198	24-05-2000	
TOWN AND COUNTRY PLANNING (DEVELOPMENT CONTROL) ACT [1984 Ed.]	CAP. 143	19-09-1972	
TRADE DISPUTES ACT [1984 Ed.]	CAP. 129	21-01-1962	
TRADE MARKS ACT [2000 Ed.]	CAP. 98	01-06-2000	
TRADE UNIONS ACT [1984 Ed.]	CAP. 128	20-01-1962	
TRAFFICKING AND SMUGGLING OF PERSONS ORDER, 2004	S 82/2004	20-12-2004	
TRANSFER OF FUNCTIONS OF THE MINISTER OF LAW ACT [2000 Ed.]	CAP. 186	16-09-1998	
TRAVEL AGENTS ACT [1984 Ed.]	CAP. 103	01-01-1982	
TREATY OF FRIENDSHIP AND CO-OPERATION [1984 Ed.]	SUP. I		
TRESPASS ON ROYAL PROPERTY ACT [1984 Ed.]	CAP. 23	01-01-1918	
UNDESIRABLE PUBLICATIONS ACT [1984 Ed., Amended by S 60/07]	CAP. 25	01-12-1986	
UNFAIR CONTRACTS TERMS ACT [1999 Ed.]	CAP. 171	18-06-1994	
UNIVERSITI BRUNEI DARUSSALAM ACT [1999 Ed., Amended by S 22/00, S 17/03, S 84/06]	CAP. 157	01-07-1988	

UNIVERSITI ISLAM SULTAN SHARIF ALI ORDER, 2008	S 71/2008	14-08-2008	
UNLAWFUL CARNAL KNOWLEDGE ACT [1984 Ed.]	CAP. 29	15-01-1938	
VALUERS AND ESTATE AGENTS ORDER, 2009	S 30/2009	01-07-2009	
VETERINARY SURGEONS ORDER, 2005	S 30/2005	02-06-2008	
VICAR APOSTOLIC OF KUCHING (INCORPORATION) ACT [1984 Ed.]	CAP. 110	11-08-1973	
WATER SUPPLY ACT [1984 Ed.]	CAP. 121	01-01-1968	
WEIGHTS AND MEASURES ACT [1986 Ed.]	CAP. 151	01-01-1987	
WILD FAUNA AND FLORA ORDER, 2007	S 77/2007	31-12-2007	
WILD LIFE PROTECTION ACT [1984 Ed.]	CAP. 102	01-08-1981	
WILLS ACT [2000 Ed.]	CAP. 193	21-10-1999	
WOMEN AND GIRLS PROTECTION ACT [1984 Ed., Amended by GN 649/03]	CAP. 120	19-04-1973	
WORKMEN'S COMPENSATION ACT [1984 Ed., Amended by GN 273/02]	CAP. 74	01-04-1957	
YAYASAN SULTAN HAJI HASSANAL BOLKIAH ACT [2008 Ed.]	CAP. 166	05-10-1992	

STRATEGIC GOVERNMENT CONTACT IN BRUNEY

Prime Minister's Office
E-Mail: PRO@jpm.gov.bn
Telephone: 673 - 2 - 229988
Fax: 673 - 2 - 241717
Telex: BU2727
Address:
Prime Minister's Office
Istana Nurul Iman
Bandar Seri Begawan BA1000

Audit Department
Prime Minister's Office
Jalan Menteri Besar
Bandar Seri Begawan BB 39 10
Brunei Darussalam
Telephone: (02) 380576
Facsimile: (02) 380679
E-mail: jabaudbd@brunet.bn

Information Department
Prime Minister's Office
Berakas Old Airport
Bandar Seri Begawan
BB 3510
Brunei Darussalam.
E-mail:- pelita@brunet.bn

Fax: 673 2 381004
Tel: 673 2 380527

Narcotics Control Bureau
Prime Minister's Office
Jalan Tungku Gadong
Bandar Seri Begawan BE 2110
Tel No: 02-448877 / 422479 / 422480 / 422481
Fax No: 02-422477
E-mail: ncb@brunet.bn

One-Stop Agency
The Ministry of Industry and Primary Resources
Bandar Seri Begawan 1220
Brunei Darussalam

Telefax: (02) 244811
Telex: MIPRS BU 2111
Cable: MIPRS BRUNEI

Head Policy and Administration Division
Ministry of Industry and Primary Resources
Jalan Menteri Besar, Bandar Seri Begawan

1220
Brunei Darussalam
Tel: (02) 382822

Secretary of Public Service Commission
Old Airport
Bandar Seri Begawan BB 3510
Tel No: 02-381961
E-mail: bplspa@brunet.bn

Semaun Holdings Sdn Bhd
Unit 2.02, Block D, 2nd Floor
Yayasan Sultan Haji Hassanal Bolkiah
Complex
Jalan Pretty
Bandar Seri Begawan BS8711
Brunei Darussalam
E-mail address: semaun@brunet.bn

Department of Agriculture
Ministry of Industry & Primary
Resources
BB3510
Brunei Darussalam
Telephone: + 673 2 380144
Fax: + 673 2 382226
Telex: PERT BU 2456

Land Transport Department
KM 6, Jalan Gadong,
Beribi BE1110,
Brunei Darussalam.
Tel : (673-2) 451979
Fax : (673-2) 424775
Email : latis@brunet.bn

FOREIGN MISSIONS

AUSTRALIA

Australian High Commission
(His Excellency Mr. Neal Patrick Davis -
High Commissioner)
4th flr Teck Guan Plaza, Jln Sultan
Bandar Seri Begawan BS8811
Brunei Darussalam
or
P.O. Box 2990
Bandar Seri Begawan, BS8675
Brunei Darussalam
Tel: 673 2 229435/6
Fax: 673 2 221652

AUSTRIA

Austrian Consulate General
No. 5 Taman Jubli, Spg 75,
Jalan Subok,
Bandar Seri Begawan BD2717
Brunei Darussalam
or
P.O. Box 1303,
Bandar Seri Begawan, BS8672
Brunei Darussalam
Tel : 673 2 261083
Email: austroko@brunet.bn

BANGLADESH

High Commission of People's Republic of Bangladesh
(His Excellency Mr. Muhammad Mumtaz
Hussain - High Commissioner)
AAR Villa, House No. 5,
Simpang 308, Jalan Lambak Kanan,
Berakas, BB1714
Brunei Darussalam
Tel: 673 2 394716
Fax: 673 2 394715

BELGIUM

Consulate of Belgium
2nd Floor, 146 Jln Pemancha
Bandar Seri Begawan BS8711
Brunei Darussalam
or
P.O.Box 65,
Bandar Seri Begawan, BS8670
Brunei Darussalam
Tel: 673 2 222298
Fax: 673 2 220895

BRITAIN

British High Commission
(His Excellency Mr. Stuart Laing - High
Commissioner)
Unit 2.01, Block D of Yayasan Sultan
Hassanal Bolkiah
Bandar Seri Begawan BS8711
Brunei Darussalam
or
P.O.Box 2197
Bandar Seri Begawan, BS8674

Brunei Darussalam
Tel: 673 2 222231
Fax: 673 2 226001

CAMBODIA

Royal Embassy of Cambodia
(His Highness Prince Sisowath
Phandaravong - Ambassador)
No. 8, Simpang 845
Kampong Tasek Meradun, Jalan Tutong,
BF1520
Brunei Darussalam
Tel: 673 2 650046
Fax: 673 2 650646

CANADA

High Commission of Canada
(His Excellency Mr. Neil Reeder - High
Commissioner)
Suite 51 - 52, Britannia House, Jalan Cator
Bandar Seri Begawan, BS8811
Brunei Darussalam
Tel: 673 2 220043
Fax: 673 2 220040

CHINA

Embassy of People's Republic of China
(His Excellency Mr. Wang Jianli -
Ambassador)
No. 1, 3 & 5, Simpang 462
Kampong Sungai Hanching,
Jln Muara, BC2115
Brunei Darussalam
or
P.O.Box 121
M.P.C, Berakas BB3577
Brunei Darussalam
Tel: 673 2 339609
Fax: 673 2 339612

DENMARK

Consulate of Denmark
Unit 6, Bangunan Hj Tahir,
Spg 103, Jln Gadong
Bandar Seri Begawan
Brunei Darussalam
or
P.O.Box 140

Bandar Seri Begawan, BS8670
Brunei Darussalam
Tel: 673 2 422050, 427525, 447559
Fax: 673 2 427526

FINLAND

Consulate of Finland
Bee Seng Shipping Company
No.7 1st Floor Sufri Complex
KM 2, Jalan Tutong
Bandar Seri Begawan, BA2111
Brunei Darussalam
or
P.O.Box 1777
Bandar Seri Begawan, BS8673
Brunei Darusslaam
Tel: 673 2 243847
Fax: 673 2 224495

FRANCE

Embassy of the Republic of France
(His Excelleny Mr. Jean Pierre Lafosse -
Ambassador)
#306-310 Kompleks Jln Sultan,
3rd Floor, 51-55 Jln Sultan
Bandar Seri Begawan BS8811
Brunei Darussalam
or
P.O.Box 3027
Bandar Seri Begawan, BS8675
Brunei Darussalam
Tel: 673 2 220960 / 1
Fax: 673 2 243373

GERMANY

Embassy of the Federal Republic of Germany
(His Excellency Klaus-Peter Brandes -
Ambassador)
6th flr, Wisma Raya Building
Lot 49-50, Jln Sultan
Bandar Seri Begawan, BS8811
Brunei Darussalam
or
P.O.Box 3050
Bandar Seri Begawan, BS8675
Brunei Darussalam
Tel: 673 2 225547 / 74
Fax: 673 2 225583

For additional analytical, business and investment opportunities information,
please contact Global Investment & Business Center, USA
at (703) 370-8082. Fax: (703) 370-8083. E-mail: ibpusa3@gmail.com
Global Business and Investment Info Databank - www.ibpus.com

INDIA

High Commission of India
(His Excellency Mr. Dinesh K. Jain - High Commissioner)
Lot 14034, Spg 337,
Kampong Manggis, Jln Muara, BC3515
Brunei Darussalam
Tel: 673 2 339947 / 339751
Fax: 673 2 339783
Email: hicomind@brunet.bn

INDONESIA

Embassy of the Republic of Indonesia
(His Excellency Mr. Rahardjo Djojonegoro - Ambassador)
Lot 4498, Spg 528
Sungai Hanching Baru, Jln Muara, BC3013
Brunei Darussalam
or
P.O.Box 3013
Bandar Seri Begawan, BS8675
Brunei Darussalam
Tel: 673 2 330180 / 445
Fax: 673 2 330646

IRAN

Embassy of the Islamic Republic of Iran
No. 2, Lot 14570, Spg 13
Kampong Serusop, Jalan Berakas, BB2313
Brunei Darussalam
Tel: 673 2 330021 / 29
Fax: 673 2 331744

JAPAN

Embassy of Japan
(His Excellency Mr. Hajime Tsujimoto - Ambassador)
No 1 & 3, Jalan Jawatan Dalam
Kampong Mabohai
Bandar Seri Begawan, BA1111
Brunei Darussalam
or
P.O.Box 3001
Bandar Seri Begawan, BS8675
Brunei Darussalam
Tel: 673 2 229265 / 229592, 237112 - 5
Fax: 673 2 229481

KOREA

Embassy of the Republic of Korea
(His Excellency Kim Ho-tae - Ambassador)
No.9, Lot 21652
Kg Beribi, Jln Gadong, BE1118
Brunei Darussalam
Tel: 673 2 650471 / 300, 652190
Fax: 673 2 650299

LAOS

Embassy of the Lao People's Democratic Republic
(His Excellency Mr. Ammone Singhavong - Ambassador)
Lot. No. 19824, House No. 11
Simpang 480, Jalan Kebangsaan Lama
Off Jalan Muara, BC4115
Brunei Darussalam
or
P.O.Box 2826
Bandar Seri Begawan, BS8675
Brunei Darussalam
Tel: 673 2 345666
Fax: 673 2 345888

MALAYSIA

Malaysian High Commission
(His Excellency Wan Yusof Embong - High Commissioner)
No.27 & 29, Simpang 396-39
Kampong Sungai Akar
Jalan Kebangsaan, BC4115
Brunei Darussalam
or
P.O.Box 2826
Bandar Seri Begawan, BS8675
Brunei Darussalam
Tel: 673 2 345652
Fax: 673 2 345654

MYANMAR

Embassy of the Union of Myanmar
(His Excellency U Than Tun - Ambassador)
No. 14, Lot 2185 / 46292
Simpang 212, Kampong Rimba, Gadong
BE3119
Brunei Darussalam

Tel: 673 2 450506 / 7
Fax: 673 2 451008

NETHERLANDS

Netherlands Consulate
c/o Brunei Shell Petroleum Co. Sdn Bhd
Seria KB3534
Brunei Darussalam
Tel: 673 3 372005, 373045

NEW ZEALAND

New Zealand Consulate
36A Seri Lambak Complex,
Jalan Berakas, BB1714
Brunei Darussalam
or
P.O.Box 2720
Bandar Seri Begawan, BS8675
Brunei Darusslam
Tel: 673 2 331612, 331010
Fax: 673 2 331612

NORWAY

Royal Norwegian Consulate
Unit No. 407A - 410A
4th Floor, Wisma Jaya
Jalan Pemancha
Bandar Seri Begawan, BS8811
Brunei Darussalam
Tel: 673 2 239091 / 2 / 3 / 4
Fax: 673 2 239095/6

OMAN

Embassy of the Sultanate of Oman
(His Excellency Mr. Ahmad Moh,d Masoud
Al-Riyami - Ambassador)
No.35 Simpang 100,
Jalan Tungku Link
Kampong Pengkalan, Gadong BE3719
Brunei Darussalam
or
P.O.Box 2875
Bandar Seri Begawan, BS8675
Brunei Darussalam
Tel: 673 2 446953 / 4 / 7 / 8
Fax: 673 2 449646

PAKISTAN

Pakistan High Commission
(His Excellency Major General (Rtd) Irshad
Ullah Tarar - High Commission)
No.5 Kampong Sungai Akar
Jalan Kebangsaan, BC4115
Brunei Darussalam
Tel: 673 2 6334989, 339797
Fax: 673 2 334990

PHILIPPINES

Embassy of the Republic of Philippines
His Excellency Mr. Enrique A. Zaldivar -
Ambassador)
Rm 1 & 2, 4th & 5th floor
Badiah Building, Mile 1 1/2 Jln Tutong
Brunei Darussalam, BA2111
or
P.O.Box 3025
Bandar Seri Begawan, BS8675
Brunei Darussalam
Tel: 673 2 241465 / 6
Fax: 673 2 237707

SAUDI ARABIA

Royal Embassy of Kingdom of Saudi Arabia
No. 1, Simpang 570
Kampong Salar
Jalan Muara, BU1429
Brunei Darusslam
Tel: 673 2 792821 / 2 / 3
Fax: 673 2 792826 / 7

SINGAPORE

Singapore High Commission
(His Excellency Tee Tua Ba - High
Commissioner)
No. 8, Simpang, 74,
Jalan Subok, BD1717
Brunei Darussalam
or
P.O.Box 2159
Bandar Seri Begawan, BS8674
Brunei Darussalam
Tel: 673 2 227583 / 4 / 5
Fax: 673 2 220957

SWEDEN

For additional analytical, business and investment opportunities information,
please contact Global Investment & Business Center, USA
at (703) 370-8082. Fax: (703) 370-8083. E-mail: ibpusa3@gmail.com
Global Business and Investment Info Databank - www.ibpus.com

Consulate of Sweden
Blk A, Unit 1, 2nd Floor
Abdul Razak Plaza,
Jalan Gadong,
Bandar Seri Begawan, BE3919
Brunei Darussalam
Tel: 673 2 448423, 444326
Fax: 673 2 448419

THAILAND

Royal Thai Embassy
(His Excellency Thinakorn Kanasuta -
Ambassador
No. 2, Simpang 682,
Kampong Bunut, Jalan Tutong, BF1320
Brunei Darussalam
Tel: 673 2 653108 / 9
Fax: 673 2 262752

UNITED STATE OF AMERICA

Embassy of the United States of America
3rd Flr, Teck Guan Plaza,
Jalan Sultan
Bandar Seri Begawan BS8811
Brunei Darussalam
Tel: 673 2 229670
Fax: (02) 225293

VIETNAM

Embassy of the Socialist Republic of Vietnam
(His Excellency Tran Tien Vinh -
Ambassador)
No. 10, Simpang 485
Kampong Sungai Hanching
Jalan Muara,BC2115
Brunei Darussalam
Tel: 673 2 343167 / 8
Fax: 673 2 343169

BRUNEI'S MISSIONS IN ASEAN, CHINA, JAPAN AND KOREA

CAMBODIA
Embassy of Brunei Darussalam
No : 237, Pasteur St. 51
Sangkat Boeung Keng Kang I
Khan Chamkar Mon
Phnom Penh

Kingdom of Cambodia
Tel : (855) 23211 457 & 23211 458
Fax : (855) 23211 456
E-Mail : Brunei@bigpond.com.kh

CHINA
Embassy of Brunei Darussalam
No. 3 Villa, Qijiayuan Diplomatic Compound
Chaoyang District
Beijing 100600
People's Republic of China 1000600
Tel : 86 (10) 6532 4093 - 6
Fax : 86 (10) 6532 4097
E-Mail : bdb@public.bta.net.cn

INDONESIA
Embassy of Brunei Darussalam
Wisma GKBI
 (Gabungan Koperasi Batik Indonesia)
Suite 1901, Jl. Jend. Sudirman No. 28
Jakarta 10210
Indonesia
Tel : 62 (21) 574 1437 - 39 / 574 1470 - 72
Fax : 62 (21) 574 1463

JAPAN
Embassy of Brunei Darussalam
5-2 Kitashinagawa 6-Chome
Shinagawa-ku
Tokyo 141
Japan
Tel : 81 (3) 3447 7997 / 9260
Fax : 81 (3) 344 79260

REPUBLIC OF KOREA
Embassy of Brunei Darussalam
7th Floor, Kwanghwamoon Building
211, Sejong-ro, Chongro-Ku
Seoul
Republic of Korea.
Tel : 82 (2) 399 3707 / 3708
Fax : 82 (2) 399 3709
E-Mail : kbrunei@chollian.net

LAOS
Embassy of Brunei Darussalam
No. 333 Unit 25 Ban Phonxay
Xaysettha District
Lanexang Avenue
Vientiane
Laos People's Democratic Republic
Tel : (856) 2141 6114 / 2141 4169

For additional analytical, business and investment opportunities information,
please contact Global Investment & Business Center, USA
at (703) 370-8082. Fax: (703) 370-8083. E-mail: ibpusa3@gmail.com
Global Business and Investment Info Databank - www.ibpus.com

Fax : (856) 2141 6115
E-Mail : kbnbd@laonet.net

MALAYSIA
High Commission of Brunei Darussalam
Tingkat 8 Wisma Sin Heap Lee (SHL)
Jalan Tun Razak
50400 Kuala Lumpur
Malaysia.
Tel : 60 (3) 261 2828
Fax : 60 (3) 263 1302
E-Mail : Sjtnbdkl@tm.net.my

THE UNIION OF MYANMAR
Embassy of Brunei Darussalam
No : 51 Golden Valley
Bahan Township
Yangon
The Union of Myanmar.
Tel: 95 (1) 510 422
Fax: 95 (1) 512 854

PHILIPPINES
Embassy of Brunei Darussalam
11th Floor BPI Building
Ayala Avenue, Corner Paseo De Roxas
Makati City, Metro Manila
Philippines
Tel : 63 (2) 816 2836 - 8

Fax : 63 (2) 816 2876
E-Mail : kbnbdmnl@skynet.net

SINGAPORE
High Commission of Brunei Darussalam
325 Tanglin Road
Singapore 247955
Tel : (65) 733 9055
Fax : (65) 737 5275
E-Mail : comstbs@singnet.com.sg

THAILAND
Embassy of Brunei Darussalam
No. 132 Sukhumvit 23 Road
Watana District
Bangkok 10110
Thailand
Tel : 66 (2) 204 1476 - 9
Fax : 66 (2) 204 1486

VIETNAM
Embassy of Brunei Darussalam
No. 4 Thien Quang Street
Hai Ba Trung District
Hanoi
Vietnam
Tel : (84) 4 826 4816 / 4817 / 4818
Fax : (84) 4 822 2092
E-Mail : bruemviet@hotmail.com

FOOD AND RESTAURANTS

Brunei restaurants, including western style fast food centres, cater to a wide range of tastes and palates.
Visitors can also sample authentic local food offered at the tamu night market in the capital.
The market, along the Kianggeh river, is actually open from early morning. It takes on a special atmosphere at night when crowds throng its alleys to shop and eat at the lowest prices in town.
Tropical fruits like watermelon, papaya, mango and banana are also available.
Locals are fond of the Malay-style satay, bits of beef or chicken in a stick, cooked over low fire and dipped in a tangy peanut sauce.

Brunei's first Chinese halal restaurant is Emperor's Court, owned by Royal Brunei Catering, which caters to Cantonese and Western tastebuds.

A list of restaurants in the capital and Seria-Kuala Belait areas follows:
Bandar Seri Begawan
Aumrin Restaurant, 1 Bangunan Hasbullah, 4 Jalan Gadong
Airport Restaurant, Brunei International Airport
Coffee Tree, Unit 3, top floor ,Mabohai Shopping Complex
Emperor's Court, 1st Floor, Wisma Haji Mohd Taha, Jalan Gadong
Excellent Taste, G5 Gadong Properties Centre, Jalan Gadong
Express Fast Food, 22/23 Jalan Sultan
Ghawar Restaurant, 3 Ground Floor Bang Hasbullah 4

Jade Garden Chinese Restaurant, Riverview Inn, Km 1 Jalan Gadong
Jolibee Family Restaurant, Utama Bowling Centre, Km 11/2 Jalan Tutong
Kentucky Fried Chicken (B) Sdn Bhd, G15-G16 Plaza Athirah
Lucky Restaurant, Umi Kalthum Building, Jalan Tutong
McDonald's Restaurant, 10-12 Block H, Abdul Razak Complex, Simpang 137, Gadong
Phongmun Restaurant, Nos. 56-60, 2nd Floor Teck Guan Plaza
Pizza Hut, Block J, Unit 2 & 3 Abdul Razak Complex
Pondok Sari Wangi, 12 Blk A, Abdul Razak Complex, Jalan Gadong
Popular Restaurant, 5, Ground floor, PAP Hajjah Norain Building
QR Restaurant, Blk C, Abdul Razak Complex, Jalan Gadong
Rainbow Restaurant, 110 Jalan Batu Bersurat, Gadong
Rasa Sayang Restaurant, 607 Bangunan Guru-Guru Melayu
Rose Garden Restaurant, 8 Blk C, Abdul Razak Complex, Jalan Gadong
Season's Restaurant, Gadong Centrepoint
SD Cafe, 6-7 Bangunan Hj Othman, Simpang 105, Jalan Gadong
Seri Kamayan Restaurant, 4 & 5 Bangunan Hj Tahir ,Simpang 103, Jalan Gadong
Seri Maradum Baru, Block C6, Abdul Razak Complex
Sugar Bun Fast Food, Lot 16397 Mabohai Complex, Jalan Kebangsaan
Schezuan's Dynasty Restaurant, Gadong Centrepoint
Swensen's Ice Cream and Fine Food Restaurant, 17-18 Ground Floor Bagunan Halimatul Sa'adiah, Gadong
Tenaga Restaurant, 6 1st Floor Bangunan Hasbollah 4
The Stadium Restaurant, Stadium Negara Hassanal Bolkiah
Tropicana Seafood Restaurant, Block 1 Ground Floor, Pang's Building,Muara
Kuala Belait/Seria
Belait Restaurant, Jalan Bunga Raya
Buccaneer Steak House, Lot 94 Jalan McKerron
Cottage Restaurant, 38 Jalan Pretty
Jolene Restaurant, 83,1st Jalan Bunga Raya
New China Restaurant, 39/40 3rd Floor, Ang's Building, Jalan Sultan Omar Ali, Seria
New Cheng Wah Restaurant, 14 Jalan Sultan Omar Ali, Seria
Orchid Room, B5, 1st Floor, Jalan Bunga Raya
Red Wing Restaurant, 12 Jalan Sultan Omar Ali, Seria
Tasty Cake Shop/Pretty Inn, 26 Jalan Sultan Omar Ali, Seria
Tasconi's Pizza, Simpang 19, Jalan Sungai Pandan

WHERE TO SHOP

For many travellers one of the pleasures of visiting another country is finding something of interest and value for one's self, family or friends. There are many shops in Brunei offering a wide variety of goods at competitive prices. These range from modern department stores to small market stalls where bargaining is still commonly practised.

Modern department stores are found in the major towns of Bandar Seri Begawan, Tutong, Kuala Belait and Seria. In addition to these departmental stores there is a wide variety of old-fashioned shophouses as well as more modern air-conditioned shops.

Most items ranging from the latest electronic goods and imported luxury goods to common household items and groceries can be conveniently found in these shops.

Traditional items that reflect the culture of Brunei like the brass cannon, kris and kain songket, better known as "jong sarat" are excellent souvenirs to bring home from a visit to the country.

These can be purchased at the Arts and Handicrafts Centre which is located off Kota Batu, and also at the airport.

Before leaving Brunei make sure you stop by the Duty Free shops at the airport. These offer a wide range of luxury goods, garments, jewellery, writing instruments, perfumes, handicrafts, Brunei souvenirs, books and chocolates at very reasonable prices.

SHOPPING CENTRES

Hua Ho Department Store, Jln Gadong, Bandar Seri Begawan

Kota Mutiara Department Store, Bangunan Darussalam, Bandar Seri Begawan

Lai Lai Department Store, Mile 1 Jln Tutong, Bandar Seri Begawan

Millimewah Department Store (BSB), Bangunan Darussalam, Bandar Seri Begawan

Millimewah Department Store (Tutong),Tutong

Millimewah Department Store (Seria), Seria

Princess Inn Department Store, Mile 1 Jln Tutong , Bandar Seri Begawan

Tiong Hin Superstore,Jln Muara, Bandar Seri Begawan

Megamart,Jln Gadong, Bandar Seri Begawan

Wisma Jaya Complex, Jln Pemancha, Bandar Seri Begawan

First Emporium & Supermarket, Mohammad Yussof Complex, Jln Kubah Makam DiRaja, Bandar Seri Begawan

Seria Plaza, Seria

Seaview Department Store, Jln Maulana, Kuala Belait

TRAVEL AGENTS

BANDAR SERI BEGAWAN

Antara Travel & Tours Sdn Bhd 02-448805/808
Anthony Tours & Travel Sdn Bhd 02-228668
Borneo Leisure Travel Sdn Bhd 02-223420
Brunei Travel Services Sdn Bhd 02-236006
Century Travel Centre Sdn Bhd 02-227296
Churiah Travel Service 02-224422
Darat Dan Laut 02-426321
Freme Travel Services Sdn Bhd 02-234277
Halim Tours & Travel Sdn Bhd 02-226688
Intan Travel & Trading Agencies 02-427340
Jasra Harrisons (B) Sdn Bhd 02-236675

JB Travel & Insurance Agencies 02-239132
JJ Tour Service (B) Sdn Bhd 02-224761
Ken Travel & Trading Sdn Bhd 02-223127
Mahasiswa Travel Service 02-243452
Oriental Travel Services 02-226464
Overseas Travel Services Sdn Bhd 02-445322
Sarawak Travel Service Sdn Bhd 02-223361
Seri Islamic Tours & Travel Sdn Bhd 02-243341
Straits Central Agencies (B) Sdn Bhd 02-229356
Sunshine Borneo Tours & Travel Sdn Bhd 02-441791
SMAS 02-234741
Travel Centre (B) Sdn Bhd 02-229601
Travel Trade Agencies Sdn Bhd 02-229601/228439
Tai Wah Travel Service Sdn Bhd 02-224015
Tenega Travel Agency Sdn Bhd 02-422974
Titian Travel & Tours Sdn Bhd 02-448742
Twelve Roofs / Perusahaan Hj. Asmakhan 02-340395
Wing On Travel & Trading Agencies 02-220536
Zizen Travel Agency Sdn Bhd 02-236991
Zura Travel Service Sdn Bhd 02-234738

KUALA BELAIT

Freme Travel Services Sdn Bhd 03-335025
Jasra Harrisons Sdn Bhd 03-335391
JJ Tour Service Sdn Bhd 03-334069
Limbang Travel Service Sdn Bhd 03-335275
Overseas Travel Service Sdn Bhd 03-222090
Southern Cross Travel Agencies Sdn Bhd 03-334642
Straits Central Agencies Sdn Bhd 03-334589
Usaha Royako Travel Agency 03-334768

SELECTED COMPANIES

- Advance Computer Supplier and Services
- AJYAD Publishing
- Akitek SAA Home Page
- Amalgamated Electronic Sdn. Bhd.
- Anthony Tours & Travel Agency
- Baharuddin & Associates Consulting Engineers
- Beseller Sdn Bhd Homepage
- BIT Computer Services
- BruDirect Business Centre
- Brunei Hotel
- Brupost
- CfBT Homepage
- Compunet Computer & Office Systems
- Dalplus Technologies, Brunei
- DN Private Investigation and Security Consultant
- DP Happy Video House
- Elite Computer Systems Sdn. Bhd.
- Fabrica Interior Furnishing Co
- Glamour Homepage

- HSBC
- HSE Engineering Sdn. Bhd.
- Indah Sejahtera Development & Services
- Insurans Islam Taib
- Interhouse Marketing Sdn. Bhd.
- International School Brunei
- IP and Company
- ISS Thomas Cowan Sdn. Bhd.
- Jerudong Park Medical Centre
- Kristal
- L & M Prestressing Sdn. Bhd.
- Megamas Training Company Sdn. Bhd.
- Mekar General Enterprise Homepage
- Micronet Computer School
- National Insurance Company Berhad
- Paotools Supplies & Services Co.
- Petar Perunding Sdn. Bhd.
- Petrel Jaya Sdn Bhd
- Phongmun Restaurant Homepage
- Poh Lee Trading Company
- Q-Carrier
- Sabli Group of Companies - Brunei Darussalam
- Scanmark Design Sdn Bhd
- SDS System (B) Sdn. Bhd.
- SEAMEO VOCTECH Homepage
- Singapore Airlines
- Sistem Komputer Alif Sdn Bhd
- SPCastro And Associates Sdn Bhd
- Sunshine Borneo Tour & Travel Sdn.Bhd.
- Survey Service Consultants
- Syabas Publishers
- Syarikat Suraya Insan
- Syarikat Intellisense Technology
- Tabung Amanah Islam Brunei
- Tang Sung Lee Sdn. Bhd.
- The Lodge Resort (In Brunei)
- Trinkets Enterprise
- Twelve Roofs / Perusahaan Hj. Asmakhan
- Unicraft Enterprises
- Utama Komunikasi

BASIC TITLES ON BRUNEI

IMPORTANT!
All publications are updated annually!
Please contact IBP, Inc. at ibpusa3@gmail.com for the latest ISBNs and additional information
Global Business and Investment Info Databank: www.ibpus.com

Title
Brunei A "Spy" Guide - Strategic Information and Developments
Brunei A "Spy" Guide - Strategic Information and Developments

For additional analytical, business and investment opportunities information, please contact Global Investment & Business Center, USA at (703) 370-8082. Fax: (703) 370-8083. E-mail: ibpusa3@gmail.com
Global Business and Investment Info Databank - www.ibpus.com

Title
Brunei Air Force Handbook
Brunei Air Force Handbook
Brunei Business and Investment Opportunities Yearbook
Brunei Business and Investment Opportunities Yearbook
Brunei Business and Investment Opportunities Yearbook Volume 1 Strategic Information and Opportunities
Brunei Business and Investment Opportunities Yearbook Volume 2 Leading Export-Import, Business, Investment Opportunities and Projects
Brunei Business Intelligence Report - Practical Information, Opportunities, Contacts
Brunei Business Intelligence Report - Practical Information, Opportunities, Contacts
Brunei Business Law Handbook - Strategic Information and Basic Laws
Brunei Business Law Handbook - Strategic Information and Basic Laws
Brunei Business Law Handbook - Strategic Information and Basic Laws
Brunei Business Law Handbook - Strategic Information and Basic Laws
Brunei Company Laws and Regulations Handbook
Brunei Constitution and Citizenship Laws Handbook - Strategic Information and Basic Laws
Brunei Country Study Guide - Strategic Information and Developments
Brunei Country Study Guide - Strategic Information and Developments
Brunei Country Study Guide - Strategic Information and Developments Volume 1 Strategic Information and Developments
Brunei Customs, Trade Regulations and Procedures Handbook
Brunei Customs, Trade Regulations and Procedures Handbook
Brunei Diplomatic Handbook - Strategic Information and Developments
Brunei Diplomatic Handbook - Strategic Information and Developments
Brunei Ecology & Nature Protection Handbook
Brunei Ecology & Nature Protection Handbook
Brunei Ecology & Nature Protection Laws and Regulation Handbook
Brunei Energy Policy, Laws and Regulation Handbook
Brunei Energy Policy, Laws and Regulations Handbook
Brunei Energy Policy, Laws and Regulations Handbook
Brunei Export-Import Trade and Business Directory
Brunei Export-Import Trade and Business Directory
Brunei Foreign Policy and Government Guide
Brunei Foreign Policy and Government Guide
Brunei Immigration Laws and Regulations Handbook - Strategic Information and Basic Laws
Brunei Industrial and Business Directory
Brunei Industrial and Business Directory
Brunei Investment and Business Guide - Strategic and Practical Information
Brunei Investment and Business Guide - Strategic and Practical Information
Brunei Investment and Business Guide - Strategic and Practical Information
Brunei Investment and Business Guide - Strategic and Practical Information
Brunei Investment and Business Guide Volume 2 Business, Investment Opportunities and Incentives
Brunei Investment and Trade Laws and Regulations Handbook
Brunei Labor Laws and Regulations Handbook - Strategic Information and Basic Laws
Brunei Land Ownership and Agriculture Laws Handbook
Brunei Mineral & Mining Sector Investment and Business Guide - Strategic and Practical Information
Brunei Mineral & Mining Sector Investment and Business Guide - Strategic and Practical Information
Brunei Mining Laws and Regulations Handbook
Brunei Oil & Gas Sector Business & Investment Opportunities Yearbook

Title
Brunei Oil & Gas Sector Business & Investment Opportunities Yearbook
Brunei Oil and Gas Exploration Laws and Regulation Handbook
Brunei Recent Economic and Political Developments Yearbook
Brunei Recent Economic and Political Developments Yearbook
Brunei Recent Economic and Political Developments Yearbook
Brunei Starting Business (Incorporating) in....Guide
Brunei Sultan Haji Hassanal Bolkiah Mu'izzaddin Waddaulah Handbook
Brunei Sultan Haji Hassanal Bolkiah Waddaulah Handbook Economic and Foreign Policy Handbook
Brunei Tax Guide Volume 1 Business Taxation
Brunei Tax Guide Volume 2 Personal Taxation
Brunei Taxation Laws and Regulations Handbook
Brunei Telecommunication Industry Business Opportunities Handbook
Brunei Telecommunication Industry Business Opportunities Handbook
Brunei: How to Invest, Start and Run Profitable Business in Brunei Guide - Practical Information, Opportunities, Contacts

BASIC LAWS AND REGULATIONS AFFECTING BUSINESS AND TRADE

COUTRY	LAW TITLE
Brunei	Admiralty Jurisdiction Act
Brunei	Advocates and Solicitors (Practice and Etiquette) Rules
Brunei	Advocates and Solicitors Rules
Brunei	Agricultural Pests and Noxious Plants
Brunei	Air Navigation Act
Brunei	Airport Passenger Service Charge Act
Brunei	Anti Terrorism (Financial and other Measure) Act
Brunei	Antiquities and Treasure Trove Act
Brunei	Application of Laws
Brunei	Arbitration Act
Brunei	Arms and Explosive Act
Brunei	Arms and Explosives Rules
Brunei	Asian Development Bank Act 2009
Brunei	Audit Act
Brunei	Banishment Act
Brunei	Banker's Book Act
Brunei	Banking Act
Brunei	Bankruptcy Act
Brunei	Bill of Sale Act
Brunei	Bills of Exchange Act
Brunei	Biological Weapons Act
Brunei	Bishop of Borneo Act
Brunei	Bretton Woods Agreement Act
Brunei	Broadcasting Act
Brunei	Brunei Board of Examination Act Brunei Economic Development Board Act
Brunei	Brunei Fishery Limits Act
Brunei	Brunei Investment Agency Act
Brunei	Brunei Malay Silversmiths Guild (Incorporation) Act
Brunei	Brunei National Archives Act
Brunei	Brunei Nationality Act
Brunei	Brunei Nationality Act Designation of Areas under Regulation 9
Brunei	Buffaloes Act
Brunei	Burial Grounds Act
Brunei	Business Name Act
Brunei	Censorship of Films and Public Entertainments Act
Brunei	Census Act
Brunei	Chinese Marriage Act
Brunei	Coin (Import and Export) Act
Brunei	Commission of Inquiry Act
Brunei	Commissioner for Oaths Act
Brunei	Common Gaming Houses Act
Brunei	Companies Act
Brunei	Computer Misuse Act

For additional analytical, business and investment opportunities information, please contact Global Investment & Business Center, USA at (703) 370-8082. Fax: (703) 370-8083. E-mail: ibpusa3@gmail.com Global Business and Investment Info Databank - www.ibpus.com

Brunei	Computer Misuse Order
Brunei	Constitution of Brunei
Brunei	Consular Relations Act
Brunei	Contract Act
Brunei	Cooperative Societies Act
Brunei	Criminal Appeal Rules
Brunei	Criminal Law Act
Brunei	Criminal Procedure Code
Brunei	Criminals Registration Act 2009
Brunei	Currency Act
Brunei	Customs Act
Brunei	Debtors Act
Brunei	Defamation Act
Brunei	Description of Land Act
Brunei	Diplomatic Privilege Act
Brunei	Disaffected and Dangerous Persons Act
Brunei	Dissolution of Marriage Act
Brunei	Dogs Act
Brunei	Education (Non-Government Schools) Act
Brunei	Election Offences Act
Brunei	Electricity Act
Brunei	Electronic Transaction Order
Brunei	Electronic Transactions Act
Brunei	Emblems and Names Act
Brunei	Emergency Regulations Act
Brunei	Employment Information Act
Brunei	Evidence Act
Brunei	Exchange Control Act
Brunei	Excise Act
Brunei	Extradition (Malaysia and Singapore) Act
Brunei	Extradition Act
Brunei	Fatal Accident and Personal Injuries Act
Brunei	Finance Companies Act
Brunei	Fire Service Act
Brunei	Fisheries Act
Brunei	Forest Act 2002
Brunei	Geneva and Red Cross Act
Brunei	Guardianship of Infants
Brunei	Immigration Act
Brunei	Income tax Act
Brunei	Intermediate Courts
Brunei	Internal Security Act
Brunei	Internationally Protected Persons Act
Brunei	Interpretation and General Clauses Act
Brunei	Intoxicating Substances Act
Brunei	Inventions Act
Brunei	Investments Incentives Act
Brunei	Islamic Banking Act
Brunei	Kidnapping Act

Brunei	Labor Act
Brunei	Land Acquisition Act
Brunei	Land Code Act
Brunei	Law Reform (Contributory Negligence) Act
Brunei	Law Revision Act
Brunei	Legal Profession (Practicing Certificate) Rules
Brunei	Legal Profession Act
Brunei	Licensed Land Surveyors Act
Brunei	Limitation Act
Brunei	Local Newspaper Act Official Secrets Act
Brunei	Marriage Act
Brunei	Married Women Act
Brunei	Medical Practitioners Dentists Act
Brunei	Merchandise Marks Act
Brunei	Mining Act
Brunei	Minor Offences Act
Brunei	Miscellaneous Licenses Act
Brunei	Misuse of Drugs Act
Brunei	Money-Changing and Remittance Businesses Act
Brunei	Moneylenders Act
Brunei	Monopolies Act
Brunei	Municipal Board Act
Brunei	National Bank of Brunei Act
Brunei	National Registration Regulations
Brunei	Nationality Registration Act
Brunei	Oaths and Affirmations
Brunei	Old Age and Disability Pensions Act
Brunei	Passport Act
Brunei	Pawnbrokers Act
Brunei	Penal Code
Brunei	Pensions Act
Brunei	Petroleum (Pipe-Lines) Act
Brunei	Petroleum Mining Act
Brunei	Petroleum Mining Act
Brunei	Poisons Act
Brunei	Post Office Act
Brunei	Powers of Attorney Act
Brunei	Preservation of Books Act
Brunei	Prevention of Corruption Act
Brunei	Price Control Act
Brunei	Prisons Act
Brunei	Probate and Administration Act
Brunei	Public Entertainment Act
Brunei	Public Health (Food)
Brunei	Public Officers (liability) Act
Brunei	Public Order Act
Brunei	Public Service Commission Act
Brunei	Quarantine and Prevention of Disease Act
Brunei	Reciprocal Enforcement of Foreign Judgments

For additional analytical, business and investment opportunities information, please contact Global Investment & Business Center, USA at (703) 370-8082. Fax: (703) 370-8083. E-mail: ibpusa3@gmail.com
Global Business and Investment Info Databank - www.ibpus.com

Brunei	Registration of Adoptions Act
Brunei	Registration of Guests Act
Brunei	Registration of Marriages Act
Brunei	Religious Council and Kadis Court Act
Brunei	Road Traffic Act
Brunei	Royal Brunei Police Force Act
Brunei	Rubber Dealers Act
Brunei	Sale of Goods Act
Brunei	Second-Hand Dealers Act
Brunei	Security Agencies Act
Brunei	Sedition Act
Brunei	Societies Act
Brunei	Specific relief Act
Brunei	Stamp Act
Brunei	Statistics Act
Brunei	Statutory Declarations Act
Brunei	Subordinate Courts Act
Brunei	Subscriptions Control Act
Brunei	Summonses and Warrants (Special Provision) Act
Brunei	Supreme Court (Appeals to Privy Council) Act
Brunei	Supreme Court Act
Brunei	Syariah Courts
Brunei	Telecommunications Act
Brunei	Territorial Waters of Brunei Act
Brunei	Tokyo Convention
Brunei	Trade Disputes Act
Brunei	Trade Marks Act
Brunei	Trade Union Act
Brunei	Transfer of the Functions of the Minister of Law Act
Brunei	Travel Agents Act
Brunei	Trespass on Royal Property Act
Brunei	Undesirable Publications Act
Brunei	Unfair Contact Terms Act
Brunei	University Brunei Darussalam Act
Brunei	Unlawful Carnal Knowledge Act
Brunei	Vicar Apostolic of Kuching Act
Brunei	Water Supply Act
Brunei	Weights and Measure Act
Brunei	Wild Life Protection Act
Brunei	Wills Act
Brunei	Women and Girls Protection Act
Brunei	Workmen's Compensation Act
Brunei	Workmen's Unemployment Indemnity Act

For additional analytical, business and investment opportunities information,
please contact Global Investment & Business Center, USA
at (703) 370-8082. Fax: (703) 370-8083. E-mail: ibpusa3@gmail.com
Global Business and Investment Info Databank - www.ibpus.com

INTERNATIONAL BUSINESS PUBLICATIONS, USA

ibpusa@comcast.net. http://www.ibpus.com

WORLD ISLAMIC BUSINESS LIBRARY
Price: $149.95 Each

Islamic Banking and Financial Law Handbook
Islamic Banking Law Handbook
Islamic Business Organization Law Handbook
Islamic Commerce and Trade Law Handbook
Islamic Company Law Handbook
Islamic Constitutional and Administrative Law Handbook
Islamic Copyright Law Handbook
Islamic Customs Law and Regulations Handbook
Islamic Design Law Handbook
Islamic Development Bank Group Handbook
Islamic Economic & Business Laws and Regulations Handbook
Islamic Environmental Law Handbook
Islamic Financial and Banking System Handbook vol 1
Islamic Financial and Banking System Handbook Vol. 2
Islamic Financial Institutions (Banks and Financial Companies) Handbook
Islamic Foreign Investment and Privatization Law Handbook
Islamic Free Trade & Economic Zones Law and Regulations Handbook
Islamic International Law and Jihad (War(Law Handbook
Islamic Labor Law Handbook
Islamic Legal System (Sharia) Handbook Vol. 1 Basic Laws and Regulations
Islamic Legal System (Sharia) Handbook Vol. 2 Laws and Regulations in
Selected Countries
Islamic Mining Law Handbook
Islamic Patent & Trademark Law Handbook
Islamic Taxation Law Handbook
Islamic Trade & Export-Import Laws and Regulations Handbook

For additional analytical, business and investment opportunities information,
please contact Global Investment & Business Center, USA
at (202) 546-2103. Fax: (202) 546-3275. E-mail: rusric@erols.com

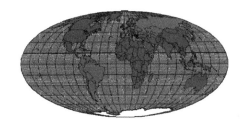

GLOBAL
SOCIAL SECURITY SYSTEM, POLICIES LAWS AND REGULATIONS HANDBOOK - STRATEGIC INFORMATION AND BASIC LAWS LIBRARY
Price: $9995 Each

1.	Albania Social Security System, Policies, Laws and Regulations Handbook
2.	Algeria Social Security System, Policies, Laws and Regulations Handbook
3.	Andorra Social Security System, Policies, Laws and Regulations Handbook
4.	Angola Social Security System, Policies, Laws and Regulations Handbook
5.	Antigua and Barbuda Social Security System, Policies, Laws and Regulations Handbook
6.	Argentina Social Security System, Policies, Laws and Regulations Handbook
7.	Armenia Social Security System, Policies, Laws and Regulations Handbook
8.	Australia Social Security System, Policies, Laws and Regulations Handbook
9.	Austria Social Security System, Policies, Laws and Regulations Handbook
10.	Azerbaijan Social Security System, Policies, Laws and Regulations Handbook
11.	Bahamas Social Security System, Policies, Laws and Regulations Handbook
12.	Bahrain Social Security System, Policies, Laws and Regulations Handbook
13.	Bangladesh Social Security System, Policies, Laws and Regulations Handbook
14.	Barbados Social Security System, Policies, Laws and Regulations Handbook
15.	Belarus Social Security System, Policies, Laws and Regulations Handbook
16.	Belgium Social Security System, Policies, Laws and Regulations Handbook
17.	Belize Social Security System, Policies, Laws and Regulations Handbook
18.	Benin Social Security System, Policies, Laws and Regulations Handbook
19.	Bermuda Social Security System, Policies, Laws and Regulations Handbook
20.	Bhutan Social Security System, Policies, Laws and Regulations Handbook
21.	Bolivia Social Security System, Policies, Laws and Regulations Handbook
22.	Botswana Social Security System, Policies, Laws and Regulations Handbook
23.	Brazil Social Security System, Policies, Laws and Regulations Handbook
24.	British Virgin Islands Social Security System, Policies, Laws and Regulations Handbook
25.	Brunei Social Security System, Policies, Laws and Regulations Handbook
26.	Bulgaria Social Security System, Policies, Laws and Regulations Handbook
27.	Burkina Faso Social Security System, Policies, Laws and Regulations Handbook
28.	Burma (Myanmar)
29.	Burundi Social Security System, Policies, Laws and Regulations Handbook
30.	Cameroon Social Security System, Policies, Laws and Regulations Handbook
31.	Canada Social Security System, Policies, Laws and Regulations Handbook
32.	Cape Verde Social Security System, Policies, Laws and Regulations Handbook
33.	Central African Republic Social Security System, Policies, Laws and Regulations Handbook
34.	Chad Social Security System, Policies, Laws and Regulations Handbook
35.	Chile Social Security System, Policies, Laws and Regulations Handbook
36.	China Social Security System, Policies, Laws and Regulations Handbook
37.	Colombia Social Security System, Policies, Laws and Regulations Handbook
38.	Congo (Brazzaville) Social Security System, Policies, Laws and Regulations Handbook
39.	Congo (Kinshasa) Social Security System, Policies, Laws and Regulations Handbook
40.	Costa Rica Social Security System, Policies, Laws and Regulations Handbook
41.	Cote d'Ivoire Social Security System, Policies, Laws and Regulations Handbook
42.	Croatia Social Security System, Policies, Laws and Regulations Handbook

**For additional analytical, business and investment opportunities information,
please contact Global Investment & Business Center, USA
at (703) 370-8082. Fax: (703) 370-8083. E-mail: ibpusa3@gmail.com
Global Business and Investment Info Databank - www.ibpus.com**

43.	Cuba Social Security System, Policies, Laws and Regulations Handbook
44.	Cyprus Social Security System, Policies, Laws and Regulations Handbook
45.	Czech Republic Social Security System, Policies, Laws and Regulations Handbook
46.	Denmark Social Security System, Policies, Laws and Regulations Handbook
47.	Djibouti Social Security System, Policies, Laws and Regulations Handbook
48.	Dominica Social Security System, Policies, Laws and Regulations Handbook
49.	Dominican Republic Social Security System, Policies, Laws and Regulations Handbook
50.	Ecuador Social Security System, Policies, Laws and Regulations Handbook
51.	Egypt Social Security System, Policies, Laws and Regulations Handbook
52.	El Salvador Social Security System, Policies, Laws and Regulations Handbook
53.	Equatorial Guinea Social Security System, Policies, Laws and Regulations Handbook
54.	Estonia Social Security System, Policies, Laws and Regulations Handbook Estonia
55.	Ethiopia Social Security System, Policies, Laws and Regulations Handbook
56.	Fiji Social Security System, Policies, Laws and Regulations Handbook
57.	Finland Social Security System, Policies, Laws and Regulations Handbook
58.	France Social Security System, Policies, Laws and Regulations Handbook
59.	Gabon Social Security System, Policies, Laws and Regulations Handbook
60.	Gambia Social Security System, Policies, Laws and Regulations Handbook
61.	Georgia Social Security System, Policies, Laws and Regulations Handbook
62.	Germany Social Security System, Policies, Laws and Regulations Handbook
63.	Ghana Social Security System, Policies, Laws and Regulations Handbook
64.	Greece Social Security System, Policies, Laws and Regulations Handbook
65.	Grenada Social Security System, Policies, Laws and Regulations Handbook
66.	Guatemala Social Security System, Policies, Laws and Regulations Handbook
67.	Guinea Social Security System, Policies, Laws and Regulations Handbook
68.	Guyana Social Security System, Policies, Laws and Regulations Handbook
69.	Haiti Social Security System, Policies, Laws and Regulations Handbook
70.	Honduras Social Security System, Policies, Laws and Regulations Handbook
71.	Hong Kong Social Security System, Policies, Laws and Regulations Handbook
72.	Hungary Social Security System, Policies, Laws and Regulations Handbook
73.	Iceland Social Security System, Policies, Laws and Regulations Handbook
74.	India Social Security System, Policies, Laws and Regulations Handbook
75.	Indonesia Social Security System, Policies, Laws and Regulations Handbook
76.	Iran Social Security System, Policies, Laws and Regulations Handbook
77.	Iraq Social Security System, Policies, Laws and Regulations Handbook
78.	Ireland Social Security System, Policies, Laws and Regulations Handbook
79.	Isle of Man Social Security System, Policies, Laws and Regulations Handbook
80.	Israel Social Security System, Policies, Laws and Regulations Handbook
81.	Italy Social Security System, Policies, Laws and Regulations Handbook
82.	Jamaica Social Security System, Policies, Laws and Regulations Handbook
83.	Japan Social Security System, Policies, Laws and Regulations Handbook
84.	Jordan Social Security System, Policies, Laws and Regulations Handbook
85.	Kazakhstan Social Security System, Policies, Laws and Regulations Handbook
86.	Kenya Social Security System, Policies, Laws and Regulations Handbook
87.	Kuwait Social Security System, Policies, Laws and Regulations Handbook
88.	Kyrgyzstan Social Security System, Policies, Laws and Regulations Handbook
89.	Laos Social Security System, Policies, Laws and Regulations Handbook
90.	Latvia Social Security System, Policies, Laws and Regulations Handbook
91.	Lebanon Social Security System, Policies, Laws and Regulations Handbook
92.	Lesotho Social Security System, Policies, Laws and Regulations Handbook
93.	Liberia Social Security System, Policies, Laws and Regulations Handbook
94.	Libya Social Security System, Policies, Laws and Regulations Handbook
95.	Liechtenstein Social Security System, Policies, Laws and Regulations Handbook
96.	Lithuania Social Security System, Policies, Laws and Regulations Handbook
97.	Luxembourg Social Security System, Policies, Laws and Regulations Handbook
98.	Madagascar Social Security System, Policies, Laws and Regulations Handbook

**For additional analytical, business and investment opportunities information,
please contact Global Investment & Business Center, USA
at (703) 370-8082. Fax: (703) 370-8083. E-mail: ibpusa3@gmail.com
Global Business and Investment Info Databank - www.ibpus.com**

99. Malawi Social Security System, Policies, Laws and Regulations Handbook
100. Malaysia Social Security System, Policies, Laws and Regulations Handbook Malaysia
101. Mali Social Security System, Policies, Laws and Regulations Handbook Mali
102. Malta Social Security System, Policies, Laws and Regulations Handbook Malta
103. Marshall Islands Social Security System, Policies, Laws and Regulations Handbook
104. Mauritania Social Security System, Policies, Laws and Regulations Handbook
105. Mauritius Social Security System, Policies, Laws and Regulations Handbook
106. Mexico Social Security System, Policies, Laws and Regulations Handbook
107. Micronesia Social Security System, Policies, Laws and Regulations Handbook
108. Moldova Social Security System, Policies, Laws and Regulations Handbook
109. Monaco Social Security System, Policies, Laws and Regulations Handbook
110. Morocco Social Security System, Policies, Laws and Regulations Handbook
111. Namibia Social Security System, Policies, Laws and Regulations Handbook Namibia
112. Nepal Social Security System, Policies, Laws and Regulations Handbook Nepal
113. Netherlands Social Security System, Policies, Laws and Regulations Handbook Netherlands
114. New Zealand Social Security System, Policies, Laws and Regulations Handbook New Zealand
115. Nicaragua Social Security System, Policies, Laws and Regulations Handbook Nicaragua
116. Niger Social Security System, Policies, Laws and Regulations Handbook Niger
117. Nigeria Social Security System, Policies, Laws and Regulations Handbook Nigeria
118. Norway Social Security System, Policies, Laws and Regulations Handbook Norway
119. Oman Social Security System, Policies, Laws and Regulations Handbook Oman
120. Pakistan Social Security System, Policies, Laws and Regulations Handbook Pakistan
121. Panama Social Security System, Policies, Laws and Regulations Handbook Panama
122. Papua New Guinea Social Security System, Policies, Laws and Regulations Handbook Papau New Guinea
123. Paraguay Social Security System, Policies, Laws and Regulations Handbook Paraguay
124. Peru Social Security System, Policies, Laws and Regulations Handbook Peru
125. Philippines Social Security System, Policies, Laws and Regulations Handbook Philippines
126. Poland Social Security System, Policies, Laws and Regulations Handbook Poland
127. Portugal Social Security System, Policies, Laws and Regulations Handbook Portugal
128. Qatar Social Security System, Policies, Laws and Regulations Handbook Qatar
129. Romania Social Security System, Policies, Laws and Regulations Handbook Romania
130. Russia Social Security System, Policies, Laws and Regulations Handbook Russia
131. Rwanda Social Security System, Policies, Laws and Regulations Handbook Rwanda
132. Samoa Social Security System, Policies, Laws and Regulations Handbook
133. San Marino Social Security System, Policies, Laws and Regulations Handbook
134. Sao Tome and Principe Social Security System, Policies, Laws and Regulations Handbook
135. Saudi Arabia Social Security System, Policies, Laws and Regulations Handbook
136. Senegal Social Security System, Policies, Laws and Regulations Handbook
137. Serbia Social Security System, Policies, Laws and Regulations Handbook
138. Seychelles Social Security System, Policies, Laws and Regulations Handbook
139. Sierra Leone Social Security System, Policies, Laws and Regulations Handbook
140. Singapore Social Security System, Policies, Laws and Regulations Handbook
141. Slovak Republic Social Security System, Policies, Laws and Regulations Handbook
142. Slovenia Social Security System, Policies, Laws and Regulations Handbook S
143. Solomon Islands Social Security System, Policies, Laws and Regulations Handbook
144. South Africa Social Security System, Policies, Laws and Regulations Handbook
145. South Korea Social Security System, Policies, Laws and Regulations Handbook
146. Spain Social Security System, Policies, Laws and Regulations Handbook
147. Sri Lanka Social Security System, Policies, Laws and Regulations Handbook
148. Sudan Social Security System, Policies, Laws and Regulations Handbook
149. Swaziland Social Security System, Policies, Laws and Regulations Handbook
150. Sweden Social Security System, Policies, Laws and Regulations Handbook
151. Switzerland Social Security System, Policies, Laws and Regulations Handbook
152. Syria Social Security System, Policies, Laws and Regulations Handbook
153. Taiwan Social Security System, Policies, Laws and Regulations Handbook

**For additional analytical, business and investment opportunities information,
please contact Global Investment & Business Center, USA
at (703) 370-8082. Fax: (703) 370-8083. E-mail: ibpusa3@gmail.com
Global Business and Investment Info Databank - www.ibpus.com**

154.	Tajikistan Social Security System, Policies, Laws and Regulations Handbook
155.	Tanzania Social Security System, Policies, Laws and Regulations Handbook Tanzania
156.	Thailand Social Security System, Policies, Laws and Regulations Handbook
157.	Togo Social Security System, Policies, Laws and Regulations Handbook
158.	Trinidad and Tobago Social Security System, Policies, Laws and Regulations Handbook
159.	Tunisia Social Security System, Policies, Laws and Regulations Handbook
160.	Turkey Social Security System, Policies, Laws and Regulations Handbook
161.	Turkmenistan Social Security System, Policies, Laws and Regulations Handbook
162.	Uganda Social Security System, Policies, Laws and Regulations Handbook
163.	Ukraine Social Security System, Policies, Laws and Regulations Handbook
164.	United Kingdom Social Security System, Policies, Laws and Regulations Handbook
165.	United States Social Security System, Policies, Laws and Regulations Handbook
166.	Uruguay Social Security System, Policies, Laws and Regulations Handbook
167.	Uzbekistan Social Security System, Policies, Laws and Regulations Handbook
168.	Vietnam Social Security System, Policies, Laws and Regulations Handbook
169.	Yemen Social Security System, Policies, Laws and Regulations Handbook
170.	Zambia Social Security System, Policies, Laws and Regulations Handbook
171.	Zimbabwe Social Security System, Policies, Laws and Regulations Handbook

**For additional analytical, business and investment opportunities information,
please contact Global Investment & Business Center, USA
at (703) 370-8082. Fax: (703) 370-8083. E-mail: ibpusa3@gmail.com
Global Business and Investment Info Databank - www.ibpus.com**

GLOBAL LABOR LAWS AND REGULATIONS HANDBOOK - STRATEGIC INFORMATION AND BASIC LAWS LIBRARY

Price: $149.95 Each

1.	Albania Labor Laws and Regulations Handbook - Strategic Information and Basic Laws
2.	Algeria Labor Laws and Regulations Handbook - Strategic Information and Basic Laws
3.	Andorra Labor Laws and Regulations Handbook - Strategic Information and Basic Laws
4.	Angola Labor Laws and Regulations Handbook - Strategic Information and Basic Laws
5.	Antigua & Barbuda Labor Laws and Regulations Handbook - Strategic Information and Basic Laws
6.	Antilles (Netherlands) Labor Laws and Regulations Handbook - Strategic Information and Basic Laws
7.	Argentina Labor Laws and Regulations Handbook - Strategic Information and Basic Laws
8.	Armenia Labor Laws and Regulations Handbook - Strategic Information and Basic Laws
9.	Australia Labor Laws and Regulations Handbook - Strategic Information and Basic Laws
10.	Austria Labor Laws and Regulations Handbook - Strategic Information and Basic Laws
11.	Azerbaijan Labor Laws and Regulations Handbook - Strategic Information and Basic Laws
12.	Bahamas Labor Laws and Regulations Handbook - Strategic Information and Basic Laws
13.	Bangladesh Labor Laws and Regulations Handbook - Strategic Information and Basic Laws
14.	Barbados Labor Laws and Regulations Handbook - Strategic Information and Basic Laws
15.	Belarus Labor Laws and Regulations Handbook - Strategic Information and Basic Laws
16.	Belgium Labor Laws and Regulations Handbook - Strategic Information and Basic Laws
17.	Belize Labor Laws and Regulations Handbook - Strategic Information and Basic Laws
18.	Bermuda Labor Laws and Regulations Handbook - Strategic Information and Basic Laws
19.	Bolivia Labor Laws and Regulations Handbook - Strategic Information and Basic Laws
20.	Bosnia and Herzegovina Labor Laws and Regulations Handbook - Strategic Information and Basic Laws
21.	Botswana Labor Laws and Regulations Handbook - Strategic Information and Basic Laws
22.	Brazil Labor Laws and Regulations Handbook - Strategic Information and Basic Laws
23.	Brunei Labor Laws and Regulations Handbook - Strategic Information and Basic Laws
24.	Bulgaria Labor Laws and Regulations Handbook - Strategic Information and Basic Laws
25.	Cambodia Labor Laws and Regulations Handbook - Strategic Information and Basic Laws
26.	Cameroon Labor Laws and Regulations Handbook - Strategic Information and Basic Laws
27.	Canada Labor Laws and Regulations Handbook - Strategic Information and Basic Laws
28.	Cayman Islands Labor Laws and Regulations Handbook - Strategic Information and Basic Laws
29.	Chile Labor Laws and Regulations Handbook - Strategic Information and Basic Laws
30.	China Labor Laws and Regulations Handbook - Strategic Information and Basic Laws
31.	Colombia Labor Laws and Regulations Handbook - Strategic Information and Basic Laws
32.	Comoros Labor Laws and Regulations Handbook - Strategic Information and Basic Laws
33.	Cook Islands Labor Laws and Regulations Handbook - Strategic Information and Basic Laws
34.	Costa Rica Labor Laws and Regulations Handbook - Strategic Information and Basic Laws

For additional analytical, business and investment opportunities information,
Please contact Global Investment & Business Center, USA
at (202) 546-2103. Fax: (202) 546-3275. E-mail: ibpusa3@gmail.com

35. Croatia Labor Laws and Regulations Handbook - Strategic Information and Basic Laws
36. Cuba Labor Laws and Regulations Handbook - Strategic Information and Basic Laws
37. Cyprus Labor Laws and Regulations Handbook - Strategic Information and Basic Laws
38. Czech Republic Labor Laws and Regulations Handbook - Strategic Information and Basic Laws
39. Denmark Labor Laws and Regulations Handbook - Strategic Information and Basic Laws
40. Dominica Labor Laws and Regulations Handbook - Strategic Information and Basic Laws
41. Dominican Republic Labor Laws and Regulations Handbook - Strategic Information and Basic Laws
42. Dubai Labor Laws and Regulations Handbook - Strategic Information and Basic Laws
43. Ecuador Labor Laws and Regulations Handbook - Strategic Information and Basic Laws
44. Egypt Labor Laws and Regulations Handbook - Strategic Information and Basic Laws
45. El Salvador Labor Laws and Regulations Handbook - Strategic Information and Basic Laws
46. Equatorial Guinea Labor Laws and Regulations Handbook - Strategic Information and Basic Laws
47. Estonia Labor Laws and Regulations Handbook - Strategic Information and Basic Laws
48. Falkland Islands Labor Laws and Regulations Handbook - Strategic Information and Basic Laws
49. Fiji Labor Laws and Regulations Handbook - Strategic Information and Basic Laws
50. Finland Labor Laws and Regulations Handbook - Strategic Information and Basic Laws
51. France Labor Laws and Regulations Handbook - Strategic Information and Basic Laws
52. Georgia Labor Laws and Regulations Handbook - Strategic Information and Basic Laws
53. Germany Labor Laws and Regulations Handbook - Strategic Information and Basic Laws
54. Gibraltar Labor Laws and Regulations Handbook - Strategic Information and Basic Laws
55. Greece Labor Laws and Regulations Handbook - Strategic Information and Basic Laws
56. Grenada Labor Laws and Regulations Handbook - Strategic Information and Basic Laws
57. Guam Investment & Business Guide
58. Guatemala Labor Laws and Regulations Handbook - Strategic Information and Basic Laws
59. Guernsey Labor Laws and Regulations Handbook - Strategic Information and Basic Laws
60. Guyana Labor Laws and Regulations Handbook - Strategic Information and Basic Laws
61. Haiti Labor Laws and Regulations Handbook - Strategic Information and Basic Laws
62. Honduras Labor Laws and Regulations Handbook - Strategic Information and Basic Laws
63. Hungary Labor Laws and Regulations Handbook - Strategic Information and Basic Laws
64. Iceland Labor Laws and Regulations Handbook - Strategic Information and Basic Laws
65. India Labor Laws and Regulations Handbook - Strategic Information and Basic Laws
66. Indonesia Labor Laws and Regulations Handbook - Strategic Information and Basic Laws
67. Iran Labor Laws and Regulations Handbook - Strategic Information and Basic Laws
68. Iraq Labor Laws and Regulations Handbook - Strategic Information and Basic Laws
69. Ireland Labor Laws and Regulations Handbook - Strategic Information and Basic Laws
70. Israel Labor Laws and Regulations Handbook - Strategic Information and Basic Laws
71. Italy Labor Laws and Regulations Handbook - Strategic Information and Basic Laws
72. Jamaica Labor Laws and Regulations Handbook - Strategic Information and Basic Laws
73. Japan Labor Laws and Regulations Handbook - Strategic Information and Basic Laws
74. Jersey Labor Laws and Regulations Handbook - Strategic Information and Basic Laws
75. Jordan Labor Laws and Regulations Handbook - Strategic Information and Basic Laws
76. Kazakhstan Labor Laws and Regulations Handbook - Strategic Information and Basic Laws
77. Kenya Labor Laws and Regulations Handbook - Strategic Information and Basic Laws

For additional analytical, business and investment opportunities information,
Please contact Global Investment & Business Center, USA
at (202) 546-2103. Fax: (202) 546-3275. E-mail: ibpusa3@gmail.com

78.	Kiribati Labor Laws and Regulations Handbook - Strategic Information and Basic Laws
79.	Korea, North Labor Laws and Regulations Handbook - Strategic Information and Basic Laws
80.	Korea, South Labor Laws and Regulations Handbook - Strategic Information and Basic Laws
81.	Kuwait Labor Laws and Regulations Handbook - Strategic Information and Basic Laws
82.	Kyrgyzstan Labor Laws and Regulations Handbook - Strategic Information and Basic Laws
83.	Laos Labor Laws and Regulations Handbook - Strategic Information and Basic Laws
84.	Latvia Labor Laws and Regulations Handbook - Strategic Information and Basic Laws
85.	Lebanon Labor Laws and Regulations Handbook - Strategic Information and Basic Laws
86.	Libya Labor Laws and Regulations Handbook - Strategic Information and Basic Laws
87.	Liechtenstein Labor Laws and Regulations Handbook - Strategic Information and Basic Laws
88.	Lithuania Labor Laws and Regulations Handbook - Strategic Information and Basic Laws
89.	Luxemburg Labor Laws and Regulations Handbook - Strategic Information and Basic Laws
90.	Macao Labor Laws and Regulations Handbook - Strategic Information and Basic Laws
91.	Macedonia, Republic Labor Laws and Regulations Handbook - Strategic Information and Basic Laws
92.	Madagascar Labor Laws and Regulations Handbook - Strategic Information and Basic Laws
93.	Malaysia Labor Laws and Regulations Handbook - Strategic Information and Basic Laws
94.	Malta Labor Laws and Regulations Handbook - Strategic Information and Basic Laws
95.	Man Labor Laws and Regulations Handbook - Strategic Information and Basic Laws
96.	Mauritius Labor Laws and Regulations Handbook - Strategic Information and Basic Laws
97.	Mauritius Labor Laws and Regulations Handbook - Strategic Information and Basic Laws
98.	Mexico Labor Laws and Regulations Handbook - Strategic Information and Basic Laws
99.	Micronesia Labor Laws and Regulations Handbook - Strategic Information and Basic Laws
100.	Moldova Labor Laws and Regulations Handbook - Strategic Information and Basic Laws
101.	Monaco Labor Laws and Regulations Handbook - Strategic Information and Basic Laws
102.	Mongolia Labor Laws and Regulations Handbook - Strategic Information and Basic Laws
103.	Morocco Labor Laws and Regulations Handbook - Strategic Information and Basic Laws
104.	Myanmar Labor Laws and Regulations Handbook - Strategic Information and Basic Laws
105.	Namibia Labor Laws and Regulations Handbook - Strategic Information and Basic Laws
106.	Netherlands Labor Laws and Regulations Handbook - Strategic Information and Basic Laws
107.	New Caledonia Labor Laws and Regulations Handbook - Strategic Information and Basic Laws
108.	New Zealand Labor Laws and Regulations Handbook - Strategic Information and Basic Laws
109.	Nicaragua Labor Laws and Regulations Handbook - Strategic Information and Basic Laws
110.	Nigeria Labor Laws and Regulations Handbook - Strategic Information and Basic Laws
111.	Northern Mariana Islands Labor Laws and Regulations Handbook - Strategic Information and Basic Laws
112.	Norway Labor Laws and Regulations Handbook - Strategic Information and Basic Laws
113.	Pakistan Labor Laws and Regulations Handbook - Strategic Information and Basic Laws
114.	Panama Labor Laws and Regulations Handbook - Strategic Information and Basic Laws
115.	Peru Labor Laws and Regulations Handbook - Strategic Information and Basic Laws
116.	Philippines Labor Laws and Regulations Handbook - Strategic Information and Basic Laws
117.	Poland Labor Laws and Regulations Handbook - Strategic Information and Basic Laws
118.	Portugal Labor Laws and Regulations Handbook - Strategic Information and Basic Laws
119.	Romania Labor Laws and Regulations Handbook - Strategic Information and Basic Laws
120.	Russia Labor Laws and Regulations Handbook - Strategic Information and Basic Laws

For additional analytical, business and investment opportunities information,
Please contact Global Investment & Business Center, USA
at (202) 546-2103. Fax: (202) 546-3275. E-mail: ibpusa3@gmail.com

121. Samoa (American) Investment & Business Guide
122. Samoa (Western) Labor Laws and Regulations Handbook - Strategic Information and Basic Laws
123. Saudi Arabia Labor Laws and Regulations Handbook - Strategic Information and Basic Laws
124. Scotland Labor Laws and Regulations Handbook - Strategic Information and Basic Laws
125. Serbia Labor Laws and Regulations Handbook - Strategic Information and Basic Laws
126. Singapore Labor Laws and Regulations Handbook - Strategic Information and Basic Laws
127. Slovakia Labor Laws and Regulations Handbook - Strategic Information and Basic Laws
128. Slovenia Labor Laws and Regulations Handbook - Strategic Information and Basic Laws
129. South Africa Labor Laws and Regulations Handbook - Strategic Information and Basic Laws
130. Spain Labor Laws and Regulations Handbook - Strategic Information and Basic Laws
131. Sri Lanka Labor Laws and Regulations Handbook - Strategic Information and Basic Laws
132. St. Helena Labor Laws and Regulations Handbook - Strategic Information and Basic Laws
133. Sudan Labor Laws and Regulations Handbook - Strategic Information and Basic Laws
134. Suriname Labor Laws and Regulations Handbook - Strategic Information and Basic Laws
135. Sweden Labor Laws and Regulations Handbook - Strategic Information and Basic Laws
136. Switzerland Labor Laws and Regulations Handbook - Strategic Information and Basic Laws
137. Syria Export Import & Business Directory
138. Taiwan Labor Laws and Regulations Handbook - Strategic Information and Basic Laws
139. Tajikistan Labor Laws and Regulations Handbook - Strategic Information and Basic Laws
140. Thailand Labor Laws and Regulations Handbook - Strategic Information and Basic Laws
141. Tunisia Labor Laws and Regulations Handbook - Strategic Information and Basic Laws
142. Turkey Labor Laws and Regulations Handbook - Strategic Information and Basic Laws
143. Turkmenistan Labor Laws and Regulations Handbook - Strategic Information and Basic Laws
144. Uganda Labor Laws and Regulations Handbook - Strategic Information and Basic Laws
145. Ukraine Labor Laws and Regulations Handbook - Strategic Information and Basic Laws
146. United Arab Emirates Labor Laws and Regulations Handbook - Strategic Information and Basic Laws
147. United Kingdom Labor Laws and Regulations Handbook - Strategic Information and Basic Laws
148. United States Labor Laws and Regulations Handbook - Strategic Information and Basic Laws
149. Uruguay Labor Laws and Regulations Handbook - Strategic Information and Basic Laws
150. US Labor Laws and Regulations Handbook - Strategic Information and Basic Laws
151. Uzbekistan Labor Laws and Regulations Handbook - Strategic Information and Basic Laws
152. Venezuela Labor Laws and Regulations Handbook - Strategic Information and Basic Laws
153. Vietnam Labor Laws and Regulations Handbook - Strategic Information and Basic Laws

For additional analytical, business and investment opportunities information,
Please contact Global Investment & Business Center, USA
at (202) 546-2103. Fax: (202) 546-3275. E-mail: ibpusa3@gmail.com